RELIGION AND PROGRESSIVE ACTIVISM

RELIGION AND SOCIAL
TRANSFORMATION
General Editors: Anthony B. Pinn and Stacey M. Floyd-Thomas

Religion and Progressive Activism

New Stories about Faith and Politics

Edited by
Ruth Braunstein,
Todd Nicholas Fuist, and
Rhys H. Williams

NEW YORK UNIVERSITY PRESS
New York

NEW YORK UNIVERSITY PRESS
New York
www.nyupress.org

© 2017 by New York University

References to Internet websites (URLs) were accurate at the time of writing. Neither the author nor New York University Press is responsible for URLs that may have expired or changed since the manuscript was prepared.

ISBN: 978-1-4798-5476-9 (hardback)
ISBN: 978-1-4798-5290-1 (paperback)

For Library of Congress Cataloging-in-Publication data, please contact the Library of Congress.

New York University Press books are printed on acid-free paper, and their binding materials are chosen for strength and durability. We strive to use environmentally responsible suppliers and materials to the greatest extent possible in publishing our books.

Manufactured in the United States of America

10 9 8 7 6 5 4 3 2 1

Also available as an ebook

CONTENTS

ACKNOWLEDGMENTS

This volume emerged out of conversations that the three co-editors had at the 2012 American Sociological Association conference in Denver, Colorado. Discussing our own research on religion and progressive activism, we noted there had been an uptick in the number of our colleagues who were conducting research on similar topics, but that there had not yet been an effort to consolidate what we had collectively learned. We agreed that a volume that brought together both emerging and established scholars in the field to share ideas, theoretical insights, and findings would be a useful contribution to the discipline, to emerging researchers in this area, and to public conversations on this topic.

We are incredibly grateful to the amazing group of scholars who agreed to participate in this project. Their rigor in presenting analyses of progressive religion that are both innovative and accessible have made this volume possible. We must note that every person who committed to writing a chapter did indeed come through, and authors responded to our suggestions for revision with alacrity and good humor. A number of other groups and individuals have also helped to bring this project to fruition. We are especially thankful for the support of Jennifer Hammer and NYU Press, as well as the scholars who reviewed this work on their behalf in the early stages of the process. Their comments and guidance have been immensely useful in shaping the final outcome. Dr. Jane Jones provided invaluable editing and commentary on the manuscript, further helping us create the most coherent volume possible.

We also express our appreciation to Christopher Ellison, who as president of the Association for the Sociology of Religion invited us to organize a conference session jointly sponsored by the American Sociological Association and the Association for the Sociology of Religion, in which several of our authors presented their papers. Other conference sessions, at the Midwest Sociological Society meetings and the Society for the Scientific Study of Religion meetings, allowed other contributors to present and "workshop" their ideas and paper drafts. At points in the process we received useful feedback from David Smilde, Brian Steensland, and R. Stephen Warner; our appreciation to them all.

Finally, this volume was also made possible, in part, through generous grants and funding from Western Washington University, the University of Connecticut's Scholarship Facilitation Fund, the Graduate School at Loyola University Chicago, and the McNamara Center for the Social Study of Religion in the Department of Sociology at Loyola University Chicago. We are truly grateful for the contribution of each of these groups and individuals.

Ruth Braunstein
Todd Nicholas Fuist
Rhys H. Williams

Introduction

Religion and Progressive Activism—Introducing and Mapping the Field

TODD NICHOLAS FUIST, RUTH BRAUNSTEIN, AND
RHYS H. WILLIAMS

Well, I don't know what will happen now. We've got some difficult days ahead. But it really doesn't matter with me now, because I've been to the mountaintop. And I don't mind. Like anybody, I would like to live a long life. Longevity has its place. But I'm not concerned about that now. I just want to do God's will. And He's allowed me to go up to the mountain. And I've looked over. And I've seen the Promised Land. I may not get there with you. But I want you to know tonight, that we, as a people, will get to the Promised Land! And so I'm happy, tonight. I'm not worried about anything. I'm not fearing any man! Mine eyes have seen the glory of the coming of the Lord!
—Martin Luther King, Jr., April 3, 1968[1]

When Martin Luther King, Jr., delivered the above address at the Mason Temple in Memphis, Tennessee, on the eve of his assassination, he prophetically cast himself as an American Moses, leading a long-suffering chosen people to a land of freedom promised to them by a just God (see Gutterman 2005). The civil rights movement, of which King was a prominent figure, forever changed the way our nation thinks about public morality. This movement—like many movements before it and many that would follow—did so in part by linking its claims with religious rhetoric, symbols, and meaning.

King repurposes language from the Biblical narrative of Exodus, in which Hebrew slaves escaped from bondage only to face forty years as sojourners in the wilderness, to narrate the history of slavery and racism faced by African Americans. Aligning their experience with the Biblical narrative, King promises a future time, after "difficult days ahead," when African Americans will see "the glory of the coming of the Lord," just as the ancient Israelites in the story of Exodus eventually reached the Promised Land.

King remains a powerful symbol of how religious values and language can be marshaled toward progressive political goals. In the decades since his death, however, the well-organized forces of the religious Right have overshadowed progressive religious voices in the public sphere. Using the politics of gender and sexuality as a nonnegotiable wedge, the religious Right has been highly successful in persuading Americans that religion and social progress are at odds (see Williams 2002). Traditionally religious people have fled the Democratic Party in droves; in turn, progressive stalwarts have left the churches of their youth. Taking stock of these trends, many observers have seen two warring camps: religious conservatives concerned with the nation's moral decay pitted against secular progressives championing civil liberties. Through the lens of this "culture wars" narrative (Hunter 1991), the topography of U.S. politics resembles the Grand Canyon: a great moral chasm allegedly divides the American people.

Forty years after King's speech, however, a charismatic young political figure turned heads by powerfully integrating progressive and religious languages on the public stage. During his first presidential campaign, Barack Obama spoke of working together toward a more perfect union, drawing on the themes of Scripture:

> This was one of the tasks we set forth at the beginning of this campaign—to continue the long march of those who came before us, a march for a more just, more equal, more free, more caring and more prosperous America. I chose to run for the presidency at this moment in history because I believe deeply that we cannot solve the challenges of our time unless we solve them together—unless we perfect our union by understanding that we may have different stories, but we hold common hopes; that we may not look the same and we may not have come from the same

place, but we all want to move in the same direction—towards a better future for our children and our grandchildren. . . . In the end, then, what is called for is nothing more, and nothing less, than what all the world's great religions demand—that we do unto others as we would have them do unto us. Let us be our brother's keeper, Scripture tells us. Let us be our sister's keeper. Let us find that common stake we all have in one another, and let our politics reflect that spirit as well. (March 18, 2008)[2]

Obama repeatedly reminded the American people that "the world's great religions demand" that they pursue justice, equality, freedom, and the common good. By forcefully arguing that these progressive goals were not just right, but also *good*, he disrupted the religious Right's monopoly on public morality. In the process, he became a highly visible reminder to Americans that progressive religion, focused on justice and equality, was possible.

Of course, progressive religion had never truly disappeared. Obama must be understood not as the *cause* of a progressive religious resurgence, but as the *product* of progressive religious efforts that have been operating in the background of U.S. politics throughout the country's history. It is true that there have been periods when progressive religious voices were drowned out by louder and more visible actors. At other times, though, such as at the height of the civil rights movement, progressive religion has been impossible to ignore, and millions have mobilized in answer to its call to action.

During the four years before Obama emerged on the national stage, there was a marked increase in attention to progressive religion within Washington, D.C. Following the religiously tone-deaf performance of Senator John Kerry during the 2004 election, and in light of perceptions that the Democratic Party was "anti-religious," a group of Democrats began discussing how to close the "God gap" between the two parties (Sullivan 2008; see also Dionne 2008 and Sager's chapter in this volume). In this context, Obama's artful merging of prophetic and civil religious rhetoric was music to many Democrats' ears. He was not just trying to make the Democratic Party palatable to conservative religious voters; he was presenting a renewed, progressive religious vision.

Obama's progressive religious rhetoric was forged both through his immersion in the prophetic tradition of the Black Church as well as in his foray into the world of congregation-based community organizing. As a young community organizer in Chicago, he worked with the Gamaliel Foundation, one of a handful of national faith-based community organizing networks—including the PICO National Network, the Industrial Areas Foundation, and the DART Center—that bring congregations and other local institutions together to address political and economic inequalities within their communities.[3] Taken as a whole, the national field of faith-based community organizing coalitions represents one of the largest and most diverse grassroots movements for social justice today.

Although many Americans may not have taken note of groups like these until President Obama raised awareness of them, contributors to this volume have been on the ground studying progressive religious activism for years. They have observed local faith-based community organizing coalitions from New York to Chicago and from Oakland to Los Angeles, including efforts that organize low-income and middle-class Americans to solve problems related to healthcare, immigration, the financial crisis, affordable housing, and education.

Although two of our most prominent progressive religious voices— King and Obama—are African American, and their activism and rhetoric were forged in the traditions of the Black Church, this broader field of progressive religious activity comprises a surprisingly diverse collection of people—racially, ethnically, socioeconomically, and religiously. And while much attention has been paid to, and many books written about, the role of the Black Church in the civil rights movement (e.g., Morris 1984), less is known about this broader field of progressive religious actors, including how they work together, across myriad social divides and multiple issue areas, to achieve shared goals.

While these efforts are often quite localized, they are also connected in a variety of ways to national activist campaigns and social movements. For example, many congregations that participate in local faith-based community organizing (FBCO) coalitions have also, in recent years, been involved in the New Sanctuary Movement, an immigrant rights movement that, using specifically Biblical language, emphasizes the faith community's obligation to embrace the "strangers" among us and to keep families at risk of deportation together. The New Sanctuary Movement is one part of a larger immigrant rights and border justice movement that has fruitfully drawn on religious communities, symbols, and values to work for a more open, humane, and just immigration system (Yukich 2013).

All of these collective efforts, in turn, reference historical movements that have used religion toward progressive ends. While civil rights activists and nineteenth-century abolitionists loom large in our historical imagination, contemporary movements also borrow tactics, symbols, and rhetoric from the earlier Sanctuary Movement, the Central America Solidarity Movement, the Plowshares Movement, and others.[4] While social movements staging public protests tend to garner the most attention, people of faith are also pursuing progressive social and political change within faith-based volunteer and civic organizations. From Midwestern towns to coastal cities, these groups have been using their moral authority to confront racism, poverty, and inequality within local communities for decades.

Least visible of all are the ongoing efforts *within* congregations and local faith communities to ask hard questions about persistent racial inequality, LGBT issues, changing family dynamics, and the poverty faced by both members in their pews and neighbors in their communities. Some have responded by fashioning alternative communities in which to prefigure their visions of a more just and loving society. The burgeoning "emergent church" movement has largely drawn young members disillusioned with the conservative churches in which they grew up, who are seeking something just as theologically rigorous yet more inclusive and politically liberal (Burge and Djupe 2014). Many congregations also funnel their members into volunteer work, often by developing partnerships with broader change-making organizations, such as the Catholic Worker Movement or Soulforce, an organization "devoted to changing the hearts and minds of religious leaders who engage in anti-homosexual campaigns." Religion is being put toward progressive ends in diverse settings.

Although these efforts are quite varied, they all complicate the dominant vision of a culture war between religious conservatives and secular liberals. Attention to progressive religion forces us to draw a more accurate map of the American political landscape—past, present, and future—and has the potential to refine our understanding of the relationship between religion, politics, and civic life. Yet there has been little effort to organize and assess what we know about progressive religion in the United States. This volume offers a corrective to this lacuna. Below, we advance a framework for understanding our object of study and begin mapping the field of progressive religious social activism.

Goals of This Volume

This volume has two interrelated goals. First, by bringing together cutting-edge work on progressive religion, it offers readers interested in American politics, religion, and civic life insight into this often overlooked field. Moreover, by carefully demonstrating how these efforts are related to those of both the religious Right and the secular Left, it contributes to a more grounded and nuanced understanding of religion and the American political landscape as a whole. Second, for readers interested in the theoretical implications of this knowledge, contributors assess the varied ways that progressive religious activism forces us to deconstruct common political binaries (like Right/Left and progress/tradition), and to rethink long-accepted theories of religion and social movements as well as the role of faith in democratic politics and civic life.

For example, although political theorists have long argued that there is no place for religious discourse in the public sphere, more recent reappraisals suggest that much of this anxiety emanated from concerns about *conservative* religious voices, seen as advancing a policy agenda that runs counter to liberal democratic values. Pointing to the role of religion in the civil rights movement, Jürgen Habermas (2006) acknowledged that some religious values have played a productive role in "stabilizing and advancing a liberal political culture" (6–7). This reconsideration of the role of religion in the public sphere suggests a need to turn our analytic attention to the issues raised by *progressive* religious voices.

Moreover, attention to progressive religious voices sheds light on the often-invisible moral and religious underpinnings of progressive politics. Although the American Left has been critiqued for lacking a clear moral vision (Hart 2001), this might be overstated due to a focus on *secular* progressives. Progressive religious groups have long promoted a morally grounded view of progressive politics, used faith-infused languages and symbolism to express their political commitments, and lent moral authority to progressive movements' claims. While these movements' public claims may ultimately be expressed in secular terms that are stripped of their religious particularism, this should not suggest that people of faith have not played formative roles in these efforts.

By analyzing progressive religion, we do not suggest that we are pioneering a new area of study, or making a new discovery. Rather, the value of this volume lies in its effort to identify a distinct field of study and to highlight the work of scholars whose research offers a multifaceted view of the progressive religious field. We turn now to a consideration of the dimensions and characteristics of our object of study, before moving on to explore the idea of progressive religion as a field of action.

The Object of Study: What Is Progressive Religion?

When people speak of progressive religion, they often refer to two things: first, politically liberal or left-wing activists who also happen to be religious; and second, theological liberals who happen to be engaged in social action or political activism. Yet many religious groups and individuals may avoid calling themselves "liberal," "progressive," or "left-wing" even while participating in social action that could mark them as such. Likewise, many religious groups and individuals may embrace aspects of a progressive agenda even as they also promote certain beliefs or engage in practices commonly identified as conservative.

Our tendency to conceptualize the political field in the United States in terms of a liberal/conservative dichotomy makes it difficult to categorize the sociopolitical beliefs of many groups, particularly groups that do not easily fit onto the main left-right axis (see Kniss 2003). Additionally, because our standard ideological axis is often conflated with an orientation toward or against *progress*, religious activism is particularly difficult to situate in these terms (Calhoun 2012). After all, many religious movements combine a desire for progress—for example, advancing toward a more just, more loving, and more God-like society—with a desire to return to or preserve certain *traditional* social forms or practices—such as an elevation of the community over the individual or a return to collective, public standards of morality. Many such groups even argue that these forms of "tradition" are necessary to achieve the kinds of progress they pursue (Calhoun 2012). This complicates the task of categorizing their efforts.

Also at issue here is whether we are considering "activism" or "civic engagement" when we examine progressive religion and, moreover, whether this distinction is a matter of degree, rather than of kind. Civic engagement is typically defined as the social action taken by individuals, groups, and organizations within "civil society"—a term used to connote the nebulous space between the state, the market, and the family (see Ehrenberg 1999; Alexander 2006). Despite this broad definition, however, scholars often draw a line between allegedly *cooperative* forms of social action like charity work or service provision, and more *contentious* activism, which is assumed to target state entities (see Allahyari 2000); and between the relatively *enduring* organizational structures of civic organizations and the more *emergent* mobilizations of social movements (Wuthnow 1999; 2006; Lichterman and Potts 2009).

Yet as Davis and Robinson (2012) point out, the line between religious activism and civic engagement is blurry, and much seemingly "civic" work done in congregations, such as running soup kitchens or providing educational services, has a political dimension. By identifying mechanisms through which faith communities politicize religious talk, practices, and identities (see Beyerlein and Hipp 2006), much of the work in this volume shows how seemingly neutral acts of civic engagement may actually promote larger moral visions for society. Chapters also highlight the ways in which many progressive religious organizations straddle the line between these organizational fields, publicly (and sometimes contentiously) exercising their political power, but also focusing on building enduring organizations that can address a broad range of issues over the long term (Braunstein, Fulton, and Wood 2014). Together, these cases challenge our often-bifurcated understandings of the distinction between civic engagement and activism, which has made it difficult for scholars to categorize and understand the kinds of progressive religious action highlighted in this book.

Progressive religion clearly complicates our prevailing understandings of American politics. This begs the question as to how we recognize "progressive religion" when we see it. What we may call progressive religion refers to multiple groups and social categories, making simple definitions elusive. Laura Desfor Edles (2013), for example, identifies two poles in progressive Christianity: "spiritual progressives," who stress their difference from conservative Christians and promote a questioning attitude toward faith, and "prophetic Christians," who are more traditional in their beliefs and practices, but seek to imbue progressive politics with sacred significance. Yet, Edles says, these two poles are united by "an emphasis on Jesus' life and teachings, and . . . an emphasis on social justice and inclusivity" (7). We see here that groups with very different theological orientations can, nonetheless, share political values or identifications.

In light of these tensions, we propose four overlapping dimensions of progressive religion, which may be found in various combinations in different groups and instances of collective action.

- *Progressive action*: A religious group that participates in social action oriented toward greater economic, political, and/or social equality—including anti-poverty activism or mobilization around the issue of universal health care.
- *Progressive values*: A religious group that espouses a commitment to reform-oriented change and/or social justice—including those claiming anti-racist or feminist values.
- *Progressive identities*: A religious group that actively identifies with other groups and individuals generally accepted to be progressive—for example, by hanging pictures of Martin Luther King, Jr., in its meeting space or understanding itself as connected to the peace movement.
- *Progressive theology*: A religious group that seeks to deconstruct, reform, or challenge faith traditions toward the end of making them more inclusive or just—for example, by promoting Biblical feminism or queer theology.

Identifying these four overlapping dimensions is important because doing so allows us to recognize the difficulty and complexity of religious and political labels, and to highlight their fluid nature. While these dimensions are connected and often bundled together, they are not inherently a complete package, and may appear in various combinations in different groups. For example, a Mennonite community studied by one of the authors participated in protests against war and housing discrimination because they believe strongly that Christians should promote both peace and economic equality. Yet some in the community bristled at being called "progressive," and many in the community rejected postmodern readings of scripture. This made certain issues, such as the place of LGBT people in the church, difficult for the group to approach. Their undeniably *progressive values* pushed them toward a desire for LGBT inclusion, while many members' lack of a *progressive identity* and *progressive theology* suggested a less reconciling approach. As such, the group could be considered a progressive religious group on certain dimensions, while demonstrating the complexity of such a label when other dimensions are taken into account.

This complexity exists because the various dimensions of progressivism detailed above are not produced in a vacuum. Rather, they are shaped simultaneously by macro cultural and structural factors, by meso and micro group dynamics, and by history. At the macro level, the existing structure of social institutions and relations, both within religion in the U.S. and outside of it, shapes how religious groups act and interact (Morris 1984; Smith 1996b; Wood 2002). Moreover, groups draw on wider public discourses of moral motivation, including shared religious languages, which both constrain and enable claim making (Gusfield 1986; Smith 1996a; Williams 1999; 2007; Wood 2002; Polletta 2006; Zubrzycki 2006; Moore 2008; Braunstein 2012; Bean 2014).

At the meso and micro level, organizational culture, talk, and practices matter for how individuals understand and act in the social world (Eliasoph 1998; Eliasoph and Lichterman 2003; Moon 2004; Lichterman 2005; Perrin 2006; Fine 2012). Following from this, there is much evidence that sense-making talk within religious organizations affects their ability to explore and confront social issues (Bender 2003; Moon 2004; Yukich 2010). Lichterman (2005), for example, finds that groups' customs, including how they conceptualize the role of religion in public life, shape their ability to build bridges with other social groups, enabling (and constraining) wider civic participation.

These dynamics can also impact groups' abilities to manage racial, socioeconomic, and religious diversity within their own communities, an issue we will see play out in various ways in the following chapters. This is particularly important because, compared to conservative religious groups, many progressive religious efforts intentionally recruit groups from a wide range of social backgrounds to work together toward a common cause—with varying results.

Finally, these organizations' practices are invariably shaped by the specific historical juncture in which they are acting. As discussed, contemporary groups situate themselves in historical lineages that include past progressive religious efforts, and distinguish themselves from conservative religious and secular liberal efforts of the past. Like all activists, they also draw on the "repertoire" of discourses, organizational styles, and tactics that are historically and culturally available to them (Clemens 1993; Tilly 1993; Williams 1995). Progressive religious groups do not define themselves and engage in action in a historical vacuum; consciously or not, they are fundamentally shaped by historical intersections between religion and politics (Warner 2013).

These levels of analysis combine in any consideration of how actual groups reconfigure existing streams of thought and discourses in creative ways to deal with the local problems and situations they confront (see Moore 2008). Religious groups, in particular, tend to give their content a moral character (Williams 2003). Haedicke (2012) suggests that this process involves the creative work of "[mobilizing] existing values and understandings to interpret new practices and adapt them to local organizational settings" (61–62). For example, Fuist, Stoll, and Kniss (2012) demonstrate that existing institutional languages and cultures shape how denominationally affiliated LGBT religious organizations pursue their agendas. More generally, a religious group may put existing progressive values toward new uses within the organization by drawing on public discourses about equality as well as religious narratives about Christ's love to espouse progressive values about LGBT inclusion, or conduct progressive action such as joining a march for universal health care (see Dillon 1999; O'Brien 2004; Wilcox 2009).

In sum, we use the term "progressive religion" as a marker, realizing that it is not entirely accurate, but lacking a more appropriate term that would be recognizable to both other scholars studying this field and individuals within the field. Beyond being recognizable, this term offers a necessary distinction between these efforts and those often associated with both secular progressives and religious conservatives. Because the public image of *progressive politics* in America is informed by liberals' and leftists' uneasy relationships with religion (or at least with public religion), and because the public image of *religion* in America is so deeply shaped by the religious Right, most Americans (and sociologists) assume that all religious activism is conservative in nature. By lifting up "liberal" or "progressive" religious activism as a distinct object of study, this volume challenges that assumption.

A Progressive Religious Field of Action

As noted above, the term "progressive religion" serves as a useful marker of what these efforts are not—namely, secular or conservative—and of some of the positive characteristics that are shared by the diverse efforts we identify with progressive religion. Still, the lack of a clearly bounded category of social actors that identify as religious progressives poses certain analytical challenges to studying this phenomenon. As an alternative to a clearly bounded category, we conceptualize our object of study as a progressive religious *field of action*[5] (Bourdieu 1991; Klawiter 2008; Fligstein and McAdam 2011; Calhoun 2012; Edgell 2012). By this we mean a set of individuals and organizations that are defined by knowledge of each other, relationships to shared discourses, symbols and historical referents, and a shared orientation toward a set of common stakes and overlapping values, such as social justice, peace, community, equality, and the common good. Importantly, the field is also defined in part through these actors' work to distinguish their efforts from forms of action cast as either conservative religious or secular progressive.

Our approach has two major benefits. First, the field concept allows us to conceptualize not only interactions *within* fields but also *between* fields. While we have already noted the ways in which these actors define themselves through *distinction from* other fields—specifically the secular and conservative religious fields—we are also able to ask questions about how they *work across and bridge between* multiple fields, variously defined. For example, Moore (2008) studied Quaker scientists who protested and argued against science's involvement with defense-based research after World War II. The scientists were surely participating in a religious field of action, but also had deep professional networks within the academy, among other research scientists, and with secular political movements. As such, the progressive religious field must be examined in relation to these other overlapping fields of activity (Edles 2013).

Second, conceptualizing these efforts as part of a progressive religious field of action allows us to assert certain loose connections among a range of different efforts that may not fit squarely into a self-conscious social category. A categorical approach, for example, would have a difficult time situating faith-based community organizations (FBCOs).

While FBCOs pursue policy goals that are typically described as liberal or progressive, they do so using methods that might—from a secular Left perspective—appear traditional, conservative, or even backward. They root their claims in their religious values and collective experiences rather than economic statistics or scientific facts. They identify issues and mobilize through relationships with others in their local communities, rather than through strategic leadership and expertise in identifying political opportunities and marshaling resources to draft individuals into action (Hart 2001; Wood 2002; Stout 2010). In short, these efforts pursue progress toward an alternative future that remains rooted in traditional forms of sociality (Calhoun 2012).

Conceptualizing such groups as part of a progressive religious field of action allows us to overcome this apparent contradiction. It is not necessary that the efforts of these social actors cluster on a particular end of a left-right continuum. Instead, we see that they exist in relation to a variety of other actors pursing similar goals, which share certain overlapping values and histories, and define themselves as distinct from groups identifying as either conservative religious or liberal secular. For example, FBCOs connected to national networks like PICO (Wood 2002; Wood, Fulton, and Partridge 2012) increasingly work in partnership with a range of liberal religious advocacy organizations that promote public policies to advance peace, justice, and the common good (Braunstein 2012; see also Hertzke 1988; Fowler et al. 2004).

And although FBCOs are strictly non-partisan and maintain their openness to working with congregations ranging from theologically liberal to conservative, the reality is that most of the religious communities that become involved in faith-based community organizing tend to be theologically liberal (Wood, Fulton, and Partridge 2012). This has made them prime targets of outreach by the Democratic Party and by the small but growing group of Democratic candidates who have sought to "close the God Gap" (Sullivan 2008; see also Dionne 2008). Moreover, the FBCO networks and their member congregations participate in social movement activism that would typically be cast as progressive. Some of these movements—like the New Sanctuary Movement (Yukich 2013)—have explicit religious identities. Others—like Occupy Wall Street and efforts to hold big banks accountable—maintain looser connections to religious communities, although they often mobilize through congregations, use religious language, and pursue goals that religious participants believe are aligned with their faith values (Schneider 2013).

As mentioned above, some of these groups would chafe at a political label like "progressive," preferring instead to present themselves as nonideological and values-based. But these labels have little analytic purchase, as groups on the religious Right would make the same claim. While we do not wish to dismiss potential similarities between religious progressives and conservatives, we also see a need for a framework that can identify and analyze the differences between them. The notion of a progressive religious field of action allows us to conceptualize FBCOs, national liberal religious advocacy organizations, progressive social movements, some para-church organizations, progressive religious media entities and figures, faith-based voter outreach efforts, and liberal congregations as an overlapping set of efforts with certain similarities to one another and, taken together, certain differences from both conservative religious and secular action fields.

Thinking of what we are studying as a field of action, rather than a category of social actors, additionally allows us to highlight the *relational* content of social positions and the constructed nature of political categories. This approach suggests that the ways in which groups define themselves and their positions can be interpreted only through close attention to the fields in which they are operating. While we believe a relational approach fruitfully opens up important lines of analysis, we also recognize that it obscures others. Indeed, because this approach places an emphasis on how groups define themselves in relation to shared reference points and political contexts, it is more difficult to trace connections between groups situated in different political (namely, national) contexts. As a result, most of the chapters in this book focus on groups working in the United States. This should not suggest that parallel progressive efforts are not underway outside of the U.S. (e.g., Nepstad 2008), and indeed future work should assess the ways in which a transnational religious action field intersects with various nationally bounded religious action fields (e.g., Bandy and Smith 2005).

In sum, our approach is rooted in our observation that groups are most fruitfully defined by the actions they take, the identifications they hold, and their relationship to other groups within the same field or other fields, rather than by any categorical box that we could place them in. It is also, importantly, rooted in a desire to highlight similarities between organizations and forms of action that are often placed in separate analytic categories. Indeed, while the contributors to this volume overlap significantly in their empirical subjects, their theoretical concerns, and their findings, they participate in several different academic debates and conversations. This volume was created as a way of bringing together this diverse body of research.

Organization of This Volume

All forms of activism share similar challenges, including how to motivate people to disrupt their everyday lives in order to focus on potentially abstract issues, to continue to be involved with social change efforts following both defeats and victories, or to persuade bystander publics that their cause is righteous. Progressive religious groups in the U.S., however, face particular versions of these challenges and have developed particular strategies to overcome them, drawing on the specific sets of resources that are available to them. At the same time, these efforts take a variety of forms, are dispersed across a wide array of organizational arenas, and engage a number of different issues.

The chapters that follow demonstrate the varied patterns of progressive religious mobilization and engagement; the cultural challenges associated with being progressive and religious and the "cultural work" required to overcome these challenges; the complex and varied roles that religion plays in progressive political action; and the ways in which actors assert their progressive religious voices and values in the public sphere. Through close attention to the various ways that individuals and groups engage in progressive religious action, this volume represents the most comprehensive effort to date to map this field.

Patterns of Progressive Religious Mobilization and Engagement

The first section includes four chapters that examine organizational patterns in progressive religious activism. Brad R. Fulton and Richard L. Wood begin by using a national dataset of faith-based community organizing coalitions to examine the different types of organizations and different modes of action they employ. Through this, they provide us with the "landscape" of one central set of groups and organizations that comprise this field, focusing particularly on how these coalitions mobilize diverse social groups, and the opportunities and challenges that arise from their diversity.

Rebecca Sager focuses on a broader ecology of progressive religious organizations and actors working at the national level. She considers in particular a group of Democratic Party activists' efforts to reach out to religious voters, and the ways in which their work was connected to a variety of new progressive religious movement organizations that have emerged as a loosely coordinated force to offset the power of the religious Right in the public sphere.

Kraig Beyerlein and A. Joseph West's chapter examines what qualities congregations that mobilize for progressive causes share. Generally speaking, progressive political mobilization out of congregations is rare, but Beyerlein and West identify several "causal recipes" that suggest which congregations are most likely to engage in progressive politics. In particular, they focus on combinations of variables including the presence of a liberal ideology and social justice orientation in the congregation and the presence of educated clergy and laity. In doing this, Beyerlein and West provide broad templates of the kind of congregations that we may see engage in progressive action.

Finally, drawing on datasets that examine ideas and attitudes of religious activists on both the Left and the Right, Laura R. Olson asks whether religious progressives share a collective identity as activists and whether they are committed to specific social movement organizations within their fields of action. It appears that when compared to conservatives, progressive religious activists are less committed to specific organizations and are less mobilized behind a coherent public agenda. Olson discusses the extent to which this difference may affect movement efficacy in political arenas.

Cultural Challenges of Progressive Religious Activism

The next three chapters offer insight into the varied cultural challenges associated with being progressive and religious, and the cultural work that groups engage in to overcome them. Several contradictory images of progressive religious activism comingle in the American historical imagination. The role of the Black Church in the civil rights movement looms large, yet liberal religious activism has also been closely associated with middle-class white Protestants and, to a lesser extent, with Catholics and Jews, who have long been vocal advocates for moral reform, peace, and social justice. And more recently, the progressive religious scene has been transformed by the influx of new immigrant communities and social movement organizations, which have brought greater racial, ethnic, socioeconomic, and religious diversity to this field. Together, the authors grapple with the challenges associated with different dimensions of this complex heritage, and the political context in which these diverse groups operate.

Beginning with a focus on theologically liberal Mainline Protestants—who have historically been at the forefront of many progressive religious actions—Paul Lichterman and Rhys H. Williams outline some of the distinctive challenges Mainliners face when they try to bring a specifically religious voice to progressive political advocacy. They show how liberal Protestant identity and communication style, as well as the larger reputation of vocal Christianity in public, all create cultural gaps that politically progressive Protestants must confront and engage.

Mia Diaz-Edelman sheds light on the challenges associated with cultivating cultural diversity within the Immigrant Rights Movement. Asking how this movement maintains solidarity across immigrant and nonimmigrant activists from faith-based, interfaith, and secular organizations, she finds that the movement has developed a "multicultural activist etiquette," a unifying mechanism within activist meeting spaces rooted in the common values of equality and the physical and emotional security of all persons.

Finally, Kristin Geraty complicates this picture by focusing on a faith-based community organizing coalition that engages in *progressive* action around issues of fair housing, education, and workforce development, but in which many participants are registered *Republicans* and consider themselves theologically *conservative*. She shows how the coalition struggles to construct a call to action that resonates with members, and to negotiate how their religious identity is communicated and interpreted in an affluent, suburban environment where the intersection of religion and politics is almost always conservative.

The Roles of Religion in Progressive Political Action

The third section includes four chapters that, in various ways, reveal the complex and varied roles that religion plays in progressive political action. The section begins with a historical analysis of the somewhat counterintuitive, yet central, role that Protestant institutions played in the emergence of the New Left. Through a case study of the Christian Faith-and-Life Community at the University of Texas at Austin from 1955 to 1962, Joshua Z. Gahr and Michael P. Young document how a group of liberal Presbyterian, Methodist, and Baptist clergy pushed UT students to reconceive the Church's "mission-in-the-world" and their personal witness to this mission in ways that unleashed a moral "breakthrough."

Moving from past to present, Juan R. Martinez argues that religious institutions today offer unique resources that encourage civic participation among noncitizens. Drawing on five years of ethnographic fieldwork, he shows that social movement organizations use and customize recognizable aspects of religious culture to promote progressive values and action among undocumented immigrants. By using religion to cast undocumented immigrants as deserving citizens, these organizations generate religious meanings that encourage calls for citizenship and civic engagement among marginalized populations.

Grace Yukich observes that most of the research in the field (including in this volume) focuses on activism emerging out of Christian congregations, and on the ways their efforts are positioned in relation to the religious Right and/or secular progressives. She argues that this focus limits the field's understanding of progressive political action by Buddhist, Hindu, and Muslim groups. She notes that these faith traditions are not necessarily "congregational" in form and do not necessarily orient themselves toward these U.S.-centric political reference points, and discusses alternative paths through which members of these groups understand and engage in social change.

Finally, Sharon Erickson Nepstad hones our understanding of how religion can shape activists' interpretations of repression. Through a comparative analysis of the U.S. and Swedish Plowshares movements, Nepstad argues that long prison sentences did not harm the U.S. Plowshares movement in part because activists' Catholic beliefs and identity led them to view repression in religious terms that deepened their commitment, motivation, and unity. She contrasts the U.S. case to the experience of the secular Swedish Plowshares activists, who interpreted their repression in ways that made them susceptible to internal disputes, waning commitment, and cooptation.

Distinctive Styles of Progressive Religious Talk in the Public Sphere

The fourth section includes four chapters that reveal the varied ways in which progressive religious actors assert their voices and values in the public sphere, with attention to the distinctive rhetorical styles and discourses they have developed. In each case, the authors attend to the unique communications challenges these individuals and groups face, and how their distinctive styles of talk were crafted in response to these challenges.

First, Philip S. Gorski provides historical context for these groups' use of civil religious rhetoric. Through an analysis of Barack Obama's efforts to resurrect the civil religious tradition during his two campaigns and terms as president, Gorski revisits and reconstructs the vision of "American civil religion" (ACR) that was originally advanced by Robert Bellah in 1967. Gorski's chapter shows that the ACR is woven out of two main threads: the prophetic religion of the Hebrew Bible and an Anglo-American version of civic republicanism. It also distinguishes the civil religious tradition from its two main rivals: religious nationalism and radical secularism.

Ruth Braunstein then zeroes in on one group of progressive religious actors—"Nuns on the Bus"—showing that in addition to voicing certain civil religious themes, they also engaged in certain distinctive forms of public communication that helped them to navigate challenges associated with being progressive and religious. Namely, the chapter shows that the nuns leveraged their moral authority as storytellers to channel media attention toward Americans' economic suffering, while also asserting the moral necessity of taking stories seriously when making policy decisions.

Two subsequent chapters then demonstrate the complicated ways in which participants in politically progressive religious communities use—or *avoid*—religious language when talking about politics. Gary J. Adler, Jr., finds that in discussions about undocumented immigration, progressive religious organizations and actors employ a style of "formal neutrality," which allows them to represent "all sides" of this contentious debate and protect their "non-partisan" status. Based on participant observation with BorderLinks, a transnational organization that leads weeklong immersion trips across the U.S.-Mexico border, Adler finds that this "neutral" style of talk may not generate the activism that its practitioners hope, since it fails to fully connect the experiences of participants with narratives of injustice or pathways to potential action.

Todd Nicholas Fuist, conversely, examines communities that talk openly about politics, and use extensive religious language to do so. The communities Fuist studies use three models for understanding the connection between faith and politics: the Teacher Model, where religious exemplars are understood as promoting progressive action; the Community Model, where groups promote specific, progressive understandings of what it means to be a community; and the Theological Model, where existing beliefs are creatively applied to contemporary politics. Through the combination of these three models, these communities create pathways to understanding and action by sacralizing progressive ideologies and practices.

Conclusion

In a concluding chapter, Rhys H. Williams assesses the ways in which attention to the complexities of progressive religion forces us to reassess longstanding theoretical understandings of religion, social movements, civic life, and political action. Drawing out key themes and questions that emerge from this volume, he examines the factors that have led to the low public visibility of progressive religious social action in the media and academic research, and points to several conceptual and empirical benefits of taking progressive religion into account.

This volume brings together a collection of scholars focused on an important, if too often overlooked, field of action in American religion and politics. Existing in almost every community, and involved with almost every possible issue or area of public concern, progressive religion is a driving force in the collective attempts by religious Americans to shape their worlds. Progressive religion has also become increasingly important in contemporary public debates. In the process of lifting up, describing, and analyzing these social worlds, we find new ways of thinking about the American religio-political landscape, and new challenges for how we conceptualize religiously motivated social action more generally.

NOTES

1 Martin Luther King, Jr., "I've Been to the Mountaintop," April 3, 1968, *American Rhetoric*, www.americanrhetoric.com.

2 "Remarks of Senator Barack Obama: 'A More Perfect Union,'" March 18, 2008, https://my.barackobama.com.

3 PICO stands for People Improving Communities through Organizing; DART stands for Direct Action and Research Training.

4 The Central America Solidarity Movement challenged U.S. intervention in Central American conflicts during the 1980s by supporting Nicaraguans, Salvadorans, and Guatemalans fighting for human rights and economic justice. The Sanctuary Movement, which provided assistance and "sanctuary" to Central American refugees to the U.S., was among the faith-based organizations involved in the broader Central America Solidarity Movement (Nepstad 2004). The Plowshares Movement is an international anti-nuclear and pacifist movement started by radical Catholic activists in the U.S. (Nepstad 2008).

5 Fligstein and McAdam's work on "strategic action fields" is the most recent in a long line of arguments for a *field*-based approach to studying the meso-level of social interaction. In citing this work, we note its influence on our adoption of this approach, but we do not wholly embrace their conceptualization of "strategic action" (see also Avishai 2008). For example, many of the groups we study have made choices that they felt were morally, politically, or spiritually "correct," but which blunted their "strategic" goals when defined in narrowly political terms or as materialist interests alone (Swartz 1996; 1997). Strategy, at least as typically conceived of in social movement research, seems to map only loosely onto these actions. For this reason, we use the term "fields of action," leaving open the possibility that some fields may orient themselves around stakes and rules that are inconsistent with traditional notions of strategic action.

REFERENCES

Alexander, Jeffrey C. 2006. *The Civil Sphere*. New York: Oxford University Press.

Allahyari, Rebecca Anne. 2000. *Visions of Charity: Volunteer Workers and Moral Community*. Berkeley: University of California Press.

Avishai, Orit. 2008. "'Doing Religion' in a Secular World: Women in Conservative Religions and the Question of Agency." *Gender & Society* 22(4): 409–433.

Bandy, Joe, and Jackie Smith, eds. 2005. *Coalitions across Borders: Transnational Protest and the Neoliberal Order*. Boulder, CO: Rowman & Littlefield.

Bean, Lydia. 2014. "Compassionate Conservatives? Evangelicals, Economic Conservatism, and National Identity." *Journal for the Scientific Study of Religion* 53(1): 164–186.

Bender, Courtney. 2003. *Heaven's Kitchen: Living Religion at God's Love We Deliver.* Chicago: University of Chicago Press.

Beyerlein, Kraig, and Mark Chaves. 2003. "The Political Activities of Religious Congregations in the United States." *Journal for the Scientific Study of Religion* 42(2): 229–246.

Beyerlein, Kraig, and John R. Hipp. 2006. "From Pews to Participation: The Effect of Congregational Activity and Context on Bridging Civic Engagement." *Social Problems* 53(1): 97–117.

Bourdieu, Pierre. 1991. *Language and Symbolic Power.* Cambridge, MA: Harvard University Press.

Braunstein, Ruth. 2012. "Storytelling in Liberal Religious Advocacy." *Journal for the Scientific Study of Religion* 51(1): 110–127.

Braunstein, Ruth, Brad R. Fulton, and Richard L. Wood. 2014. "The Role of Bridging Cultural Practices in Racially and Socioeconomically Diverse Civic Organizations." *American Sociological Review* 79(4): 705–725.

Burge, Ryan P., and Paul A. Djupe. 2014. "Truly Inclusive or Uniformly Liberal? An Analysis of the Politics of the Emerging Church." *Journal for the Scientific Study of Religion* 53(3): 636–651.

Calhoun, Craig. 2012. *The Roots of Radicalism: Tradition, the Public Sphere and Early 19th Century Social Movements.* Chicago: University of Chicago Press.

Clemens, Elisabeth S. 1993. "Organizational Repertoires and Institutional Change: Women's Groups and the Transformation of U.S. Politics, 1890–1920." *American Journal of Sociology* 98(4): 755–798.

Davis, Nancy J., and Robert V. Robinson. 2012. *Claiming Society for God: Religious Movements and Social Welfare in Egypt, Israel, Italy, and the United States.* Bloomington: Indiana University Press.

Dillon, Michele. 1999. *Catholic Identity: Balancing Reason, Faith, and Power.* New York: Cambridge University Press.

Dionne, E. J., Jr. 2008. *Souled Out: Reclaiming Faith and Politics after the Religious Right.* Princeton, NJ: Princeton University Press.

Edgell, Penny. 2012. "Cultural Sociology of Religion: New Directions." *Annual Review of Sociology* 38: 247–265.

Edles, Laura Desfor. 2012. "Contemporary Progressive Christianity and Its Symbolic Ramifications." *Cultural Sociology* 7(3): 3–22.

Ehrenberg, John R. 1999. *Civil Society: The Critical History of an Idea.* New York: New York University Press.

Eliasoph, Nina. 1998. *Avoiding Politics: How Americans Produce Apathy in Everyday Life.* New York: Cambridge University Press.

Eliasoph, Nina, and Paul Lichterman. 2003. "Culture in Interaction." *American Journal of Sociology* 108(4): 735–794.

Fine, Gary Alan. 2012. "Group Culture and the Interaction Order: Local Sociology on the Meso-Level." *Annual Review of Sociology* 38: 159–179.

Fligstein, Neil, and Doug McAdam. 2011. "Toward a General Theory of Strategic Action Fields." *Sociological Theory* 29(1): 1–26.

Fowler, Robert Booth, Allen D. Hertzke, Laura R. Olson, and Kevin R. den Dulk. 2004. *Religion and Politics in America: Faith, Culture, and Strategic Choices*. 3rd ed. Boulder, CO: Westview Press.

Fuist, Todd Nicholas, Laurie Cooper Stoll, and Fred Kniss. 2012. "Beyond the Liberal-Conservative Divide: Assessing the Relationship between Religious Denominations and Their Associated LGBT Organizations." *Qualitative Sociology* 35(1): 65–87.

Gusfield, Joseph R. 1986. *Symbolic Crusade: Status Politics and the American Temperance Movement*. 2nd ed. Champaign: University of Illinois Press.

Gutterman, David S. 2005. *Prophetic Politics: Christian Social Movements and American Democracy*. Ithaca, NY: Cornell University Press.

Habermas, Jürgen. 2006. "Religion in the Public Sphere." *European Journal of Philosophy* 14(1): 1–25.

Haedicke, Michael A. 2012. "'Keeping Our Mission, Changing Our System': Translation and Organizational Change in Natural Foods Co-ops." *The Sociological Quarterly* 53(1): 44–67.

Hart, Steven. 2001. *Cultural Dilemmas of Progressive Politics: Styles of Engagement among Grassroots Activists*. Chicago: University of Chicago Press.

Hertzke, Allen D. 1988. *Representing God in Washington: The Role of Religious Lobbies in the American Polity*. 1st ed. Knoxville: University of Tennessee Press.

Hunter, James Davison. 1991. *Culture Wars: The Struggle to Control the Family, Art, Education, Law, and Politics in America*. New York: Basic Books.

Klawiter, Maren. 2008. *The Biopolitics of Breast Cancer: Changing Cultures of Disease and Activism*. Minneapolis: University of Minnesota Press.

Klemp, Nathaniel. 2010. "The Christian Right: Engaged Citizens or Theocratic Crusaders?" *Politics and Religion* 3(1): 1–27.

Kniss, Fred. 2003. "Mapping the Moral Order: Depicting the Terrain of Religious Conflict and Change." In *Handbook of the Sociology of Religion*, edited by Michele Dillon, 331–347. New York: Cambridge University Press.

Lichterman, Paul. 2005. *Elusive Togetherness: Church Groups Trying to Bridge America's Divisions*. Princeton, NJ: Princeton University Press.

Lichterman, Paul, and C. Brady Potts, eds. 2009. *The Civic Life of American Religion*. Stanford, CA: Stanford University Press.

Moon, Dawne. 2004. *God, Sex, and Politics: Homosexuality and Everyday Theologies*. Chicago: University of Chicago Press.

Moore, Kelly. 2008. *Disrupting Science: Social Movements, American Scientists, and the Politics of the Military, 1945–1975*. Princeton, NJ: Princeton University Press.

Morris, Aldon D. 1984. *The Origins of the Civil Rights Movement: Black Communities Organizing for Change*. New York; London: Free Press; Collier Macmillan.

Nepstad, Sharon Erickson. 2004. *Convictions of the Soul: Religion, Culture, and Agency in the Central America Solidarity Movement*. New York: Oxford University Press.

Nepstad, Sharon Erickson. 2008. *Religion and War Resistance in the Plowshares Movement*. New York: Cambridge University Press.

O'Brien, Jodi. 2004. "Wrestling the Angel of Contradiction: Queer Christian Identities." *Culture and Religion* 5(2): 179–202.

Perrin, Andrew J. 2006. *Citizen Speak: The Democratic Imagination in American Life*. Chicago: University of Chicago Press.

Polletta, Francesca. 2006. *It Was Like a Fever: Storytelling in Protest and Politics*. Chicago: University of Chicago Press.

Powell, Rachel. 2011. "Frames and Narratives as Tools for Recruiting and Sustaining Group Members: The Soulforce Equality Ride as a Social Movement Organization." *Sociological Inquiry* 81(4): 454–476.

Schneider, Nathan. 2013. *Thank You Anarchy: Notes from the Occupy Apocalypse*. Oakland: University of California Press.

Smith, Christian. 1991. *The Emergence of Liberation Theology: Radical Religion and Social Movement Theory*. Chicago: University of Chicago Press.

Smith, Christian, ed. 1996a. *Disruptive Religion: The Force of Faith in Social-Movement Activism*. New York: Routledge.

Smith, Christian. 1996b. *Resisting Reagan: The U.S. Central America Peace Movement*. 1st ed. Chicago: University of Chicago Press.

Stout, Jeffrey. 2010. *Blessed Are the Organized: Grassroots Democracy in America*. Princeton, NJ: Princeton University Press.

Sullivan, Amy. 2008. *The Party Faithful: How and Why Democrats Are Closing the God Gap*. New York: Scribner.

Swartz. David. 1996. "Bridging the Study of Culture and Religion: Pierre Bourdieu's Political Economy of Symbolic Power." *Sociology of Religion* 57(1): 71–85.

Swartz, David. 1997. *Culture and Power: The Sociology of Pierre Bourdieu*. Chicago: University of Chicago Press.

Tilly, Charles. 1993. "Contentious Repertoires in Great Britain, 1758–1834." *Social Science History* 17(2): 253–280.

Warner, R. Stephen. 2013. "Evangelicals of the 1970s and 2010s: What's the Same, What's Different, and What's Urgent." In *The New Evangelical Social Engagement*, edited by Brian Steensland and Philip Goff, 280–291. New York: Oxford University Press.

Wilcox, Melissa M. 2009. *Queer Women and Religious Individualism*. Bloomington: Indiana University Press.

Williams, Rhys H. 1995. "Constructing the Public Good: Social Movements and Cultural Resources." *Social Problems* 42(1): 124–144.

Williams, Rhys H. 1999. "Visions of the Good Society and the Religious Roots of American Political Culture." *Sociology of Religion* 60(1): 1–34.

Williams, Rhys H. 2002. "From the 'Beloved Community' to 'Family Values': Religious Language, Symbolic Repertoires, and Democratic Culture." In *Social Movements: Identity, Culture, and the State*, edited by David S. Meyer, Nancy Whittier, and Belinda Robnett, 247–265. New York: Oxford University Press.

Williams, Rhys H. 2003. "Religious Social Movements in the Public Sphere: Organization, Ideology, and Activism." In *Handbook of the Sociology of Religion*, edited by Michele Dillon, 315–330. New York: Cambridge University Press.

Williams, Rhys H. 2007. "Social Movements and Culture." In *Blackwell Encyclopedia of Sociology*, edited by George Ritzer, 954–955. Malden, MA: Blackwell.

Wood, Richard L. 2002. *Faith in Action: Religion, Race, and Democratic Organizing in America*. Chicago: University of Chicago Press.

Wood, Richard L., Brad Fulton, and Kathryn Partridge. 2012. *Building Bridges, Building Power: Developments in Institution-Based Community Organizing*. Interfaith Funders. www.interfaithfunders.org.

Wuthnow, Robert. 1999. "Mobilizing Civic Engagement: The Changing Impact of Religious Involvement." In *Civic Engagement in American Democracy*, edited by Theda Skocpol and Morris P. Fiorina, 331–363. Washington, DC; New York: Brookings Institution Press; Russell Sage Foundation.

Wuthnow, Robert. 2006. *Saving America? Faith-Based Services and the Future of Civil Society*. Princeton, NJ: Princeton University Press.

Yukich, Grace. 2010. "Boundary Work in Inclusive Religious Groups: Constructing Identity at the New York Catholic Worker." *Sociology of Religion* 71(2): 172–196.

Yukich, Grace. 2013. *One Family under God: Immigration Politics and Progressive Religion in America*. New York: Oxford University Press.

Zubrzycki, Genevieve. 2006. *The Crosses of Auschwitz: Nationalism and Religion in Post-Communist Poland*. Chicago: University of Chicago Press.

PART I

Patterns of Progressive Religious Mobilization and Engagement

The chapters in this section examine patterns of progressive religious mobilization and engagement at the individual, organizational, and field levels. After reading this section, both longtime observers of political life and students being introduced to this world for the first time will better understand the following questions: Why do religious people become involved in progressive activism? Once they are involved, how do they organize and interact with other political groups, including political parties? Do participants within the progressive religious field share a common set of views, characteristics, and ideas about how to engage in political life? Or are there important sources of difference and diversity, including ethnic, religious, and even political diversity, within this group of Americans and the organizations they represent?

Moreover, for readers who are interested in how progressive religious activism differs from conservative religious and secular progressive activism, the chapters in this section illuminate the following three points of divergence. First, as we will see, many individuals who hold progressive religious views do not identify strongly as "progressive religious activists" per se, and progressive religious organizations vary in their identification with a broader progressive religious movement. This lack of collective consciousness stands in marked contrast to the conservative religious activist field. Although it is certainly not monolithic, the religious Right enjoys comparatively high levels of internal coherence and identification—especially concerning traditional views of gender and sexuality—albeit only after decades of intentional movement building by both local and national actors.

Second, we will learn about the complex relationship between progressive religious movement organizations and American political parties. In contrast to the religious Right, which has forged a close, albeit fraught, relationship with the Republican Party over the past several decades, we learn that progressive religious organizations have not been welcomed as fully into the Democratic Party coalition, which is dominated by secular (and secularist) progressive actors. This has limited progressive religious actors' political influence and visibility, at least in electoral politics, but also shaped their tactical choices in important ways, including leading them to pursue action primarily at more local levels.

Finally, these chapters show the extent to which progressive religious organizations differ in their demographic composition from most conservative religious and secular progressive groups. High levels of religious, racial, and socioeconomic diversity within progressive religious organizations are reflections of these groups' commitment to values like inclusion and equality as well as an important source of political legitimacy in an increasingly diverse society. Overall, by highlighting the field's internal composition, coherence, diversity, and relationship to other political organizations, the chapters in this section provide readers with a multifaceted picture of this often-overlooked field as well as the actors that comprise it, and necessary context for the sections that follow.

1

Achieving and Leveraging Diversity through Faith-Based Organizing

BRAD R. FULTON AND RICHARD L. WOOD

After a perceived hiatus of several decades—"perceived" for reasons discussed below—religious progressives have reappeared in the public eye in recent years. Though mostly very marginal players in the Occupy Wall Street movement that made inequality a prominent public issue in American life by framing it as a struggle between "the one percent and the ninety-nine percent," religious progressives have been prominent participants in the subsequent debates over house foreclosures, banking reform, racial inequities in law enforcement and sentencing, and comprehensive immigration reform (Sanati 2010; Waters 2010; Wood and Fulton 2015). Even before the Great Recession, religious progressives had been among the crucial sectors articulating why access to healthcare was a fundamental moral issue (Wood 2007). Their advocacy helped lead to renewal of the State Children's Health Insurance Program that was twice vetoed by President George W. Bush before being signed by President Barack Obama; their subsequent moral advocacy was crucial to the passage of national healthcare reform in 2009—and particularly to its inclusion of significant subsidies for healthcare for the poor and lower middle class (Parsons 2010; Pear 2009).

The perception of religious progressives as absent from the public arena is itself an interesting phenomenon (Fulton 2016a). It is hard to argue that they have indeed been absent, given the presence of religious voices in favor of the successful immigration reform of the 1980s (Hondagneu-Sotelo 2001; Hondagneu-Sotelo et al. 2004), in favor of peace and human rights (Nepstad 2004; 2008; 2011) and against apartheid in South Africa in the 1980s and 1990s (Comaroff and Comaroff 1991; Kairos Theologians Group 1986; Wood 2000), in defense of social welfare in the 1990s (Marsh 2006), and in support of civil rights and against the American-led war in Iraq after 2001 (Religious News Service 2003). Rather than an actual *absence* of religious progressives, then, the key dynamic has been of vastly reduced *efficacy* of religious voices and organizations in claiming a strong position in favor of politically liberal and progressive social policy within public discourse.

We suggest this reduced efficacy of religious progressives—and thus the perception of their absence from public discourse—has less to do with religious progressivism itself than with three related factors: First, American political culture has shifted dramatically rightward since the Reagan administration, meaning that the arguments and policy positions of religious progressives get less of a public hearing. Second, religious conservatives have mobilized so effectively for a media-oriented political culture that they have crowded out religious voices supporting other policy alternatives. Third, as noted in the introduction to this volume, secular voices—sometimes simply non-religious voices, sometimes clearly anti-religious ones—increasingly dominate progressive policy discourse. The key question then is not whether religious progressives exist, but rather whether they can claim space in public discourse and power relations commensurate with their continuing presence in American society.

We explore that question by analyzing the field of faith-based community organizing (FBCO), which has enabled one sector of religious progressives to gain greater political influence. Our analysis suggests that religion need not be condemned to being a politically conservative force, nor to exist without effective public voice. It also suggests that progressive politics need not do without resonance with the moral instincts and religious ethical teachings that undergird many American communities. Progressive politics can draw on religious commitments rooted in many communities and across all social strata to bridge the racial/ethnic and socioeconomic divides that currently eviscerate progressive policy-making.

We focus on the high levels of diversity across religious, racial/ethnic, and socioeconomic divides that the FBCO field's organizational infrastructure in congregations and other institutions has generated. That diversity and the sheer scale of mobilization enabled by the FBCO infrastructure together constitute faith-based organizing's most significant sources of power and most important credentials for legitimacy in the public arena. Most crucially for the FBCO field and its potential contribution to progressive politics and deepening democracy in the United States, the field bridges social divides in ways rarely seen within American civil society. Faith-based community organizing thus deepens the wells of "bridging social capital" that Robert Putnam and others have found so desiccated in the United States, and leverages that social capital to build power and influence in the political arena.[1] Furthermore, we argue that the FBCO field has the potential to advance progressive socioeconomic priorities at a scale that will matter for the future direction of American society. Realizing its potential, though, will require navigating and leveraging its internal social differences for the collective good and overcoming the challenges facing progressive politics in general.

Faith-Based Community Organizing and Progressive Politics

The full history of the field of community organizing and its most prominent variants today has been told in a number of venues.[2] Rather than retell that history here, we note simply that the field emerged from foundations in the work of Saul Alinsky and prior organizers in American civic life, but over the last twenty years the field has also significantly transcended those origins by drawing on innovative work within and beyond its own boundaries. Nonetheless, most political work that falls under the rubric of "community organizing" today sustains Alinsky's focus on a particular set of socioeconomic issues: those that affect residents' quality of life in communities falling somewhere on the spectrum from the desperately poor to the working class to the middle class made newly vulnerable by recent economic restructuring and its attendant insecurity and "fear of falling" into poverty.

We use the term "religious progressives" to identify political progressives who trace their political views to their religious and spiritual commitments. Religious progressives thus may or may not be "progressive" in theological or religious or spiritual terms; rather, we use the term to denote political progressives, noting that relatively conservative theological and religious positions sometimes undergird rather progressive political views. Of course, the term "progressive" as applied to politics in turn raises a host of ambiguities: Must one hold to progressive ortho-doxy across every issue to be considered politically progressive? Who gets to determine that list of issues, and what counts as the progressive view on each?

To avoid these conundrums, for the purposes of this chapter we use the term "progressive" to denote only those who are active in the public arena in a way that places substantial political emphasis on one or both of two efforts: first, the effort to expand the effective representation of socioeconomic, racial/ethnic, or immigrant groups previously marginal-ized in American political decision-making at all levels; second, the effort to roll back the staggeringly high levels of economic inequality (i.e., in-come and wealth) that have been rebuilt in the United States over the last few decades and were previously unprecedented in American life since the Gilded Age. In this, we follow the lead of one of the recent classics of American political sociology in emphasizing the role of *voice* and *equal-ity* as central to the effort to defend and deepen democracy in America.[3]

The FBCO field embraces both of these aspirations. As documented below, most FBCO coalitions are organizing a highly diverse base of communities, addressing issues related to poverty and economic in-equality (see Figure 1.1), and seeking to empower voices that had previ-

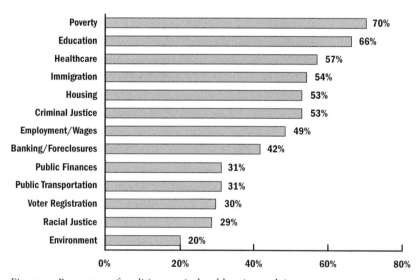

Figure 1.1. Percentage of coalitions actively addressing each issue category

ously been politically marginalized. Although this chapter focuses on the FBCO field, we by no means claim (or believe) that this field or the issues it addresses are the only important foci of "progressive" political engagement.

The National Study of Community Organizing Coalitions

To document and analyze the current state of the FBCO field, we conducted the National Study of Community Organizing Coalitions, which surveyed the entire field of FBCO coalitions (see Figure 1.2) (Fulton et al. 2011).[4] This study achieved a response rate of 94 percent—gathering data on 178 of the 189 coalitions in the country and demographic information on the 4,145 member organizations, 2,939 board members, and 628 paid staff affiliated with these coalitions (Fulton 2016b). To measure diversity, the data include the religious affiliation and predominant race of each member organization, and the gender, age, religion, race, income, education, and occupation of each board member and paid staff.

Since 1999, the FBCO field experienced a net growth of 42 percent—102 new coalitions were established and 46 had become inactive. In most areas where a coalition had become inactive, another coalition still exists.

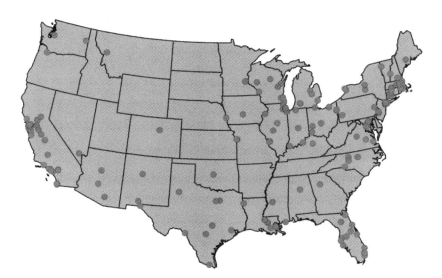

Figure 1.2. Map of the entire field of FBCO coalitions in 2011

The overall growth of the field corresponds with an increase in its geographic spread. In 1999, 33 states had active coalitions; now, coalitions are active in 40. As the field extended into new areas, it also deepened its presence in former areas, with the highest concentrations being in major urban areas.

The base of the FBCO field is its member organizations, of which there are approximately 4,500. Congregations remain the large majority of member organizations and 30 percent of the coalitions have a member base comprised exclusively of congregations. Furthermore, the members' shared identity as people of faith often provides the cultural glue that holds a socially diverse coalition together (Braunstein, Fulton, and Wood 2014). Most coalitions regularly incorporate religious practices into their organizing activities and many support "congregational development" initiatives designed to use organizing as a means to strengthen member congregations.[5]

Since 1999, the number of non-congregational member organizations has doubled from approximately 500 to 1,000 (see Figure 1.3). These organizations include schools, faith-based nonprofits, unions, immigrant associations, economic development corporations, and other civic associations. Although congregations and their faith commitments remain central to the FBCO organizing model, non-congregational members

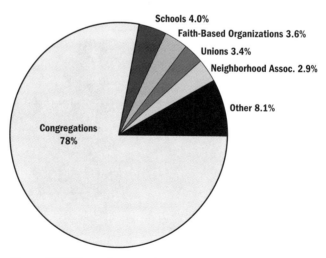

Figure 1.3. Types of FBCO member organizations

now make up 22 percent of all member organizations; 70 percent of coalitions have at least one non-congregational member (Fulton and Wood 2012).

Beyond the field's ability to form enduring coalitions with organizations across multiple organizational sectors, we here document its effectiveness in building a socially diverse base. We examine religious, racial/ethnic, and socioeconomic diversity in turn. FBCO coalitions achieve this diversity through their member organizations, which individually may be relatively homogenous, but collectively represent substantial diversity along religious, racial/ethnic, and socioeconomic lines. FBCO coalitions pursue this diversity intentionally, believing that they gain political credibility in the public sphere by organizing a base that is representative of its surrounding community.

Religious Diversity

Since at least the 1970s, religious congregations have been the primary institutional members that organizers have recruited. As of 2012, 7 percent of all U.S. congregations are involved in some form of faith-based community organizing.[6] Mainline Protestant, Catholic, and Black Protestant congregations have been the core of this membership base, while Conservative Protestant, Jewish, Unitarian Universalist, and Muslim congregations represent a much smaller share.[7] Over the last decade, however, the religious composition of the field has become more evenly distributed among the various religious traditions (see Figure 1.4).[8]

Even though congregations from every major religious tradition are involved in faith-based community organizing, the participating congregations do not represent the religious composition of congregations in the United States (see Figure 1.5). While Mainline Protestant and Catholic congregations represent a majority in the FBCO field, they represent a minority among congregations in the United States. On the other hand, almost half of the congregations in the U.S. are Conservative Protestant, yet they represent a small minority in the FBCO field. Black Protestantism is the only religious tradition in which the percentage of congregations in the field matches its percentage among all U.S. congregations. With regard to the minority religious traditions, Jewish, Unitarian Universalist, and Muslim congregations are relatively well represented in the

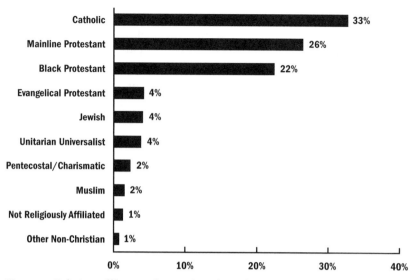

Figure 1.4. Religious affiliation of FBCO board members

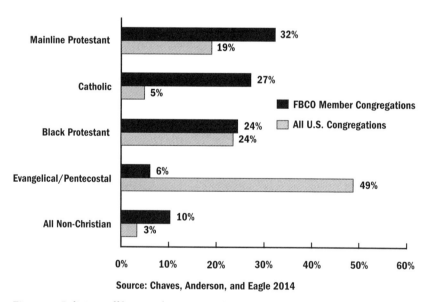

Source: Chaves, Anderson, and Eagle 2014

Figure 1.5. Religious affiliation of FBCO member congregations compared with all congregations in the U.S.

FBCO field. Jewish synagogues, for example, make up roughly 2 percent of all U.S. congregations, whereas they make up 5 percent of all FBCO member congregations. Unitarian Universalist and Muslim congregations each make up less than 1 percent of U.S. congregations, and respectively they make up 4 percent and 1.3 percent of all FBCO member congregations.

The substantial religious diversity of the field is also reflected within most individual coalitions. The percentage of coalitions that have only Mainline Protestant, Catholic, and/or Black Protestant congregations—the historic religious core of the FBCO field—decreased from 25 percent to 15 percent between 1999 and 2011. Almost half of the coalitions have at least one Conservative Protestant, Jewish, or Unitarian Universalist congregation, 20 percent have at least one Muslim congregation, and 15 percent have at least one Jewish *and* one Muslim congregation. Furthermore, over 50 percent of the coalitions have at least one secular member organization and 20 percent of the member organizations of a typical coalition are non-congregations.[9]

Through its religiously diverse member base, the FBCO field is building power by bridging the divides that separate religious traditions from one another and from secular institutions. Moreover, religious diversity within individual coalitions indicates that this bridging is occurring on the ground locally, rather than only at aggregate state and national levels (which might not constitute "bridging" at all). This base in diverse religious traditions allows these organizations to project influence more effectively in two ways. First, by drawing communities linked to divergent faith traditions into shared work in the public arena, faith-based organizing coalitions broaden their mobilizing base and increase their legitimacy in the religiously pluralistic political arena of the United States. Second, by drawing on religious sources of meaning, these coalitions infuse their work with moral authority and a sense of transcendence that not only mobilizes constituents but also links their political interests and real-life struggles to moral traditions that are broadly shared by diverse publics.

Racial/Ethnic Diversity

Similarly, the FBCO field is building power by bridging racial/ethnic divides. Figure 1.6 shows the racial/ethnic composition of the field's

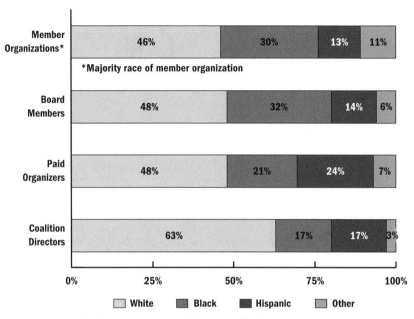

Figure 1.6. Racial/ethnic composition of the FBCO field

member organizations, board members, paid organizers, and coalition directors.[10] Over 50 percent of FBCO coalition board members are nonwhite (see Figure 1.7). For purposes of comparison, note that only 19 percent of all nonprofit board members in the U.S. and 13 percent of Fortune 500 board members are nonwhite (Ostrower 2007; Lang et al. 2011).

The field's substantial racial/ethnic diversity is also reflected within most individual coalitions.[11] We calculate the racial diversity of a coalition's board using the Blau index, which takes into account both the number of racial/ethnic groups and the proportion of each group represented on the board.[12] It generates a diversity score that ranges from 0 to .80, and the score can be interpreted as the probability that two randomly selected board members of a coalition are of a different race/ethnicity.[13] Based on this index, a coalition with a mono-racial board has a diversity score of 0, and as the number of different racial/ethnic groups represented on a coalition's board increases and as the proportion of each group becomes more evenly distributed, the coalition's diversity score approaches .80. Figure 1.8 shows the distribution of coali-

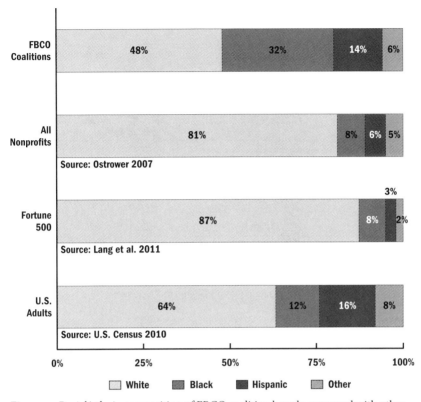

Figure 1.7. Racial/ethnic composition of FBCO coalition boards compared with other boards and all U.S. adults

tions based on their board's diversity score, the percentage of the majority race/ethnicity, and the identity of the majority race/ethnicity.

Using the Blau index enables us to compare the racial/ethnic diversity of FBCO coalitions with that of other community-based institutions.[14] The mean diversity score for FBCO coalitions is .47, whereas the mean diversity score for public schools is .33, for U.S. counties is .28, and for congregations is .12.[15] FBCO coalitions thus tend to be more diverse than public schools and U.S. counties, and much more diverse than congregations. In an era of declining social capital, it appears that the FBCO field plays a crucial role in bolstering bridging capital by linking Americans across the divides that otherwise separate them.

No simple summary can fully capture the complex patterns of racial/ethnic diversity within FBCO coalitions. However, by all measures, their

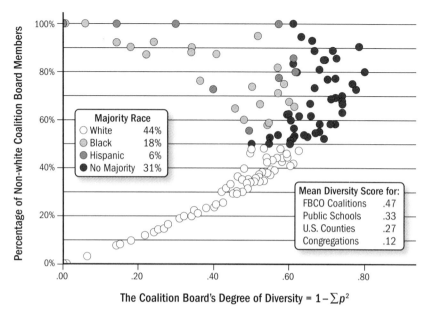

Figure 1.8. Racial/ethnic diversity score of FBCO coalition boards

Sources: Aud et al. 2010; 2010 U.S. Census; Chaves, Anderson, and Eagle 2014

boards are much more racially/ethnically diverse than most corporate and nonprofit boards, and their member base is more diverse than most schools, neighborhoods, and congregations. In this way, the field's ability to bring Americans together across racial and ethnic divides is extraordinary within American political culture and institutions. Currently, that capacity allows some of these coalitions to simultaneously: (i) organize effectively in communities heavily made up of racial/ethnic minorities and recent immigrants; (ii) confront "colorblind" ideologies that refuse to take seriously continuing racial divides of American life; and (iii) advance "universalist" policy solutions that transcend race-based politics (Wood and Fulton 2015).

Socioeconomic Diversity

Similarly, assessing the education and household income level of the coalition board members shows that the FBCO field also exhibits substantial socioeconomic diversity. This dimension of diversity is among the most unique and most important characteristics of the FBCO field. Twenty-three percent of the coalition board members have less than a bachelor's degree. Although this figure is lower than the proportion in the U.S. population as a whole, it demonstrates that these boards are not comprised solely of the highly educated. More significant is the spread of household incomes among the coalition board members (see Figure 1.9). Twenty-three percent have a household income of less than $25,000 per year (an amount slightly above the 2011 federal poverty level for a family of four). Another 35 percent have a household income between $25,000 and $50,000 per year. Although no nationally representative data on the socioeconomic status of nonprofit or corporate board members exist, the field of FBCO board members clearly reflects much greater socioeconomic diversity than most other fields.

Altogether, the proportion of board members with a household income below $50,000 per year almost precisely matches the proportion of American households below that income level. This substantial socioeconomic diversity is also reflected within most individual coalitions. Over 90 percent of the coalitions have at least one board member who has no more than a high school degree, and over 75 percent of the

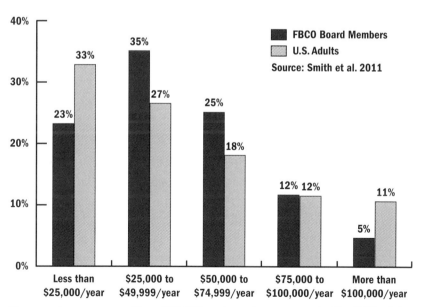

Figure 1.9. Income composition of FBCO board members compared with all U.S. adults

coalitions have at least one board member with a household income of less than $25,000 per year. Although systematic comparative data on the class composition of social movement organizations do not appear to exist, such organizations are rarely class diverse and when they are, internal class differences often undermine their work (Leondar-Wright 2014). This makes the socioeconomic diversity of the FBCO coalitions and their success all the more noteworthy.

The combination of socioeconomic and racial/ethnic diversity documented above makes these coalitions unusual within American civil society, rivaled only by those labor unions that have successfully organized in diverse settings in recent years (Bronfenbrenner 1998; Martin 2007; Voss and Sherman 2000). Adding in their religious diversity—and (in some cases) fluency in religious ethical teachings—appears to position them uniquely to offer a credible moral voice on issues of economic and racial inequality in American life.[16]

The Effects of Internal Social Diversity on Organizing Activities

Given the high levels of diversity documented above, one might expect this field of faith-based and progressively oriented political activity to struggle to maintain internal cohesion. Yet many of these coalitions have maintained a stable presence and unified voice on socioeconomic issues in the political arena for years or decades. How do they navigate these differences?

Although many coalitions simultaneously exhibit substantial levels of religious, racial/ethnic, and socioeconomic diversity, they navigate each dimension of diversity in distinct ways. While most coalitions are religiously diverse and leaders are often encouraged to draw on their specific religious traditions, participants seldom focus on their religious differences. The majority of coalitions reported discussing religious differences only "rarely" to "sometimes," and most indicated that religious differences had a minimal effect on their planning meetings. Interestingly, the coalitions that reported "often" discussing religious differences were more likely to report that those differences affected their planning meetings (the direction of causality is not clear). Yet a coalition's propensity to discuss religious differences is unrelated to its degree of religious diversity. Furthermore, the directors of religiously diverse coalitions did not report it to be any more difficult to accommodate different religious traditions in their organizing work than did directors of less diverse coalitions.

These patterns along with ethnographic research in these coalitions suggest that, as coalition members from different religious traditions work together to improve their communities, they navigate their religious differences by downplaying them. Instead of focusing on potentially divisive differences, they leverage their shared commitment to address common concerns about inequality and social policy that disproportionately affect poor, low-, and middle-income families. In an increasingly polarized political culture, in which religious differences are often used to amplify political disagreements, FBCO coalitions are strikingly counter-cultural. Rather than pitting religious traditions against each other (or advancing one strand within a particular tradition over other strands), they seek to transcend religious differences by focusing on shared values, engaging in mutually acceptable spiritual practices, and pursuing common socioeconomic goals—often by emphasizing the ways their religious ethical teachings overlap on socioeconomic terrain.

In contrast to how coalitions handle religious differences, some now handle racial/ethnic differences by addressing them directly. Even though historically faith-based organizing typically downplayed racial/ethnic differences, in 2011 most coalitions reported discussing racial/ethnic differences either "sometimes" or "often," and coalitions that are more racially/ethnically diverse tend to discuss racial/ethnic differences more often. In addition, the racial/ethnic diversity of a coalition is significantly associated with the extent to which racial/ethnic differences complicate, prolong, hinder, and enhance its planning meetings.[17]

FBCO coalitions respond to religious differences and racial/ethnic differences in contrasting ways. They tend to talk less about religious differences, and religious differences tend to have little impact on their planning meetings. Conversely, they tend to talk more about racial/ethnic differences, and racial/ethnic differences tend to have a greater impact their planning meetings. Moreover, these opposite ways of responding to differences become amplified as the respective level of diversity of the coalition increases.[18]

This suggests that a substantial portion of coalitions do not operate with a "colorblind" disposition, as they strove to do in the past. Rather they are cognizant of racial/ethnic differences, focus on addressing them, and shape their organizing activity with an eye toward their internal diversity. This change in orientation toward race represents a significant shift in the culture of these coalitions, prompted in part from "below" by a younger and more diverse generation of organizers and in part from "above" by decisions taken in some of the organizing networks to systematically foster explicit attention to racial justice (Wood and Fulton 2015).

The Role of Religion in Faith-Based Organizing

Despite the FBCO field's tendency to deemphasize religious differences and the growing proportion of secular member organizations and religiously unaffiliated organizers, drawing on religious faith continues to be an integral part of the FBCO ethos. Sixty percent of the coalitions' offices contain objects with religious references and 80 percent of the coalitions reported that their promotional material contains religious content. Furthermore, the directors of the coalitions are, on average, more religious than the general U.S. population (i.e., they pray, read sacred texts, and attend religious services more often than the average U.S. adult).[19]

Most coalitions actively integrate religious practices into their organizing activities. Over 90 percent of the coalitions reported that they often open and close their meetings with a prayer, and over 75 percent often have discussions about the connection between faith and organizing. Most coalitions incorporate some form of religious teaching into their organizing activities; however, it is less common for their activities to include people singing or reading religious-based content together. The least common practice within coalitions is people making announcements about upcoming religious events. This presumably reflects the tendency in FBCO culture to focus on shared commitments and avoid giving preference to or promoting specific religious traditions. Furthermore, greater religious diversity in a coalition does not seem to dampen the influence of religious faith in the coalition. In fact, religiously diverse coalitions are *more* likely to incorporate religious practices into their organizing activities, and the directors of religiously diverse coalitions reported feeling more comfortable doing so.

FBCO coalitions *led* by people who engage in the spiritual practices of their religious tradition tend to incorporate religion into their organizing activities more often, and religiously active directors were also more likely to report that religious differences *enhanced* their coalition's planning meetings. It appears that religiously active directors help to cultivate an organizational environment that is at ease with religious differences and comfortable with incorporating religion into their activities, *or* that coalitions more grounded in religion tend to recruit directors who reflect that orientation.

Alongside the above patterns, all FBCO coalitions in the U.S. are facing the challenges presented by the stagnant or declining number of congregations from the field's three core religious traditions. As the number of Mainline Protestant, Catholic, and Black Protestant churches declines, some coalitions are responding by developing ways to retain current congregational members and recruit new members. They have generally adopted one of the following three strategies. Some coalitions are investing organizational resources to help member congregations strengthen their congregational life in an effort both to reinvigorate existing members and reverse denominational decline. Other coalitions are actively recruiting congregations from *other* religious traditions and/ or secular institutions to become members. Finally, some coalitions see congregational decline as widespread and irreversible, and they have decided to dedicate their resources to starting new kinds of institutions (such as community schools, homeowners' associations, after-school care programs, food co-ops, and day labor centers) in poor and middle-class communities, essentially striving to create their own organizational members.

Faith-based community organizing thus intersects with religion in complex ways. Although each individual coalition adopts its own practices, an overall pattern exists. Many coalitions tend to ignore religious *differences*, yet they do not ignore religion altogether. Rather than being venues for interfaith dialogue, FBCO coalitions are vehicles for inter-faith action. In addition to employing non-religious principles rooted in the American democratic tradition, these coalitions incorporate faith into their organizing efforts, drawing on various religious teachings, narratives, prayers, and symbols. These practices serve to motivate and mobilize their faith-oriented members around issues of common concern, while building relationships between leaders from different religious traditions. Moreover, these effects are amplified among coalitions that are more religiously diverse and led by religiously active directors. All this is occurring within the context of a shifting American religious landscape, with decline in some sectors presenting new challenges to the faith-based organizing field.

Overall, these findings indicate that many FBCO coalitions are quite comfortable with bringing religion into the public arena. Their comfort with public religion combined with their strong interfaith cooperation contrasts sharply with *both* radical secularism and intolerant forms of faith-based politics (see also Bretherton 2011; 2014; Jacobsen 2001). The former would drive all religious voices from the public sphere, while the latter have alienated many from religion altogether.

Approaches to Political Engagement

Coupled with the field's growing diversity are its more sophisticated approaches to political engagement. A decade ago, it was rare for FBCO coalitions to address issues beyond the city level; since then, however, this organizing strategy has become much more commonplace (see Figure 1.10). In 2011, 87 percent of the coalitions reported addressing at least one issue at the state or national level. In addition, many coalitions have become more intentional about engaging political officials personally in order to be more effective at influencing decisions in public life. In 2011, 92 percent of the coalitions had met with a city-level political official in the last year to discuss a particular issue. These meetings do not always focus exclusively on winning a particular issue; they are also used to lay the relational groundwork for future negotiations or to gain political knowledge. Although many coalitions restrict their organizing area to a city, most are engaging political officials beyond the city level. Eighty-four percent had met with a state-level official within the last year and 66 percent had met with a national-level official (see Figure 1.11).

Overall, the picture of higher-level issue work and extensive meetings with state and federal officials, along with specific issue victories in those higher arenas, provide evidence of intensified power projection in the FBCO field over the last decade.[20] That power has been achieved despite a decline in attendance at the largest public actions—previously the field's primary tactic for bolstering its influence. Instead, FBCO coalitions have developed a wider array of tactics. They now turn out

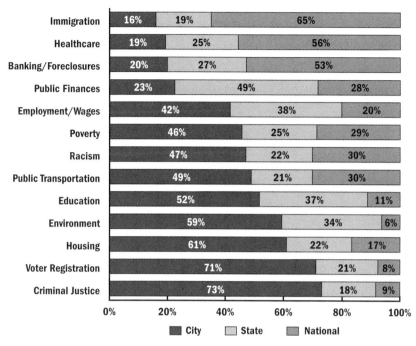

Figure 1.10. Highest level at which FBCO coalitions are addressing each issue category

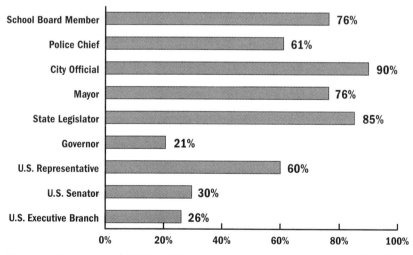

Figure 1.11. Percentage of FBCO coalitions that met with the above political officials sometime in the last year

people for more events, coordinate efforts at multiple political levels simultaneously, and cultivate strategic relationships with political officials and institutional leaders. For example, those addressing racial injustice in American law enforcement have organized locally for "ban-the-box" and transition-to-work initiatives at the county level, advocated new reduced sentencing legislation at the state level, and pressed federal officials for new policy intervention at the national level. Beyond this, some coalitions and organizing networks now systematically use electronic communication technologies, actively cultivate media coverage, and draw on outside policy expertise more routinely than in the past. In addition, some coalitions that previously collaborated only within their own organizing network (if at all) now operate within broader strategic partnerships in nationwide efforts. Beneath these diverse strategic and tactical differences, all FBCO coalitions share a common commitment to build democratic power, reverse rising inequality, and strengthen public life while bridging social divides.

Opportunities and Challenges for Religious Progressives and Progressive Politics

With the decline of liberal hegemony in American political culture in recent decades, religious progressives seeking to influence public policy cannot rely on moral sermonizing about injustice. They have been largely outmaneuvered on that terrain, to such a degree that what counts as a "moral argument" in much of American political culture already prejudges many issue areas in favor of the conservative position. That is, the Moral Majority, Christian Coalition, and their successor organizations of the religious Right have redefined the cultural terrain of morality such that the policy preferences of religious progressives are simply excluded from being embraced as moral concerns.[21]

To be taken seriously in the broad American political arena, while simultaneously swimming upstream against this narrow definition of morality, will require religious progressives to construct political space within which to articulate their own moral-political vision—and to attain sufficient influence to have that vision actually heard. In turn, this will involve establishing the organizational infrastructure to undergird such political space. This chapter has described such an organizational infrastructure to illustrate what building this political space might entail for a wider and deeper movement among religious progressives. We do so not because faith-based community organizing is the only example of such an organizational infrastructure; the introduction of this volume, as well as groups such as Interfaith Worker Justice, Domestic Workers United, and the living-wage campaigns of various labor unions and community-labor coalitions offer other examples (Medina and Scheiber 2015).

Among the opportunities religious progressives face, perhaps the key insight from the above analysis is that it is indeed possible to build an organizational infrastructure to sustain political work on this terrain. Religion is not condemned to being a politically conservative force, and progressive politics are not condemned to "thin" moral ground without recourse to the deep ethical traditions that flow in American life—many of them religious. Likewise, because religious commitment reaches widely across the racial/ethnic and socioeconomic divides that bedevil American society, and reaches deeply into most communities and social strata, faith-based progressive politics can create precisely the kind of bridging social capital that transcends the cleavages that are used to prevent policy reform that strives to address our nation's challenges.

Achieving this outcome, however, requires overcoming not only conservative definitions of what counts as "moral," but also the vast power of those whose wealth and/or privilege leads them to oppose all progressive socioeconomic policy, from universal healthcare to living wages to immigration reform to reasonable checks on the ability of the financial sector to endanger American and global economic growth. Thus, despite all the evidence here for the promise of an organizational infrastructure for religious progressivism, our underlying argument is somber: the faith-based community organizing field, religious progressives more broadly, and the entire movement for more progressive social policy face enormous challenges.

If any of those sectors are to achieve widespread influence, several challenges must be met: First, the best practices of progressive organizing models must be identified, replicated, and multiplied extensively beyond current strongholds—along with the "softer" skills of organizing that can creatively adapt such practices to fit emerging strategic needs. Second, religious progressives must deepen their ability and orientation toward collaborating with other religious and secular political actors who possess complementary political skills and practices. Third, religious progressives must bolster their locally rooted organizing work while coordinating it with higher-level organizing work at the state and national levels, in order to create leverage across all of the arenas in which social policy innovation and adoption occur.

All that would require a pragmatic orientation that only a minority of religious progressives have demonstrated up to now. But if more religious progressives embrace this orientation, a decade from now the American political landscape may be less distorted by economic inequality and the dearth of full democratic voice for all who inhabit that landscape.

ACKNOWLEDGMENTS

We gratefully acknowledge the generosity of those who made the National Study of Community Organizing Coalitions possible. Primary funding was provided by Interfaith Funders and secondary grants supporting this research came from Duke University, the Hearst Foundation, the Society for the Scientific Study of Religion, the Religious Research Association, the W. K. Kellogg Foundation, and the Louisville Institute. In addition, we greatly appreciate the lead organizers and directors of the community organizing coalitions who participated in the study and the leaders of the organizing networks who endorsed and promoted it. We are also thankful for the editors of this volume for their insightful comments on earlier versions of this chapter.

NOTES

1 On the paucity of bridging social capital in America, see Putnam (2000; 2007) and Putnam, Feldstein, and Cohen (2004).

2 On the background of the faith-based organizing field (also called broad-based, congregation-based, and institution-based community organizing) and other variants that emerged partly from Alinsky's work, see Boyte and Kari (1996), Bretherton (2014), Chambers and Cowan (2003), Delgado (1986), Fisher (1994), Gecan (2009), Hart (2001), Horwitt (1989), Swarts (2008), Warren (2001), and Wood (2002).

3 See Verba, Schlozman, and Brady (1995) for a now-classic study of how democratic skills are developed in American society.

4 This study was conducted as a follow-up to a 1999 study of the FBCO field (Warren and Wood 2001), and when we estimate changes in the field over the last decade, we compare data from the 1999 study with data from the 2011 study. The

organizing networks included in this study are the Gamaliel Foundation, Industrial Areas Foundation, National People's Action, and PICO National Network. The regional networks include the Direct Action Research Training (DART) Center, Inter-Valley Project, and Regional Congregations and Neighborhood Organizations (RCNO).

5 Denominations and congregations that have sponsored efforts to use faith-based community organizing as a strategy for congregational development (also termed "institutional development") include the Evangelical Lutheran Church in America, the Unitarian Universalist Association, and many Jewish faith communities (see Interfaith Funders 2004 and Flaherty and Wood 2004).

6 All statistics related to U.S. congregations are based on estimates from the 2012 National Congregations Study (Chaves, Anderson, and Eagle 2014).

7 The category "Conservative Protestant" includes all Evangelical, Pentecostal, and Charismatic congregations.

8 Also noteworthy is the increase in the number of religiously unaffiliated (i.e., secular) member organizations. This is the result of an increase in involvement among non-congregational organizations.

9 Similar levels of religious diversity exist among the coalition board members as well. This is not surprising, since coalitions' boards are comprised of representatives from their member organizations.

10 We define the racial/ethnic identity of a member organization to be the racial/ethnic group that represents a majority in that organization. If no group represents more than 50 percent, then the organization is identified as being multiracial.

11 Only 8 percent of the coalition boards are mono-racial (i.e., all of the board members have the same racial/ethnic identity). Furthermore, "mono-racial" looks different in different settings. Five of the thirteen mono-racial coalitions are all black and practice a model of organizing that focuses explicitly on organizing in black churches. One of the thirteen is all Hispanic and is located in the Rio Grande Valley of Texas—an overwhelmingly Hispanic region. The remaining seven coalitions have only white board members and are located in Maine, Vermont, New Hampshire, Wisconsin, Missouri, and Oregon—states with relatively low racial diversity.

12 Diversity $= 1 - \sum_{k} \rho_{k}^{2}$ where ρ_{k} is the proportion of board members in group k.

13 Because the racial diversity score is calculated using four racial groups (i.e., $k = 5$), the maximum possible score is .80.

14 We use the racial/ethnic composition of a coalition's board to calculate the racial/ethnic diversity of the coalition. We obtain similar results when we use the racial/ethnic composition of a coalition's member organizations.

15 The mean diversity score for public schools is based on the 2009–10 NCES Common Core of Data Public Elementary/Secondary School Universe Survey, the score for counties is based on the 2010 U.S. Census, and the score for congregations is based on the 2012 National Congregations Study.

16 Compared to 1999, when men predominated in professional FBCO organizer roles, gender representation has also shifted significantly in the field: in 2011, 55 percent of organizers and 46 percent of coalition directors were female.

17 Even when controlling for the effects of language differences, racial/ethnic differences continue to effect planning meetings. Language differences have the strongest effect on coalitions that have at least one immigrant member organization.

18 Further research might delve into these dynamics more fully—including the fact that roughly 70 percent of the coalitions have a policy in place for dealing with religious differences, and 50 percent for dealing with racial/ethnic differences. Also urgent is further research on the dynamics of class diversity within organizations (Leondar-Wright 2014).

19 Source: Smith et al. 2011.

20 For analysis of higher-level issue engagement in the field, see Wood (2007), Wood and Fulton (2015). For examples, see Pear (2009), Sanati (2010), and Waters (2010).

21 The Catholic tradition here represents a complex picture: the American Catholic bishops have preserved progressive teachings on immigrant rights, racism, labor rights, and inequality, but in recent decades have given far greater prominence to teaching on abortion and sexuality (even while continuing major funding for anti-poverty work, including faith-based organizing). This disparity makes particularly interesting Pope Francis's current efforts to revitalize Catholic teachings against inequality and exclusion, as well as Ruth Braunstein's chapter in this volume on the "Nuns on the Bus" phenomenon.

REFERENCES

Aud, Susan, William Hussar, Michael Planty, Thomas Snyder, Kevin Bianco, Mary Ann Fox, Lauren Frohlich, Jana Kemp, and Lauren Drake. 2010. "The Condition of Education 2010" (NCES 2010–028). National Center for Education Statistics, Institute of Education Sciences, U.S. Department of Education. Washington, D.C.

Boyte, Harry and Nancy Kari. 1996. *Building America: The Democratic Promise of Public Work*. Philadelphia: Temple University Press.

Braunstein, Ruth, Brad R. Fulton, and Richard L. Wood. 2014. "The Role of Bridging Cultural Practices in Racially and Socioeconomically Diverse Civic Organizations." *American Sociological Review* 79(4): 705–25.

Bretherton, Luke. 2011. *Christianity and Contemporary Politics: The Conditions and Possibilities of Faithful Witness*. Oxford: Wiley.

Bretherton, Luke. 2014. *Resurrecting Democracy: Faith, Citizenship, and the Politics of the Common Good*. New York: Cambridge University Press.

Bronfenbrenner, Kate. 1998. *Organizing to Win: New Research on Union Strategies*. Ithaca, NY: ILR Press.

Chambers, Edward T., and Michael A. Cowan. 2003. *Roots for Radicals: Organizing for Power, Action, and Justice*. New York: Continuum.

Chaves, Mark, Shawna Anderson, and Alison Eagle. 2014. *National Congregations Study: Cumulative Datafile and Codebook*. Durham, NC: Duke University, Department of Sociology.

Comaroff, Jean, and John Comaroff. 1991. *Of Revelation and Revolution*. Chicago: University of Chicago Press.

Delgado, Gary. 1986. *Organizing the Movement: The Roots and Growth of ACORN*. Philadelphia: Temple University Press.

Fisher, Robert. 1994. *Let the People Decide: Neighborhood Organizing in America*. New York: Twayne Publishers.

Flaherty, Mary Ann, and Richard L. Wood. 2004. *Faith and Public Life: Faith-Based Community Organizing and the Development of Congregations*. New York: Interfaith Funders.

Fulton, Brad R. 2016a. "Trends in Addressing Social Needs: A Longitudinal Study of Congregation-Based Service Provision and Political Participation." *Religions* 7(5): 51–57.

Fulton, Brad R. 2016b. "Organizations and Survey Research: Implementing Response Enhancing Strategies and Conducting Nonresponse Analyses." *Sociological Methods & Research*. Advance online publication. doi:10.1177/0049124115626169.

Fulton, Brad R., and Richard L. Wood. 2012. "Interfaith Organizing: Emerging Theological and Organizational Challenges." *International Journal of Public Theology* 6(4): 398–420.

Fulton, Brad R., Richard L. Wood, and Interfaith Funders. 2011. "National Study of Community Organizing Coalitions: Data File." Duke University. Durham, North Carolina.

Gecan, Michael. 2009. *After America's Midlife Crisis*. Boston: MIT Press.

Hart, Stephen. 2001. *Cultural Dilemmas of Progressive Politics: Styles of Engagement among Grassroots Activists*. Chicago: University of Chicago Press.

Hondagneu-Sotelo, Pierrette. 2001. *Domestica: Immigrant Workers Cleaning and Caring in the Shadows of Affluence*. Berkeley: University of California Press.

Hondagneu-Sotelo, Pierrette, Genelle Gaudinez, Hector Lara, and Billie Ortiz. 2004. "There's a Spirit That Transcends the Border: Faith, Ritual, and Postnational Protest at the U.S-Mexico Border." *Sociological Perspectives* 47(2): 133–59.

Horwitt, Sanford D. 1989. *Let Them Call Me Rebel: Saul Alinsky, His Life and Legacy*. New York: Knopf.

Interfaith Funders. 2004. *Renewing Congregations: The Contribution of Faith-Based Community Organizing*. New York: Interfaith Funders.

Jacobsen, Dennis A. 2001. *Doing Justice: Congregations and Community Organizing*. Minneapolis: Fortress Press.

Kairos Theologians Group. 1986. *The Kairos Document: Challenge to the Church—A Theological Comment on the Political Crisis in South Africa*. Grand Rapids, MI: Eerdmans.

Lang, Ilene, Arnold W. Donald, Carlos F. Orta, and J. D. Hokoyama. 2011. *Missing Pieces: Women and Minorities on Fortune 500 Boards. 2010 Alliance for Board Diversity Census*. New York: Catalyst.

Leondar-Wright, Betsy. 2014. *Missing Class: How Seeing Class Cultures Can Strengthen Social Movement Groups*. Ithaca, NY: Cornell University Press.

Marsh, Charles. 2006. *The Beloved Community: How Faith Shapes Social Justice from the Civil Rights Movement to Today*. New York: Basic Books.

Martin, Andrew. 2007. "Organizational Structure, Authority and Protest: The Case of Union Organizing in the United States, 1990–2001." *Social Forces* 85(3): 1413–35.

Medina, Jennifer, and Noam Scheiber. 2015. "Los Angeles Lifts Its Minimum Wage to $15 per Hour." *New York Times*. May 19.

Nepstad, Sharon Erickson. 2004. *Convictions of the Soul: Religion, Culture, and Agency in the Central America Solidarity Movement*. New York: Oxford University Press.

Nepstad, Sharon Erickson. 2008. *Religion and War Resistance in the Plowshares Movement*. New York: Cambridge University Press.

Nepstad, Sharon Erickson. 2011. *Nonviolent Revolutions: Civil Resistance in the Late 20th Century*. New York: Oxford University Press.

Ostrower, Francie. 2007. "Nonprofit Governance in the United States: Findings on Performance and Accountability from the First National Representative Study." Washington, DC: Urban Institute.

Parsons, Christi. 2010. "Obama Plan Would Curb Health Insurers on Rate Hikes." *Los Angeles Times*. February 22.

Pear, Robert. 2009. "Obama Signs Children's Health Insurance Program Bill." *New York Times*. February 5.

Putnam, Robert. 2000. *Bowling Alone: The Collapse and Revival of American Community*. New York: Simon & Schuster.

Putnam, Robert. 2007. "E Pluribus Unum: Diversity and Community in the Twenty-First Century." *Scandinavian Political Studies* 30(2): 137–74.

Putnam, Robert, Lewis Feldstein, and Don Cohen. 2004. *Better Together: Restoring the American Community*. New York: Simon & Schuster.

Religious News Service. 2003. "Religious Groups Issue Statements on War with Iraq." Washington, DC: Pew Research Religion and Public Life Project.

Sanati, Cyrus. 2010. "Protests Planned for Banks' Shareholder Meetings." *New York Times*. April 8.

Smith, Tom W., Peter V. Marsden, Michael Hout, and Jibum Kim. 2011. *General Social Survey, 1972–2010: Cumulative Codebook*. Chicago: National Opinion Research Center.

Swarts, Heidi. 2008. *Organizing Urban America: Secular and Faith-Based Progressive Movements*. Minneapolis: University of Minnesota Press.

United States Census Bureau. 2010. 2010 Census. *www.census.gov*.

Verba, Sidney, Kay Lehman Schlozman, and Henry Brady. 1995. *Voice and Equality: Civic Voluntarism in American Politics*. New York: Cambridge University Press.

Voss, Kim, and Rachel Sherman. 2000. "Breaking the Iron Law of Oligarchy: Union Revitalization in the American Labor Movement." *American Journal of Sociology* 106(2): 303–49.

Warren, Mark. 2001. *Dry Bones Rattling: Community Building to Revitalize American Democracy*. Princeton, NJ: Princeton University Press.

Warren, Mark, and Richard Wood. 2001. *Faith-Based Community Organizing: The State of the Field*. New York: Interfaith Funders.

Waters, David. 2010. "Immigration Reform Advocates to Pray, Rally and March in Washington." *Washington Post*. March 19.

Wood, Elisabeth Jean. 2000. *Forging Democracy from Below: Insurgent Transitions in South Africa and El Salvador*. New York: Cambridge University Press.

Wood, Richard L. 2002. *Faith in Action: Religion, Race, and Democratic Organizing in America*. Chicago: University of Chicago Press.

Wood, Richard L. 2007. "Higher Power: Strategic Capacity for State and National Organizing." In *Transforming the City: Community Organizing and the Challenge of Political Change*, edited by Marion Orr, 164–92. Lawrence: University of Kansas Press.

Wood, Richard L., and Brad R. Fulton. 2015. *A Shared Future: Faith-Based Community Organizing for Racial Equity and Ethical Democracy*. Chicago: University of Chicago Press.

2

Progressive Religious Activists and Democratic Party Politics

REBECCA SAGER

When most Americans think of someone who is both religious and political, one image comes to mind—a Republican voter that is against same-sex marriage and abortion. For much of the last several decades this is not only the image of the intersection of religion and politics in the United States, but also, by and large, the reality (Conger and Green 2002). Actors on the religious and political right have swayed political campaigns in their favor, enacted a wide variety of policy, and shaped political discourse, creating a political stronghold in much of the South and at many levels of the government (Conger and Green 2002; Green, Rozell, and Wilcox 2003; Sager 2010). For those who are not students of history, it may seem odd that there was a time when the religious Right was not the dominant religious political voice, when voices from the religious Left dominated political discourse and were also the most politically engaged religious actors in the United States (Hart 2001).

While this may not be the current reality, there are some working diligently from within the religious Left to shape American politics and policy. This chapter examines how a group of progressive religious activists within the Democratic Party attempted to engage religious voters, specifically through one campaign effort. Using extensive interview and field research data collected over the last eight years, I examine the strategies and tactics employed by this political campaign, what was successful and challenging about these efforts, and why in the long run the Democratic Party abandoned this work. This is part of a larger project that delves deeply into the role of progressive religious activism in modern-day politics.

Religious Left in Political History

There is a long history of religiously driven political activism from the progressive or liberal side of the theological spectrum. Progressive religious political activism was key to victories in the abolitionist, women's rights, and civil rights movements (Hart 2001). Activists in these movements registered voters, protested, and brought a moral side to the issue that many argued would not have been there without their presence. While these successes in shaping politics were present throughout US history, there is a distinct period of time where political actions and success by the religious Left seemed to be absent from American institutional politics. Beginning in the late 1970s and continuing, many would argue, until today, progressive religious voices seemed to have largely disappeared from political life (Hart 2001). While there were many progressive religious activists working in community organizing (Wood 2002), their voices were often below the public's radar. And the once prominent liberal ministers and religious voices of the past were largely silent when it came to institutional-level politics (Stanley 2010).

In their place a very successful and very active religious Right came to the forefront of American politics. Winning on issues ranging from abortion to gay marriage bans and increased enactment of religiously infused laws (Conger and Green 2002; Sager 2010), the religious Right became arguably the most successful voice in political activism from the late 1970s until today. This did not mean that the voices on the religious Left did not care about American politics or did not want to be active anymore. On the contrary, while they lacked clear organizing efforts, many religious voters who were liberal wanted to be more active. However, they had not created new ways to become relevant in a changing religious landscape when their numbers in the pews were shrinking (Hart 2001).

This is slowly changing. While the names and organizations may not be well known to the majority of Americans, in a few places there is a new and vibrant spirit from within the religiously progressive community, striving to reshape American politics (Wood 2002; Yukich 2013). Though these efforts have not achieved anything close to the success of the religious Right, these efforts show that a new way of being both religious and politically active is building in the United States. If they can build on some recent successes with tax policy and prison reform (Sager 2014), these actors will be able to become long-lasting players in American politics.

The Political Activism of the Religious Left

While there is no doubt the religious Right is a fully formed social movement (Conger and Green 2002), the status of the efforts by the religious Left is not so clear. There is no central leader like Jerry Falwell, nor even a central organization like the Christian Coalition. There are some politically engaged actors that are more well known, like Jim Wallis of Sojourners and Rick Cizik, the former head of the National Association of Evangelicals, who later in life defected to the more "Left" side of things. None of these, however, command the centralized political power of a James Dobson or former president George Bush. Further, because of the diversity of those who belongs to the religious Left, racially, religiously, and geographically, bringing these actors together is a challenge that the religious Right does not face (Jones et al. 2013). Finally, and perhaps most important, there is deep disagreement amongst those on the religious Left about whether or not religious groups should even be involved in politics (Jones et al. 2013). These factors often combine to inhibit political activism by those claiming a progressive religious and political identity.

So with all these obstacles, how are there some within the religious Left who have become so political? What sets them apart? I argue that activists involved in these political efforts have what social movement scholars describe as a "revolutionary consciousness" (Yukich 2013, 237). That is, they see themselves as being effective political actors among a group of like-minded thinkers; therefore, they view their efforts to organize and shape US politics not as a solitary pursuit, but rather as part of something bigger than their own individual efforts. As described by the editors in the introduction, while these efforts may be limited and not yet a full social movement, it does not mean that their efforts to shape politics are unimportant or ineffectual. Rather, by viewing their work through a revolutionary lens, these politically engaged actors are able to create political change in often seemingly impossible circumstances.

To better understand how and why progressive religious actors were becoming engaged in institutional politics I examined the efforts of progressive religious political activists within the Democratic Party who were hoping to reinvigorate the party's religious voter outreach. I conducted 22 weeks of participant observation at the faith-saturated political campaign of Democratic congressional candidate Tom Perriello in 2008 and 2010 in Virginia, including attendance at numerous congregation-related campaign events, as well as attendance at non-religious political functions such as campaign speeches. I also conducted over 80 in-depth interviews with movement activists from the campaigns, as well as other long-time political activists (not all were related directly to the Perriello case). These were formal taped interviews lasting between 30 minutes and 3 hours. I asked a variety of questions about their activism, their religious feelings and background, their political views, and how well they thought their efforts were working. The majority of my interviewees were on-the-ground field organizers and ministers who were working to build a new voter and movement base. These interviews allowed me real-time access to the thoughts, feelings, and strategies these actors were employing at the time of the campaigns. This real-time access to activists and their engagement strategies creates a new way of looking at a social movement's political activism, one that focuses on the day-to-day activities of a movement in the present, rather than on its past, however recent. Crucially, my work moves away from looking at religion as tradition and ritual to examining how religion is an active part of the political world.

A Call to Act: Reinvigorating Religiously Progressive Political Efforts

By 2004 the religious Right had cemented itself as arguably the most successful political movement of the last 30 years, transforming politics at all levels of government. Progressive religious activists had been outmanned, outspent, and outmaneuvered. But at this point there was also a feeling that this could change and political victories for progressives could be achieved if political organizing began to change. One of the reasons for this new perspective was the 2004 presidential election, when John Kerry, a Catholic, lost the Catholic vote to George Bush, an

Evangelical. While the Democratic Party had long ago ceded the Evangelical vote to the Republican Party, losing the Catholic vote with a Catholic candidate signaled that they had a real problem with engaging religious voters. This led some within the party to fundamentally rethink religious outreach and begin a new campaign to organize religious voters for the Democrats.

In her book on the role of religion in the Democratic Party following the unsuccessful Kerry campaign, Amy Sullivan (2008) argues that the Democrats were finally beginning to get their "soul" back and were focusing on religious voters as a key demographic they could begin to win. Sullivan was one of the early members of a small, but influential group of religious Left activists that were finding that the party they belonged to and sometimes worked for was not friendly to their faith. Kerry had in fact been advised to incorporate his faith into his run for the presidency. Instead he downplayed his religion and was more concerned about the secular wing of his party, which saw any discussion of religion in politics as an anathema (Stanley 2010). After he lost, activists took the opportunity to argue that the Democrats could win by reengaging religious voters.

Creating a Renewed Movement—from the Top Down

Following the 2004 election, some of these activists began to meet at the Virginia home of Tom Perriello, an original and influential leader in this group, to discuss strategies to create a new voice for progressive religious believers within the Democratic Party. Known as the "Grassmere group," after the house's name, the participants included various activists who would eventually go on to found progressive religious groups such as Faith in Public Life, a media-engagement organization, and Common Good Strategies, a campaign-consulting group. These members were focused on something that the religious Left had not discussed for some time—how to influence electoral politics. Their vision of a new role for the religious Left within Democratic Party politics culminated in a plan of action that focused on multiple levels of influence on the party. What was important about this plan was its focus on influencing political *power* through institutional political means. Of course there were many religious Left organizations working to create social change through non-profits and community organizing; what set this group apart was its strategic focus on creating new organizations to change institutional politics.

New Organizations, New Conversations—2005 to 2007

Starting around 2005, new organizations such as Faith in Public Life and Common Good Strategies all became players in Democratic Party politics, helping to shape elections, media relationships, and voter action. Rather than developing a centralized political organization like the Christian Coalition, these progressive religious activists—who were largely evangelical and progressive Catholics—decided that they wanted to create a variety of organizations, each with their own specific strengths. These original activists felt that taking a decentralized approach would allow them to do a variety of tasks to accomplish one uniting strategy: moving the role of religion in politics away from the Christian Right and taking a broader view of morality and faith into politics. Leaders of these organizations hoped by doing this to transform the Democratic Party and ameliorate the discomfort many members of Democratic institutional politics have with discussing religion and matters of faith.

Early Signs of Success

In 2004 the religious Left was something that most people did not even know existed. Between 2000 and 2004 the *New York Times* only mentions the "religious Left" 8 times. Between 2004 and 2008 this jumps to 78 times. Clearly these organizations had begun to change the conversation, and a number of Democratic political candidates had taken on serious efforts to reach religious voters; however, by 2007 there were also signs this work was in some trouble. Splits about who to support for president (Obama vs. Clinton) had divided key members, and there were a number of Democratic Party activists who thought this was not a good strategy. But in 2008 these early signs of difficulty were being eclipsed by one of their own, Tom Perriello, who had decided to run for Congress and put into play the faith-based outreach strategies they had developed to engage religious voters. This was going to be a pivotal year for the renewed religious Left and its efforts to transform Democratic Party politics.

Perriello's New Brand of Faith-Based Politics

In 2008, Tom Perriello ran for a seat in Congress in Virginia's 5th District, one of the most religious areas in the entire country. This high level of religiosity, combined with some support for Democratic policies, made it the perfect place to build a Democratic campaign based on religious engagement. His campaign was long in the making, stemming from beliefs held by some in the Democratic Party that by abandoning faith and ceding what it meant to be a religious or moral voter to the Republican Party, Democrats had lost the soul of the country. In order to reach religious voters, Perriello's campaign used a number of strategies they hoped would show through deeds over words that their candidate's faith was real. Their goal was to create an intensely faith-saturated campaign, moving away from merely doing some level of "god talk" to doing a "god walk."

Perriello's campaign used a number of faith-based strategies to reach out to voters, including Christian radio commercials, meetings with area pastors, tithing campaign time to volunteer agencies, and regular church visits. Perriello (who one campaign worker called the Jerry Falwell of the religious Left) argued that Democratic politicians can effectively engage religious voters if the campaign and candidate take faith seriously and signal their faith commitment to voters via deeds over words. The campaign wanted to create something very new, a self-consciously religiously infused campaign that sought to spark both religious innovation and social change.

To articulate the authenticity of his religious faith on the campaign trail, Perriello frequently told his life story to voters. After graduating from Yale, Perriello says he was called to Sierra Leone and spent two years there working with tribal leaders to help to end the Blood Diamonds war and unseat despot Charles Taylor. The compelling nature of his life story and spiritual call to action were fused with attempts to make connections to voters through both pointing to his own personal sacrifice and communicating to them that he was one of them, a person of faith, who would listen to them. This way of interacting with voters led people I spoke with to refer to him as a "true believer" and someone who "walked the walk," with one woman referring to him as "her hero" (Campaign Event, 7/31/2010). These various mechanisms were designed to reimagine what role religion could play in campaigning and how campaigns were run.

Religious Messaging

One early and key component of this religious outreach strategy was religious messaging. Beginning in 2006 Democratic politicians and organizers on the religious Left began making claims that the Democratic Party and its policies represent the real party of Christianity. As James Clyburn (D-SC), head of the Democrats' Faith Working Group, stated in an open letter to the faith community, "The message contained in Proverbs 14:31, 'He who oppresses the poor shows contempt for their Maker, but whoever is kind to the needy honors God,' is evident in the politics and positions promoted by my Democratic colleagues" (Clyburn 2006). In the case of Perriello, the first step in this strategy was to create a candidate-specific religious platform. For example, his campaign slogan was "Common Good for the Commonwealth." The term "common good" is religiously coded language that was intended to create a bond between the candidate and the voters. As one participant in the campaign's Common Good Summer Fellows program (described later) said, "the religious motifs help frame things in a way that resonates with people. You know instead of talking past them about health care policy . . . you talk about it in a language that people understand" (Jane, CGS Fellow Interview, 7/22/2008). What is important about these messaging strategies is that they cost very little, required almost no time from the campaigns, and were designed to reach out to a large swath of voters; however, they would only be impactful if the messenger was perceived as religiously authentic. For many voters in Virginia's 5th, Perriello was the right messenger.

Christian Radio Commercials

In addition to communicating specific religious messages in his slogan, Perriello used Christian radio commercials to reach voters. These commercials cost very little and, according to supporters, had the potential for a tremendous impact on the voters; however, this impact was difficult if not impossible to measure. Despite the lack of data, organizers believed that they created at least some benefit. In the first 2008 campaign some of the commercials were actually made by the Common Good Summer Fellows, young people hired by the campaign to live, work, and go to church throughout the district. What was perhaps most interesting about this process was that making the commercials brought up feelings in the interns of religious uncertainty and questions about the role of religion in the campaign; this was especially true for the interns who were not religious. As one woman stated, "I'm not religious. I don't know how to talk about this" (Common Good Summer Training Session, 6/3/2008), bringing up early in the campaign a problem they would continue to encounter. The campaign worker who was directing the commercials told her that he was not interested in a purely religious perspective, but rather in morality.

In Perriello's first ad on Christian radio, he linked a biblical imperative to his running for Congress. "In the book of Micah, the prophet asks, what does the Lord require of you? The answer: to do justice, to love mercifully, and to walk humbly with our God. I'm Tom Perriello, and my attempt to answer this call has taken my life in some interesting directions. . . . And now I'm running for Congress in the community where I was born and raised because I believe we deserve leaders who will focus on right and wrong instead of right and left" (teacherken 2008). Commercials similar to this were created and played not just in the Perriello campaign, but throughout the United States. Perriello did not use them again in 2010; instead, they were replaced by ads featuring bluegrass music on country radio stations to reach a broader audience.

Listening Meetings

Another outreach strategy was the "listening meeting," with groups of 5 to 15 local pastors. The organizers behind the tactic felt it was particularly relevant because many pastors had been ignored by the Democrats. They argued that many of the pastors they reached were grateful for their message because they felt that the conservative movement often did not represent their "Christian" ideals of helping the needy. When done correctly, these meetings allowed pastors to come together and air their feelings about what was happening in their communities. As one pastor I spoke with noted, Perriello speaks to people about faith and politics in a way that other Democrats, like John Kerry, did not. "I think he's really been willing to engage. . . . The one comment made even by people who are not Democrats, they say, 'When you talk to him, when he's at those meetings, he listens to everything everyone says.' . . . He gives me hope" (Pastor Interview, 7/27/2010). Quite simply, they were listened to, something that they felt was very rare.

Sacred Places, Secular Purposes: Congregations as Political Organizing Ground

In the campaign, congregations were at the heart of the strategies employed to sway religious voters. Like many candidates before him (Olson 2000; Djupe and Gilbert 2009), Perriello gave a series of speeches at local congregations, addressing congregants with religiously tinged political messages and using the pastor's pulpit as a way to increase votes and reach out to the community. How much interaction he had varied greatly. For example, some congregations would let Perriello give a speech or say a prayer, while others simply acknowledged his presence. This varied consistently by race, with black churches almost always letting Perriello or a member of his staff give a speech, while white churches would allow attendance but not a speech. The reactions to his visits also varied—while some parishioners and church leaders appeared uninterested (one pastor even mispronounced his name), there was usually a fair amount of enthusiasm and joy, with congregants stopping to shake his hand after the service, applauding his speech, and discussing afterward their feelings of joy at having a candidate for Congress take the time to come to their church.

Common Good Summer

In the summer of 2008, Eleison Group (a faith consulting organization) and Tom Perriello created the Common Good Summer Fellows program. The program gave a small stipend to local college and high school students to live and work in the district and do outreach to religious voters. The program was modeled after Freedom Summer, the effort in 1969 to bring mostly white college students to the south to register African American voters. The intention was for the Fellows to become part of these communities. They attended churches, went to farmers' markets, volunteered at local organizations, and went out to eat at local restaurants. By funding this effort, many voters saw the Perriello campaign as one that was about being part of the community for the long term, not just hiring outsiders to collect votes. As one Fellow noted, "People in this campaign are genuinely out there to do community service, to help the community" (Mark, CGS Fellow Interview, 7/22/2008). The hope was that by having Fellows become embedded within religious communities, faith voters would interpret this as a demonstration of Perriello's commitment to religious values. Fellows acted essentially as surrogates for Perriello and received training on how to message the candidate as a person of faith. This training in messaging was key because many of these students—like many Democrats in general—were secular and had little idea how to talk about religion, much less authentically connect with Christian voters.

One of the main responsibilities of the Common Good Summer Fellows was to attend church at local congregations and talk to parishioners about Perriello. While reactions among congregants were almost always positive, Fellows had very divergent feelings about their tasks. Many of the Fellows saw congregations as "sacred spaces," spaces made profane by the inclusion of politics; however, others felt that the inclusion of politics into congregational settings seemed natural. While some of the Fellows were open to including faith messages and reaching out to faith voters, my interviews also show that many were deeply uncomfortable with these actions and resisted the inclusion of faith into campaign outreach. It is important to note, however, that even the ones who were uncomfortable with integrating faith by the end of the campaign had begun to have a religious political awakening in which they could see that there was a role for faith in politics.

Tithing Campaign

In conjunction with their other efforts, the faith-infused Perriello campaign wanted to show that they were *really* different when it came to religion influencing their politics. They were not the religious Right's politicians who claimed moral superiority without doing anything to demonstrate their faith to the public. This required a reimaging of what role religion could play in a political campaign. To do this they created a tithing initiative, which required campaign workers and volunteers to partner with local congregations and social services and volunteer 10 percent of their time on the campaign to helping these organizations do community service. Over the two campaign seasons, I went to a number of these tithing events, including helping the campaign to build Habitat for Humanity houses in Martinsville and Bedford, Virginia, working at several area soup kitchens, and gardening at a senior citizens center. By the end of Perriello's 2008 and 2010 campaigns, his workers had tithed over 2,000 hours to local services. One campaign worker put it this way: "How great would this be if people looked forward to election year as the year not just that everyone comes out and panders, but the year that everyone comes out and works . . . how great to help our community" (Scott, CGS Fellow Interview 8/4/2008).

Of all the myriad ways the campaign tried to reach religious voters, I found that this strategy resonated most with voters; even with those who told me they were Republican. This meant that the tithing initiative made for both good practice as well as good politics. As one Fellow told me about his first tithing experience, "When I showed up there were like 6 media people there . . . so the moral reasons why we do the tithing I think are great and having seen the effect of it [on the campaign] then sure why not?" (Luke, CGS Fellow Interview 8/4/2008). The initiative was so popular because voters saw it making a positive impact on the community, even if the candidate did not win. Another fellow described it as "the most exciting part of the campaign . . . because win or lose we accomplish something other than putting one of the two people in office" (Scott, CGS Fellow Interview, 8/4/2008). As one minister told me over lunch after the Perriello campaign had visited his church, tithing "was the single best addition to a progressive faith agenda" he had ever seen (Church Visit, 6/27/2010).

Through this initiative Perriello linked his personal political agenda to his faith, creating a campaign that effectively showed his faith to voters. In an interview he described his reasons for tithing: "We wanted to put our principles in action, so we needed to give our time. . . . While it's important to tackle the culture of corruption in Washington, it's just as important to replace it with a culture of service" (McNeill 2008). This message and mandate from Perriello reached people and for some changed how they interacted in their own communities. As one volunteer told me at a campaign office opening, "Well Tom being involved in his campaign, that's what got me tithing, and Obama too, both of them asking us to do something to be a part of the community to go out there and make a difference. . . . I'm religious but it wasn't because of my religion that I got involved in going to Shepherd's Table [a local charity]. It was because of the campaign, because of his tithing campaign. I am a Christian and I want to serve, but it was the campaigns that got me doing this, not my religious background" (Field Notes, 6/6/2010).

Winning the Day

Tom Perriello's victory did not come right away. In fact it did not come for two weeks. The vote was so close that a recall was issued; Perriello narrowly beat out his competitor, Virgil Goode, a six-term Republican incumbent, by 727 votes. But he was not able to enjoy this moment for long. Unfortunately, it occurred against the backdrop of the worst economic crisis the United States had encountered since the Great Depression. Soon, conservative forces that had seemed to dissipate were plotting, planning, and working to undo the Democratic political sweep that gave the party control of all three levels of the federal government. So while November 2008 held much promise for activists, by January this hope began to give way to massive unemployment, confusing health care changes, and political foes that were able to outmaneuver and outspend progressive religious voices.

From Hope to Nope—2008 to 2009

If 2008 could be described by the terms "hope" and "change," the following two years could be described by "disappointment" and "disillusionment." The progressive religious movement went from creating new organizations, feeling a sense of hope and empowerment, and having key movement actors such as Mara Vanderslice and Alexia Kelly offered key federal government positions, to disarray and disengagement. Crucially, once their goal of electing a new Democratic president was achieved and many of the leaders of this movement were put in positions of largely symbolic power within the Obama administration, the influence they had gained was overwhelmed by traditional Democratic Party insiders. As one faith activist told me, "We have our elbows on the table, but we are not a trusted member" (Patrick, Activist Interview, 6/23/10).

While Obama had won and progressive religious activists were elated with this victory, his presidency happened against the backdrop of the second worst economic crisis the United States has ever seen. This meant that many of the goals the movement had—including immigration reform and work on climate change—had to be put on the back burner. Instead, crucial time and political capital had to be spent just ensuring there was no further economic disintegration and the one major initiative that did get passed, health care reform, turned out to be politically disastrous.

Health Care Reform

Democratic presidents since Lyndon Johnson had been trying to pass some form of universal health care, so the fact that Obama was able to do this seemed like a great accomplishment; however, the eventual complexities, costs, and confusion surrounding the law turned the policy victory into a political defeat. The passage of health care not only proved to be politically costly to Democratic elected officials, but also to the Democratic and progressive policy activists within Washington, DC. The fights between traditional Democratic activists and new progressive religious activists led to a great amount of bitterness—particularly around issues related to abortion. These battles created significant problems for new faith leaders who saw the influence and power they had hoped for quickly diminished by Democratic allies with much stronger connections and more money. In the end a health care bill passed, but its passage ushered in a reshaped Republican Party that was more conservative, wealthier, and determined to bring the federal government to its knees. And it left a bitterly divided Democratic Party that viewed the law with much skepticism.

The Democratic Party and the Decline of Faith Organizing

In addition to significant problems stemming from the politics of Obama's health care law, the 2010 election also marked the loss of concerted religious outreach support from the Democratic Party. For all of its talk about being more open to faith and wanting to reach faith voters, the political machine of the Democratic Party is still dominated by secular political activists who view religion with skepticism, at best, and often with outright hostility. Unlike the religious Right, the religious Left within the Democratic Party did not have the critical mass to make its voice heard. In my research I observed how movement actors had to face the entrenched secular culture of the Democratic Party, which more often than not dismisses their concerns out of hand and views faith-infused political action by members of its own party as an unwelcome intrusion. In 2007 Howard Dean, then head of the DNC, had declared a new kind of Democratic Party and put considerable resources into faith organizing, sponsoring some level of faith outreach in seven races in 2006 and in a number of battleground states in 2008. But by 2010, with the departure of Dean from the DNC, the party abandoned its faith outreach at the state level and had only one part-time employee doing religious outreach to traditional allies in the Black Church. Because of this, many of the activists I spoke with felt that their work was shuffled off to the "religion desk," creating a general disenchantment with the Democratic Party infrastructure.

While some activists became part of the federal government, an unintended consequence of this new administrative power was a brain drain out of movement organizations and into the administration. Many of the organizations, such as Catholics in Alliance for the Common Good, which had assumed an "if we build it they will come" attitude, became shells of their former selves, losing many members as soon as their leaders went into the government. In addition, movement members began to doubt that working from within institutional politics was really the best idea. Critics began calling such top-down political efforts the "religion-industrial complex," arguing that they were not actually in the best interest of progressive religious political activism. Instead, as one interviewee noted, there was "a lot more energy happening outside of the partisan context" (George, Activist Interview, 7/1/2010). So while 2008 had originally appeared a positive turning point, it was clear by early 2010 that things were not going to go the way that many activists had expected.

Perriello and the 2010 Election

Against this backdrop Tom Perriello had to run for reelection in a conservative Southern district. The campaign knew they had to use many of the faith outreach strategies that helped them win in 2008; however, they were also running a congressional office at the same time. Thus, they could no longer focus only on campaigning. In 2010, I returned to southern Virginia to see how they were trying to meet these challenges and still run a faith-infused campaign that would engage religious voters.

Tea Party Time

Perhaps the biggest challenge Perriello faced in 2010 was how to address health care and the Tea Party. In 2009 he held more town halls than any other congressman in the entire country. Unfortunately, these meetings were not able to counter the new Tea Party politics. After he voted for health care reform, he received death threats; even more distressing, someone responded to Tea Party demands that voters confront Perriello in person and actually came onto his brother's property and tried to engineer an explosion that could have destroyed his home and killed his family (Barr 2010). While I had met many Democrats in southern Virginia who had told me they hid their political views or parked far away from Democratic political meetings, this was a step further than many had thought possible. The problems that were occurring in Washington, DC, were playing out on a personal level in Perriello's campaign in southern Virginia.

2010 and the Retooling of Faith-Based Campaigning Strategies

While faith organizing was something that Perriello remained strongly committed to, there were signs that struggles with how to do this were emerging in 2010. Though the strategies Perriello relied on were successful in 2008, leaving activists and ministers feeling that the campaign had achieved its goal of moving beyond traditional politics, for some involved this changed in 2010. Some people involved in 2008 felt that the campaign had become politics as usual, leaving behind what one activist described as "its soul" (Campaign Event, 11/2/2010). Additionally, several of the ministers I spoke with argued that the campaign no longer had the same religious feeling it had in 2008 and were disappointed in how things were going, but were still rooting for Perriello and his message. While this was certainly not the case for everyone, and there were a number of people who felt the religious outreach was going very well, there had been none of the doubt that was expressed in 2010 back in 2008.

Additionally some of the ways the campaign was doing outreach shifted in 2010. For example, in 2008 the campaign only requested church visits from Fellows; however, by 2010 they were mandating church visits and requiring Fellows to read a letter of faith at their visits. Some Fellows felt this took away from the authenticity of their religious message, making it appear that their efforts were coming more from political concerns than from a desire to be part of the religious community. Additionally, whether or not to read the letter or how to approach churches also seemed to be more challenging this time around, leading to confusing and conflicting church visits (Church Visit, 7/4/2010).

In addition to changes in religious outreach strategy, the Fellows were also different than the 2008 campaign Fellows. In 2008, the Fellows largely came to the program because they believed in Perriello. They had heard about his work in Africa or were excited about his faith outreach. In 2010, the Fellows were much more likely to come to the campaign because of *political* ties, rather than personal or religious reasons. Unlike 2008, when all the Fellows were aware of Perriello's religion and his faith as the root of his political activism, there was little awareness in 2010. I would like to note here that I do not think that these changes in religious outreach strategies necessarily had much of an impact on the outcome of the campaign. As many observers noted, the voting population was also very different in 2010 than in 2008 (much older and whiter), and the Tea Party had poisoned the well for Democrats, especially in the South. Additionally, as one observer argued, "Perriello hasn't been able to replicate what he did in 2008. . . . His TV ads were some of the best in the country in 2008. This year, they've been more typical-type ads" (Goldsmith 2010). So while the deck was stacked against him in 2008, by 2010 Perriello faced a number of new obstacles that turned out to be insurmountable.

Perriello's Loss and the End of Democratic Party Faith Outreach

Whether it was the commercials, the changes in strategy, or the extreme turn of the political climate, a number of factors aligned and turned out to be insurmountable for the Perriello campaign. While he lost by much less than most of his Democratic counterparts (4 percent), it was still a loss; however, unlike most other candidates, this was a loss not just for one person or one party, but also for what many felt was the beginning of a new movement. While Perriello's 2008 campaign showed the potential for a progressive faith-based politics, his loss in 2010 illustrated many of the problems in religious engagement of voters, including problems with organizing a disparate group who often did not like politics in their religion and a lack of institutional support for faith-based organizing from groups with money, like the Democratic Party.

The once ascendant idea of a faith-infused Democratic Party began to fade in Washington, DC. Eleison Group, which had been in charge of faith-based campaigning efforts, started a new organization, American Values Network, which moved to focusing on policy change and several once growing groups restricted themselves to Internet-based activism. Further, without the support of the Democratic Party, there was increased infighting for scarce resources. Consequently, despite the discussion in 2008 of a renewed religious Left (Sullivan 2008), there was still a significant lag in the way religion was perceived and acted upon by voters in the United States. In short, the "god gap" remained alive and well.

Where to Next? Policy over Politicians

After the Kerry campaign there were many people who had hoped that building a politically engaged religious Left would lead to a series of political victories for the Democratic Party. Instead, while there was some success, the limited accomplishments were followed by significant problems. Tom Perriello lost his seat in Congress, and the religious Left lost its main supporter on the Hill; the organizations that had supported that strategy were losing influence, and the Democratic Party leadership no longer supported their efforts. This series of setbacks meant that many activists had to rethink what direction would lead to political success.

For most of these actors and new ones, the next phase of progressive faith-based activism was not working to get specific politicians elected, but rather to get specific policies passed. In my book I examine two electoral political campaigns waged in part by a congregation-based community-organizing group in California. In 2012 and 2014 this group was instrumental in passing two statewide ballot initiatives that fundamentally altered the tax policy and justice system in California (Sager 2014). In some ways the legacy of Perriello and Democratic faith organizing are not changes within the Democratic Party, but a renewed energy by progressive religious groups to shape politics by shaping social policy. Instead of moving away from institutional political change, progressive faith activists are concentrating on making change by directly enacting state and local policy, not worrying about getting representatives elected and then asking representatives to make those policy changes. As the editors note in the introduction, progressive faith activism is not new, but the changes to our political system it can bring about through influencing institutional politics fundamentally are. By exploring how and why these campaigns have worked we can see the once great political power of progressive religion in America once again come alive.

ACKNOWLEDGMENTS
This project could not have been completed without the generous support of the National Science Foundation, Princeton University's Center for the Study of Religion, the Louisville Institute, Loyola Marymount University, the Haynes Foundation, my always understanding and generous family, colleagues who were always eager to help, and everyone on the campaign trail who took the time to talk to me, let me into their lives, and helped me better understand how invigorating religion can be to political life.

REFERENCES

Barr, Andy. 2010. "Perriello Gas Line 'Intentionally Cut.'" *Politico*. March 25. www.politico.com.

Clyburn, James E. 2006. "An Open Letter to Leaders of the Faith Community." *Christian Recorder*. October 20. http://tcr-online.blogspot.com.

Conger, Kimberly, and John Green. 2002. "Spreading Out and Digging In: Christian Conservatives and State Republican Parties." *Campaigns and Elections Magazine*. February: 58.

Djupe, Paul A., and Christopher P. Gilbert. 2009. *The Political Influence of Churches*. New York: Cambridge University Press.

Goldsmith, Will. 2010. "Perriello Headed Towards another Recount?" *C-Ville*. October 19. www.cville.com.

Green, John, Mark Rozell, and Clyde Wilcox. 2003. *The Conservative Christian in American Politics: Marching to the Millennium*. Washington, DC: Georgetown University Press.

Hart, Stephen. 2001. *Cultural Dilemmas of Progressive Politics*. Chicago: University of Chicago Press.

Jones, Robert, Daniel Cox, Juhem Navarro-Rivera, E. J. Dionne Jr., and William A. Galston. 2013. "Findings From the Economic Values Survey." *Public Religion Research Institute*. July 18. http://publicreligion.org.

McNeill, Brian. 2008. "Volunteerism a Requirement for Perriello Workers." *Daily Progress*. July 23. www.dailyprogress.com.

Olson, Laura R. 2000. *Filled with Spirit and Power: Protestant Clergy in Politics*. Albany: State University of New York Press.

Sager, Rebecca. 2010. *Faith, Politics, and Power: The Politics of Faith-Based Initiatives*. New York: Oxford University Press.

Sager, Rebecca. 2014. "LA Voice: Congregations and Communities Building Political Power." *Center for Religion and Civic Culture*. October 28. http://crcc.usc.edu.

Stanley, Tiffany. 2010. "How Democrats Gave Up on Religious Voters." *New Republic*. December 18. www.tnr.com.

Sullivan, Amy. 2008. *The Party Faithful: How and Why Democrats Are Closing the God Gap*. New York: Scribner.

teacherken. 2008. "Perriello Advertising on Christian Radio." *Raising Kaine* (message board). June 16. www.raisingkaine.com/14646.htm.

Wood, Richard. 2002. *Faith in Action*. Chicago: University of Chicago Press.

Yukich, Grace. 2013. *One Family under God*. New York: Oxford University Press.

3

Why Congregations Mobilize for Progressive Causes

KRAIG BEYERLEIN AND A. JOSEPH WEST

On a Tuesday in late September 2008, pastors and lay members of local religious congregations gathered at Grace St. Paul's Episcopal Church in Tucson, Arizona, to protest Proposition 102. This proposition, which Arizonans voted on later that year, called for the state constitution to be amended so that the only valid form of marriage recognized was between "one man and one woman." For those in attendance, this exclusionary legislation violated their religious convictions and they were mobilizing congregations to defeat it. As one of the pastors present said, "Proposition 102 offends my sense of justice, and my sense of justice comes right out of my religious faith" (Denogean 2008).

When we think about the hundreds of thousands of congregations spread throughout the United States, scenes such as the one above do not typically come to mind. Places of fellowship, service, and worship? For sure. Perhaps even sites of *conservative* politicking. But bases of progressive activism? Not likely. While rare, congregation-based mobilizing for greater economic, political, or social equality does happen.[1] The classic case in America is Southern black churches rallying for civil rights in the 1960s (Morris 1984). More recent examples include congregations organizing for immigrant and refugee rights (Smith 1996; Nepstad 2004; Davis, Martinez, and Warner 2010; Yukich 2013) as well as to empower people in poor communities (Warren 2001; Wood 2002).

What explains why certain congregations but not others mobilize for progressive causes?[2] This question has received relatively little attention in the scholarship on religion and politics. When this scholarship focuses on progressive social movements, it is mainly to document how congregations support them, such as by providing meeting spaces, pools of potential participants, and communication channels (for example, see Morris 1984; Smith 1996). Specifying the resources that congregations contribute to progressive social movements is valuable and highlights the significant role religious organizations can play in helping them achieve their goals. But understanding what differentiates congregations that participate in collective efforts to promote greater economic, political, or social equality from those that do not is equally important.

Drawing on the 2009 Southern Arizona Congregations Study (SACS)—a survey of nearly 300 congregations in Maricopa and Pima counties—this chapter analyzes six factors to explain variation in progressive mobilization: (1) Mainline Protestant affiliation; (2) liberal ideology; (3) social-justice orientation; (4) membership in an interfaith group; (5) educated clergy; and (6) high percentage of educated laity. Instead of treating these factors as independent predictors of whether Southern Arizonan congregations engage in activism for progressive causes, we consider how different *combinations* of them work together to produce this outcome. To do so, we employ Qualitative Comparative Analysis (QCA), which is specifically designed to identify "causal recipes" among a set of theoretically relevant factors (Ragin 1987; Ragin 2008).

The SACS was in the field at a time when Arizona politics were extremely conservative. Citizens passed the anti–gay marriage amendment Proposition 102, mentioned above, in November 2008. Moreover, in the late 2000s the Grand Canyon state was home to some of the harshest anti-immigration policies in the land. In 2006, for instance, Proposition 103—establishing English as the official state language—was enacted. These and other legislative efforts constituted important opportunities for congregations to rise up and mobilize against. Despite these opportunities, very few did. Based on our 2009 survey data, only 6 percent of Southern Arizonan congregations lobbied or protested for a progressive cause during the last year. In the next section, we develop theoretical arguments to explain why some congregations take progressive action, focusing on the *joint* occurrence of certain factors that typically leads congregations to mobilize for greater economic, political, or social equality.

Mobilizing for Progressive Causes

If congregations are to mobilize for immigrant rights, same-sex mar- riage, or other progressive causes, their identity, mission, and values must align with them (for example, see Snow et al. 1986). Congregations that oppose these causes do not tend to have progressive mobilization potential (cf. Klandermans and Oegema 1987). As a result, regardless of how many resources opposing congregations have to offer progressive social movements, they will not be put to use for them. The first piece of the puzzle, then, is figuring out what factors render congregations potentially mobilizable for causes that promote greater economic, politi- cal, or social equality.

One factor should be Mainline Protestant affiliation. Sociologists of religion have long observed that congregations and people belonging to such denominations as the Episcopal Church, the United Church of Christ, or the Presbyterian Church USA espouse progressive views on a range of social and political issues. Analyzing public opinion data, stud- ies generally find that Mainline Protestants are more likely to approve of, for instance, a woman's right to choose and gay and lesbian relation- ships relative to members of other religious traditions (for example, see Davis and Robinson 1996; Sherkat et al. 2011). As for Mainline Protestant congregations, research shows they speak out in support of progressive causes, including during sermons and group discussions (for example, see Guth et al. 1997; Olson 2000; Smidt 2004; Djupe and Gilbert 2009).

Not all Mainline Protestant congregations endorse progressive causes, however. Concerning same-sex marriage, some of them are si- lent or even take the conservative side (for example, see Moon 2004; Ammerman 2005). Moreover, concerns in the religious world for greater economic, political, or social equality are not exclusive to the Mainline Protestant tradition. The pro-life position on abortion is generally non- negotiable in Catholic circles. But on other issues, such as immigration or poverty, many Catholic parishes advocate progressive policies (for example, see Davis, Martinez, and Warner 2010; Smith 2008). Further- more, although they are a small minority, some Evangelical Protestant churches go against their tradition's broad conservatism and take pro- gressive stances for certain causes (for example, see Elisha 2011). These findings confirm what Wuthnow (1988) argued nearly three decades ago—positions on social and political issues cross-cut denominations and religious traditions.

We therefore must look beyond Mainline Protestant affiliation to identify congregations that have progressive mobilization potential. Two other factors are expected to be relevant for doing so. The first is liberal ideology. It is not surprising that religious-based progressive social movements tend to draw participants from the left end of the political and theological spectrum (for example, see Smith 1996). We also know that clergy who hold liberal theological views generally support progressive politics, and often publicize this support within congregations (for example, see Guth et al. 1997). Taken together, these findings lead us to expect that ideologically liberal congregations will be potentially mobilizable for causes that seek to advance greater economic, political, or social equality in society.

Additionally, congregations with a social-justice orientation should have progressive mobilization potential. In his study of the U.S. Central America peace movement, Smith (1996) describes how religious teachings about peace and justice motivated congregations and members of different traditions to support this movement (see also Nepstad 2004). Similarly, research shows that black churches featuring sermons about social justice are more likely to engage in social advocacy in local communities (Barnes 2005). Based on these findings, we hypothesize that congregations oriented toward social justice will be prone to take political action for progressive causes.

Mainline Protestant affiliation, liberal ideology, or social-justice orientation should each make congregations open to the idea of mobilizing for greater economic, political, or social equality. But it is their co-occurrence that should be a particularly strong force for doing so. In other words, it is hard to imagine a *Mainline Protestant* congregation that is also *ideologically liberal* and *social-justice oriented* lacking progressive mobilization potential.

With that said, being potentially mobilizable for progressive causes is not a guarantee that congregations will take action for them. From other research, we know that only a very small subset of the pool of potential activists actually takes to the streets (for example, see Beyerlein and Hipp 2006; Klandermans and Oegema 1987; Williams and Blackburn 1996). It follows, then, that Mainline Protestant affiliation, liberal ideology, and social-justice orientation are unlikely to be sufficient by themselves to generate congregation-based mobilizing for progressive causes.

Among the factors expected to propel progressively inclined congregations into political action is belonging to an interfaith group. The broader literature on social movements highlights the importance of coalitions for successful mobilization (for example, see Jones et al. 2001; Larson and Soule 2009). Furthermore, establishing collaborative networks is a core strategy of faith-based community organizing (Warren 2001; Wood 2002). When organizations join forces, they pool resources to share the costs of participation and gain access to diverse sources of information. Given the mobilizing advantages of connectedness, we posit that interfaith group membership will promote progressive activism among sympathetic congregations.

We also expect congregations' progressive mobilization potential to be realized when educated clergy are at the helm. As leaders of congregations, clergy are in a position to initiate organizing efforts and recruit parishioners to the cause. This was often how black churches got involved in the U.S. civil rights movement (Morris 1984). Importantly, research finds that higher education distinguishes activist pastors from quiescent ones (for example, see Guth et al. 1997). In this way, clergy educational level directly bears on activating congregations' progressive leanings.

Pastors need not be personally involved for congregations to engage in activism, but they must give the green light if it is to move forward. Even if congregants are ready to lead the activist charge, clergy have the power to shut it down. They may do so for a variety reasons, including the possibility of internal conflicts (for example, see Hadden 1969; Moon 2004). The more education pastors have completed, the greater the likelihood they will approve of congregations taking political action (for example, see Guth et al. 1997; McDaniel 2011). Among the possible explanations for this finding is that higher-educated clergy may believe they are better equipped to manage congregational dissent that could arise from political engagement. This leads us to predict that congregations with progressive commitments will act on them when educated clergy are in place.

The final factor that should convert congregations' progressive mobilization potential to action is a critical mass of educated laity. Obviously, larger congregations have more people who can plan and coordinate events. Not all lay members, however, are equally valuable when it comes to mobilizing social activism. For this activity, pews filled with individuals who possess leadership and organizing skills are most crucial. Given the positive relationship between educational level and these skills (Verba, Schlozman, and Brady 1995), progressively minded congregations with a high percentage of educated laity should be engaged in efforts for greater economic, political, or social equality.

In sum, our theoretical framework predicts that Mainline Protestant affiliation, liberal ideology, and social-justice orientation will make congregations potentially mobilizable for progressive causes. But without a tie to an interfaith group, educated clergyperson, or high percentage of educated laity, these predisposing factors are *not* likely to generate progressive activism. While we expect that one of the above action-inducing conditions must be present for congregations' progressive mobilization potential to be activated, the particular combinations most likely to do so are an empirical question. For instance, when congregations possess all three predisposing factors, perhaps just one action-inducing condition (such as belonging to an interfaith group) is required to mobilize for greater economic, political, or social equality. At the same time, it is possible that congregations with an educated clergyperson and a sizable educated laity need only a social-justice orientation to lobby or protest for progressive causes. In what follows, we use a novel methodology to identify the specific combinations that explain why congregations engage in political action for immigrant rights, same-sex marriage, or similar causes.

Data, Measures, and Methods

Data for this chapter come from the 2009 Southern Arizona Congregations Study (SACS). Based on lists from various sources, including denominational directories and telephone books, a master list ("sampling frame") of all known congregations in Pima and Maricopa, the two most populous counties in Arizona, was constructed. Congregations on the list were sorted into groups ("stratum") according to the major religious traditions.[3] We then randomly selected congregations from within each tradition.[4] The SACS collected information about a variety of topics—including worship practices, civic and political activity, and demographic characteristics—from a single key informant, usually a clergyperson. The majority of surveys were conducted over the phone, while a few were done in person. This information was collected between January and November 2009. A total of 477 congregations were selected to participate in the study and 293 did, for a response rate of 61 percent.

Our analysis explores whether congregations engaged in *Progressive Mobilization* (P) or not, which we measured based on whether congregations lobbied or protested for a cause promoting greater economic, political, or social equality in the last 12 months.[5] As mentioned above, only 6 percent, or 50 congregations in the SACS, took political action for progressive causes.[6]

In descending order, Table 3.1 shows the progressive causes for which congregations in Southern Arizona lobbied or protested in 2008–9. Because key informants could nominate up to three causes for each political activity, the total number of causes exceeds 50. Looking at this table, we see that two causes stand out: pro–gay marriage and pro–immigrant rights. The third and fourth progressive causes for which congregations rallied the most during this time were economic equality and reducing poverty. Anti-war and human rights tie for fifth. All of the remaining causes were present in no more than three Southern Arizonan congregations.

TABLE 3.1. Progressive Causes for Which Congregations Mobilize

Cause	Cases Present
Pro–Gay Marriage	23
Pro–Immigrant Rights	21
Economic Equality	10
Anti-Poverty	9
Anti-War	5
Human Rights	5
Support Homeless	3
Pro-Education	2
Pro-Environment	2
Anti–Health/Social Service Cuts	1
Prison Reform	1
Help HIV-Positive Persons	1

To explain why some congregations but not others mobilized for progressive causes, we focus on six different theoretical factors. As we argued in the prior section, Mainline Protestant affiliation, liberal ideology, and social-justice orientation are expected to make congregations potentially mobilizable for these causes. Congregations were coded as *Mainline Protestant* (M) or not using Steensland et al.'s (2000) classification scheme for denominations. The next predisposing factor was *Liberal Ideology* (L), which was measured based on whether key informants identified their congregations as either politically or theologically liberal, or not. Key informants were also asked if their congregations were more oriented toward social justice, personal salvation, or both equally. The first option was used to measure a *Social-Justice Orientation* (S).

Theoretically, we do not expect the above factors to be sufficient in themselves (or in combination) to generate congregation-based progressive mobilization. But in the presence of action-inducing factors, we expect progressive mobilization to occur. The first action-inducing factor is membership in an *Interfaith Group* (G), which we measured based on whether a congregation was a member of such a group or not. Next, we identified whether congregations' clergyperson (or head clergy if there was more than one) completed a master's degree or higher (*Educated Clergy* (C)). The last factor that should activate congregations' progressive mobilization potential is a *Large Educated Laity* (E), or whether at least 50 percent of the adult members of the congregation had completed a bachelor's degree or more.

We use Qualitative Comparative Analysis (QCA) (Ragin 1987) to identify the specific combinations that promote congregation-based mobilizing for greater economic, political, or social equality. The goal of QCA is "to aid causal interpretation, in concert with knowledge of cases" and "to explore evidence descriptively and configurationally, with an eye toward the different ways causally relevant conditions may combine to produce a given outcome" (Ragin 1987, 141). Put simply, QCA helps identify what conditions combine to produce an outcome. For those who are interested in learning more about the technical aspects of QCA and our analysis, see the methodological appendix at the end of this chapter.

Empirical Findings

Table 3.2 presents relationships between each of the six theoretical factors mentioned above and progressive mobilization (P). As expected, each one is present in many instances of the outcome. Looking down the first column, we see that among the 50 congregations that lobbied or protested for a progressive cause, 40 congregations (or 80 percent) were affiliated with a Mainline Protestant denomination. Most progressive mobilization thus happens within congregations of this tradition. Of the ten non–Mainline Protestant cases that took political action for a progressive cause, eight were Catholic parishes and two were Evangelical Protestant churches. Nearly three out of four congregations that mobilized for greater economic, political, or social equality identified as ideologically liberal (L), while just under half had a social-justice orientation (S). All but ten cases of progressive mobilization occurred within congregations connected to an interfaith group. Education was also very important, though more so for clergy. Of congregations that mobilized for a progressive cause, over 90 percent had an educated clergyperson, while less than 60 percent had a critical mass of educated laity.

While the six theoretical factors vary in the extent to which they are present in progressive mobilization, none of them perfectly overlap with it. In other words, they are *not* sufficient by themselves to generate congregation-based progressive mobilization. This does not mean, however, that they are insignificant. For example, as the QCA models illustrate below, liberal ideology and social-justice orientation are key causal conditions explaining why congregations engage in activism for greater economic, political, or social equality, but only in combination with other theoretical factors.

Before turning to the QCA results, it is also useful to consider variation *within* each theoretical factor. Doing so, we observe that less than a third of all Mainline Protestant congregations mobilized for a progressive cause. At 47 percent, not even half of all ideologically liberal congregations engaged in progressive mobilization. Among social-justice-oriented congregations, 62 percent lobbied or protested for same-sex marriage, immigrant rights, or similar issues. But this still means that over a third of these congregations remained on the sidelines. Most congregations with a tie to an interfaith group, educated clergyperson,

TABLE 3.2. Relationship between Theoretical Factors and Progressive Mobilization (P)

Theoretical Factors	Percent of Mobilized Congregations	Percent of Congregations that Mobilized
Mainline Protestant (M)	80	29
Liberal Ideology (L)	72	47
Social Justice Organization (S)	48	62
Interfaith Group (G)	80	29
Educated Clergy (C)	92	20
Educated Laity (E)	58	25

or large educated laity did not mobilize for a progressive cause (the percentages that did so were 29, 20, and 25, respectively).

Together with the results from the first column in Table 3.2, these data underscore the point that the presence of any one theoretical factor does *not* produce congregation-based progressive mobilization. In what follows, we employ QCA to explicate what particular set(s) of theoretical factors generate this outcome. Our analyses focus on six causal conditions, which implies 64 possible combinations of causal conditions. If combinations of causal conditions found in reality were equally distributed across all logically possible combinations, inference would be easier. However, what researchers almost always find is what is known as "limited diversity" among combinations of causal conditions. This is when many or most possible combinations of causal factors are not found in empirical reality (Ragin 2008, 174–8). Table 3.3 illustrates the

TABLE 3.3. QCA Outcomes by Combination

Outcome	Total	Success	Consistency	Coverage
lsCgmE	46	2	0.04	0.04
lscgmE	31	0	0.00	0.00
lsCGmE	30	2	0.07	0.04
lsCgME	26	1	0.04	0.02
LsCGME	25	10	0.40	0.20
lsCGME	25	4	0.16	0.08

(*continued*)

TABLE 3.3. QCA Outcomes by Combination (*continued*)

Outcome	Total	Success	Consistency	Coverage
LSCGME	**17**	**14**	**0.82**	**0.28**
lscgme	12	0	0.00	0.00
lscGmE	7	0	0.00	0.00
lsCgme	7	0	0.00	0.00
lsCGme	6	1	0.17	0.02
LsCgME	6	2	0.33	0.04
lsCgMe	5	0	0.00	0.00
lsCGMe	5	0	0.00	0.00
LsCGmE	5	1	0.20	0.02
LSCgME	5	2	0.40	0.04
lscGme	4	1	0.25	0.02
LScGME	**4**	**3**	**0.75**	**0.06**
lSCgME	3	0	0.00	0.00
LsCgmE	3	0	0.00	0.00
lSCGmE	**2**	**2**	**1.00**	**0.04**
LsCgMe	**2**	**2**	**1.00**	**0.04**
lscgMe	2	0	0.00	0.00
lSCGME	2	1	0.50	0.02
LSCGmE	**1**	**1**	**1.00**	**0.02**
LSCgMe	**1**	**1**	**1.00**	**0.02**
lscGMe	1	0	0.00	0.00
lscGME	1	0	0.00	0.00
lSCgme	1	0	0.00	0.00
LscgMe	1	0	0.00	0.00
LscgME	1	0	0.00	0.00
LscGME	1	0	0.00	0.00
LsCGme	1	0	0.00	0.00
LsCGMe	1	0	0.00	0.00
LScgmE	1	0	0.00	0.00
LScgMe	1	0	0.00	0.00
LSCGMe	1	0	0.00	0.00
Totals	293	50	N/A	1.00

Note: "L" is a measure of liberal ideology, "S" is a measure of social-justice orientation, "C" is a measure of clergy education, "G" indicates membership in an interfaith group, "M" indicates Mainline Protestant, "E" is a measure of large-educated laity. Only 37 out of 64 logically possible combinations are presented. No instances of the 27 remaining possible combinations were found in our data.

combinations of causal conditions found in our data. We find empirical cases fitting over half (37 out of 64) of the possible combinations.

In Table 3.3, we highlight the rows with the most relevant combinations. These are the combinations of causal conditions that are reasonably consistent with the presence of progressive mobilization within congregations. As discussed in the methodological appendix at the end of this chapter, the consistency measure is related to claims of causal sufficiency. Perfect consistency of 1.0 indicates that in every instance in which this combination of causal conditions was found, the outcome was also present. There are six total combinations that lead to congregation-based progressive mobilization. Table 3.4 displays the six relevant combinations from Table 3.3, which can then be reduced into three more general recipes for progressive mobilization. The analysis thus suggests that there are three possible combinations of causal conditions, or "paths," that are more or less sufficient to generate congregation-based mobilization for progressive causes. We discuss each of these combinations in turn.

Ultra-Progressive Combination

The first reduced combination (L*S*G*M*E) is also the most empirically and theoretically relevant. Its interpretation is that within Mainline Protestant congregations (M), those with a liberal ideology (L), a social-justice orientation (S), an interfaith group (G), and a sizable educated laity (E), mobilize for progressive causes. This combination—which we label "Ultra-Progressive"—covers 21 cases, 17 of which mobilized for a progressive cause. This particular configuration explains 34 percent of

TABLE 3.4. QCA Solutions for Progressive Mobilization

Label	True Combinations (unique coverage)	Reduced Solution	Solution Coverage	Solution Consistency
Ultra-Progressive	LSCGME (0.28) LScGME (0.06)	(L*S*G*M*E) +	0.460	0.852
Non-Mainliner	lSCGmE (0.04) LSCGme (0.02)	(S*C*G*m*E) +		
Lone-Operator	LsCgMe (0.04) LSCgMe (0.02)	(L*C*g*M*e)		

Note: The [*] symbol indicates the logical operator "and" or set intersection. The [+] symbol indicates the logical operator "or" or set union.

all instances of congregation-based progressive mobilization. A representative example from this group was a United Methodist congregation. It was a highly educated congregation with an educated pastor, a liberal identity, membership in an interfaith group, and a social-justice orientation. In an interview, the pastor describes their social engagement:

> Well, we're very socially active. Our mission statement . . . is to inspire and guide each other . . . through engaging with each other, our community, the earth, and the divine. So we have all four. We do engage with each other and our engagement with the community takes the form of intimate and active ministries of social justice in terms of the poor, homelessness, revision of our immigration laws, a revised or a new healthcare initiative that will be inclusive of everyone . . . we not only welcome gays, lesbians, bisexual and transgendered persons of sacred worth, but we're working towards their full civil rights; marriage, insurance, et cetera. So we're, I hesitate to say this, but we're probably one of the most socially active churches in town.

One way to understand this solution is to imagine a Venn diagram in which the intersection of these five theoretical factors also overlaps with approximately a third of all the cases of the outcome. Consistent with our theoretical expectation, Mainline Protestant affiliation, liberal ideology, and social-justice orientation are insufficient by themselves to produce lobbying or protesting for progressive causes. The joint presence of other factors is necessary for these predisposing factors to generate mobilization for greater economic, political, or social equality. This makes sense given the relatively low occurrence of this mobilization in our data. While the "net effect" of the three predisposing factors on the probability that a congregation will mobilize for a progressive cause is certainly positive, our analyses show the specific conditions under which these factors are activated.

Another implication of the first reduced solution is that when the five above theoretical factors are present, clergy education (C) can be present or absent, and progressive mobilization will still occur. This does not mean that having an educated clergy is unimportant for explaining why congregations engage in activism for greater economic, political, or social equality. For other combinations, we find that it is a significant factor. But for the "Ultra-Progressive" combination, the presence of educated clergy is not required for the outcome to occur.

Non-Mainliner Combination

The next reduced combination (S*C*G*m*E) means that among *non*–Mainline Protestant congregations (m), those with a social-justice orientation (S), interfaith group membership (G), educated clergy (C), and a large educated laity (E) mobilize for progressive causes. We call this combination "Non-Mainliner." It is less empirically relevant than the first, covering three cases, all of which mobilized. Its importance, however, is that it sheds light on how progressive mobilization operates outside of Mainline Protestant channels. Recall from above that there were only ten cases of lobbying or protesting for progressive causes in congregations that were *not* Mainline Protestant. So this combination explains almost a third of those cases. There are good reasons to think that the processes of congregation-based progressive mobilization may work differently among non–Mainline Protestants given that this mobilization outcome is so rare. The striking feature of this combination is that liberal ideology is not an important factor. For congregations unaffiliated with Mainline Protestantism, this ideology can be either present or absent in the joint presence of other theoretically relevant conditions. For example, one particular case from the "Non-Mainliner" category was a large Catholic parish, which did not identify as either theologically or politically liberal, but had a strong social-justice orientation and belonged to an interfaith group. This parish was involved in pro–immigrant rights activism.

Lone-Operator Combination

The final reduced combination is (L*C*g*M*e), which means that among Mainline Protestant congregations (M), those that are ideologically liberal (L), led by an educated clergy (C), do not belong to an interfaith group (g), and lack a critical mass of educated laity (e) mobilize for progressive causes. We call this combination "Lone-Operator" because they are uniquely characterized by the fact of *not* belonging to an interfaith group. This combination of causal conditions covers three cases, all of which mobilized for progressive causes. The low level of coverage means that this combination is not as empirically relevant as the other two. One way to interpret this solution is that in all instances of congregations without connections to an interfaith group and a low percentage of educated laity, the presence of a liberal ideology and an educated clergyperson are still sufficient to produce progressive mobilization. For example, a United Church of Christ (UCC) congregation was a liberal, social-justice oriented congregation that was not involved with an interfaith group, but was still very active in pro–gay marriage advocacy.

Conclusion

While it is a rare event, we know from case studies that congregations can provide important resources for social movements fighting for greater economic, political, or social equality in society (for example, see Davis, Martinez, and Warner 2010; Morris 1984; Nepstad 2004; Smith 1996; Warren 2001; Wood 2002; Yukich 2013). But why do certain congregations but not others mobilize for these movements? This question has generally not been addressed in the extant literature. By explicating the conditions under which congregations mobilized for progressive causes, this chapter contributes new knowledge to the scholarship on religion and politics.

Drawing on a sample of nearly 300 congregations in Southern Arizona and employing QCA, we found that no *one* single causal recipe emerged to explain progressive mobilization. Rather, several pathways were identified. As expected, if congregations were engaged in progressive activism, one of the following conditions needed to be present: Mainline Protestant affiliation, liberal ideology, or social-justice orientation. This makes sense because congregations that are unsympathetic would not be open to mobilizing for progressive causes. But none of these conditions by themselves led to lobbying or protesting for immigrant rights, same-sex marriage, or similar issues. That is, while a Mainline Protestant affiliation, liberal ideology, or social-justice orientation was a necessary ingredient, they were not sufficient (even together) to generate progressive mobilization. Rather, only in combination with other theoretically relevant factors did these predisposing characteristics promote action for greater economic, political, or social equality.

The most empirically relevant result found that among ideologically liberal, social-justice-oriented Mainline Protestant congregations, belonging to an interfaith group and having a large educated laity was sufficient to produce mobilizing for progressive causes. That clergy education was not needed in the "Ultra-Progressive" combination is counter to findings of research based on more traditional statistical regression analyses, which stress the importance of this variable in isolation for predicting congregation-based activism (for example, see Guth et al. 1997; McDaniel 2011). At least for congregations in Southern Arizona, however, educated clergy are not necessary for progressive mobilization to occur when other factors are present.

Interestingly, while the majority of cases of progressive activism were found within Mainline Protestant or ideologically liberal congregations, these factors were not always necessary. As long as *all* of the action-inducing characteristics (interfaith group membership, educated clergy, and large educated laity) were present, a social-justice orientation was enough for congregations to participate in lobbying or protesting efforts for progressive causes. Combined with the above finding, this suggests that there are unique pathways to progressive mobilization for ideologically liberal, Mainline Protestant congregations and those falling outside this camp. It thus seems that the factors (or sets of them) required to explain activism for progressive causes depends on congregations' particular religious tradition.

While we identified three important combinations that generated congregation-based progressive mobilization, some of the combinations that were insufficient in doing so were surprising. For example, the causal combination of liberal ideology (L), highly educated clergy (C), interfaith group membership (G), Mainline Protestant (M), and large educated laity (E), but without a social-justice orientation (s) failed the test for sufficiency (see Table 3.3). Congregations in this combination exhibited every relevant causal condition, *except* for a social-justice orientation. Twenty-five congregations fit into this combination, and only ten of them (or 40 percent) mobilized for a progressive cause. The benchmark for combinations that are consistent with an argument for causal sufficiency is at least 75–80 percent. Similarly, the combination

LSCgME (all causal conditions present except for membership in an interfaith group) had five cases, only two of which were mobilized. This shows the power of this kind of "configurational" analysis by highlighting the necessity of the right combination of causal conditions. There is no one single causal condition that was necessary in all of the combinations. Liberal ideology (L) is important, but the "Non-Mainliner" category shows that it is not absolutely necessary. Social-justice orientation (S) is crucial as well, but again not required for the "Lone-Operators." An educated clergy seems to matter quite a bit, but not necessarily for the "Ultra-Progressives." QCA enabled us to explicate the specific combinations of relevant causal conditions that are sufficient to produce progressive mobilization within congregations.

Because of the many conservative political victories in Arizona when our study was in the field, congregations had plenty of targets against which to mobilize. The conditions under which congregations take action for progressive causes could be very different in more favorable political environments. In states with more liberal social policies in place, progressively inclined congregations should generally be less aggrieved. Perhaps in such situations more and diverse conditions are needed to activate sympathetic congregations. Future research is needed to identify whether different combinations explain progressive mobilization among congregations embedded in more supportive settings.

Given the rarity of congregation-based mobilization for progressive causes, even a fairly large sample of congregations (like the one featured in this chapter) did not allow these causes to be examined separately. Rather, it was necessary for us to combine different progressive causes into a single category to have enough cases to analyze. But the causal combinations that lead to mobilizing could vary from one progressive cause to the next. For instance, the combinations that generate congregation-based activism for immigrant rights may be very different from those that promote marriage equality. Addressing this issue is challenging, as it requires collecting data from several thousands of congregations so that each progressive cause could be individually represented. Despite the challenge, doing so would add additional insight into how congregation-based progressive mobilization works.

To conclude, while it is not easy to find, congregation-based progressive mobilization does exist. It is unlikely that this mobilization will ever be the norm in society. But this does not mean that congregations are insignificant actors for advancing causes for greater economic, political, or social equality. Since grassroots movements tend to lack sufficient funding, volunteers, and other resources, even a handful of congregations mobilizing for progressive causes can make a big difference. Furthermore, when congregations lobby or protest for immigrant rights, same-sex marriage, or similar causes, like those we observed in Southern Arizona, they remind us that despite conventional wisdom equating faith-based mobilizing and conservative politics, there is a progressive side to religion.

Methodological Appendix

Standard multivariate regression techniques allow researchers to understand the "net effect" of an independent variable on a dependent variable by including control variables. QCA is different in that it enables understanding how different variables combine in different ways to produce a specified outcome (in our case, congregation-based mobilization for progressive causes). This appendix provides additional details about QCA and our analysis that some readers might find helpful.

Two central ideas of QCA are causal *necessity* and *sufficiency*. A causal condition or set of conditions is said to be causally *necessary* if the outcome does not occur in its absence. A combination of causal conditions is *necessary* if the set of cases exhibiting the specified combination of causal conditions is a *superset* of the set of cases exhibiting the outcome in question. A causal condition or set of conditions is said to be causally *sufficient* if the outcome does occur in all cases exhibiting the specified combination of conditions. A combination of causal conditions is *sufficient* if the set of cases exhibiting the specified combination is a *subset* of cases exhibiting the outcome in question.

There are two important measures used to assess these distinct aspects of set relations: consistency and coverage. *Consistency* is a measure from 0 to 1, which indicates "how closely a perfect subset relation is approximated" (Ragin 2008, 44) between a set of causal conditions and an outcome set. A consistency score of 1.0 is therefore consistent with an argument for causal sufficiency. Ragin (2008) suggests a heuristic baseline of consistency scores of 0.75 or higher before substantive interpretation is permissible. Consistency can be thought of as loosely analogous to statistical significance in traditional regression. If a coefficient is not statistically significant in a regression model, interpreting it is generally not warranted. Similarly with QCA, if consistency falls below 0.75, interpretation of that combination of causal conditions is problematic. *Coverage* is a measure from 0 to 1 of the degree to which "a cause or causal combination accounts for instances of an outcome" (Ragin 2008, 44). A coverage score of 1.0 is therefore consistent with an argument for causal necessity. Imagine an instance in which there are several different combinations of causal conditions that are sufficient to produce an outcome. In this case the coverage of any particular combination of causal conditions may be small. Coverage can be thought of as a measure of the empirical relevance of a particular combination of causal conditions. Coverage is measured as the proportion of the cases in the outcome for which the solution accounts. It can be thought of as somewhat analogous to the explained variance (R-squared) measure in traditional quantitative analysis.

ACKNOWLEDGMENTS
We thank Christian Smith for helpful comments on earlier versions of our chapter.

NOTES
1 This reflects the *action* dimension of progressive religion that Fuist, Braunstein, and Williams discuss in the introduction to this volume.
2 By progressive causes, we mean those focused on greater economic, political, or social equality.
3 Because of the low number of black Protestant congregations in Southern Arizona, they were placed with either Evangelical Protestants or Mainline Protestants. For instance, the Church of God in Christ (COGIC) was put with the former, while the African Methodist Episcopal (AME) Church was put with the latter.
4 The SACS pulled more congregations from the Mainline Protestant stratum than from the other tradition strata. Since we know the rate by which Mainline Protestant congregations were oversampled, they can be weighted appropriately to make the SACS data representative of all congregations in Pima and Maricopa counties.
5 These cases were coded as "one," and those that did not mobilize were coded as "zero."

6 This figure is based on the SACS data being weighted to be representative of all congregations in Maricopa and Pima counties. Among other things, the weighting accounts for the oversample of Mainline Protestant congregations (see note 4). If we do *not* weight the data and let Mainline Protestant congregations represent a greater share of congregations than they are in the population (see note 4), the number jumps to 17 percent. While weighting the data affects descriptive statistics, it does not change the actual number of congregations identified as having mobilized for a progressive cause.

REFERENCES

Ammerman, Nancy T. 2005. *Pillars of Faith*. Berkeley: University of California Press.

Barnes, Sandra L. 2005. "Black Church Culture and Community Action." *Social Forces* 84(2): 967–994.

Beyerlein, Kraig, and John R. Hipp. 2006. "A Two-Stage Model for a Two-Stage Process: How Biographical Availability Matters for Social Movement Mobilization." *Mobilization* 11(3): 219–240.

Davis, Nancy J., and Robert V. Robinson. 1996. "Are the Rumors of War Exaggerated? Religious Orthodoxy and Moral Progressivism in America." *American Journal of Sociology* 102(3): 756–787.

Davis, Stephen P., Juan R. Martinez, and R. Stephen Warner. 2010. "The Role of the Catholic Church in Chicago Immigrant Mobilization." In *¡Marcha!: Latino Chicago and the Immigrant Rights Movement*, edited by A. Pallares and N. Flores-González, 79–96. Urbana: University of Illinois Press.

Denogean, Anne T. 2008. "Some Clergy Oppose Gay Marriage Ban." *Tucson Citizen*, September 26.

Djupe, Paul A., and Christopher P. Gilbert. 2009. *The Political Influence of Churches*. Cambridge, UK: Cambridge University Press.

Elisha, Omri. 2011. *Moral Ambition: Mobilization and Social Outreach in Evangelical Megachurches*. Berkeley: University of California Press.

Guth, James L., John C. Green, Corwin E. Smidt, Lyman A. Kellstedt, and Margaret M. Poloma. 1997. *The Bully Pulpit*. Lawrence: University of Kansas Press.

Hadden, Jeffrey K. 1969. *The Gathering Storm in the Churches*. Garden City, NY: Doubleday.

Jones, Andrew W., Richard N. Hutchinson, Nella Van Dyke, Leslie Gates, and Michelle Companion. 2001. "Coalition Form and Mobilization Effectiveness in Local Social Movements." *Sociological Spectrum* 21(2): 207–231.

Klandermans, Burt, and Dirk Oegema. 1987. "Potentials, Networks, Motivations, and Barriers: Steps towards Participation in Social Movements." *American Sociological Review* 52(4): 519–531.

Larson, Jeff A., and Sarah A. Soule. 2009. "Sector-Level Dynamics and Collective Action in the United States, 1965–1975." *Mobilization* 14(3): 293–314.

McDaniel, Eric L. 2011. *Politics in the Pews: The Political Mobilization of Black Churches* Ann Arbor: University of Michigan Press.

Moon, Dawne. 2004. *God, Sex, and Politics*. Chicago: University of Chicago Press.

Morris, Aldon. 1984. *The Origins of the Civil Rights Movement*. New York: Free Press.

Nepstad, Sharon Erickson. 2004. *Convictions of the Soul*. New York: Oxford University Press.

Olson, Laura R. 2000. *Filled with Spirit and Power*. Albany: State University of New York Press.

Ragin, Charles. 1987. *The Comparative Method: Moving beyond Qualitative and Quantitative Strategies*. Berkeley: University of California Press.

Ragin, Charles. 2008. *Redesigning Social Inquiry: Fuzzy Sets and Beyond*. Chicago: University of Chicago Press.

Sherkat, Darren, Melissa Powell-Williams, Gregory Maddox, and Kylan Mattias de Vries. 2011. "Religion, Politics, and Support for Same-Sex Marriage in the United States, 1988–2008." *Social Science Research* 40(1): 167–180.

Smidt, Corwin, ed. 2004. *Pulpit and Politics*. Waco, TX: Baylor University Press.

Smith, Christian. 1996. *Resisting Reagan*. Chicago: University of Chicago Press.

Smith, Gregory A. 2008. *Politics in the Parish*. Washington, DC: Georgetown University Press.

Snow, David A., E. Burke Rockford, Jr., Steven K. Worden, and Robert D. Benford. 1986. "Frame Alignment Processes, Micromobilization, and Movement Participation." *American Sociological Review* 51(4): 464–481.

Steensland, Brian, Jerry Z. Park, Mark D. Regnerus, Lynn D. Robinson, W. Bradford Wilcox, and Robert D. Woodberry. 2000. "The Measure of American Religion: Toward Improving the State of the Art." *Social Forces* 79(1): 291–318.

Verba, Sidney, Kay Lehman Schlozman, and Henry E. Brady. 1995. *Voice and Equality*. Cambridge, MA: Harvard University Press.

Warren, Mark R. 2001. *Dry Bones Rattling*. Princeton, NJ: Princeton University Press.

Williams, Rhys H., and Jeffrey Blackburn. 1996. "Many Are Called but Few Obey: Ideological Commitment and Activism in Operation Rescue." In *Disruptive Religion*, edited by Christian Smith, 167–185. New York: Routledge.

Wood, Richard L. 2002. *Faith in Action*. Chicago: University of Chicago Press.

Wuthnow, Robert. 1988. *The Restructuring of American Religion*. Princeton, NJ: Princeton University Press.

Yukich, Grace. 2013. *One Family under God*. New York: Oxford University Press.

4

Collective Identity and Movement Solidarity among Religious Left Activists in the U.S.

LAURA R. OLSON

Collective action has long been a major component of the complex relationship between religion and American politics (Morris 1984; Hertzke 1988, 2006; Guth, Kellstedt et al. 1993; Guth, Smidt et al. 1993; Noonan 1998; Hofrenning 2002; Gutterman 2005; Conger 2009; Djupe and Lewis 2015). Organized political activity by religious people frequently manifests itself, as it does in the secular world, through social movements and the interest groups that often double as social movement organizations on the ground. For decades, political observers and scholars alike have focused on two broad, polarized religio-political movements in the United States: the religious Right and (albeit to a lesser extent) the "religious Left" (e.g., Hunter 1991). Even though the religious Right and religious Left ought not to be classified as protest movements (Olson 2011), it is nevertheless appropriate to think of each as social movements (Smith 1996a; Noonan 1998; Hart 2001; Gutterman 2005).

Although the religious Right has enjoyed much more political influence than the religious Left has in recent times, progressive interfaith coalitions historically have been highly significant agents of change in American society (Wuthnow 1988; Hart 2001; Putnam and Campbell 2010; Porterfield 2012). Some scholars would contend that for most of the twentieth century, the dominant faith-based impetus in American politics was in fact a progressive one (Hertzke 1988). The Social Gospel Movement of the late nineteenth and early twentieth centuries gave rise to the teaching that Mainline Protestants have a duty to combat injustice, poverty, and discrimination (Hart 2001; Steensland 2002; Bartkowski and Regis 2003; Evans 2004; Gutterman 2005; Wilson 2009; see also Lichterman and Williams in this volume).

Meanwhile, the longstanding social justice imperatives inherent in Catholic Social Teaching have undergirded significant antipoverty work by American Catholics (Wuthnow 1988; Cochran and Cochran 2003; Putnam and Campbell 2010). Reform-minded Mainline Protestant, Catholic, and Jewish religious leaders lent their support to African Americans' struggle for civil rights (Findlay 1993; Friedland 1998). Religious progressives have lent their voices to a range of other high-profile political movements as well, including the anti–Vietnam War movement of the 1960s and 1970s (Hall 1990) and the Sanctuary Movement of the 1980s, which gave shelter to refugees of Latin American civil wars (Smith 1996b). In recent decades, however, the political clout of the American religious Left has been rather minimal. Despite the election and reelection of President Barack Obama (who cut his political teeth doing progressive faith-based community organizing work in Chicago) and a concomitant warming of the climate in Washington for progressives, some might wonder whether there even is a religious Left in the United States any longer, much less one that would be powerful enough to offset the influence of the religious Right.

On the other hand, some analysts recently have suggested that the religious Left might be well positioned to rebound in light of various demographic, political, and cultural changes since the turn of the century (e.g., Sullivan 2008; Dionne 2009; Jones et al. 2013). Such resurgence would require the religious Left to overcome several longstanding challenges that hinder its ability to mobilize potential supporters on the ground (Olson 2007, 2011). The religious Right's sustained political influence has been a direct result of a high level of commitment among its activists to a relatively narrow—and thus effective—agenda (Wilcox and Robinson 2010). The religious Left instead has tended to pursue a broad, sometimes inchoate agenda. Moreover, the religious Left is a diverse, loosely knit web of religious people who do not just tolerate, but celebrate, differences in opinion (Alpert 2000; Hart 2001; Kellstedt et al. 2007; Olson 2007, 2011). For these reasons and beyond, the question of whether meaningful resurgence is a viable possibility for the religious Left is an open one.

Against this backdrop, this chapter examines progressive and conservative religio-political activists' degree of commitment to their respective movements: the religious Left and Right. As social psychological work on social movements contends, successful movements tend to be those in which activists demonstrate high levels of unity and commitment to the cause (Cohen 1985; Gamson 1992; Hunt and Benford 2004). Two concepts from this literature are especially relevant here. *Collective identity* refers to "how individuals' sense of who they are becomes engaged with a definition shared by co-participants in some effort at social change" (Gamson 1992, 55; the notion of "group consciousness" fits in here as well: see Miller et al. 1981). Movement *solidarity* concerns "how individuals develop and maintain loyalty to . . . groups or organizations [that] act as carriers of social movements" (Gamson 1992, 55). If the religious Left is poised to increase its political influence in the twenty-first century, we should expect to see evidence of collective identity and solidarity among its adherents that might outstrip that of its rival movement, the religious Right.

My general contention is that despite an increasingly advantageous political *zeitgeist*, the religious Left in the United States lacks influence because its activists tend not to be unified. Although I cannot directly test this hypothesis, I am able to make some inferences about its viability on the basis of three empirical questions that allow me to compare progressive religio-political activists with their conservative counterparts. First, do religio-political activists actually perceive themselves as belonging to the religious Right or religious Left? If a movement has substantive integrity, individuals who can reasonably be called "activists" within it should say that they do, in fact, identify with the movement. Such personal identification is one of the most basic building blocks of collective identity (Miller et al. 1981). Second, belief in a movement's potential effectiveness also contributes to collective identity. Do activists perceive their movement as being capable of effecting meaningful change? Do they see the main goals articulated by their movement as being achievable? Third, to what extent do activists demonstrate movement solidarity, as measured by their support for key affiliated social movement organizations (SMOs)? This question is another way of asking about the depth and strength of individuals' identification with a movement. I analyze each of these questions in turn by comparing separate samples of religio-political activists on the Left and on the Right.

Data and Method

The analyses that follow rely on data gathered in 2009 by the Public Religion Research Institute (PRRI). For its Conservative and Progressive Religious Activists study, PRRI undertook two separate mail surveys (using a nearly identical survey) of people they identified as religious activists, of which 1,886 can be considered of the religious Left and 1,123 of the religious Right. Their data-gathering strategy began with the development of lists of core religious Left and religious Right SMOs. PRRI then generated random samples from membership lists of six progressive organizations and four conservative ones.[1] They augmented these samples with additional random samples of: (1) clergy/religious professionals who made financial contributions to federal campaigns in 2008; and (2) publicly available lists of leaders of local faith-based advocacy groups.[2] I analyze each dataset separately, using parallel items from the two surveys to address the three questions I proposed.

First, how do progressive and conservative religio-political activists compare in their identification with "their" movement? To answer this question, I rely on a question in the PRRI survey instrument that asks respondents "Do you consider yourself to be part of the [progressive/conservative] religious movement?" (the answers were either "yes" or "no"). I recognize that this item does not ask about affiliation with a religio-*political* movement per se, but it was asked alongside a variety of other questions that did ask specifically about politics.

Second, how influential, and potentially influential, do activists perceive their movement to be? PRRI asked both sets of activists how much influence they felt "religious progressive groups" and "religious conservative groups" had "on the 2008 election results." Separately, the progressive sample was asked whether "political action by religious people can help establish justice in American society," and the conservative sample was asked whether "political action by religious people can help restore traditional morality in America." The religious Left emphasizes the need to fight for justice in the world, especially by assisting the poor and disadvantaged; in particular, many religious progressives perceive flaws in the distribution of wealth in the United States (Guth et al. 1997; Hart 2001; Steensland 2002; Olson 2007; Wilson 2009). Meanwhile, the religious Right concerns itself primarily with returning American society to what it perceives as traditional moral and family values (Wilcox and Robinson 2010). The first item measures perceptions of *actual* (electoral) influence, while the second is a much broader indicator of the respondent's belief in *potential* influence with regard to their movement's most central priority. I use the latter measure as the dependent variable to be explained in the statistical analyses.

Third, to what extent does each set of activists support SMOs affiliated with their own movement—and those of the "other side"? Respondents were asked their opinions about groups typically identified with the movement to which they (supposedly) belong.[3] Progressives were asked about the American Civil Liberties Union, Bread for the World, the Human Rights Campaign, the Interfaith Alliance, the NAACP, and Sojourners (see Olson 2011 for more detail about the constellation of religious Left organizations). Conservatives were asked about the American Center for Law and Justice, Christian Coalition, Concerned Women for America, the Family Research Council, Focus on the Family, National Right to Life, and Prison Fellowship (see Wilcox and Robinson 2010 for further information about religious Right organizations). Respondents on each side also were asked about one or two groups commonly identified with the *other* movement; progressives were asked about Focus on the Family and Prison Fellowship while conservatives were asked about Bread for the World. First, I explore activists' evaluations of each SMO; then I calculate each respondent's average evaluation of same-movement SMOs as the way to answer my third question.[4]

In each of the analyses that follow, I include several religious and political independent variables alongside a set of standard demographic control variables. I chose the independent variables as the most obvious hypothetical predictors of affiliation with each of the two movements. In analyses for progressives, I include variables that indicate whether or not respondents identify as an observant Mainline Protestant or observant Catholic; for conservatives, the relevant variables asked whether or not respondents identified as an observant Evangelical Protestant or observant Catholic.[5] Mainline Protestants historically have been associated with the religious Left, or at least not with the religious Right; Evangelicals have been the backbone of the religious Right; Catholics have fitted themselves into both movements depending on contextual factors (Smidt 2001; Fowler et al. 2010; Putnam and Campbell 2010).

The political independent variables include political ideology, partisanship, and a seven-point measure of support for religio-political activism for which respondents answered the question "Some religious leaders have argued that religious people should withdraw from politics and rededicate themselves to non-political pursuits. What is your view on this matter?" Demographic control variables include gender, region (with the West as the excluded group), community size, age, education, and income.

Collective Identity I: Movement Identification

In purely descriptive terms, respondents in the religious Left sample are fully ten percentage points less likely than religious Right respondents to say they identify with "their" movement: 74.1 percent of the religious Left sample say they "consider [themselves] a part of the progressive religious movement," as compared to 84.5 percent of the religious Right sample who identify with the "conservative religious movement." Separate statistical analyses, using a technique called logistic regression, are presented in Table 4.1. The dependent variable, or the thing to be explained, is movement identification. The religious and political independent variables discussed above are included, as are demographic controls.

The religion variables are strong predictors in both models in Table 4.1. Being an observant Catholic predicts identification with the religious Left but with not the religious Right, which supports the frequent assumption that Catholics in the aggregate lean mildly toward the left. As expected, being an observant Mainline Protestant predicts religious Left identification, while being an observant Evangelical drives religious Right identification. The results for ideology and partisanship also are as expected. Meanwhile, living in a more densely populated community and being older both predict identification with the religious Left, while being female, living in the South, and having a lower income all boost identification with the religious Right. Above all, the fact that the model for conservatives is more statistically significant and explanatory than the one for progressives squares with the assertion that religious progressives are difficult to characterize (Alpert 2000; Olson 2007, 2011)

TABLE 4.1. Logistic Regression Analysis of Identification with Movement

	Progressives	Conservatives
Observant Mainline Protestant	2.02***	—
Observant Evangelical Protestant	—	3.33***
Observant Catholic	1.68**	.72
Liberal ideology	1.30***	.49***
Democratic party identification	1.28***	.67**
Stay focused on politics (vs. withdraw)	1.43***	1.49***
Male	1.18	.53*
Region: Northeast	.79	.84
Region: Midwest	1.06	1.42
Region: South	1.03	1.85*
Community size	1.09*	.93
Age category	.77**	.97
Education	1.18	.95
Income	.99	.85**
(Constant)	.02***	20.2**
N	1406	805
Log likelihood	−710.68	−258.20
P	<.001	<.001
Pseudo R²	.13	.26

Note: Figures reported are odds ratios.

and lends support to my underlying contention that the religious Left lacks unity.

Collective Identity II: Perceptions of Movement Influence

To what degree do religious Left and religious Right activists believe their movements can be effective? Both groups of activists were asked how influential each movement was in the 2008 elections. Progressives were more than three times as likely as conservatives (10.6 percent versus 3.4 percent) to perceive their movement as having had "great influence" on the elections. This result is unsurprising considering that a Democrat, Barack Obama, was elected to the presidency and Democrats posted net gains in the U.S. Senate, House of Representatives, and governors' mansions. However, both sets of activists rated the *opposite* group's influence almost equally: 7.9 percent of progressives thought the religious Right had "great influence," while 7.6 percent of conservatives said the same of the religious Left.

The two groups also registered similar levels of belief in their movements' potential to be influential in achieving its principal advocacy priority. Among progressives, 69.6 percent agreed with the statement "politics can restore justice," whereas 71.9 percent of the conservative sample concurred with the assertion "politics can restore morality." Table 4.2 presents the results of more statistical analyses (again using logistic regression) of activists' belief that their movement's main advocacy priority can be successful (progressives: "politics can restore justice"; conservatives: "politics can restore morality"). I include the same independent variables and controls as in Table 4.1.

Table 4.2 indicates that many of the same factors predict belief in movement effectiveness for both groups. Observant Catholics and those who prefer religious actors to "stay focused on politics" are significantly more likely to believe that their movement's main cause can be successful. Being an observant Mainline Protestant drives belief in potential effectiveness in the progressive model, as does older age in the conservative model. Surprisingly, whether one is an observant Evangelical Protestant is not significant in the conservative model, but notice that this statistical model is not especially powerful; perhaps this is a function of the fact that a large majority (71.9 percent) of religious Right activists *do* believe that politics can restore morality. Neither ideology nor party identification is significant for either Left or Right. Education is significant in both models, but works in opposite directions: better-educated progressives are more likely to perceive the potential of success, while better-educated conservatives are less so. Especially when compared with Table 4.1, Table 4.2 suggests that progressive religio-political activists do share a certain degree of collective identity revolving around belief in the viability of their cause. The roots of such identity seem to lie more in individual religious characteristics than in political orientation. In this sense, religion trumps politics: having a progressive religious outlook drives certainty of movement effectiveness much more powerfully than having a progressive political outlook.

TABLE 4.2. Logistic Regression Analysis of Attitudes about Movement Influence

	Progressives "Politics can restore justice"	Conservatives "Politics can restore morality"
Observant Mainline Protestant	1.60**	—
Observant Evangelical Protestant	—	.88
Observant Catholic	2.18***	1.96*
Liberal ideology	1.12	.98
Democratic party identification	1.02	1.06
Stay focused on politics (vs. withdraw)	1.71***	1.36***
Male	1.21	1.19
Region: Northeast	.69	1.01
Region: Midwest	.91	1.03
Region: South	.96	.77
Community size	.94	.99
Age category	.93	1.29*
Education	1.39**	.80*
Income	1.01	1.06
(Constant)	.03**	.28
N	1406	812
Log likelihood	−701.24	−452.27
P	<.001	<.001
Pseudo R²	.16	.07

Note: Figures reported are odds ratios.

Movement Solidarity: Support for Social Movement Organizations

Do religio-political activists register movement solidarity through support for the SMOs most commonly identified with the religious Left or Right? Table 4.3a provides descriptive data about progressive respondents' attitudes toward various SMOs, while Table 4.3b does the same for conservatives' attitudes. Generally speaking, larger percentages of conservatives register support for same-movement SMOs; not one religious Left SMO receives a "very favorable" rating from more than half of the progressive respondents. The average evaluation scores among conservatives are uniformly more positive as well. Distaste among progressives for the more prominent of the two religious Right SMOs about which they were asked—Focus on the Family—is palpable, with an evaluation average of 1.86. This result suggests that the religious Left might know more about what it stands against (the religious Right) than what it stands for. This result might well reflect the fact that much of the religious Left's more recent mobilization efforts really have been counter-mobilization efforts against the religious Right. For example, until recently the Interfaith Alliance described itself as "the faith-based voice countering the radical right and promoting the positive role of religion."

TABLE 4.3A. Support for Movement SMOs among Progressives

	Percent "very favorable"	Mean (range: 1–5; 5 = very favorable)
ACLU	31	3.89
Bread for the World	30	3.99
Focus on the Family	3	1.86
Human Rights Campaign	26	3.91
Interfaith Alliance	41	3.87
NAACP	19	3.36
Prison Fellowship	15	3.47
Sojourners	32	3.51

Note: Opposite-movement SMOs are noted in italics.

TABLE 4.3B. Support for Movement SMOs among Conservatives

	Percent "very favorable"	Mean (range: 1–5; 5 = very favorable)
American Center for Law and Justice	46	4.30
Bread for the World	7	3.29
Christian Coalition	25	3.92
Concerned Women for America	38	4.13
Family Research Council	44	4.30
Focus on the Family	60	4.56
National Right to Life	65	4.58
Prison Fellowship	46	4.35

Note: Opposite-movement SMOs are noted in italics.

Table 4.4 presents statistical analyses (this time using a technique called "ordinary least squares" regression) of average support for one's "own" SMOs conducted separately using the progressive and conservative samples. Again, independent and control variables are the same as in the previous analyses (Tables 4.1 and 4.2). Several findings stand out in Table 4.4. Being an observant Catholic reduces the likelihood of support for both sets of SMOs, but as expected, being an observant Evangelical increases the likelihood of support for religious Right SMOs. Indeed, Table 4.4 might offer evidence of the cross-pressures observant Catholics encounter when attempting to sort out their political allegiances

TABLE 4.4. OLS Regression Analysis of Average Support for Movement SMOs[1]

	Progressives[2]	Conservatives[3]
Observant Mainline Protestant	.06	—
Observant Evangelical Protestant	—	.22***
Observant Catholic	−.10**	−.21**
Liberal ideology	.19***	−.14***
Democratic party identification	.08***	−.03
Stay focused on politics (vs. withdraw)	.03***	.07***
Male	−.06*	−.11**
Region: Northeast	.03	.11
Region: Midwest	.02	.06
Region: South	.01	.03
Community size	.02**	−.01
Age category	.07***	.04
Education	.02	.05*
Income	−.03**	−.04***
(Constant)	1.85***	4.00***
N	1050	630
P	<.001	<.001
Adjusted R^2	.28	.26

Note: Figures reported are standardized regression coefficients (beta).
[1] The dependent variable is a ratio of (summed ratings of SMOs) to (total SMOs rated).
[2] Progressive SMOs: ACLU, Bread for the World, Human Rights Campaign, Interfaith Alliance, NAACP, Sojourners.
[3] Conservative SMOs: American Center for Law and Justice, Christian Coalition, Concerned Women for America, Family Research Council, Focus on the Family, National Right to Life, Prison Fellowship.

(Cochran and Cochran 2003; Hussey and Layman 2014). Ideology is a strong predictor of SMO support as well, working in the expected direction in each model. Party identification is highly significant in the progressive model but not the conservative model; religious orientation clearly trumps partisanship in shaping activists' support for their movement's SMOs. Notice that the values of the R^2 coefficients (the amount of variation the models can predict) are very similar in these two models as well, suggesting that, overall, the hypothesized influences of religious and political orientations on movement solidarity are roughly the same for the religious Left and the religious Right.

Discussion and Conclusion

This brief comparative exploration of factors that might shape collective identity and movement solidarity among religio-political activists reveals that both the religious Left and the religious Right enjoy sources of deep commitment among their activists—but also that both movements face potential challenges with regard to mobilization. Religious Left activists seem less willing to be labeled as adherents of a "progressive religious movement" than their conservative counterparts are to claim affiliation with a "conservative religious movement." Perhaps this reluctance is due to lack of clarity about what such a movement entails in comparison with the religious Right, even among those who reasonably may be classified as religious Left activists. The basic descriptive fact that fewer than three in four individuals in the religious Left activist sample said they identify with the movement is rather striking, and this result cannot be explained away by sampling error. I cannot comment on whether these survey respondents mostly dislike the term "religious Left," its SMOs, or its various political tactics, but it is fair to conjecture that multiple factors contribute to activists eschewing outright identification with the movement. A separate, but no less significant, challenge for the religious Left is the fact that observant Mainline Protestants and observant Catholics do exhibit collective identity—but not movement solidarity—with the movement. The same cannot be said of Evangelicals and the religious Right, which is one explanation of its enduring political clout.

The underlying contention framing this inquiry has been that the religious Left lacks influence because of a lack of unity among its activists. The empirical results do not, however, indicate that this is necessarily true. Liberal Mainline Protestant and Catholic respondents clearly believe it is possible for collective action to bring about justice. The statistical results presented here, however, suggest that such activists are neither terribly likely to identify with the religious Left movement per se nor to place a great deal of faith in the effectiveness of existing religious Left SMOs. There may be willing activists on the ground, but if national-level organizations lack the clout and legitimacy to take advantage of the present American political *zeitgeist*, the religious Left's prospects for future success are no brighter today than they have been since at least 1980.[6]

External conditions create and destroy opportunities for social movements (McAdam 1982; Tarrow 2011). The religious Left learned this lesson in the late twentieth century when the religious Right emerged and began reshaping the "morality politics" discourse, emphasizing issues such as abortion and homosexuality instead of inequality and social justice. During this period religious progressives remained complacent—and some paid a steep price when moderate-to-conservative laity began leaving due to perceptions that white Mainline Protestantism (in particular) had grown too liberal (Hadden 1969; Finke and Stark 2005). The religious Right capitalized on its strategic advantages, engaged around a narrow and effective agenda, and has been rewarded for decades with a unified activist base and significant political clout (especially in the context of elections). What might change the religious Left's political fortunes in the decades ahead?

First, progressive religious groups would need to find a way of overcoming the challenges of maintaining a wide-ranging issue agenda. Stepping away from this agenda would be disingenuous, particularly because of the broad swath cut by the longstanding traditions of the Social Gospel, Catholic Social Teaching, and Jewish public witnesses for justice, tolerance, and equality. And as my empirical analysis shows, religious Left activists believe in the social justice cause. Pursuing a broad political agenda can be both a blessing and a curse. Embracing a broad agenda means there will be many opportunities for coalition building, which is essential if the relatively weak organizations that comprise the religious

Left today hope to exercise any clout (Hertzke 2006). However, movements with broad agendas often find it challenging to carve out niches for themselves on the vast frontier of American political pluralism. Instead, resources must be spread thinly across a wide range of policy priorities, meaning that no one priority can ever get the attention it needs.

If it hopes to return to political prominence, the American religious Left also will need to marshal key resources. At present, there are few nationally visible progressive Protestant leaders. Sojourners' Jim Wallis is probably the religious Left's most prominent representative, but one leader does not a movement make. The existence of so many organizations within the movement sector undoubtedly makes it difficult for individual leaders to rise to prominence. An important component of the movement's challenge will be finding ways of joining these organizations together in common cause rather than duplicating efforts and wasting resources, which appears to be a tendency among religious Left organizations (Olson 2011).

Moreover, one previous study also suggests that religious liberals are especially likely to say they are *satisfied* with the social status quo (Olson 2007). It takes a certain "fire in the belly" stemming from deep dissatisfaction with the status quo to move people toward political action (Miller et al. 1981; Marx and McAdam 1994). Perhaps the religious Left had become overly complacent by the time the religious Right emerged in the 1980s, assuming (incorrectly) that progressivism would continue to be the most audible faith-based voice in American politics (Hertzke 1988). And if Mainline Protestantism, the natural home of most progressive Protestants, is in numerical decline (Finke and Stark 2005), clergy might be unwilling to engage in political activism for fear of scaring away current and potential members (Crawford and Olson 2001). Congregations facing serious survival challenges are likely to curtail their participation in political action, turning inward in an attempt to survive. Such congregations also are likely to avoid any activities that might be perceived as controversial for fear of accelerating numerical decline.

Whether the American religious Left will rise again to national prominence remains to be seen. At the elite level, there is organization and energy. Among the activists studied here, there is a continuing belief in the viability of the religious Left's core agenda item: the fight for social justice. Of course, all social movements wax and wane. Some go dormant for decades before reemerging when the *zeitgeist* is right. Even though the religious Left may now have more *potential* energy than has been the case since the Vietnam war era, it will be up to current and future activists and elite-level organizations to address the challenges of coordination and mobilization that presently prevent the religious Left from converting its potential energy into the most desired kinetic energy in politics: meaningful, transformative clout.

ACKNOWLEDGMENTS

This chapter is dedicated to the memory of my parents, Robert and Mary Olson. I would like to thank the editors of this volume for their helpful recommendations about earlier drafts of this piece and for their patience with and support of me during a difficult time in my life. Portions of this chapter are adapted from two of the author's previous publications (Olson 2011 and Olson 2016).

NOTES

1 PRRI does not disclose a full list of the organizations from which they drew their samples, but they cite examples: the Interfaith Alliance and Sojourners for progressives, and Concerned Women for America and the National Right to Life Committee for conservatives (Green, Jones, and Cox 2009, 32n10).

2 See Green, Jones, and Cox (2009, 31–32) for additional information on PRRI's sampling strategy.

3 I include only those organizations rated "very favorably" by at least 30 percent of activists, with the exception of the opposite-movement organizations.

4 The dependent variable is a ratio of the summed evaluation scores for same-movement SMOs to the number of SMOs evaluated.

5 I use these variables as coded by PRRI (Green, Jones, and Cox 2009). I decided against using religious affiliation alone on the assumption that activists in a religio-political movement are likely to be individuals of relatively high religiosity (see, e.g., Green 2007 for background on the need to measure religious affiliation and religiosity separately in research on religion and politics).

6 It is important to note that these data were collected shortly after Barack Obama was first elected to the presidency, so replication might reveal somewhat different results. Nevertheless, since 2009 the political climate in the United States has remained somewhat more favorable to liberals than it has to conservatives (for instance, the Affordable Care Act has been passed and upheld as constitutional and same-sex marriage is now legal across the country)—and the religious Left has shown no obvious signs of rebirth during the Obama years.

REFERENCES

Alpert, Rebecca T., ed. 2000. *Voices of the Religious Left: A Contemporary Sourcebook*. Philadelphia: Temple University Press.

Bartkowski, John P., and Helen A. Regis. 2003. *Charitable Choices: Religion, Race, and Poverty in the Post- Welfare Era*. New York: New York University Press.

Cochran, Clarke E., and David Carroll Cochran. 2003. *Catholics, Politics, and Public Policy: Beyond Left and Right*. Maryknoll, NY: Orbis.

Cohen, Jean L. 1985. "Strategy or Identity: New Theoretical Paradigms and Contemporary Social Movements." *Social Research* 52(4): 663–716.

Conger, Kimberly H. 2009. *The Christian Right in Republican State Politics*. New York: Palgrave Macmillan.

Crawford, Sue E. S., and Laura R. Olson, eds. 2001. *Christian Clergy in American Politics*. Baltimore: Johns Hopkins University Press.

Dionne, E. J. Jr. 2009. *Souled Out: Reclaiming Faith and Politics after the Religious Right*. Princeton, NJ: Princeton University Press.

Djupe, Paul A., and Andrew R. Lewis. 2015. "Solidarity and Discord of Pluralism: How the Social Context Affects Interest Group Learning and Belonging." *American Politics Research* 43(3): 394–424.

Evans, Christopher H. 2004. *The Kingdom Is Always but Coming: A Life of Walter Rauschenbusch*. Grand Rapids, MI: Eerdmans.

Findlay, James F. Jr. 1993. *Church People in the Struggle: The National Council of Churches and the Black Freedom Movement, 1950–1970*. New York: Oxford University Press.

Finke, Roger, and Rodney Stark. 2005. *The Churching of America, 1776–2005: Winners and Losers in our Religious Economy*. New Brunswick, NJ: Rutgers University Press.

Fowler, Robert Booth, Allen D. Hertzke, Laura R. Olson, and Kevin R. den Dulk. 2010. *Religion and Politics in America: Faith, Culture, and Strategic Choices*, 5th ed. Boulder, CO: Westview.

Friedland, Michael B. 1998. *Lift Up Your Voice like a Trumpet: White Clergy and the Civil Rights and Antiwar Movements, 1954–1973*. Chapel Hill: University of North Carolina Press.

Gamson, William A. 1992. "The Social Psychology of Collective Action." In *Frontiers in Social Movement Theory*, edited by Aldon D. Morris and Carol McClurg Mueller, 53–76. New Haven, CT: Yale University Press.

Green, John C. 2007. *The Faith Factor: How Religion Influences American Elections*. Westport, CT: Praeger.

Green, John C., Robert P. Jones, and Daniel Cox. 2009. "Faithful, Engaged, and Divergent: A Comparative Portrait of Conservative and Progressive Religious Activists in the 2008 Election and Beyond. Available at http://publicreligion.org.

Guth, James L., John C. Green, Corwin E. Smidt, Lyman A. Kellstedt, and Margaret M. Poloma. 1997. *The Bully Pulpit: The Politics of Protestant Clergy*. Lawrence: University Press of Kansas.

Guth, James L., Lyman A. Kellstedt, Corwin E. Smidt, and John C. Green. 1993. "Theological Perspectives and Environmentalism among Religious Activists." *Journal for the Scientific Study of Religion* 32(4): 373–382.

Guth, James L., Corwin E. Smidt, Lyman A. Kellstedt, and John C. Green. 1993. "The Sources of Antiabortion Attitudes: The Case of Religious Political Activists." *American Politics Research* 21(1): 65–80.

Gutterman, David S. 2005. *Prophetic Politics: Christian Social Movements and American Democracy.* Ithaca, NY: Cornell University Press.

Hadden, Jeffrey K. 1969. *The Gathering Storm in the Churches.* Garden City, NY: Doubleday.

Hall, Mitchell K. 1990. *Because of Their Faith: CALCAV and Religious Opposition to the Vietnam War.* New York: Columbia University Press.

Hart, Stephen. 2001. *Cultural Dilemmas of Progressive Politics: Styles of Engagement among Grassroots Activists.* Chicago: University of Chicago Press.

Hertzke, Allen D. 1988. *Representing God in Washington: The Role of Religious Lobbies in the American Polity.* Knoxville: University of Tennessee Press.

Hertzke, Allen D. 2006. *Freeing God's Children: The Unlikely Alliance for Global Human Rights.* Lanham, MD: Rowman & Littlefield.

Hofrenning, Daniel J. B. 2002. *In Washington but Not of It: The Prophetic Politics of Religious Lobbyists.* Philadelphia: Temple University Press.

Hunt, Scott A., and Robert D. Benford. 2004. "Collective Identity, Solidarity, and Commitment." In *The Blackwell Companion to Social Movements*, edited by David A. Snow, Sarah A. Soule, and Hanspeter Kreisi, 433–457. Malden, MA: Blackwell.

Hunter, James Davison. 1991. *Culture Wars: The Struggle to Define America.* New York: Basic Books.

Hussey, Laura, and Geoffrey C. Layman. 2014. "Coping with Cross-Pressures: Electoral Choice and Political Perceptions among American Catholics." Paper presented at the Annual Meeting of the American Political Science Association.

Jones, Robert P., Daniel Cox, Juhem Navarro-Rivera, E. J. Dionne Jr., and William A. Galston. 2013. "Do Americans Believe Capitalism and Government Are Working? Religious Right, Religious Left, and the Future of the Economic Debate." Available at http://publicreligion.org.

Kellstedt, Lyman A., Corwin E. Smidt, John C. Green, and James L. Guth. 2007. "A Gentle Stream or a 'River Glorious'? The Religious Left in the 2004 Election." In *A Matter of Faith: Religion in the 2004 Presidential Election*, edited by David E. Campbell, 232–256. Washington, DC: Brookings Institution.

Marx, Gary T., and Douglas McAdam. 1994. *Collective Behavior and Social Movements: Process and Structure.* Upper Saddle River, NJ: Prentice Hall.

McAdam, Doug. 1982. *Political Process and the Development of Black Insurgency.* Chicago: University of Chicago Press.

Miller, Arthur H., Patricia Gurin, Gerald Gurin, and Oksana Malanchuk. 1981. "Group Consciousness and Political Participation." *American Journal of Political Science* 25(3): 494–511.

Morris, Aldon D. 1984. *The Origins of the Civil Rights Movement: Black Communities Organizing for Change*. New York: Free Press.

Noonan, John T. 1998. *The Lustre of Our Country: The American Experience of Religious Freedom*. Berkeley: University of California Press.

Olson, Laura R. 2007. "Whither the Religious Left? Religiopolitical Progressivism in Twenty-first Century America." In *From Pews to Polling Places: Faith and Politics in the American Religious Mosaic*, edited by J. Matthew Wilson, 53–80. Washington, DC: Georgetown University Press.

Olson, Laura R. 2011. "The Religious Left in Contemporary American Politics." *Politics, Religion and Ideology* 12(3): 271–294.

Olson, Laura R. 2016. "Movement Commitment among Progressive and Conservative Religio-Political Activists in the United States." *Politics and Religion* 9(2): 296–308.

Porterfield, Amanda. 2012. *Conceived in Doubt: Religion and Politics in the New American Nation*. Chicago: University of Chicago Press.

Putnam, Robert D., and David E. Campbell. 2010. *American Grace: How Religion Divides and Unites Us*. New York: Simon & Schuster.

Smidt, Corwin E. 2001. "Religion and American Public Opinion." In *In God We Trust? Religion and American Public Life,* edited by Corwin E. Smidt, 96–117. Grand Rapids, MI: Baker.

Smith, Christian. 1996a. "Correcting a Curious Neglect, or Bringing Religion Back In." In *Disruptive Religion: The Force of Faith in Social Movement Activism*, edited by Christian Smith, 1–28. New York: Routledge.

Smith, Christian. 1996b. *Resisting Reagan: The U.S. Central America Peace Movement*. Chicago: University of Chicago Press.

Steensland, Brian. 2002. "The Hydra and the Swords: Social Welfare and Mainline Advocacy, 1964–2000." In *The Quiet Hand of God: Faith-Based Activism and the Public Role of Mainline Protestantism*, edited by Robert Wuthnow and John H. Evans, 213–236. Berkeley: University of California Press.

Sullivan, Amy. 2008. *The Party Faithful: How and Why Democrats Are Closing the God Gap*. New York: Scribner.

Tarrow, Sidney. 2011. *Power in Movement: Social Movements and Contentious Politics*, 3rd ed. New York: Cambridge University Press.

Wilcox, Clyde, and Carin Robinson. 2010. *Onward Christian Soldiers? The Religious Right in American Politics*, 4th ed. Boulder, CO: Westview.

Wilson, J. Matthew. 2009. "Religion and American Public Opinion: Economic Issues." In *Oxford Handbook of Religion and American Politics*, edited by Corwin Smidt, James L. Guth, and Lyman A. Kellstedt, 191–217. New York: Oxford University Press.

Wuthnow, Robert. 1988. *The Restructuring of American Religion: Society and Faith since World War II*. Princeton, NJ: Princeton University Press.

PART II

Cultural Challenges of Progressive Religious Activism

While the previous section introduced the progressive religious field and illuminated several ways in which it is distinctive from other activist fields, this section turns to the ways in which the characteristics that set the progressive religious field apart also present a variety of cultural and political challenges for participants.

For example, many progressive religious organizations' commitment to social diversity and multiculturalism complicates the tasks of organizing, maintaining commitment, and speaking collectively. Yet the degree to which groups are able to overcome these challenges varies, as the chapters in this volume detail. While Fulton and Wood's chapter demonstrates that groups with high levels of internal racial and socioeconomic diversity can nonetheless find common ground as "people of faith," the chapters in this section also show that without mechanisms in place to manage these challenges, high levels of religious, racial, ethnic, and socioeconomic diversity can generate internal power imbalances, distrust, and disagreement within groups, all of which can threaten organizational stability.

These challenges are complicated further by the *political* diversity that is also found within progressive religious organizations—especially related to gender and sexuality issues. Indeed, as we will see, many actors within this field hold socially conservative views alongside economically progressive commitments. These individuals may identify as conservatives, or even Republicans, despite also participating in social change efforts that we would consider progressive. This phenomenon raises questions about the relationship between political identity and action.

Finally, some readers may be surprised to learn that some progressive religious groups struggle to frame their efforts in explicitly "religious" terms, as they endeavor to speak *for* religiously diverse memberships and *to* religiously diverse (and nonreligious) publics. In part, their discomfort appears to be rooted in concerns that religious language is too narrow and particularistic. But it also appears to stem from the fact that, for some individuals engaged in progressive religious action, their *religious* identities are not as salient to their activist efforts as other identities—as progressives, as Americans, as immigrants, as members of diverse communities, or even as humans.

In sum, for readers interested in the practical realities of progressive religious activism, this section sheds new light on the inner workings of this field. These chapters not only deepen our understanding of the complex challenges these actors face, but also highlight the creative ways in which organizations have sought to overcome these challenges. Meanwhile, for scholars of political and civic life, this section also offers more general insights into the challenges of collective action and the public exercise of power, as well as into how organizations navigate challenges arising from internal diversity.

5

Cultural Challenges for Mainline Protestant Political Progressives

PAUL LICHTERMAN AND RHYS H. WILLIAMS

Even a moderate amount of attention to current events and American politics leads one to notice the significant attention by news media, political pundits, and scholars to the role of religion in politics. Those analyzing electoral outcomes often point to a "God gap" in which Republican candidates fare much better than Democratic candidates among voters who attend church weekly and say that their religion is highly important in their lives. In reporting on many "hot-button" political issues there is the formulation of a "culture war" in which the religious "Right" and the secular "Left" battle over issues such as access to abortion, same-sex marriage, prayer in the public schools, and legalization of pornography. And recently much attention has been devoted to a collection of writings and books coming from a group of authors collectively referred to as the "New Atheists." Richard Dawkins, Sam Harris, Bill Maher, and others are regularly counterpoised, either in print or as panelists on television talk shows, to religious fundamentalists.

And yet, any serious attention to the civically engaged world—not to mention the pages of this volume—reveals scores of examples of progressive religious activism. Many immigrant rights organizations have religious activists and organizations at their center (Yukich 2013). "Moral Monday" protests—whether denouncing state budget cuts in North Carolina or police shootings of unarmed African Americans—are organized by clergy and other religious actors. The "Nuns on the Bus" toured the country to advance a religious case for social welfare spending, as Braunstein's chapter illustrates. Local programs combating hunger, or homelessness, or organizing tenants' rights, often are headquartered in religious congregations. As Fulton and Wood demonstrate in this volume's opening chapter, faith-based community organizing (FBCO) is widespread across the country and across a multitude of political and social causes.

Courtesy of the Occupy movement, journalists and social critics have recently been talking a great deal more than before about a stark divide between the super-rich and the 99 percent. For religious or religiously literate people in many Mainline Protestant congregations, it is hardly a new topic. People in denominations and congregations that we call Mainline Protestant are heir to a long history of public engagement on social issues—such as anti-slavery, the civil rights movement, the farm workers movement. That legacy of activism and civic engagement remains current in the contemporary United States; many of the activists being studied in this volume are from Mainline Protestant traditions—for example, they can be found in the chapters by Geraty, Diaz-Edelman, Beyerlein and West, Gahr and Young, Fuist, and Olson. Whether acting on their own or in multifaith coalitions, Mainline Protestants have often been at the center of progressive religious social action in the United States.

So why is there this disconnect between public perception and the on-the-ground reality? Some of this is a failure of the news media. But part of grabbing media attention is the dynamics of cultural and political communication. In this chapter we offer an analysis of what we call the "cultural challenges" that politically progressive religious activists—particularly those in Mainline Protestant groups—face when trying to communicate *as religious actors* to wider publics, to policy makers, to news media, and even to those within their own social and religious communities. Our fundamental claim is that public audiences view the civic involvement and understand the political statements that these civic actors communicate, but often do not link these actors and activities to a religious authority or sensibility. We think there are three cultural dimensions to this disjuncture: identity, communicative style, and the discursive field in which Mainline Protestant progressives find themselves. The first two are aspects of Mainline Protestantism in the U.S., and the latter is an attribute of the wider American political and religious culture. After a brief discussion of the religious sector we are centrally concerned with, we discuss each dimension in turn.

Who Are Mainline Protestants?

In general, "Mainline Protestants" refers to Presbyterian, Episcopalian, Lutheran, United Church of Christ, and Methodist denominations. These are denominational families with long histories in the United States, and once constituted a majority of the American population. Their symbolic place in American life is also significant; for example, more presidents of the United States have been Episcopalian than any other denomination, followed by Presbyterian (admittedly, changes in the denominational structures of American religion over time have made tallies of affiliation a bit imprecise, but the general distribution remains clear).

Groups such as the Episcopalians, Presbyterians, and United Church of Christ are the descendants of what were the established churches in colonial America. They have an old pedigree and a deep association with American national identity and civil religion. In this regard they contrast with "Evangelical Protestants" such as Baptists, Pentecostal groups, and many Methodists, who are descendants of the pietest Protestant groups who began immigrating to the U.S. in large numbers in the first quarter of the nineteenth century (Fischer 1989; Hatch 1989).

Since the social and cultural turmoil of the 1960s these "Mainline" groups are sometimes referred to as "liberal Protestants," often to be contrasted with "conservative Protestants," and sometimes with "Evangelical" Protestants (Roof and McKinney 1987). The designation as "liberal" has the advantage of calling attention to the variety and divisions within Mainline denominational groups. Robert Wuthnow's (1988) account of the "restructuring" of American religion demonstrated that along many dimensions, particularly politically relevant ones, liberal Christians have more in common with other liberal Christians in different denominations, whether "Mainline" or not, than they have in common with conservative members of their own denomination. Thus, Presbyterians and Methodists, and to a lesser extent Lutherans, have both liberal/Mainline and conservative/Evangelical wings. The liberal designation also draws attention usefully to the ways in which political distinctions have permeated much of American religion (see also Putnam and Campbell 2012).

However, one disadvantage of the "liberal Protestant" label is that it doesn't specify what exactly is liberal. Is it their theology? Is it their political commitments? And if it is intended to indicate relative political commitments, does that mean on all issues or just some—and which ones? Public opinion research has consistently shown that for many people, liberal or conservative positions on economic issues do not necessarily align with attitudes toward cultural and personal morality issues (e.g., see Williams 1997). This is particularly true for many people in the white and educated middle class. There is a distinct tendency among many in this demographic to take positions that would be considered "liberal" on the so-called "social issues" such as abortion or same-sex marriage, but to have "conservative" attitudes toward economic policies. So, for example, in much of the Midwest, these Protestants have long been a core constituency of the Republican Party, but are much less supportive of the party's recent shift to the right on racial, gender, and other social issues (e.g., Barlow and Silk 2004).

That is why we will use the "Mainline" designation both to call attention to the historic centrality of these denominations to American culture and religion, and to avoid characterizing their political leanings in blanket terms. This chapter concerns itself with cultural challenges for Mainline *progressive* activists; it may turn out that Mainline Protestants pursuing conservative stances face some similar challenges, though these would play out somewhat differently given different political allies, issues, and targets.

Given the historical importance of this swath of American religion, it is reasonable to view today's Mainline Protestants as the inheritors of the late-nineteenth-century "Social Gospel" that saw Christians as living out their faith by engaging in social action to remedy injustice (e.g., Wuthnow and Evans 2002). Thus, they should have powerful theological resources for thinking about the growing economic divide, other forms of inequality, and their effects on the social fabric. Mainline Protestant denominations are more likely than their theologically conservative Protestant counterparts to affirm efforts to change the social world rather than to see social change as a distraction from personal piety focused on the next world.

It is no surprise, then, that the Mainline Protestant denominational bodies in North America—Presbyterian, Lutheran, Episcopalian, Methodist, and Congregationalist—do not lack for texts on economic justice, the primacy of people and God over profits, the urgency of global climate change, and other progressive issues (Reynolds 2015). The Evangelical Lutheran Church in America (the "Mainline" Lutherans, notwithstanding the "Evangelical" in their name), for example, teaches not only that climate change is real and pressing but a matter of justice:

> The great paradox of climate change is that those least responsible for emission of pollutants harmful to the earth will be most severely affected and least able to adapt to changing conditions. Christ taught us to seek justice, care for our neighbor, and to provide special care and consideration for "the least of these"—those living in poverty. Our response to climate change must heed this call to justice.[1]

The Episcopal Public Policy network meanwhile concerns itself with America's culture of violence, among other issues. It urges policy makers both to pass "common-sense gun laws" and increase federal support for mental healthcare. It dramatized the issue with a 2013 Stations of the Cross procession in Washington, D.C., reciting prayers to end violence "and the economic conditions that spawn violence."[2]

We want to use the question of Mainliners' relation to public political conversations to propose that theologically liberal and politically progressive Protestants face some special cultural challenges in their efforts to bring a distinctive voice to the debate about the most vibrant political issues of the day. All "challenges" are relative and we are not saying these dilemmas are fatal. Rather, we think of these in relation to the political claims-making and cultural "successes" that theologically conservative, Evangelical Protestants have experienced in the U.S. the past forty years.

Religious Identity and Political Commitment

Even if Mainline Protestant churchgoers have access to denominationally endorsed language that frames political issues such as inequality as profound moral problems for people of God, that language does not necessarily circulate widely. Social researchers who put a lot of emphasis on the power of message framing recognize that the publics who receive a message may agree with it yet not care that much, or want to do anything about it. It is not enough that a message "resonate," it must also be salient (Williams and Kubal 1999). We would elaborate:

liberal Mainline Protestants who hear a critique of economic inequality or homelessness or military spending may not hear it as *religious* people. They may care mainly as citizens, political progressives, or employees. That means they may act on that concern by endorsing e-petitions, or more rarely by writing a check to, or even attending a meeting of, a non-religious interest group or coalition—rather than a church-sponsored forum. For Mainliners, Protestant identity is one identity among others. Religious identity may well be an important or special one, but need not be the one that "hears" the message. Many relate their religious life most directly to their personal behavior and interactional dealings with others. They often emphasize a type of "Golden Rule Christianity" (Ammerman 1997) that does not necessarily link to issues that they categorize as "political" or "economic."

It may also be the case, as Putnam and Campbell (2012) suggest, that many people are attracted to particular religious congregations, if not traditions, because of their political orientation. They find a place comfortable because of like-minded people—it is as much about the politics as about theology. This might also explain why they hear issues as political actors in the first place.

Contrast this identity centrality and salience with Evangelical Protestants. As Christian Smith (1998) has argued, Evangelicals make their Christian identity the center of their existence. Working to keep that identity foremost whenever possible is part of what it is to be an Evangelical. This is reinforced by their social networks. Evangelical Protestants, compared to Mainliners, are more likely to spend more time at their church or in church-related activities each week, and are more likely to have more of their close friends in their church or at least share a denominational identity with them (Olson 1993; Olson and Perl 2011). Their networks are simply more insular, reinforcing the importance of their religious identities. Put simply, Evangelical and Mainline Protestants do not inhabit their religious identities in the same ways. Proponents of a Mainline voice in progressive discussions of economic inequality and other political issues need to give Mainline Protestant publics an additional reason for speaking and listening *as religious people*, a reason that Evangelical Protestants do not need.

One of those reasons could be that many Americans associate a "Christian" identity in political life with loud religious conservatives.

For example, Lichterman (2005) spent time observing and participating alongside a social justice education group made up of church representatives who wanted to publicize to their congregations the dangers of shrinking government social welfare programs for poor and unemployed people. The group hosted long discussions of "neoliberalism," the worldwide move to shrink national governmental responsibilities and expand reliance on businesses and market relations to address social needs and fix social problems. Some talked about how political tourism in poor villages in Central America woke them up to soulless American materialism and commercialism. Lichterman asked at a meeting one night why they did not talk more often *in religious terms* about public issues that concerned them. One replied (in this group of churchgoing activists), "That's what fundamentalists do." Over two years' time, the group—Mainline Protestants and two Catholics—mentioned several times but never made good on a plan to devote one night's meeting to discussing the religious grounding of their work. The churchgoers seemingly most committed to criticizing the politics of wealth and poverty were not so comfortable, or interested, in discussing distinctly religious reasons for caring.

We would venture another reason that Mainline progressive activism sounds less *distinctively* religious than the social advocacy of Evangelical Protestants. In the past several decades, Mainline Protestants have been more likely than Evangelicals to express their religious identities in the name of inclusivity. They draw less sharply defined boundaries between "we" and "they," producing a larger if fuzzy religious "us" in which Mainline Protestants represent one faith commitment among others. Robert Wuthnow (2005) has portrayed this sensibility as the "many mansions" approach to religious truth: Mainline Protestants are more likely than others to take their religious commitments as "true for me" or true for Mainline Protestants but not necessarily better or truer than others' religious commitments are for others. In this view, many religions cultivate worthwhile approaches to ultimate reality. Add to that increasing attempts since the 1930s by Mainline leaders to practice some degree of interreligious civility in public (Cuddihy 1978) and we arrive at a distinctive distaste for claiming exclusive religious truth or for gathering in religiously exclusive coalitions. That does not mean that Mainline Protestants engage in interreligious coalitions as cultural equals. Old, Mainline Protestant understandings are institutionalized in the very fabric of American society, including a "personal" understanding of God and a voluntaristic, individualistic, and congregational understanding of religious community (Williams 2007). American religious pluralism continues to map out as concentric if expanding circles of acceptability, with Protestant and often Mainline Protestant customs in the center (see Bender and Klassen 2010; Nabors 2015).

Mainline Protestant inclusivity thus can make Mainline progressives' advocacy sound less *specifically* religious or specifically Christian than that of Evangelical Protestants, who often identify as "Christ-centered" and not merely "religious." Much as some would say inclusivity itself *is* a religiously cultivated virtue—a regard for all God's children—it is easy to hear it as a hedge against a more specific or demanding religious inspiration. In his research on homeless advocacy, for example, Lichterman (2012) heard the Mainline leader of a loose network of church leaders appeal earnestly and repeatedly to the network's cause as one supported at least potentially by "churches and synagogues and mosques." But no Muslim-identified advocate ever attended monthly meetings, and only rarely did one or two Jews visit, so the careful listener would take this multi-religious identification as a normative statement, to the effect that we are people who *should* work interreligiously.

Appeals to inclusivity can have complicated consequences. The leader of the network described above requested that network participants write together an interreligious prayer on homelessness, for distributing to interested congregations, but he only received a lukewarm response. The leader's understanding of interfaith expression did not comport well with an African American attendee's liturgical practice, nor with that of the synagogue that an occasional participant attended. Sometimes the most heartfelt commitment to inclusivity makes the inclusion proponent's own specificity obscure to her, and risks looking to others like presumptuousness instead of solidarity.

Mainline commitments to inclusivity, ironically, may hinder coalitions with other Christians on progressive issues. The case of one Midwestern anti-racism coalition can illustrate (Lichterman 2008): Unnerved by the prospect of a Ku Klux Klan march in their town, Mainline and Evangelical Protestant pastors collaborated easily on a position statement denouncing racism in the name of God. The position statement took roughly twenty-five minutes to write; coalition participants debated at monthly meetings over the next year, however, whether they should identify a public counter-event, timed for the KKK march, as Christian or interreligious. Mainline pastors said they would not participate if the event was *not* inclusively interreligious; Evangelical pastors said they could not participate if the event was not specifically Christian, perhaps with non-Christian spectatorship. The pastors eventually arrived at a compromise, calling the event "cultural, not religious," and focusing very specifically on the issue of racism—relieving the event of some of its original religious significance. It makes little sense to say that Mainline Protestants were any more divisive than Evangelicals. The point is that identifying as part of a religiously inclusive effort does not necessarily facilitate collective action even when coalition members all share a progressive stance on the issue.

All this is not to say that Mainline Protestants do not take their religious identities seriously. Rather, research shows that people in Mainline denominations often have multiple identities and dispersed social networks. They also have a history of thinking that religious commitments and political involvements are not necessarily linked tightly. As a result, the use of religious authority to push progressive political involvements often falls less convincingly on the ears of many within Mainline denominations. Further, Mainline Protestants also value interreligious diversity highly, and are consistently wary of religious proclamations that seem to be exclusionary, sometimes making interreligious organizing a challenge (see the chapter by Diaz-Edelman in this volume). Finally, Mainline Protestants also have a cultural style of manifesting their religious identities that is less overt and expressive than that of many Evangelical Christians. This often leads Mainline activists to use communicative styles in their activism that are not as effective as they might be—a topic to which we turn now.

Communicative Style and Engaging Politics

Even if Mainline Protestant groups use their religious identities, and their theological traditions, to make claims about political and civic issues, the communicative styles of Mainline and Evangelical Protestant claims-making are different—quite apart from the claims themselves—in ways that matter for political activism. In fact, the communicative style is part of what makes the communicator's religious identity evident to others. Evangelicals *sound* certain and are clear about their specific religious identity—communicating a message of certainty and clear boundaries, a message of a deeply held and primary identity. Whether this means that religiously conservative leaders are transferring a heartfelt sensibility to the political world, or exploiting it cynically to make "ordinary Americans" fear and disdain other Americans, the language the public hears is striking: There is one (right) way and we know the one. All social activists learn to "frame" claims simply and telegraphically, and to mark off the claims-making "we" clearly from one or more kinds of "they" who stand in opposition. It is not just a difference of opinion or an expression of preference—it is a matter of right and wrong, morality and (often) evil. We certainly need not discount decades of sophisticated Evangelical theology to observe that there may be an affinity between popular Evangelical language and social movement leaders' perception that they need "catchy" and direct communication in a competitive market of political ideas (Strong 2012).

In contrast, Mainline or liberal Protestantism prefers to speak more "quietly" and subtly about religious authority (e.g., Wuthnow and Evans 2002). Bible-thumping is not a Mainline Protestant custom, no matter what political issue the Bible is being used to justify. Another scenario from Lichterman's social justice outreach group is instructive: One night, the African American host of a radical radio talk show visited the group and listened alongside others while one member spoke for nearly an hour on neoliberalism. With frustration evident in his voice, he told the group, "I represent a race that doesn't live as long. . . . There are a lot of Blacks who don't care about ideology." He sounded surprised that the group was hosting an extended ideological critique of capitalism but not talking about the religious commitments that should have given the critique its moral and emotional power. He blurted out, "We know who the number-one activist is, the one who risked everything: Jesus!" No one else spoke up for Jesus, and Lichterman did not see the radio announcer at another meeting. The radio announcer made a charismatic statement of religious certainty, inviting the others to affirm a tight, collective faith—ordinary and comfortable expression in many African American religious circles (Lincoln and Mamiya 1990; Pattillo-McCoy

1998). Mainline Protestant subtlety or circumspection easily sounded like diluted or uncertain faith in this context. Mainline Protestant progressives who hope to engage multi-racial progressive coalitions may disaffect would-be allies who agree on the issues but articulate those issues' religious significance very differently.

The Mainline Protestant tendency for circumspection regarding religious authority also suggests a preference for statements that do not claim to be the final and complete word. An anecdote might help: Not long ago the progressive United Church of Christ congregation on Lichterman's bike route to work hung a banner over the church entryway, announcing "God is still speaking." The passing bicyclist might recognize the critical allusion to conservatives' biblical literalism, and it may be a catchy counter-slogan, but it is neither a simple, nor world-ordering statement about the problem, the protagonist and the antagonists. Another phrase used by some religious liberals is "don't put a period where God used a comma"—similarly subtle, folding in a crafty allusion to grammar where conservative Protestants may prefer to entice readers with a crafty allusion to Scripture. These sound like counter-moves in a field of Christian advocacy still heavily weighted in favor of theological conservatives—clever if you can decode them.

Compare with a bumper sticker Williams has encountered in his research on conservative religious activism—"The Bible said it, I believe it, and that settles it!" Put colloquially, and at this point only anecdotally, conservative Protestantism may offer more "framing-friendly" language for social advocacy than do Mainline Protestantism's distinctive forms of inclusivity or universalism. Braunstein (2012) has shown that liberal religious discourse can be effective—but she demonstrates that it often takes the form of "storytelling" rather than proclamation. And the stories often are "secular" in content, giving them a potentially wider audience, but perhaps diluting their religious impact. Stories are often evocative and multi-message, and that can be both useful and a great appeal. But they fit less easily into the strictures of a social media world where much communication must happen within 140 characters (i.e., Twitter). Whether liberal Protestant leaders are able to offer an enticing, distinctively religious alternative route to social movement arenas may depend partly on developing clarity in their framing.

If Evangelical publicists and a few television fundamentalists have taken over the meaning of speaking as a Christian in the U.S. today, then progressive Mainline Protestant activists will need to work at widening the public's imagination for "Christian" political activism. Memories of Mainline Protestant participation in the civil rights movement a half-century ago will not be enough. Nor will it suffice to refer the curious to position papers or websites. Founded on the sense that Christian faith ought to be the driving force in life, conservative Christian political advocacy against abortion rights or gay marriage wants to speak to Americans in general. It does not engage so much as try to delegitimate progressive readings of social issues as un-American as well as un-Godly. The first task for progressive Protestant activism, in contrast, seems to be to speak back to other Christians before speaking to Americans in general. The discursive force-field in which progressive Protestant activism finds itself may force it to pursue "countermovement" strategies, apart from trying to leaven a broader, national discussion on the economic divide with subtle religious reasoning.

The "Discursive Field" of Religion in American Politics

To this point, we have focused our attention on the people who compose Mainline Protestantism, and the messages and communicative styles that they employ when engaged in attempts at reforming society. However, for a message or political claim to be effective, it needs to be heard. It must resonate with potential audiences. The most carefully crafted political argument will go nowhere if it falls on deaf ears.

Complicating that simple fact is that audiences vary in what they are able to "hear." The process of hearing a political message has three stages. First, it must be intelligible; that is, it must literally make sense to listeners irrespective of whether they agree with it. Language that is overly technical, for example, or that assumes a common frame of reference that doesn't exist, cannot connect with those hearing it. Just as academic writing is often accused of having too much jargon and thus being inaccessible to those outside a small disciplinary profession, political claims that do not use a common language are fruitless. Second, audiences must agree with the content or the implications of the claim. Such agreement may not be purely cognitive—language researchers have long demonstrated that how a message is delivered, or by whom, can be as important to audience reception as the content in and of itself. Nevertheless, at some point, audiences must respond positively to a message and its framing. Third, the resulting agreement, or the call to action that the message implies, must have salience. It must be regarded as important and worthy of action. Without these three elements, "resonance" of political claims cannot be said to have happened (e.g., Williams and Kubal 1999).

While analytically useful to lay out the elements of a successful political message, all of these dynamics happen within a particular context that we are calling the "discursive field." Inspired by the ideas of Pierre Bourdieu (see Swartz 1996), in political terms the discursive field is the set of ideas, symbols, and actors that have been active with and relevant to a particular public issue, contentious event, or movement cause. The notion goes beyond just who the "players" are in a particular political setting; it includes the symbols already in play regarding an issue or event—the array that provides the resources for how people think and talk about the issue at hand. A discursive field sets up the cues that tell people what "kind" of issue this is (e.g., Gusfield 1981), or who has knowledge that should be regarded as authoritative (e.g., Moore 2008).

The discursive field is not a "natural" fact. Social movements, interest groups, elected officials, news media, and other public actors actively sustain and sometimes alter it as they joust over social issues. Any given discursive field can change. For example, when progressive religious leaders try to reframe proposed state budget cuts as a "moral" issue and not just an "economic" one, they may offer new elements to the existing discursive field and hope those elements become predominant. We emphasize, though, that an established discursive field acts as a powerful constraint on what claims-makers can say, and what publics can understand. Claims-makers cannot just make an issue mean anything; discursive fields offer the basic categories, the basic parameters shaping communication about a given issue. Lichterman (2012) has found, for example, that while activists and volunteers widely understand the issue of homelessness as calling for compassion, especially in religious circles, issues articulated as "housing" issues rarely are understood that way (Dasgupta and Lichterman 2015). Boundaries develop in what can be said, or at least said legitimately, and heard (Williams 1995). We want to examine two aspects of the discursive field of religiously based political involvement that pose particular challenges to progressive actors in Mainline Protestant traditions. First are aspects of the contemporary scene, and second are aspects of the historical field of American religious culture and its civic engagement.

The Contemporary Scene

As we noted above, Mainline progressives are often reluctant to articulate fully a religious rationale for their causal activism due to a desire to distinguish themselves from conservative Christians, particularly Evangelical Protestants, who are active in the "Christian Right." Discursive fields run partly on group reputations and aversion to reputations (see Zubrzycki 2001). But progressive activists are not alone in a certain wariness or suspicion about overtly religious claims in public life. One indication of that is in some recent changes in Americans' religious affiliations. Over the past two decades the number of Americans who respond to questions about their religious identity or affiliation with the word "none" has more than doubled. It now comprises almost one-fifth of the American public (Pew Forum on Religion and Public Life 2012). Only a minority of these people (6 percent of the overall American public) are actually atheists, those who pointedly say that do not believe in a god. Rather, most of the religious "nones" are indicating they do not identify with any particular denominational or faith tradition within organized religion.

There are a variety of reasons people indicate they have no religious identity. But one reason, clearly identified by sociologists Claude Fisher and Michael Hout (2006) and political scientist Tobin Grant (2008), is distaste for what many see as the heavy-handed moralism and social intolerance of conservative religious groups. Since 1980 there has been a clear dominance of conservative religious voices on public issues. This dominance has been so clear that, to many people, the only type of public religion they can conceive is conservative, and they would rather leave the field of religiously based political involvement, or the larger field of religious involvement in general, than risk the reputation of conservative moralism. As Americans have generally grown more socially tolerant, particular around issues of sex and gender relations, conservative religio-politics has become less appealing, particularly to those who do not identify as conservative religiously. Thus, some Americans would rather be "nones" than admit to a religious identity. Not surprisingly, this works against progressive religious voices having much impact in convincing them on public issues. Ironically then, the style of religious voice that Mainliners avoid is also perhaps irritating to increasing numbers of Americans, who would "hear" Mainliners' own, progressive religious voice—particularly if it becomes more assertive—as simply more of the public religion that annoys them.

Another development in American religion also undercuts the efficacy of religious voices in public. Increasing numbers of Americans identify as "spiritual but not religious" (Roof 1998). For many people, of course, these two terms are intimately related—part of being religious is being spiritual and spirituality is tied up with religion. But increasingly the two concepts can be separated. When they are, people often use the term "spirituality" to mean a personal set of commitments or beliefs or practices that are aimed at some sense of the divine and have convinced the person of a power or reality beyond mundane material life. On the other hand, "religion" is taken to mean the institutional church, with its received tradition. In that way, proclaiming oneself to be "spiritual but not religious" is a rejection of the authority of organized religion, a declaration of a certain independence from tradition and doctrine. It is often accompanied by a highly developed sense of individual spiritual authority—that the individual is fully capable of discerning spiritual truths, and even practices or beliefs pulled together from several different faith traditions. Not surprisingly, this formulation, with its accent on individual subjectivity and discernment, is more popular among people with more formal education. Further, its individualism aligns with the cultural individualism long a part of American liberal traditions.

The larger contemporary field, in short, offers tough conditions for Mainline progressives. The increase in religious nones and the spiritual-but-not-religious mean that religious claims-making in general is less influential as a public discourse. Further, those who identify in those ways are often found within liberal constituencies—groups that should be a natural home for progressive religious efforts. The result is a diminished effectiveness for progressive religious activists trying to reach and mobilize their own communities *as religious communities*, let alone persuade those who are connected to other groups. In this already un-inviting climate, Mainline circumspection and nuance make it almost easier to blend in with non-religious voices than to try articulating a specific yet not exclusive, religious yet not moralistic, progressive voice.

The Historical Religious Field

While a significant number of the thirteen North American colonies were founded by groups of people who identified with the Protestant traditions we now call the "Mainline," it is also true that in the early national period the nature of American religion changed in a number of ways. As noted above, significant numbers of the immigrants from the British Isles that came to the U.S. from 1800 to 1825 were not from the established Church of England, or from the Calvinist traditions that had informed the religion of the Puritans. Rather, they were pietist Protestants who were considered "dissenters" in England—they were members of smaller sectarian groups rather than the established church. The religious ideas and practices they brought with them were quite different from those of the Anglican or Reformed Calvinist groups. The ideas and practices of these "dissenters" seeded a now deeply rooted religious populism and anti-intellectualism in the U.S. cultural environment that is not particularly hospitable terrain for the relatively cerebral, intellectually articulated religious reasoning that characterizes a lot of the Mainline Protestant approach to social concerns.

The Protestantism practiced by the newer Adventists, Methodists, Baptists, and Disciples of Christ expanded many of the religious options available, especially on the American frontier, and shifted some of the cultural meanings of what was to count as "authentic" religion. This became particularly clear during the period often called the "Second Great Awakening" (roughly dated as 1790–1840). In general terms, the revivals that swept through the U.S. during that period—from western New York state down the frontier into the Appalachian region—put an emphasis on the emotional and experiential aspects of faith, and downplayed formal education and institutionalized doctrine. Many people remained illiterate or minimally educated, and their actual exposure to Scripture or formal theology was slight. Instead, traveling revivalists and circuit-riding evangelists pushed people to be "on fire for the Lord"—to feel the Spirit, not just think about it. The individual person's experience of transformation—what we would now call being "born again"—expressed in exuberant emotions became the mark of the truly religious person.

This elevation of the common person and their personal experience was an intrinsically populist cultural impulse. One need not be highly educated, or even literate, to know God. One need not be well read in the doctrine of the institutional church to be saved. This aligned well with the democratic political impulse also sweeping the U.S.—the common sense exhibited by ordinary people was increasingly taken to be the mark of American identity, and it found expression in both religious and political culture.

Moreover, the experience of the personal transformative religious event—and the transformed behaviors it was to produce (such as abstention from spirits)—became part of the boundary marking those within the "moral community" from those outside it. The new religious consciousness continued to mark distinct lines between the saved and the damned, but it was less about the preordained elect and non-elect of the Calvinists and more dependent on the purposeful efforts of individuals themselves. The non-elect became the "unregenerate"—those who refused the transformative power of Jesus.

Of course, not all Americans accepted this approach to religion. But our point is that a deeply populist, emotional, and experiential approach to religion began to undercut the authority of institutionalized religious authorities and the style of reasoned, cognitive faith favored by Mainline groups. Educational degrees in theology could be challenged by the simple, sincere authenticity of the common person saved at a revival. This aligned easily with the ideas of *sola Scriptura* (in Scripture alone does one find religious authority) and a common-sense approach to biblical literalism. Answers to religious questions could be easy, obvious, and felt, and available to all who were pure in spirit. That such a cultural theme continues to exist in American religion is one of the reasons that the discursive field of religion and politics is not always receptive to the nuanced, tentative, and almost academic-sounding messages articulated by Mainline progressives.

Possibilities and Prospects for the Mainline

None of our argument should be taken to imply that Mainline progressives lack any real chance to pursue progressive causes successfully. Looking back for inspiration to impressive Mainline participation in the 1960s U.S. civil rights movement as some Mainline leaders do, however, will not address a lot of the conditions that exacerbate the cultural gaps Mainline progressives face today. It is worth imagining how customary, Mainline forms of religious identity and vocabulary might more readily meet the challenges of voice in an age of noisy, conservative faith and sound-bite political discourse.

Mainline progressives might, first, make the Mainline penchant for inclusive affiliations and rhetoric do more work for them. Doing sociology's work of challenging common sense with inconvenient, counterintuitive findings, we have emphasized some *downsides* of inclusivity. But certainly being inclusive has its virtues. We suggest that Mainline progressives will be able to realize more of them by practicing inclusivity more reflexively, rather than as a uniform ritual that inevitably is more comfortable for some participants—the ones culturally closer to Mainline Protestant practices— than others. Being inclusive of Evangelical Protestants could mean embracing a Christian-only coalition, situationally, on the notion that the public arena is segmented already and may call for compartmentalized engagements with a broader, longer-term goal in mind. All groups need boundaries; we already illustrated how the most well-intended Mainline inclusivity is not indefinitely open but bounded and even potentially exclusive in its consequences. A more reflexive understanding of how other religious collectivities carry and communicate religious identity can help bind diverse, progressive coalitions. Their members don't need to understand "inclusive" the same way, and can try instead to understand the differences instead of assuming there is one, trans-cultural way to be inclusive.

Second, Mainline Protestants might find this a good time to promote the political virtues of quiet faith, particularly one practiced in local communities. As more and more Americans become wary of loud faith proclamations in the public square, the Mainline approach to public religious identity may actually get a new hearing. That does not mean Mainline progressives should expect that other religious groups with whom they ally must also present a circumspect, relatively intellectualized, compartmentalized religious identity the way Mainliners do. This would not work well as a uniform strategy for coalition work with Latino/a Catholic or African American progressives, whose constituencies are more comfortable with singularly directive God talk (see Wood 2002). It means using distinct, Mainline cultural resources to fashion modest new roles, perhaps as bridge-builders who are good at hearing their God speak in diverse voices.

Religion has considerable political authority as a basis for grounds and warrants in American political culture and claims-making. It can be a powerful motivator that brings people to activism, and encourages and rewards the sacrifices they make. Mainline Protestant progressives do much of this work already, but are not as successful communicating it to their own communities, to other potential allies and constituencies, or to policy makers, as they might be. And as religion is deeply ingrained in African American, Hispanic American, and many immigrant communities, if Mainline Protestants want a more *inclusive progressive movement* there are limits on who can be reached with a purely secular discourse (Hart 2001; Wood 2002). Thus, Mainline Progressives must consider and respond to the cultural challenges we have articulated directly and unapologetically.

ACKNOWLEDGMENTS

A partial version of this essay, authored by Paul Lichterman, appeared on the blog *Mobilizing Ideas*, November 15, 2012. A co-authored draft of the current essay was presented at the annual meetings of the Eastern Sociological Society, in New York City, February 2015. Thanks to Ruth Braunstein and Todd Fuist for helpful feedback in refining the argument.

NOTES

1 "Poverty and Hunger in a Changing Climate," *Evangelical Lutheran Church of America*, www.elca.org.

2 Alexander D. Baumgarten, "EPPN Alert: Lent—Changing Our Culture of Violence," March 21, 2013, *Episcopal Church*, www.episcopalchurch.org.

REFERENCES

Ammerman, Nancy Tatom. 1997. "Golden Rule Christianity: Lived Religion in the American Mainstream." In *Lived Religion in America*, edited by David Hall, 196–216. Princeton, NJ: Princeton University Press.

Barlow, Philip, and Mark Silk, eds. 2004. *Religion and Public Life in the Midwest: America's Common Denominator?* Thousand Oaks, CA: AltaMira Press.

Bender, Courtney, and Pamela Klassen, eds. 2010. *After Pluralism: Reimagining Religious Engagement.* New York: Columbia University Press.

Braunstein, Ruth. 2012. "Storytelling in Liberal Religious Advocacy." *Journal for the Scientific Study of Religion.* 51(1): 110–127.

Cuddihy, John Murray. 1978. *No Offense: Civil Religion and Protestant Taste.* Boston: Seabury Press.

Dasgupta, Kushan, and Paul Lichterman. 2015. "How a Housing Advocacy Coalition Adds Health: A Culture of Claims-making." Paper, Department of Sociology, University of Southern California.

Fischer, David Hackett. 1989. *Albion's Seed: Four British Folkways in America.* New York: Oxford University Press.

Fisher, Claude S., and Michael Hout. 2006. *Century of Difference: How America Changed in the Last One Hundred Years.* New York: Russell Sage Foundation.

Grant, J. Tobin. 2008. "Measuring Aggregate Religiosity in the United States, 1952–2005." *Sociological Spectrum* 28(5): 460–476.

Gusfield, Joseph. 1981. *The Culture of Public Problems.* Chicago: University of Chicago Press.

Hart, Stephen. 2001. *Cultural Dilemmas of Progressive Politics: Styles of Engagement among Grassroots Activists.* Chicago: University of Chicago Press.

Hatch, Nathan O. 1989. *The Democratization of American Christianity.* New Haven, CT: Yale University Press.

Lichterman, Paul. 2005. *Elusive Togetherness: Church Groups Trying to Bridge America's Divisions.* Princeton, NJ: Princeton University Press.

Lichterman, Paul. 2008. "Religion and the Construction of Civic Identity." *American Sociological Review* 73(1): 83–104.

Lichterman, Paul. 2012. "Religion in Public Action: From Actors to Settings." *Sociological Theory* 30(1): 15–36.

Lincoln, C. Eric, and Lawrence Mamiya. 1990. *The Black Church in the African American Experience.* Durham, NC: Duke University Press.

Moore, Kelly. 2008. *Disrupting Science: Social Movements, American Scientists, and the Politics of the Military, 1945–1975.* Princeton, NJ: Princeton University Press.

Nabors, Bradly. 2015. "The Regime of Religious Pluralism: Uncovering the Cultural Dimensions of American Religious Belonging." Ph.D. dissertation, Department of Sociology, University of Southern California.

Olson, Daniel. V. A. 1993. "Fellowship Ties and the Transmission of Religious Identities." In *Beyond Establishment: Protestant Identity in a Post-Protestant Age*, edited by Jackson W. Carroll and Wade Clark Roof, 32–53. Louisville, KY: Westminster/John Knox Press.

Olson, Daniel V. A., and Paul Perl. 2011. "A Friend in Creed: Does the Religious Composition of Geographic Areas Affect the Religious Composition of a Person's Close Friends?" *Journal for the Scientific Study of Religion* 50(3): 483–502.

Pattillo-McCoy, Mary. 1998. "Church Culture as a Strategy of Action in the Black Community." *American Sociological Review* 63(6): 767–784.

Pew Forum on Religion and Public Life. 2012. "'Nones' on the Rise: One-in-Five Adults Have No Religious Affiliation." October 9. www.pewforum.org.

Putnam, Robert D., and David E. Campbell. 2012. *American Grace: How Religion Divides and Unites Us*. New York: Simon & Schuster.

Reynolds, Amy. 2015. *Free Trade and Faithful Globalization: Saving the Market*. New York: Cambridge University Press.

Roof, Wade Clark. 1998. *Spiritual Marketplace*. Princeton, NJ: Princeton University Press.

Roof, Wade Clark, and William McKinney. 1987. *American Mainline Religion: Its Changing Shape and Future*. New Brunswick, NJ: Rutgers University Press.

Smith, Christian. 1998. *American Evangelicalism: Embattled and Thriving*. Chicago: University of Chicago Press.

Strong, Susan C. 2012. *Move Our Message: How to Get America's Ear*. Orinda, CA: Metaphor Project.

Swartz, David. 1996. "Bridging the Study of Culture and Religion: Pierre Bourdieu's Political Economy of Symbolic Power." *Sociology of Religion* 57(1): 71–85.

Williams, Rhys H. 1995. "Constructing the Public Good: Social Movements and Cultural Resources." *Social Problems* 42(1): 124–144.

Williams, Rhys H., ed. 1997. *Cultural Wars in American Politics: Critical Reviews of a Popular Myth*. Hawthorne, NY: Aldine de Gruyter.

Williams, Rhys H. 2007. "The Languages of the Public Sphere: Religious Pluralism, Institutional Logics, and Civil Society." *The Annals of the American Academy of Political and Social Sciences* 612: 42–61.

Williams, Rhys H., and Timothy J. Kubal. 1999. "Movement Frames and the Cultural Environment: Resonance, Failure, and the Boundaries of the Legitimate." *Research in Social Movements, Conflict and Change* 21: 225–248.

Wood, Richard L. 2002. Faith in Action: *Religion, Race, and Democratic Organizing in America*. Chicago: University of Chicago Press.

Wuthnow, Robert. 1988. *The Restructuring of American Religion: Society and Faith since WWII*. Princeton, NJ: Princeton University Press.

Wuthnow, Robert. 2005. *America and the Challenges of Religious Diversity*. Princeton, NJ: Princeton University Press.

Wuthnow, Robert, and John H. Evans, eds. 2002. *The Quiet Hand of God: Faith-Based Activism and the Public Role of Mainline Protestantism*. Berkeley: University of California Press.

Yukich, Grace. 2013. *One Family under God: Immigration and Progressive Politics in America*. New York: Oxford University Press.

Zubrzycki, Genevieve. 2001. "'We, the Polish Nation': Ethnic and Civic Visions of Nationhood in Post-Communist Constitutional Debates." *Theory and Society* 30: 629–668.

6

Activist Etiquette in the Multicultural Immigrant Rights Movement

MIA DIAZ-EDELMAN

Introduction

Red, yellow, white, and green feathers gracefully sway to the rhythm of the drums and to the beat of seeds adorning the ankles of Aztec dancers. They ceremoniously move down the center aisle of the San Diego Episcopal Cathedral, honoring the four directions and bowing toward the altar. Three female clergy members and activist leaders—first-generation Mexican immigrant Reverend Mary Moreno-Richardson, second-generation Italian immigrant Reverend Madre Patricia Andrews-Callori, and Rabbi Laurie Coskey—stand leading an audience of immigrant and nonimmigrant multicultural activists, empathizers, media persons, and researchers of distinct secular and faith traditions who fill the pews. Biblical readings, a sermon personally remembering the tragedies of the Holocaust, a testimony from a young man in sanctuary, and a handwritten poem by a child about an undocumented father separated from his family send a clear message. They make a plea to learn from the horrors of our past and to live by the teachings of our values in their collective demands for inclusive immigrant rights. After the media representatives and activists are asked to step forward and stand at the altar, they are collectively blessed with a prayer calling them to continue their hard work and report on it accurately.

The Immigrant Rights Movement (IRM) is made up of activists from a variety of faith traditions and belief systems who share a vision of our world in which neighbors care for one another and *everyone* is treated equitably. Furthermore, multicultural and interfaith movement participants believe that there ought to be a preferential option for the poor, vulnerable, and marginalized communities, with specific attention given to welcoming the immigrant. These values are imprinted upon the general call for just and humane comprehensive immigration reform. More specifically, they are echoed in the call for the right of immigrants to securely migrate across national boundaries and to live, gain an education, and contribute to the United States with protections and rights equal to those of citizens. For instance, IRM goals are articulated most often as legalization and equal rights for immigrants so that they can live securely (both physically and emotionally) as equal members of society with the ability to migrate freely, attend school, earn a living wage with worker protections, and preserve family unity. In addition to establishing a pathway to citizenship for undocumented immigrants, IRM goals include safely uniting unaccompanied minors with their parents and families, ending deaths along the U.S.-Mexico border, and providing spiritual counsel during immigration enforcement. Activists also work together for more equitable financial and worker protections, such as ensuring provisions for workers' rights within free trade agreements and supporting the growth of the middle class in developing nations to minimize economic disparities. Caring for the future of immigrant children, movement members collaborate to allow children to gain an education and to work legally after graduation. It is also important for IRM members to help facilitate cross-cultural bridging in diverse communities, thus creating more inclusive and safe communities for immigrants and ensuring equitable treatment to all people during emergencies regardless of immigration status.

Many of these goals were amplified beyond the walls of the cathedral on that Sunday afternoon. I remember the worship service taking the form of an impassioned political protest and watched as it transpired seamlessly. It was a vivid and powerful expression of how activists envision their role in the world—not to turn the world upside down, but rather to bring heaven to earth, making it right side up.

The IRM necessitates collaboration among many people with a variety of perspectives. Not unlike other contemporary social movements, such as the Occupy Wall Street movement, the Black Lives Matter movement, and the International Workers movement, diverse activists from unique ethnic backgrounds and faith traditions make up the IRM. Gender, age, ethnicity, level of education, geography, sexual orientation, and political affiliation were part of the multiculturalism within the IRM; however, immigrant/nonimmigrant and religious identity categories are at the forefront of my research. Focusing on these is especially useful, since "a strong majority of Americans across racial and religious lines view both race and religion as a salient source of identity and a basis for community life" (Hartmann et al. 2011, 337). Episcopal, Quaker, reform Jewish, Catholic, Muslim, Buddhist, United Church of Christ, Seventh-day Adventist, Nazarene, Rastafari, personally spiritual, and nonreligious traditions make up the vast majority of activist respondents in this study. Of the 77 percent of movement respondents that identified as religious, 86 percent were part of Christian traditions. Of the 62 percent first- and second-generation immigrant respondents in this study, 90 percent were of Mexican origin, probably due to the proximity of San Diego to Mexico.

A unique challenge in ethnic and religiously diverse groups is finding a common ground upon which to stand. *Without a single faith tradition or a common cultural heritage, what is the culture of interaction that helps hold multicultural, religious, and nonreligious activists together?* This chapter analyzes the behaviors of immigrant and nonimmigrant activists of distinct faith traditions from sixteen organizations that participated in the IRM. In doing so, it advances scholarship that considers the multidimensionality of activists, a topic that has become increasingly relevant in our multifaceted and further interconnected world.

Based on information gained from the media, activists, and local academics familiar with the social movement organizations (SMOs) in San Diego County, the linkage of activist networks was discovered and data was gathered from what appeared to be the most dominant local forces in the area. The five single-faith, three secular, and eight interfaith-based organizations chosen have collaborated in nonviolent, contentious activities with immigrant and nonimmigrant activist members whose faith perspectives differ from their own.

Between April 2006 and August 2008, I engaged in participant observation in these organizations. During the more than two years of participant observation, extensive field notes were taken at more than two hundred organizing meetings, religious services, press conferences, prayer vigils, conferences, marches, and other publicly accessible events coordinated by the selected organizations. During this time, I conducted forty-nine in-depth, open-ended, formal interviews that were designed to elaborate on the social processes observed directly. Of the forty-nine formal interviews, two interviews were not included in the activist identity calculations because the interviewees were not IRM activists. While they were not activists, their insights were valuable in better understanding the movement in San Diego, some instrumental relationships within the movement, and the lack of involvement from local key leaders. Furthermore, I researched news media archives and received up to date information from various SMOs' e-mail networks.

During this extensive period, it quickly became clear that meeting spaces were critical areas where the movement was created. Activists spend the vast majority of their time in meetings ranging from one to three hours each. Many movement participants meet as often as every week and even more frequently as the date of a protest event approaches. Others meet bimonthly or monthly. The few that do not choose to meet regularly remain in contact through other media, particularly through phone calls, e-mails, listservs (mass e-mail lists), and additional online venues that have emerged through technological advances (i.e., Facebook, Skype, Facetime, Gchat).

Previous studies have shown us that organizational resources used in social movements, such as meeting spaces, are often supplied by religious organizations and are necessary to advancing social movement goals (McCarthy and Zald 1977; Jenkins 1983; Klandermans 1984; McCarthy and Zald 2001). While this is true in the IRM, it is also important to pay attention to *how* the work is done within these spaces. This chapter focuses on the *organizational processes* within the spaces of meeting rooms, places vital for creating the bridges and bonds within and across various communities (Wood 2003) that are necessary for the cohesion that forms the overall multicultural, power-generating movement base.

Essential for the grassroots pursuit of social progress, these physical and metaphorical spaces are where immigrant and nonimmigrant activists discuss agreed upon immigration-related injustices and strategies to actualize visions of equality and security for immigrants. It is here that they invite others to join them; share movement narratives and construct new ones; and collectively negotiate and innovatively strategize around concrete actions and events to build awareness, garner media attention and support, and put pressure on those with the capacity to actualize agreed-upon movement goals. Meeting spaces are also used to disseminate information on national, state, and local legislation; learn about the latest injustices, up-to-date strategies, and tactics that have worked for other organizations elsewhere; and follow up on their responsibilities to one another, in alignment with their responsibilities to the overall advancement of the movement.

In these spaces, members of various SMOs work together, further increasing collaboration among multicultural and interfaith groups. For instance, activists work with other movement members from their own organizations while also serving as representatives within coalition settings where they partner with additional activist organizations. Quite a few participants hold membership within more than one SMO, change memberships, and also serve on the boards of other SMOs. While some are paid staff members of social justice organizations participating in the IRM, most activists volunteer their time.

Multicultural and interfaith alliance building is not a small feat; however, groups made up of diverse members have found ways to work together and construct a collective identity. Previous research on multicultural or interfaith groups found that collaborating together in protest actions (Taylor 2013) and learning about one another (Slessarev-Jamir 2011; Yukich 2013) played key roles in establishing solidarity within groups with diverse membership. Some found that interfaith and prefigurative prayers as well as certain prayer forms that include sharing religious practices and physically reaching out to one another helped bridge across faith traditions, socioeconomic backgrounds, and cultural heritages (Braunstein, Fulton, and Wood 2014). Others found that certain organizational dynamics help facilitate cohesion among culturally distinct group members, such as maintaining diverse representation of members, leaders, and symbols (Weldon 2006; Roth 2008; Yukich 2013); creating a "political arena free of hostility" (Fominaya 2010, 399); calling attention to power dynamics within groups; and expecting to disagree while moving toward consensus (Weldon 2006).

In some organizations, multicultural collaboration is inhibited by the exclusion of groups in decision-making processes that directly affect their lives (Gamson 1992) and by the organizational culture of the movement community despite intentions to promote diversity (Lichterman 1995). However, there are examples, such as in Penny Edgell Becker's work (1998), where multicultural religious congregations showed efforts that moved beyond symbolism. Such practices "includ[ed] African American members in positions of leadership and administration," "encouraged cross-racial fellowship," and provided opportunities for "small group[s] [formation], with members and leaders recruited across racial lines so that people could get to know one another informally" (468). In much the same way that these congregations were able to successfully integrate participants of varying ethnic backgrounds, the cadre of activists in the IRM practiced a code of conduct within meeting spaces that served as an inclusive method of interaction that embraced diversity. They did so, not only in a symbolic manner, but in concrete and practical ways in order to collectively and equally organize for immigrant rights. In addition to bridging across national origins, gender, social class, and lifestyle, movement participants also connected across distinct religious and secular traditions.

This chapter explores how the IRM attempted to (1) ensure *equality* within organizational processes and (2) create a physically and emotionally *secure* meeting and decision-making space to uphold the dignity and physical safety of movement activists. While activists did not refer to this code of conduct by name, I refer to this behavioral code as the "multicultural activist etiquette" (MAE). MAE, a mechanism that helped hold diverse activists together, might be described as the movement cadre's "group style" (Eliasoph and Lichterman 2003). Although some of the specific practices within MAE might have varied, the two aforementioned processes ensuring equality and security were consistently present. These were accomplished through practices authentic to the group that drew on and respected the diverse cultures and experiences of group members. Because of this, they provided patterns of interaction and decision-making that allowed the movement's transcendent liberal values to be reflected in its internal organization. Although the practices were not observably multicultural in nature (in other words, one may not be able to successfully disaggregate each component and assign it to a particular culture), they fostered respectful treatment of diverse members. This activist etiquette analyzed during movement planning meetings was practiced by multicultural, interfaith, and nonreligious activists from all sixteen organizations studied in the IRM in San Diego County.

In this multicultural setting, activists were not able to assume everyone shared in one another's cultural framework and religious worldview. However, the group style reflected in MAE created a culture of equal inclusion and security that helped trump potentially divisive differences. For instance, activists undertook organizational tasks through their constructed code of conduct that upheld the respect of one another's diverse origins and cultures. The multicultural SMOs were able to advance their work, not just by having clearer or more attainable goals, but also by adopting this particular *way* of working together based on shared, inclusive values of securing human rights, justice, dignity, and equality. Movement participants largely respected diversity and most even sought it out. Such an awareness, inclusive openness, and sensitivity to the needs of vulnerable immigrant communities rooted in progressive religious and liberal values permeated conversations and communal tasks. Meetings could not be conducted without sincere consideration of religious, ethnic, and national differences. As much of a burden as this may appear in a setting where productivity influences group bonds and the lifespan of the SMO, IRM participants welcomed this internal movement challenge as a necessary practice consistent with the kind of respectful and equal world they wished to achieve through their very movement goals.

As we will see, MAE was critical in facilitating trust among activists, helping advance movement goals, sustaining a pool of IRM allies from which to draw in subsequent movement actions, and creating a context where immigrants are leaders in a movement asserting their place in society with equal rights and protections as valuable members of the community.

The Multicultural Activist Etiquette

Equality

First, MAE aimed at facilitating a culture and practice promoting equality. "Overcoming inequality and segregation is a motivating factor. . . . [W]inning legalization and winning equality lays the basis for improving the conditions of life for a majority, not just those without papers. . . . It's a human rights framework first. It's a workers' rights framework. The utmost, underlying principle is equality between peoples and equality between workers. . . . How much equality are you willing to fight for? . . . So that people become half equal? Or . . . for people to become fully equal?" said Justin Akers-Chacón, an academic and nonreligious activist for Si Se Puede Coalition, a secular grassroots community organization made up of immigrant and nonimmigrant college students and local activist leaders.

Estela De Los Rios, a Christian immigrant activist for Justice Overcoming Boundaries (part of the larger Gamaliel Foundation) and the Immigrant Rights Consortium (IRC) in San Diego, made a similar point: "I believe that everyone . . . should have the same rights regardless of race, ethnicity, gender, age, disability, whatever it is. . . . God made us all as one. He didn't say, 'You're more valuable than another one,' or 'You're different than another one because of what you look like.' We're spiritually all the same, and I believe that we should all be respected the same."

Estela De Los Rios and Justin Akers-Chacón, like other activists in the IRM, value the equal treatment of all people, yet they hold different justifications for their beliefs. Akers-Chacón justified this commitment to equality using secular human rights language, while De Los Rios did so on the basis of the belief that "God made us all as one."

Differences between diverse religious and secular people could be an insurmountable challenge in a context where respecting differences is not practiced; however, multicultural activists in the IRM embrace multiculturalism and practice a code of conduct that focuses on equal and respectful inclusion.

Much in the same way in which activists organized for equal rights, dignity, and protections for all immigrants, they worked to create an "equal space" in the movement where all people are valued. Highly aware of and sensitive to larger societal power dynamics, activists were careful to make sure that everyone felt equally included, respected, and heard, *especially* people who are traditionally and currently underrepresented and otherwise neglected.

Being inclusive and respectful was one way that movement members cultivated equality within organizing spaces. For instance, even though activists may speak about God while referring to their own belief systems, they do not assume their religion or belief in God is shared. Rather, they choose to respect each person's unique origins and cultures, hold onto their own, and interpret their individual faith traditions as similarly encouraging them to bridge across cultural differences. Additionally, activists that do not reference any religious beliefs approach the uniqueness of members of the group in the same way, careful not to impose their faith traditions (or lack thereof) on one another.

In addition to being equally respectful of differences, they drew especially on practices common in liberal religious traditions. Even some activists who might be considered conservative when it comes to other political issues brought liberal religious practices of inclusion to their movement work. Rabbi Laurie Coskey of the Interfaith Center for Worker Justice (ICWJ) drew on her identification as a liberal Jew who "belong[s] to a tradition that is inclusive and open-ended." In much the same way, Reverend Mary Moreno Richardson from St. Paul's Episcopal Cathedral, a first-generation Mexican immigrant, explained, "Anyone and everyone is invited to that [Eucharistic] table because we really believe that it is Jesus' dinner table. And we can't imagine that He would look at someone and say, 'No, you're too young' or 'No, you're not married,' or 'No, you're gay,' or 'No, you're Jewish or Buddhist' or any of that. That *everyone* would be included in that dinner table." Such a practice of inclusion is concretely extended to nonreligious activists, as well. I observed nonreligious activists accept the invitation to partake in the Eucharist during a mass that took the form of a protest for immigrant rights and agree to give the homily during a routine Episcopal service.

The principle of inclusivity was also expressed in scheduling meetings. When IRM leaders sent out a general call to action, they tried to make sure that the time and location were convenient for the diverse constituencies among the activists. Because some lived in Barrio Logan, a Mexican ethnic enclave in San Diego, and others lived further north in La Jolla and northern San Diego County, efforts were made either to rotate locations or establish a central meeting space, thus fostering attendance among the diverse groups and linking otherwise disparate groups of activists together.

Sensitive to the multitude of personal and professional demands within and outside the movement, activists were conscious of the need to allow for enough time for the arrival of everyone in order to set the stage for a productive meeting with all the decision-makers present. Meeting organizers were attuned to the reality that the concept of time varies between cultures from an exact point (i.e., We must begin the meeting at exactly 6:00 p.m.) to a loose range (i.e., Our meeting will begin somewhere between 6:00 p.m. and 6:15 p.m.). Additionally, many activists held full-time jobs and volunteered after work hours to the movement, a reality also taken into consideration when scheduling meetings.

The principle of equality through inclusivity was also expressed in seating arrangements. Seats were almost always arranged in a circular fashion—although there may have been a facilitator for the meeting or a director for a more formal organization present, a circular seating arrangement communicates a sense of equal participation, equal footing, and equal accountability.

To help ensure that everyone was respectfully introduced and aware of the name and, where applicable, the organization of all present, meetings usually began with a round of introductions, moving from one activist to another around the circle of seats. This practice also supported the aforementioned efforts to accommodate busy schedules and honor differing cultural concepts of time. It accomplished this by delaying the heart of the meeting's start time for about fifteen minutes and giving the opportunity for late arrivals to be the last to introduce themselves while also being present for the substantive part of the meeting.

Furthermore, randomly assigned subgroups were utilized to maximize equal communication in larger meetings and promote cross-cultural relationships. For example, in the May 1st Coalition, comprising a large number of SMOs that organize an annual march for immigrant rights, some of the meetings included nearly thirty members. The members decided to section off into multiple small groups and discuss aspects of the agenda. More familiar with one another and therefore more comfortable contributing in the smaller subgroups, they then returned to the larger group to summarize their contributions, which were then addressed by the group as a whole.

Equality was also pursued in how meeting agendas were structured. In formal, director-run organizations like ICWJ, agendas were set by the director and board. However, in the more common community organizations and coalitions such as the Si Se Puede Coalition or the May 1st Coalition, agendas were collectively constructed at the end of each meeting for the following meeting. Votes were often taken regarding the inclusion of items as well as the order of discussion. Agendas usually began with a debriefing on the latest happenings during the "updates" section of the agenda so everyone was equally informed and on the same page. Agendas culminated with announcements, providing the opportunity for all of the activists and organization representatives (if in a coalition meeting) to make known their respective struggles and call for support as well as to announce any other events occurring in the area.

When multiple cultures also means multiple languages, principles of equality demand practices that make communication open to all. Perhaps most critically, great effort was made to ensure that there was a translator present, even if it was for one person. Because nearly every immigrant activist seemed to be from Mexico, Central America, or South America, the translators were predominantly English and Spanish speakers. Although some activists may have personally felt insecure in their bilingual abilities, the large majority of activists expressed acceptance of a variety of language skills.

A sense of inclusion was also promoted through communication practices that favored open language, respectful of the diversities that were present and welcoming toward all people. "Your people" or "our people" phrases were not used to refer to ethnic or religious group differences. Movement members generally used more welcoming language to talk about "our community."

Choosing culturally representative members of the SMO as public speakers for their collective efforts is another way this is accomplished. For instance, movement participants were often conscientious in requesting at least one male and at least one female, an immigrant voice, and a religious perspective whenever available. This had the added benefit of helping members communicate their movement message, best reflect their member base, and resonate with a larger pool of potential multicultural sympathizers and allies.

Efforts at equal and inclusive practices also addressed modes of conducting discussion and deliberation, elevating more introverted activists into opportunities for discovering and asserting their leadership. While it was important for participants that all members were heard, it was specifically important that the opinions and suggestions of immigrant members and those who are traditionally marginalized in society were highly considered.

For instance, in order to prevent domination by voices that often overpowered public discourse, activists talked in turn (raising their hands, especially in larger group settings), went around the circle to get everyone's point of view, and often broke off into smaller, more specialized groups for a less intimidating audience. Educated and charismatic orators in the IRM, such as clergy persons or academic activists, often succeeded in persuading the group with complex messages and supporting arguments; but ideas were taken seriously from those activists with less expertise in rhetoric, regardless of how simple the message or how much the speaker struggled to deliver it. I often saw movement leaders actively encouraging the participation of first-generation Mexican immigrants with limited educational experience. Although many came from more humble backgrounds, immigrant men and women were treated as experts with valuable insights and information regarding their needs and the needs of their immigrant community—further solidifying their place at the table as vital members of the IRM.

This practice of amplifying the immigrant voice and minimizing disparities in power is also seen in the way people of all levels of education were strongly encouraged to speak during planning meetings. Formal education was clearly valued, but the life experiences of the most vulnerable immigrants were valued even more so due to their expertise regarding the needs of the immigrant community to which they belonged. Belinda Zamacona, a first-generation Mexican immigrant and activist in La Raza Rights Coalition and contributor to the May 1st Coalition, referred to this notion as "self-determination." She explained, "The whole concept [is] that you need to . . . recognize the injustices that are happening in your community. And you need to organize around that, because no one is going to do that for you. Who better than the community itself to know what's best for that community?" With this in mind, organizers usually limited their expertise to the specific community within which they had direct contact. According to this principle, each community's needs are different, and the affected community, immigrants in the case of the IRM, knows best what those needs are. Because organizations like Justice Overcoming Boundaries (JOB) are about developing leaders, they cannot move forward on an issue "unless [their] member base gets excited about it and feels passionately about it," explained community organizer Jessica Nolan. In other words, the power and passion to reform injustices comes from the mobilized impacted community, which therefore determines the direction of the movement's efforts.

For example, I recall many incidents in which highly vocal, nonimmigrant, male activists personally asked soft-spoken immigrant women what their thoughts were. At first, caught off guard, such participants responded shyly. I specifically remember witnessing the transformation of a non-English-speaking female activist from the May 1st Coalition who courageously spoke before media cameras representing over twenty SMOs marching for immigrant rights. Just hours before, she was listening quietly to everyone in the meeting give their ideas. The anxiety on her face was evident when her opinions were requested and she was chosen to speak for the group, but their attentiveness and confidence in her brought forth her leadership skills.

In another example, a non-English-speaking, Mexican immigrant mother communicated her anxiety and concern about local police officers and immigration enforcement officials patrolling around nearby elementary schools during pick-up times. Stories were shared of undocumented parents being apprehended when picking their children up from school. This greatly upset activists who heard her story, and they began a campaign to collect testimonies of local residents and their experiences with law enforcement that would later be used by movement participants to put pressure on local legislators to end such patrols.

Representative channels of communication also provided a mechanism of inclusion in coalition settings. Each organization sent one or more representatives to contribute to the collective negotiation of coalition strategies, tactics, goals, and events in order to routinely report back to the home organization and allow other members to provide indirect input. At times, these representatives were given sole discretion to make decisions on behalf of their home organization. During other times, however, representatives were expected to hold off on decision-making until their home organization voted or agreed upon each decision and then report back to the coalition. Frequent reports relaying information back and forth between the home organization and the coalition often delayed the progress of the meeting, but it was important to many activists, nonetheless, because of the resulting full participation of all members involved.

Equality was pursued in a variety of communication strategies, but it was also embodied in the way meetings were led. Leadership was often voted upon and sometimes rotated. Andrea Guerrero provided further insights into how she decided to run the Immigrant Rights Consortium (IRC): "It was important to change leadership, so I decided [I wasn't] running for chair. I think if this consortium depends on me . . . then this consortium is not a healthy consortium; it's not going to survive. So there's a new chair. . . . She's really good at keeping the peace, and people are showing up in force every meeting." Changing leadership assures that the organization's success does not rest on only one person, but it also reflects the more progressive value of multiple perspectives and calling forth new leaders.

Furthermore, movement members distributed responsibilities in fair ways that resonated with goals rooted in equality. In only a few organizations, which were led by formal directors, were duties and tasks delegated from the top. Within the vast majority of coalition meetings, there was virtually no top-down delegation. Facilitators generally guided the group through a collectively agreed-upon agenda, usually decided upon at the end of each previous meeting. Activists self-divided into task-oriented, smaller groups based upon both the needs of the upcoming protest and activists' own individual strengths, interests, and resources. Subgroup tasks usually included publicity, press releases, canvassing, logistics, gathering needed resources (e.g., speaker system, stage, posters, fliers), creating the agreed upon agenda, and deciding upon the activist speakers.

Finally, decision-making, a critical and fundamental task within organizing meeting spaces, was accomplished by either a democratic vote (rarely, if ever, anonymous) or by consensus of the whole group—depending upon what the group decided was best. Grassroots community organizations tended to rely more on decisions by consensus of the whole group. In such a setting, movement members often went around the circle to bring up and respond to all concerns. In other organizations, members preferred an open democratic vote and longer periods of dialogue where members more frequently debated their positions. Unifying points, the facilitator role, formal codes of meeting, and agreed-upon goals were decided in these ways. Regardless of how they chose to make future decisions, IRM activists expended great efforts to ensure that all members were equally heard so as to construct optimal solutions toward immigrant rights in a fair and equitable way.

Security

The physical and psychological security of all people is another valued beacon guiding the direction of movement goals in the Immigrant Rights Movement and additionally shaping the behavioral culture in meeting spaces. Multicultural, interfaith, and nonreligious activists strategically collaborate to enable undocumented immigrants to securely emerge from their fearful and vulnerable hidden status. They collectively seek rights and legal protections for immigrants to work, raise their families, drive their cars, and leave their homes safely, without the threat looming around every corner that they will be deported and separated from their family, home, and communities. IRM activists understand the notion of security in similar ways and believe that comprehensive legalization would better protect immigrants against workplace and law enforcement abuses, while also enabling them to live as fully integrated members of society with inalienable rights.

Marco Castillo, a first-generation Mexican immigrant and Seventh-day Adventist, claimed, "I've never had any security whatsoever," due to his undocumented immigration status in the United States. However, through the IRM's New Sanctuary Movement, Joan Helland of ICWJ and the San Diego Friends Quaker organization, has forged a nurturing friendship with him. When he was terribly ill and had nowhere to go due to his limited funds and lack of health insurance, she provided him with a list of health clinics he could visit. Castillo reflected gratefully, "I thanked her and, I mean, when somebody cares about your health and cares about your spirituality, I mean that's a full package . . . and I think that sense of security is what really . . . is the biggest reward out of anything." Similarly, a female grassroots activist who comes from the Catholic tradition but does not currently consider herself religious, described security as "not fearing when you're stepping out the door that you're going to get taken away."

Dean Scott Richardson of St. Paul's Episcopal Cathedral, a non-immigrant IRM activist, acknowledged the "vulnerability of the Hispanic congregation" within his church. He emphasized, "With the Hispanic congregation . . . [i]t's different because they *really* are living it out. They are really vulnerable. They don't want to sit and talk about it in kind of an academic, theoretical way. They want to talk to an immigration attorney; they want to know what their rights are; they want to know how to deal with this; they want to know where the trouble is. They are trying to manage this thing in a very real, direct way that impacts them."

Establishing security for immigrants is at the heart of the Immigrant Rights Movement's goals. In alignment with this vision of a more secure and equitably inclusive society, they were mindful of constructing a safe organizing space for vulnerable, diverse activists to strategize about how to enact immigrant rights, a challenge specific to the organizing meetings within the IRM. In such spaces, IRM members followed patterns of behavior geared toward making sure that their undocumented colleagues were safe from apprehension and that all participants felt respected, protected, and comfortable during collective planning and organizing.

Physical safety for undocumented members was most often accomplished by not requesting disclosure of legal status and by voting upon the guest list to meetings and events. In order to give undocumented immigrant activists control over their own safety, organizations communally decided whether to invite reporters to meetings or whether to close them to the public. For instance, activists in the May 1st Coalition organized a fundraiser to assist local immigrant bakers who incurred legal fees due to a raid at their workplace. During the planning meeting, movement members and the affected bakers decided against inviting media persons to publicize this event. They expected it would attract many undocumented families and wanted the families to feel safe while enjoying the festivities, secure from media attention.

In addition to practices that protected physical security, activists also engaged in behaviors designed to protect the psychological or emotional well-being of multicultural and multi-religious activists. One way this was accomplished was by being conscientious of preserving the dignity of each participant, making sure each activist felt respected. Just as certain communication techniques were used to establish equality, other modes of communication were used to establish psychological security. This was especially important during brainstorming sessions when ideas and identities threatened to become intertwined. For instance, most activists were careful not to quickly dismiss ideas, thus preserving and respecting one another's public image. Instead, they would find valuable aspects of proposed ideas by opening with a few pros and then explaining the more convincing counterpoints in a way that separated the idea from the person. On potentially divisive topics, it became especially important for activists to listen patiently and explain themselves carefully. In this way, members were more inclined to participate and share their thoughts and suggestions. Times when these practices were ignored stand out as harsh examples. The majority mindfully managed to prevent hurt feelings and relationship rifts, and were careful to turn an idea down diplomatically.

The goal of protecting the dignity of each participant was also pursued through practices of respectful address. Participants avoided the more offensive term "illegals" and referred to immigrants without proper legal documentation as "undocumented" or "unauthorized" immigrants. I often heard movement members (including non-Spanish-speaking English speakers) call fellow activists from their own organization and from other activist organizations "brother," "sister", "señor" (Mr.), "señora" (Ms.), "Don" (reverential way of referring to a male elder in Spanish), "Doña" (reverential way of referring to a female elder), "compadres," or "comadres" (endearing masculine and feminine Spanish terms for "closer than a friend," "godparent," "protector," or "benefactor").

Establishing emotional or psychological safety in a context of religious and nonreligious diversity was valued as well. One way this was done was by avoiding proselytizing. Faith-based members steered clear of trying to convert one another or their nonreligious peers. If the topic of conversion did come up, it was only in jest. Religious leaders from other faiths were usually spoken of in a reverential manner.

Religious activists worked hard to make sure people of other faiths and nonreligious participants felt comfortable, welcomed, and respected in their diversity. Not only did they avoid obvious proselytizing, they worried that religious language, belief systems, and rituals could be seen as threatening, divisive, exclusive, or simply uncomfortable. They, therefore, developed practices designed to protect the religious (and nonreligious) traditions of their diverse coalitions. Such efforts in the IRM took the form of more universal prayer language and an invitation to pray only if one felt comfortable doing so.

Religious activists often placed extra effort in being conscientious in prayer and reflection language. Their inclusive intentions aimed at being nonthreatening to nonreligious members and those of differing faiths, even though they fell short at times. For instance, many religious leaders prayed to God during opening or closing meeting prayer by using the broader term "God" rather than specific references such as "Jesus" in order to make activists feel more secure and comfortable in their membership.

Prayer times were also predictable. For the most part, prayer occurred only if the meeting was led by a religious leader or organization, or if it was located at the site of a religious organization. Prayer times were also predictable in that they happened at the introduction and conclusion of meetings and were often included in the meeting agenda. Therefore, prayer was expected and anticipated in certain settings rather than others, rarely coming as a surprise to activists—an especially useful cue for religiously diverse members.

Multicultural and religiously diverse members did, at times, however, still feel a sense of discomfort or threat of exclusion or restriction, exposing the work that still needs to be done. For Joan Helland, the thought of a higher being, or God, "just [is] an extra concept that doesn't add anything. The best parts . . . [are that] we're stronger and more effective and more human when we work together and produce something that makes the world a better place. And that's magical." Certain kinds of prayers made some activists, like Helland, feel uncomfortable at times "because they put names on [a higher being]. But sometimes there's a sense of 'God is on our side.' And I just find that . . . I mean the other side gets to say the same thing. That's just a whole concept I'm not comfortable with." Other activists felt as though interfaith events and services watered down each faith tradition, restricting religious activists from fully expressing their religion. It was in both of these instances that focusing on movement goals and on invested activist relationships helped hold movement members together.

The sheer effort at building warm personal relationship lines across religious difference was a powerful way movement members established security in meeting spaces and in IRM events. Despite their religious discomfort and through their collective efforts, Helland and others were able to contribute to a nurturing, comfortable, and secure environment by focusing on the people with whom they connect in addition to their shared goals. "But they're also really warm, beautiful people. Madre Patricia calls me her precious one! How could you not [feel comfortable]?! I mean my mother doesn't call me her precious one! And Rabbi Laurie is very warm. She's nice to be around. It's a nice place to be. And that motivates me and makes it easy to be there." For Helland, the effort and intention to be inclusive, nonoffensive, and kind spoke volumes. It was enough to make her and others feel welcomed and committed to working together to improve the lives of immigrants. In this way, individuals, such as Helland, took it upon themselves to do the multicultural bonding and bridging work and keep focused on the goals and positive takeaways, including the relationships they have made and new ways of connecting with a higher power.

Conclusion

In sum, a group style based on the multicultural activist etiquette, within the IRM, created a culture of interaction within meeting spaces that intentionally prioritized equality and security. This, in turn, facilitated respectful interaction among multicultural and interfaith activists of varying immigration statuses and helped hold the mosaic of movement members together. These practices also demonstrated a level of sophistication and commitment to organizing in professional and productive ways that stayed true to the inclusive and humanitarian elements of their unique belief systems and distinct cultural origins.

IRM participants from distinct cultures not only understood that they needed to work together to achieve their shared goals; they also valued the diversity of which they were a part. In this spirit, they needed to establish a culture of interaction that respected their unique identities while staying productively focused on their agreed-upon claims in order to collectively move forward. This was largely accomplished by adhering to practices that were consistent with activists' liberal values, with roots in progressive religious traditions, relating to securing equality, dignity, safety, and justice for immigrants. What is striking here, is that diverse religious and nonreligious belief systems affirm and inform the shared liberal values echoed in the Immigrant Rights Movement, creating a unifying common ground among diverse movement activists.

Organizing among multicultural, immigrant and nonimmigrant, faith-based and nonreligious participants could be a difficult task. It required sensitivity to the needs of the diverse cultural subgroups within the IRM's expanding network of activists as well as to the expectations of unique activist organizations so as to build trust through recurring interactions and therefore maintain cohesion for future collaboration (Van Overwalle and Heylighen 2006; Fine 2012). When MAE was ignored, it jeopardized trust, caused rifts among activists and between organizations, and diverted energy away from productivity and toward repairing injured relationships—all of which took the focus off of movement goals and weakened the movement base.

When MAE was maintained, mutual respect, trust, and productivity toward realizing movement goals were enhanced while members simultaneously developed leadership and mobilizing skills. The practice of equal inclusion in a secure environment helped multicultural, faith-based, and nonreligious activists maintain mutual respect for one another and, in turn, feel respected and valuable, thus increasing the likelihood of future collaboration on shared movement goals. This commitment to equality and security while productively focusing on common movement claims cultivated trust upon which professional relationships and personal friendships formed. In doing so, members further strengthened the IRM movement base and their collective power. Such a cohesive network of movement organizers, what in fact makes up the social movement (Diani 1992), is a necessary asset in a context where effectiveness is generated from the quantity of movement members and the quality of their contributions and commitment.

Furthermore, activists practicing equal inclusion in a secure space benefited from the ideas proffered by equal participation. For instance, movement members had access to the rarely communicated ideas originating from people traditionally marginalized by society, such as immigrant women and non-English speakers. By practicing MAE, movement participants received additional opportunities to develop as more skillful and empowered agents of change. Over time, more timid and unassuming immigrant activists, who were encouraged by their fellow immigrant and nonimmigrant activist peers, grew more assertive and confident in their roles. They realized that their voices could be heard and, more importantly, that their opinions were eagerly sought after to help make a difference in their communities.

In such a context, where multicultural movement members with shared movement goals felt safe and equally valuable, activists were able to be more productive and focus on strategizing and developing movement tactics toward their common claims. The multicultural, faith-based, and nonreligious IRM participants operating within the framework of MAE were, therefore, able to use their collective energy to focus on movement goals while simultaneously knowing that they were creating the reality within their relatively small meeting spaces that they wish to achieve in society at large. In other words, IRM activists created a microcosm within meeting spaces of how they believe the world ought to be, consistent with their movement goals.

Beneficial outcomes to practicing MAE continue beyond current organizing efforts. In grassroots social movements where power is leveraged and originates from the masses, maintaining a healthy pool of organized and committed allies is crucial. Therefore, cultivating positive and productive working relationships by equally respecting the dignity and security of each member helps current movement efforts and plants the seeds for future collaboration.

Finally, MAE helps create an opportunity to observe the participation of immigrants themselves in a movement asserting their place in society. In a national context of restrictive immigration policies (Schuck 2007; Zolberg 2007) and hostility toward immigrants, many immigrants have chosen to act as agents of their own lives and opted for an alternative route toward upward mobility and immigrant incorporation. In this chapter, I showed how MAE, based on progressive values, formed the context in which immigrants named the injustices they faced and collaborated with others in a multicultural setting that valued the principle of self-determination. Through MAE's organizational unifying mechanism, religiously distinct immigrants and nonimmigrants were able to work together to ensure equality, security, and progress toward movement goals both inside and outside meeting spaces. By collaborating to change the practices and policies that have traditionally stood in the way of their rights, protections, and quality of life, immigrants and allies are paving an alternative route to immigrant integration into American society.

ACKNOWLEDGMENTS

I must give a heartfelt thank you to Ruth Braunstein, Todd Fuist, and Rhys H. Williams for your vision and commitment in putting this project together. Thank you, Nancy T. Ammerman, for your help in shaping me as a sociologist. Faith, family, and friends have carried me through. This work is because of you.

REFERENCES

Becker, Penny Edgell. 1998. "Making Inclusive Communities: Congregations and the 'Problem' of Race." *Social Problems* 45(4): 451–472.

Braunstein, Ruth, Brad R. Fulton, and Richard L. Wood. 2014. "The Role of Bridging Cultural Practices in Racially and Socioeconomically Diverse Civic Organizations." *American Sociological Review* 79(4): 705–725.

Diani, Mario. 1992. "The Concept of Social Movement." *Sociological Review* 40(1): 1–25.

Eliasoph, Nina, and Paul Lichterman. 2003. "Culture in Interaction." *American Journal of Sociology* 108(4): 735–794.

Fine, Gary Alan. 2012. "Group Culture and the Interaction Order: Local Sociology on the Meso-Level." *Annual Review of Sociology* 38: 159–179.

Fominaya, Cristina Flesher. 2010. "Creating Cohesion from Diversity: The Challenge of Collective Identity Formation in the Global Justice Movement." *Sociological Inquiry* 80(3): 377–404.

Gamson, William A. 1992. *Talking Politics.* Cambridge, UK: Cambridge University Press.

Hartmann, Douglas, Daniel Winchester, Penny Edgell, and Joseph Gerteis. 2011. "How Americans Understand Racial and Religious Differences: A Test of Parallel Items from a National Survey." *The Sociological Quarterly* 52(3): 323–345.

Jenkins, Craig. 1983. "Resource Mobilization Theory and the Study Of Social Movements." *Annual Review of Sociology* 9: 527–553.

Klandermans, Bert. 1984. "Mobilization and Participation: Social-Psychological Expansions of Resource Mobilization Theory." *American Sociological Review* 49(5): 583–600.

Lichterman, Paul. 1995. "Piecing Together Multicultural Community: Cultural Differences in Community-Building among Grass-Roots Environmentalists." *Social Problems* 42(4): 513–534.

McCarthy, John D., and Mayer N. Zald. 1977. "Resource Mobilization and Social Movements: A Partial Theory." *American Journal of Sociology* 82(6): 1212–1241.

McCarthy, John D., and Mayer N. Zald. 2001. "The Enduring Vitality of the Resource Mobilization Theory of Social Movements." In *Handbook of Sociological Theory,* edited by Jonathan H. Turner, 533–565. New York: Springer US.

Roth, Silke. 2008. "Dealing with Diversity: The Coalition of Labor Union Women." In *Identity Work in Social Movements (Vol. 30)*, edited by Jo Reger, Daniel J. Myers, and Rachel L. Einwohner, 213–232. Minneapolis: University of Minnesota Press.

Schuck, Peter H. 2007. "Citizenship and Nationality Policy." In *The New Americans: A Guide to Immigration Since 1965*, edited by Mary C. Waters, Reed Ueda, and Helen B. Marrow, 43–55. Cambridge, MA: Harvard University Press.

Slessarev-Jamir, Helene. 2011. *Prophetic Activism: Progressive Religious Justice Movements in Contemporary America.* New York: NYU Press.

Taylor, Verta. 2013. "Social Movement Participation in the Global Society: Identity, Networks and Emotions." In *The Future of Social Movement Research: Dynamics, Mechanisms, and Processes*, edited by Jacquelien Stekelenburg, Conny Roggeband, and Bert Klandermans, 37–58. Minneapolis: University of Minnesota Press.

Van Overwalle, Frank, and Francis Heylighen. 2006. "Talking Nets: A Multi-Agent Connectionist Approach to Communication and Trust between Individuals." *Psychological Review* 113(3): 606–627.

Weldon, S. Laurel. 2006. "Inclusion, Solidarity, and Social Movements: The Global Movement against Gender Violence." *Perspectives on Politics* 4(1): 55–74.

Wood, Richard L. 2003. "Religion, Faith-Based Community Organizing, and the Struggle for Justice." In *Handbook of the Sociology of Religion*, edited by Michele Dillon, 385–399. New York: Cambridge University Press.

Yukich, Grace. 2013. *One Family under God: Religion and Immigration Politics in the New Sanctuary Movement.* New York: Oxford University Press.

Zolberg, Aristide R. 2007. "Immigration Control Policy: Law and Implementation." In *The New Americans: A Guide to Immigration since 1965*, edited by Mary C. Waters, Reed Ueda, and Helen B. Marrow, 29–42. Cambridge, MA: Harvard University Press.

7

Challenges and Opportunities of Community Organizing in Suburban Congregations

KRISTIN GERATY

Since its founding in 2003, Lake County United (LCU) has worked with the suburban Chicago county board to boost the affordable housing budget in the county by 66 percent, obtained commitment from suburban municipalities to include affordable housing in new developments, won approval from the county board for construction of a new $31 million facility for low-income elderly residents, and battled with a local school board to open a high-performing public charter school to serve low-income students. The LCU coalition consists of 35 dues-paying institutions including 10 Catholic parishes, 15 Mainline Protestant churches, 3 synagogues, a mosque, several private elementary and secondary schools, a public library, and a few social service agencies. LCU is an affiliate of the Industrial Areas Foundation (IAF), one of a handful of national broad-based community organizing networks in the US (see chapter 1 for more details). But LCU is unique among broad-based community organizations (BBCOs) in that Lake County is suburban and affluent.

While LCU is unique, it is an important case study for several reasons. Drawing on census data of the BBCO field, Richard Wood and colleagues describe a new strategic dynamic that has developed within the field of organizing over the past ten years in that organizing networks have made a "widespread effort to better serve the interests of low-income communities by projecting power across broader geographic areas and into higher-level political arenas. This strategy has led many BBCOs to seek new members beyond core urban districts, by expanding into inner- and sometimes outer-ring suburbs" (2013, 14). Thus, LCU reflects a new trend in the BBCO field. Second, according to a Brookings Institute study, by 2002, nearly as many poor people in the US were living in suburbs as in central cities (Casey et al. 2004). Social-class stratification in suburban municipalities and school districts has important ramifications for poor suburban residents and for scholars interested in suburban political activity. Lake County, Illinois, embodies this racial and economic variation between suburban municipalities.

Like other BBCOs, LCU engages in progressive action around issues of fair housing, education, and workforce development. But many LCU participants are registered Republicans and would consider themselves theologically conservative. Based on extensive fieldwork with LCU and participant observation with another suburban IAF affiliate, I have found that there are challenges and opportunities in the suburbs that change the face of broad-based organizing. This chapter focuses specifically on the struggles that the LCU coalition faces in constructing a call to action that resonates with its institutional members and in negotiating how its participants' religious identities are communicated and interpreted in an environment where the intersection of religion and politics is almost always conservative. I begin by identifying and discussing the key factors that make LCU unique among BBCOs. The sections that follow analyze how those factors influence how organizers and leaders describe their organizing work as well as their identity as a faith-based organization.

Privilege, Perceptions, and Place

Between 2008 and 2010, I engaged in participant observation with LCU, interviewing key informants from the 30 congregations involved in LCU at the time of the study, as well as key informants from demographically similar congregations that were recruited but were not currently engaged. In total, I connected with 55 congregations in suburban Lake County.[1] Table 7.1 provides a summary of the congregations involved in the study by faith tradition.

To put these congregations in perspective, there are approximately 290 congregations in Lake County. Almost half of those are associated with the Evangelical Protestant faith tradition, including many Black

TABLE 7.1. Congregations by Faith Tradition

	Mainline Protestant	Evangelical	Catholic	Muslim	Black Protestant	Jewish	Total
Member Congregations	15	0	10	1	1	3	30
Non-Member Congregations	8	7	6	0	2	2	25
Total	23	7	16	1	3	5	55

Protestant churches. Catholic and Mainline Protestant churches make up 11 percent and 30 percent of the county's congregations respectively. Focusing only on the sample of member congregations, half of LCU's membership is Mainline Protestant and a third is Catholic. Compared with the institutional makeup of other broad-based organizations across the US, Mainline Protestant churches are overrepresented and Baptist congregations are underrepresented in LCU. LCU is also unique among BBCOs around the country in that it consists of far more affluent congregations. Of the 30 religious congregations, 10 are located in highly affluent suburbs, for which the median household income is over $150,000. Twelve LCU congregations are located in less affluent but still upper-middle-class communities, two are located in middle-class suburbs, and six are located in the most racially and economically diverse community in the county.

As Tom Gieryn explains, "place is not just a setting, backdrop, stage, or context for something else that becomes the focus of sociological attention, nor is it a proxy for demographic, structural, economic, or behavior variables" (2000, 466). In Lake County, "place" has both geographic and identity components, and each component of place impacts how congregations negotiate their engagement with LCU. Building a metropolitan coalition presents place-based challenges, mostly related to geographic sprawl and municipal governance structures. In suburban counties, people and institutions are more widely dispersed and interact less frequently as a result. People who live in close proximity interact with different municipal offices, park districts, and school districts because of community boundaries. Religious denominations are organized into groups of congregations that may or may not overlap with community boundaries, meaning that clergy and lay leaders may not be engaging with others that are located close to them. Suburban environments present particular challenges for community organizing initiatives as well. Because BBCOs operate with so few paid staff, organizers have to cover a lot of ground as they attempt to recruit and engage institutions in the work of organizing. It means they spend a lot of time in their cars and are less likely to engage in repeat conversations with institutional leaders. Suburban organizers also spend a significant amount of time trying to understand how various municipalities interact with each other.

In Helene Slessarev-Jamir's book on progressive religion (2011), she makes the important point that religion cannot be divorced from its social location. In the case of LCU, I find that the intersection of religion and organizing is strongly influenced by social location. In particular, congregants within LCU member and potential member institutions struggle to make sense of IAF founder Saul Alinsky's reputation, as well as BBCO tactics and strategies. Contemporary organizing efforts are almost always traced back to the pioneering work of Alinsky in the 1940s. While the IAF in particular, and BBCO in general, has evolved quite a bit since Alinsky's death in 1972, IAF affiliates continue to employ tactics that embrace his emphasis on power, self-interest, and tension. Because of Barack Obama's experience with community organizing, the profession and the legacy of Alinsky became part of the political discourse during both the 2008 and 2012 presidential campaigns. Newt Gingrich declared that Obama "is for the writing of Saul Alinsky. I am for the Constitution; he is for European socialism" (Sugrue 2012). Liberal commentators responded by saying that Alinsky was "a patriot in a long line of patriots, who scorned the malignant narcissism of duplicitous politicians and taught everyday Americans to think for themselves and fight together for a better life" (Moyers and Winship 2012). This polarized view of Alinsky emerged in my interviews with LCU participants and in the discourse about LCU membership with Lake County congregations.

Early on in the course of my fieldwork, I interviewed an associate pastor in a Presbyterian congregation located in an affluent part of the county. When I arrived at his office, he waived me in as he finished a phone conversation. After hanging up the phone, he recounted to me the conversation he just had with another Presbyterian pastor in the county who was considering LCU membership. He laughed as he told me that the pastor was concerned about the organization's current relationship with Saul Alinsky, and how he had to inform his colleague that Alinsky had died several decades ago. As Gary Allan Fine argues, "We live in an organizational society, and organizations develop reputations that influence their effectiveness" (2001, 4). The pastor on the phone was particularly concerned with Alinsky's emphasis on power and worried that IAF teachings would not resonate within his congregation.

Lake County's suburban setting not only influences the way that LCU brands itself as a BBCO, it also influences the religious character of the organization. While the field of broad-based community organizing has become increasingly faith-based since the days of Alinsky, the explicit use of religious symbols and discourse is subdued in some cases because of the interfaith nature of many organizations and the increasing number of secular institutions that belong to BBCOs (Wood, Fulton, and Partridge 2013). The interfaith makeup of LCU as well as the membership of secular institutions has a strong influence on the organization's religious practices and identity. However, the suburban environment is also crucial to understanding why LCU appears to be less "faith-based" than other BBCOs. As many interviewees indicated, LCU operates in an environment in which "faith-based politics" is synonymous with the religious Right.

Constructing a Call to Action in Lake County

It is difficult to convince clergy and lay leaders to join and maintain membership in a BBCO given the resources required in terms of annual dues and congregants' time. This challenge is particularly acute in Lake County as a result of factors discussed in the previous section. The majority of the individuals with whom I spoke did not immediately perceive or classify LCU's message of broad-based organizing in the way that LCU organizers would like. In fact, even after years of participation, many of them still do not perceive or classify the work in LCU's terms. While both members and non-members of LCU tend to say that they support the work of the organization, they often confess to "not really getting what it is all about." There are multiple instances of interviewees reporting that although they attended the LCU Founding Assembly, they could not describe the organization to someone. Although they approve of LCU's strategies and goals, and usually emphasize their support, it is clear that in many cases the central concepts of community organizing are foreign to them.

One stumbling block for many participants in Lake County is the IAF's focus on tension. The internal recruitment work within congregations consists of a fair amount of tension. Prior to public meetings, leaders are asked to provide expected turnout quotas for their institution, which means that these leaders have to put pressure on their fellow congregants. The IAF argues that tension is a necessary part of effecting change. At public actions, public officials are "put on the spot" to answer challenging questions. For example, in July 2008, LCU held a public meeting as part of its public charter school campaign. The meeting was held at a Catholic church in Waukegan. The event was meant to demonstrate support among community members for a public charter school in Waukegan, and LCU leaders turned out over 700 Lake County residents. At the end of the meeting, the Methodist pastor chairing the event asked the school board members in attendance to come forward and publicly state their support for the school. The board members were clearly not prepared to address this question publicly, and those that chose to speak indicated that they needed more information prior to making a decision. While LCU organizers maintained that the board members had been adequately briefed on the proposal, some members of LCU congregations expressed discomfort with the tactic at an IAF training session a few weeks later. The contentious nature of the IAF's work is often criticized and presents a unique challenge in upper-middle-class congregations where "being polite" is of particular importance. In their study of environmental factors that impact social movement activity, Jeff Larson and Sarah Soule argue that social movements have a hard time recruiting adherents without a "generalized perception" that the actions of the organization are "desirable, proper, or appropriate within some socially constructed system of norms, values, beliefs, and definitions" (2009, 295). LCU organizers clearly struggle to convince many Lake County residents that their tactics are proper or appropriate.

One Catholic pastor associates his congregants' inability to comprehend community organizing with the geographic location of his congregation:

Sometimes they've moved down from Milwaukee, sometimes they've just moved from other parts of the United States. So their understanding of life doesn't come from—isn't rooted in Chicago. So because of that you can't assume they have a direct connection with Chicago in any way shape or form. Whereas Chicago has been involved in community organizing since the '50s, it's a relatively new thing here. They hear "community organizing," and they don't automatically get that image in their head that people connected to Chicago have.

Another pastor described his congregants' inability to grasp the LCU philosophy:

I describe [LCU] as a group of people trying to empower local communities and that it gives us a method to build a sense of belonging and, to use Tom's word all the time, empowerment. That is why I had thought originally that it would be a great thing for this community. I thought people really needed a sense of some way to feel they have power to make things happen. It just doesn't work. Not it doesn't work, it hasn't struck a chord yet. I don't know if that is because people are powerful enough in the work they do or because they are so powerless they can't even conceive of taking control.

Even in congregations in which the congregational liaison understands and supports LCU's work, the ability to convey a message that makes sense to other members is a challenge. One Lutheran pastor explained it this way:

It is not on their radar. They are not aware of exactly what it is; the title doesn't tell you much. I think it would probably be more likely to engage them around a particular issue than just kind of, "would you like to be part of a community action or community advocacy." That is a little too generic for most people.

A lay leader within a Catholic church discussed her frustration with communicating LCU's philosophy to her fellow congregants:

We have a gift program at Christmas. Catholic Charities runs it, and I volunteer at Catholic Charities, people donate gifts to families that need help. The response is absolutely unbelievable. We served 12,800 people this year. Not just our parish, but Lake County. Our parish did a significant amount. They will do that. They will go out and shop, they will spend their money, they will wrap a gift, and it will go out and be delivered. They bring food for the food pantry, all kinds of stuff. They are very good about that, but just filling a chair is not enough. I think that people are pretty separated from Lake County United. I have been trying to figure out what is a better way, a good way, to get the message to the people.

A lay leader from a Presbyterian church said, "I'm still struggling with calling somebody out of the blue and just saying, 'Hey, let's have a one on one,'" while a lay leader from an Episcopal church said, "It is just hard to explain, and it sounds like communism."

The fact that LCU organizers engage in process-specific rather than issue-specific messages when recruiting potential institutions seems to make the message particularly difficult for recruits to embrace. As one pastor explained:

Honestly my initial impressions were it was an organization in search of a cause. My question that I kept coming back to was that, alright, I'm all for advocacy but what are we going to advocate? I was a little bit saying, alright. It would be easier to promote if I knew what we were promoting. It was kind of a cart-and-a-horse kind of question. . . . I was probably curious more than skeptical. I was just kind of sensitive to the irony of you are organizing to do something but you haven't decided what it is yet.

To facilitate LCU's message, organizers rely on what social movement scholars refer to as bridge leaders (Robnett 1996) within congregations and institutions. To effectively mobilize upper-middle-class congregations, bridge leaders must mediate the LCU message for fellow congregants. Bridge leaders are also important in that they engage in "frame alignment" processes (Snow et al. 1986) within their congregations that are similar to what LCU organizers do in making initial contacts. While organizers "bridge" identical recruitment frames to clergy and other leaders representing congregations that they feel will be supportive of the work, bridge leaders within congregations then "amplify" the frame.

In doing so, they highlight particular aspects of LCU's philosophy that are in line with their congregation's mission and use language that is appropriate for their audience. An important bridge leader in a Presbyterian church described the work that she does in framing the LCU philosophy for her congregation.

> I think that one of the major issues that Lake County United faces generally, and I certainly do within my church, is what we call going deeper in our own congregations. We have not done a good job of that. Within my church I have not done a good job of that. . . . This is going back to the very first presentation in 2003. Our church at that time, our mission was, A Place to Grow. We started out with Micah 6:8.[2] Then we said what is Lake County United, went through its history and purpose. We talked about the founding assembly. I use the language of focus groups instead of action teams. It's just more neutral. We now use action teams and everybody is okay with it, but in the beginning . . . we talked about housing, homelessness, shelter beyond PADS. Everybody knows what PADS is and they get involved in it, but what happens later? I tried to make some theological connections: living out Christ's mandate, building bridges, creating community, projecting a positive image in the community, witnessing for Christ, becoming a transforming influence of Lake County.

Several respondents indicated that they change LCU's language a bit in an attempt to make the message fit better with the congregation.

As is the case for all cultural messages, LCU's ideas about improving lives in Lake County enter into congregational fields that are already occupied with other ideas and solutions. Existing ideas must either be displaced or merged with LCU's solutions in order for new ideas to take hold. Bridge leaders must compete with other ideas and programs in their attempt to get LCU and the organization's work on a given congregation's agenda. Congregations in Lake County are involved in a wide spectrum of social justice or mission programs, ranging from organizing volunteers for soup kitchens and homeless shelters to coordinating international mission trips. In competing for the congregation's financial resources and visibility, as well as congregants' time, energy, and attention, LCU bridge leaders must convince organizational decision makers of the need for organizing in the county and essentially engage in a process of agenda setting.

Three aspects of bridge leaders' efforts are important in understanding congregations' engagement with LCU and are likely important in understanding participation in BBCO efforts more generally. That said, these strategies are particularly important in the Lake County context because of the disconnect between BBCO tactics and strategies and Lake County congregants' experiences and expectations about faith and public life. First, the reputation and credibility of the bridge leader within the congregation is extremely important in understanding why some congregations are able to "turn out" significant numbers of people for LCU events. The pastor of a small Methodist congregation explained that she had led a congregation in a nearby county that was a member of a BBCO but was not nearly as involved in it as her current congregation was in Lake County. When I asked why she thought this was the case, she answered that the simple explanation was the respect within the congregation for the couple who serves as bridge leaders. As she explained, "Kathy and John would not encourage people to get involved in something that wasn't right for the church." In another case, a Catholic pastor refused to talk about LCU from the pulpit and the congregation struggled with turnout until a longtime parishioner, who had been active on the parish council, took the lead on LCU. The pastor began making announcements about LCU events and the leaders of various ministry teams began incorporating aspects of LCU into their work.

Second, effective leaders need to decide how to situate LCU's work alongside other outreach projects in the congregation. The majority of congregations' outreach work in Lake County is focused on service. In cases in which LCU's message has been well received, congregational leaders have effectively tied LCU work to existing charity-focused projects or have diminished the existing emphasis on charity. When I ask clergy and lay leaders from LCU-member congregations to describe LCU's work as they would to a fellow congregant, few of them distinguish the systemic aspects of organizing from more traditional forms of charity. In almost every interview in which I asked a follow-up question about the distinction between charity and service, respondents, particularly clergy, offered a somewhat exasperated response about the obvious differences between LCU and something like the PADS program that provides temporary shelter for the homeless. As an example of a typical response, one Catholic pastor said:

> Lake County United is necessary to change the system while we are delivering the food. We obviously see that. There is no doubt that if all we did was food pantry here but never did anything to try for better employment or cheaper health care or something like that, then we are going to be a long time serving that food.

While the distinction is clear in leaders' minds, it is not an important part of the causal story they use to describe and define LCU for the congregation.

Leaders within many member congregations seem to take for granted that their congregants distinguish between charity and justice approaches. More importantly, they explain that congregants clearly see the connection between the church or synagogue's teachings and the institutions' charity-based projects. Even the most engaged leaders, however, say that they do not make that same connection when talking about LCU. In fact, they accept congregants' broad dismissal of anything perceived to be political, despite the fact that they provide elaborate explanations to me about their faith tradition's teachings about systemic justice. All of the interviewees mentioned how much easier it is to recruit fellow congregants to participate in charity-based projects.

Finally, clergy and lay leaders affiliated with the congregations most deeply involved in LCU are able to clearly articulate how they contribute to and benefit from membership in LCU. They discuss the beneficial leadership training and interfaith experiences they gain from participation in LCU while also emphasizing the role that their congregation has played in securing affordable housing or campaigning for a public charter school. Leaders within less engaged congregations do not recognize the symbiotic relationship. For example, when I asked a Methodist pastor who leads a secondary congregation whether her congregation's membership in LCU has benefits for the congregation, she answered, "I think it is primarily about serving others. I am trying to think of ways it serves the congregation. I guess it makes people feel good. . . . I can't think of anything else." Throughout our conversation, this pastor focused only on what her congregation offered the organization without articulating any benefit to the congregation itself. Similarly, when I asked a Catholic deacon specifically about how the congregation benefits internally from membership in LCU, he answered,

> Yeah, this is what I don't understand. I took the one-day training on the one on ones; but it was the transition, how does it apply to what we are doing here? What we are doing is someone stands up and makes an announcement at church and says we are short hands at the food pantry, show up in some old clothes on Thursday and we will put you to work. That doesn't build the long-term commitment; it is more "just get on this task list."

I asked him if he was familiar with LCU's program on internal congregational development, and while he had spoken with the lead organizer about it, it was clear that he could not see the application of broad-based organizing to an internal campaign of congregational development. Within the most involved congregations, on the other hand, clergy and lay leaders describe elaborate campaigns in which lay leaders involved with LCU hold listening sessions and leadership training sessions based on the principles of broad-based organizing both to contribute to LCU's agenda and to strengthen their own institution.

Negotiating LCU's Religious Identity

Despite the clear religious components of LCU's work, participants struggle with the organization's religious identity and rarely use religious language in public meetings or in interviews. The organization is an interesting case of what Nancy Ammerman describes as a "seeming paradox of religion's simultaneous presence and absence in the modern world" (2007, 4). The organizing work is rooted in religious congregations, but the organizers and participants do not engage in religious talk in the ways described by scholars who study the movements and politics of the religious Right (Diamond 1998; McGirr 2001), other community and civic organizations (Braunstein 2012; Hart 2001; Hondagneu-Sotelo 2008; Warren 2001; Wood 2002); or even the US civil rights movement

(Morris 1984; Payne 1995). While LCU is certainly connected to religion in important ways, participants use religious discourse and culture more subtly than we might expect.

In thinking about how actors incorporate religion into public life, Paul Lichterman (2008) makes an important distinction between actors using religious language to construct a religious presence versus using religious language to define the goals of an organization. In terms of constructing a religious presence, it is clear that the interfaith makeup of LCU is a crucial aspect of the organization's identity. This interfaith identity undoubtedly constrains participants insofar as they do not want to incorporate theological language that excludes particular religious groups or the handful of secular members. This identity is important for Protestant clergy in that it raises concerns among Mainline Protestant pastors who are hesitant to engage in any evangelization discourse and alienates conservative Protestant pastors for whom interfaith coalitions are unacceptable. It would be inaccurate, though, to conclude that LCU members are a group of activists who happen to represent religious congregations and who share a loosely defined identity as a "people of faith." LCU is a faith-based organization, composed of individuals who often articulate their personal motivations for participation in religious terms. Meetings and public events take place in faith-based places and incorporate religious symbols and language. However, leaders within the organization are also thoughtful about the presence of secular groups in the coalition, about differences in beliefs and practices across faith traditions represented, and about perceptions in the suburban county about what it means to be a faith-based political organization.

Historical and sociological research notes that while the early IAF spent more time with block clubs, business groups, and social service groups, modern BBCOs have relied heavily on religious congregations. Data from the Chicago IAF affiliates does not dispute the argument that institution-based organizing is now heavily reliant on congregations. In the case of LCU, 30 of 37 member institutions are congregations. The other two Chicago-area IAF affiliates have a greater proportion of secular members but are still dominated by religious institutions. Research on organizing demonstrates that particular faith traditions have been well suited to this type of political activity as a result of their theological ideas about outreach and their history with activism. Among these faith traditions are the Black Protestant tradition, the Catholic Church, the Mainline Protestant tradition, and Reform Judaism. All of the usual suspects are represented in LCU with the addition of one mosque.

As Stephen Hart (2001) describes, modern institution-based organizing has developed an "original, systematic religio-political language" that combines themes from Saul Alinsky's work with five religious social action traditions. Among these strands of religious teachings are modern Catholic teachings about social justice and the economic order dating back to Pope Leo XIII's encyclical *Rerum Novarum* in 1891, prophetic Christianity within African American faith traditions, Liberation Theology within the Catholic Church, the Social Gospel tradition within American Protestantism, and Christian realism with the work of Reinhold Niebuhr as a paradigm.

Identifying the theological ideas that contribute to the work of broad-based organizing helps to explain why Catholic and Mainline Protestant churches, in general, are more likely to participate in LCU than Evangelical Protestant churches. Congregations within religious traditions that emphasize an "other worldly" focus as opposed to social action have a more difficult time mobilizing around organizations like LCU. A pastor from an Evangelical Free Church in Lake County described the challenge he sees in participating in LCU. He explained:

> Saint Francis of Assisi . . . he talked about "preach the gospel wherever you go, whenever necessary use words." I used to think that was cool and the more I hear that I think, you know, that really misses the point because you can't . . . At some point you can't preach the gospel without using words. Good deeds aren't enough.

A pastor from an Episcopal church, on the other hand, said:

> What we are called to do is to be Christ's hand and heart in the world. And that doesn't mean to just be there. It literally means for you to go out as if Christ was in this body and look at the next person as if that was Christ there. And it doesn't matter who that is. That person will see Christ in you without mentioning his name.

I frequently encountered this dichotomy between "social action" congregations and congregations that emphasize evangelization and a focus on the next world during my research.

However, I find that this distinction is a bit more complicated in Lake County. There is evidence that both Mainline and Evangelical Protestant congregations are currently struggling with their identity as "this world" or "next world" churches. Several pastors within Mainline Protestant traditions described what they perceive as a mistake by the liberal branch of Protestantism in embracing the social gospel with its emphasis on community and public engagement at the expense of both developing members' personal faith and evangelization. The response below is from a Lutheran pastor describing his struggles with this issue:

> I can tell you all about ecclesiology. I can take apart that Hebrew and Greek and . . . But lead someone to a deeper relationship with Jesus Christ? Clueless, they don't teach us how to do that. That is the main difference between how a Mainline denomination trains its pastors and some of the non-denominational/Evangelical. . . . There is a group of pastors and lay people around here struggling to try to not unlearn, but to integrate, to help people grow this way.

An Evangelical pastor described the shift in his tradition this way:

> In the '70s when I was in grade school and my teens and then in high school I know the church I went to would not have done anything, nothing if there was a food drive with the Catholic Church or a Lutheran Church. My church leaders would have said that is ecumenical and that was a dirty word! Now, I think the approach among Evangelicals who still say we really are firm on our convictions of the Bible would say it is not an all or nothing thing. I think it was this really odd dichotomy where you had churches that were basically saying we are not really convinced of the Bible and the gospel and they championed social justice and the values of the Bible. Then, you have churches over here with beliefs that doctrinally were more accurate but somehow missed out, and I'm still baffled at how that happened. . . . We weren't out there meeting the needs of the poor. Churches I grew up in even had a name for that,

the Social Gospel, and that was a negative expression. I would think, man, those are things that go together. . . . In the last couple decades I think that Evangelical churches or churches that would say we are committed to the Bible and the gospel and the person of Jesus, that they have started to get their acts together more and have brought these emphases back together.

These quotes demonstrate how pastors struggle with the traditional division between Mainline and Evangelical Protestant congregations concerning the extent to which they value and prioritize service and outreach. Individual-level research on attitudes toward economic justice has demonstrated that conservative Protestants are as likely as Mainline Protestants to support policies related to economic justice (Davis and Robinson 1996). While this line of research and the quotes above indicate a level of similarity between the two camps that is not usually represented in academic or popular discourse about religion and politics, the difference in LCU membership between Evangelical and Mainline Protestant churches suggests that at the level of action there are still important differences.

Interview data demonstrate concern among some LCU leaders about how the use of religious discourse might be perceived by outsiders. Several of the Mainline Protestant clergy articulated a concern that if LCU portrayed itself as a faith-based organization, it might be perceived as an evangelism project. As Lichterman says about the group of white Protestants he studies, others in the community "might easily associate public, Christian-based advocacy with abrasive fundamentalism, especially when the advocates are white" (2005, 131). Participants acknowledge that they compete for the attention of local congregations with a Lake County coalition of Evangelical churches, and LCU organizers, clergy, and lay leaders continually discuss the growing presence of Evangelical congregations in the county and what this growth means for their organization moving forward. LCU participants describe their communities as mostly affluent and politically conservative, and while only a small percentage of interviewees explicitly express concerns about public perceptions, almost all of the interviewees make some reference to the fact that social justice advocacy is not the dominant paradigm for faith-based politics in the county.

Lake County has a significant number of Evangelical churches, and although LCU organizers have had some conversations with the pastors of these congregations, none have considered membership. Based on previous research, one might speculate that LCU will be unable to recruit Evangelical churches until it incorporates more explicit religious language. The Evangelical pastors with whom I spoke, however, indicated that they would be *less* inclined to partner with LCU if they presented themselves as a religious organization. Based on interviews with Evangelical pastors, there is no way to reconcile LCU's emphasis on interfaith collaboration with the conservative Protestant emphasis on evangelism. The interfaith nature of LCU is of concern to pastors of Evangelical congregations. By keeping any partnerships focused on service and outreach, they do not have to deal with theological differences. As an Evangelical pastor explained, potential collaboration between LCU and the more conservative churches would have to happen on a level that did not require a compromise on religion:

> You can kind of sense that there is kind of a gray area here. I think what we want to avoid is close partnerships with churches that we would say we just have completely different belief systems and it would be or it would at least really look like a huge . . . somehow condoning of what they are doing. But, if it is a wide enough net where everybody understands this is just a community service, this is something that maybe the United Way is doing. . . . All of that is to say we try to be creative on that and say we are not going to do things if there is some kind of religious message that is being sent out. We wouldn't want to do something where we are partnering with others who are going to be sending out a religious message that we just don't think squares with the Bible. But, if it is something that is more nonreligious in nature, then yeah, we can partner together.

The affluence of many of the LCU congregations, combined with the interfaith identity of the organization, likely contributes to a polite lack of religious discourse in both public and private conversations. A strong Evangelical Protestant presence in the county further complicates LCU's portrayal of itself as a faith-based organization.

Conclusion

While LCU is part of a broader organizational field of BBCOs, and while this field is an important part of a larger field of progressive religious organizations, LCU's message about its religious identity and organizing mission are strongly influenced by place, understood in terms of geography, identity, and privilege. Organizers must simultaneously negotiate both their politically progressive agenda in a politically conservative county and their interfaith identity in a religiously conservative environment. Despite the fact that clergy conduct most of LCU's meetings in churches and synagogues, the religious identity of the organization is less "faith-based" than previous research would predict. Based on interviews with LCU participants, the interfaith identity of the organization is extremely important, but also constrains the use of religious language. Successful congregational participants have been able to negotiate IAF strategies and teachings to fit with the identities of their institutions and have negotiated particular uses of religious symbols and discourse that allow them to engage in an unusual form of faith-based politics in their suburban environment.

NOTES

1 Lake County is made up of all or parts of 52 cities and villages north and north-west of Chicago. The Village of Mundelein, in the center of Lake County, is 35 miles from the Chicago Loop.

2 "He has shown you, O mortal, what is good. And what does the Lord require of you? To act justly and to love mercy and to walk humbly with your God."

REFERENCES

Ammerman, Nancy Tatom. 2007. *Everyday Religion: Observing Modern Religious Lives.* Oxford: Oxford University Press.

Braunstein, Ruth. 2012. "Storytelling in Liberal Religious Advocacy." *Journal for the Scientific Study of Religion* 51(1): 110–127.

Casey, Colleen, Peter Dreier, Robert Flack, and Todd Swanstrom. 2004. "Pulling Apart: Economic Segregation among Suburbs and Central Cities in Major Metropolitan Areas." Washington, DC: Brookings Institution.

Davis, Nancy, and Robert Robinson. 1996. "Are the Rumors of War Exaggerated?: Religious Orthodoxy and Moral Progressivism in America." *American Journal of Sociology* 102(3): 756–787.

Diamond, Sara. 1998. *Not by Politics Alone: The Enduring Influence of the Christian Right.* New York: Guilford Press.

Fine, Gary Allan. 2001. *Difficult Reputations: Collective Memories of the Evil, Inept, and Controversial.* Chicago: University of Chicago Press.

Gieryn, Thomas. 2000. "A Space for Place in Sociology." *Annual Review of Sociology* 26: 463–496.

Hart, Stephen. 2001. *Cultural Dilemmas of Progressive Politics.* Chicago: University of Chicago Press.

Hondagneu-Sotelo, Pierrette. 2008. *God's Heart Has No Borders: How Religious Activists Are Working for Immigrant Rights.* Berkeley: University of California Press.

Larson, Jeff, and Sarah Soule. 2009. "Sector Level Dynamics and Collective Action in the United States: 1965–1975." *Mobilization* 14(2): 293–314.

Lichterman, Paul. 2005. *Elusive Togetherness: Church Groups Trying to Bridge America's Divisions.* Princeton, NJ: Princeton University Press.

Lichterman, Paul. 2008. "Religion and the Construction of Civic Identity." *American Sociological Review* 73(1): 83–104.

McGirr, Lisa. 2001. *Suburban Warriors: The Origins of the New American Right.* Princeton, NJ: Princeton University Press.

Morris, Aldon. 1984. *The Origins of the Civil Rights Movement: Black Communities Organizing for Change.* New York: Free Press.

Moyers, Bill, and Michael Winship. 2012. "The Truth about Newt's Favorite Punching Bag." *Salon*, February 6. www.salon.com.

Payne, Charles. 1995. *I've Got the Light of Freedom: The Organizing Tradition and the Mississippi Freedom Struggle.* Berkeley: University of California Press.

Robnett, Belinda. 1996. "African-American Women in the Civil Rights Movement, 1954–1965: Gender, Leadership, and Micromobilization." *American Journal of Sociology* 101(6): 1661–1693.

Slessarev-Jamir, Helene. 2011. *Prophetic Activism: Progressive Religious Justice Movements in Contemporary America.* New York: NYU Press.

Snow, David, E. Burke Rochford, Stephen Worden, and Robert Benford. 1986. "Frame Alignment Processes, Micromobilization, and Movement Participation." *American Sociological Review* 51(4): 464–481.

Sugrue, Thomas. 2012. "Saul Alinsky: The Activist Who Terrifies the Right." *Salon*, February 7. www.salon.com.

Warren, Mark R. 2001. *Dry Bones Rattling: Community Building to Revitalize American Democracy.* Princeton, NJ: Princeton University Press.

Warren, Mark, and Richard Wood. 2001. "Faith-Based Community Organizing: The State of the Field." Comm-Org Papers, Volume 7.

Wood, Richard. 2002. *Faith in Action.* Chicago: University of Chicago Press.

Wood, Richard, Brad Fulton, and Kathryn Partridge. 2013. *Building Bridges, Building Power: Developments in Institution-Based Community Organizing.* Interfaith Funders. www.interfaithfunders.org.

PART III

The Roles of Religion in Progressive Political Action

The next four chapters deepen our understanding of religion's complex role in political action. Previous research has highlighted three main ways in which religion enables activism: first, religion can serve as a moral impetus to action; second, association with religion can supply (some) activists with moral authority to make public claims; and third, religious institutions, mostly congregations, can supply material resources, space, and skilled leaders to activists who would otherwise lack these resources.

Through a diverse set of case studies of progressive religious activism, this section complicates these previous understandings of the role that religion plays in political action. Rather than simply assuming that religion matters, each author investigates *if* and *how* religion enables political action in particular contexts.

For example, we see that religion does not necessarily directly enable activism. Rather, it can shape the ways that activists *interpret* their action and the actions of their adversaries. Moreover, this interpretive process does not happen in a vacuum—it is cultivated by leaders, and in light of the historical and cultural contexts in which action plays out. As we will see, the ways in which actors interpret their efforts through a religious lens can have measurable effects on organizations' strength and commitment. And notably, this process plays out in organizations that are closely identified with religion (e.g., the Plowshares Movement), as well as in some movements that are widely viewed as secular (e.g., the New Left).

Second, by focusing on the grounded processes through which individuals and groups imbue their religious and political actions with meaning, and the role of various religious cultures in shaping these meaning-making processes, we are forced to reconsider the boundaries around "activism" itself. As we will see, what counts as "activism" shifts markedly across groups and contexts. This finding requires researchers and more casual observers alike to consider the benefits and drawbacks of defining activism more expansively, and potentially including practices that have political significance to actors despite not generally being viewed as "political."

Finally, we find there are cases in which religion actually *undermines* political actors' moral authority to make public claims. This highlights the extent to which our assumptions about the cultural power of religion have been based on *high-status* religious actors, like Protestant pastors in the civil rights movement or Catholic Sisters in the more recent Nuns on the Bus campaign. But what happens when Muslim leaders engage in protest in the U.S. today? Does their religious identity imbue them with the moral authority to make legitimate public claims, or does Islam's cultural "otherness" in American society today undermine their claims? Overall, the chapters in this section explore these issues by examining the ways that religion shapes (and constrains) various actors' efforts to make, disseminate, and interpret political claims.

8

Religious Roots of New Left Radicalism

JOSHUA Z. GAHR AND MICHAEL P. YOUNG

We start with the theoretical assumption that social movements are a creative source of new moral outlooks and that activists can articulate emerging moral intuitions. Movements can be agents in the emergence of "a new order of life" (Blumer 1939, 255). Movement activists, like prophets, can "speak before" and articulate new visions of ways of living together (Melucci 1996, 1). We tie these theoretical assumptions to a historical observation about the United States: as the introduction and several chapters in this volume show, any shortlist of important American movements includes those deeply marked by progressive Protestants. Antislavery, women's rights, and civil rights are the most well known, but the list is longer. As we argue in this chapter it also includes the new Left in the 1960s.

Sociologists no longer doubt the important role religion played in mobilizing resources for progressive social movements, but many on the Left seem to think that when it comes to American movements this history ends with black churches in the civil rights movement—as if in the 1960s, the progressive wellspring of Protestantism dried up. When it comes to white Protestant churches, they suspect the well may have been dry decades earlier in the North. And in the South, white churches always fiercely defended the status quo and were never a force for progressive change. In this chapter, however, we look closely at the role played by progressive Protestants at the Christian Faith-and-Life Community (CFLC), a Christian dormitory at the University of Texas, in the emergence of the new Left in Austin. We seek to find in their actions keys to how religious activism guided moral change in the 1960s and how it can guide such change in the present and future.

The new Left emerged at the outset of the 1960s. It encapsulated a myriad array of causes: civil rights, anti-capitalism, Vietnam War resistance, women's liberation, and attacks on the bureaucratization of higher education. Across this array of causes, a characteristic mix of personal freedom with radical social change gave cohesive form to the movement. According to historian Doug Rossinow (1998, 9), Austin was the most important center of the new Left "east of Berkeley, west of Morningside Heights, and south of Chicago." Activists from Texas brought a fusion of rebellious lifestyle and radical politics to the wider movement, a fusion commonly referred to as prairie radicalism. In Austin, this style of radicalism started with the students at the CFLC (Evans 1980; Rossinow 1998).

The new Left was involved in a wide range of contentious episodes and supported by a diverse set of Americans. We are not claiming that the progressive dimensions of the movement can be fully captured in the events we look at here. We do claim that the new Left emerged through a sequence of episodes like the ones we describe. A social movement is not a "unified" empirical "actor" or "datum" (Tilly 2004, 7; Melucci 1989). It is instead a concatenation of episodes of contention gleaned through an analytical lens (Melucci 1996). In the concatenation of contentious episodes that gave shape to the new Left, the sequence of events in Austin that we describe here was defining.

The idea that white, Protestant Texans were important to early new Left mobilizations might sound ludicrous to many, but it is not. Participants, historians, and sociologists of the movement have long noted their contribution. Sara Evans (1980), for example, found that in the South, white women involved in the civil rights movement and the new Left almost invariably came to this involvement through religion. And Doug Rossinow (1998), who viewed Austin as a key hub of the new Left, argued that the origins of activism in this university town were strongly connected to the Christian institutions of the CFLC and the Campus YMCA/YWCA.

It may be tempting for sociologists of social movements to interpret the relationship between religion and the new Left using structural and materialist approaches that do not disrupt the common-sense wisdom that the new Left was essentially a secular movement. From this approach, the influence of religion on social movements is limited to the materialist provision of "mobilizing structures" (McAdam, McCarthy, and Zald 1996, 3; McCarthy and Zald 1977; Morris 1984). From this angle, progressive Protestantism's pervasive mark on the new Left stems from its mobilization of church resources like meeting halls and mimeograph machines for essentially secular, "extra-curricular" purposes. We move beyond this view by arguing that the contentious mobilization flowing from religious organizations often depends on a *religious will* to sacrifice church resources for deeply personal and contentious sacred purposes.

To explain progressive Protestants' religious will to sacrifice church resources, we explore their sense of the limits of the traditional church as organized. As we discuss, a range of disturbing conditions compelled the faculty and students at the CFLC to sacrifice church resources: the disillusioning experience of World War II and the anxiety of a developing Cold War centered around nuclear weapons; the shallowness of faith and worship as they saw it in traditional churches; the meaninglessness of education in the research university; and, above all, the racial bigotry that pervaded every aspect of life in the South. This will to sacrifice was also shaped by new theological conceptions of sin and renewal in Christ. And, more importantly, these new ideas were taught to young students by religious virtuosos who pushed them to discover sin where they had not seen it before, to hope for renewal in places they did not expect to find it, and to do so with a "reckless venturesomeness" that would willingly sacrifice the traditional influence and material wealth of the Church (*Letter to Laymen* 1959, vol. 6, no. 1). This inspired a quest to find personal purpose in engagement with extensive social problems like racism.

The Broader Religious-Historical Context of the 1950s

In the decade prior to the protests emerging from the CFLC, Protestants were building resource-rich and influential institutions across America and Texas. For most Protestant Americans, the 1950s felt like a decade of religious revival. They built thousands of new suburban churches. Worship attendance was up compared to the two preceding decades of depression and war, and the revenue and budgets of the major Protestant denominations expanded (Wuthnow 1988). Most of the leaders commanding these expanding organizational resources believed they were witnessing a religious revival, but among them there were some who were deeply concerned about the shallow theological commitments accompanying this revival.

Describing the Protestant establishment of the 1950s, a young and somewhat angry Peter Berger (1961, 102–3) said,

> It prevents the individual from stepping outside the routines of his every-day life in society and looking at himself in freedom. Instead, it ratifies the routines, sanctifies the values by which the social roles are rational-ized, comforts the individual if personal crises threaten adjustment.

Berger was not alone among the faithful in his disapproval of the moral flabbiness of mainstream Protestantism in the 1950s. As many Protestant leaders enjoyed the religious revivals, to the dissenters the challenges of the postwar period seemed dire and the organized Church unequal to the task. They worried that Protestantism did not have the right message or organizational forms to meet these challenges.

Many progressive Protestants complained bitterly of the superficial nature of the religious establishment. Surveys revealed that American religion failed to penetrate deeply into the lives of most. The "organiza-tion man" went to church on Sunday, but at work for the company and at leisure in the suburbs, religion did not shape his life nor that of his wife and children (Whyte 1956). The religion of most Americans did not address the threats of the postmodern rationalization of produc-tion, consumption, destruction, and communication. Instead it soothed the conscience and sacralized the "other-directed" style of life (Riesman 1961; Berger 1961).

For some religious leaders, secular forces appeared on the brink of destroying the world. The nation had only just survived the horrors of World War II to enter straight into an increasingly chilly Cold War. Secure in the possession of rich institutional resources, these dissenting leaders nonetheless felt restless. Churches and denominational organiza-tions remained the institutional centers of American Protestantism, but these religious leaders worried that if they relied solely on them, religion would fail to address the perils of the time. They needed new institutions designed for a new ministry. As their tradition taught, the faithful could not risk being *of* this world, but they also could not risk simply stand-ing apart from it. At a talk at the Austin Presbyterian Seminary in 1949,

H. Richard Niebuhr described this mission as "culture transforming" (Niebuhr 1951). This new mission called for new organizational forms.

In the 1950s, the CFLC represented a leading edge of a movement to innovate the organizational form of American Protestantism. In this setting of revival and experimentation, the distance between liberals and fundamentalists, or between progressives and Evangelicals, closed somewhat. The yawning gap of the first half of the century in American Protestantism narrowed as Evangelicals moved left of fundamentalist camps and as neo-orthodoxy challenged liberal Protestantism's facile embrace of Enlightenment principles and its attempt to "rationalize" Christianity. In the South, in places like Austin and in experimental spaces like the CFLC, some Evangelicals took to the neo-orthodox theology articulated by the likes of Paul Tillich and the Niebuhr brothers and taught at institutions like Yale and the Union Theological Seminary, and to a variety of Christian existentialism. This brought them closer to progressive Protestants in other parts of the country. The contact proved productive in terms of mobilizing in the South for social change.

Early History of CFLC

The CFLC opened in 1952. In its inaugural year it housed thirty young University of Texas students. They were all men and represented six Protestant denominations. To gain admission they were required to present letters of recommendation from their congregations back home. At the CFLC they enrolled in what was billed as a "laboratory course in Christian living" (*Letter to Laymen* 1957, vol. 3, no. 8). Frequently referred to simply as the Community, the CFLC provided students a dormitory just blocks from campus as well as a religious education to supplement their secular studies at University of Texas.

The Community sprang from the religious imagination of Presbyterian minister Rev. W. Jack Lewis. Lewis served as a chaplain in the Navy and Marine Corps during World War II. Immediately after his return from war, Lewis took over the ministerial position at the University Presbyterian Church in Austin—a congregation adjacent to the UT campus that drew many of its worshippers from the university's student body. As a campus chaplain, Lewis became profoundly discouraged by the popular versions of Christian faith propagated by churches and campus ministries. He viewed them as "inadequate and irrelevant in the face of world chaos, death, and destruction" (CFLC n.d.a, 10). The disillusioning forces of the war stirred him deeply, and the traditional campus ministry seemed a feeble response to these forces. In 1950, just as religious revival appeared to be fueling church going across America, Lewis retired his pulpit, unhappy with his ministry. As would be the case for other clergy to join him later at the CFLC, he left a successful, traditional religious career because it did not seem particularly relevant.

Unemployed, Lewis took the opportunity to study at St. Andrews University at Scotland. His sixteen-month stay in Europe with his wife and four children afforded Lewis the time to observe a postwar rise in Christian training centers for the laity across Europe. During his stay, he visited and studied such organizations as the Iona Community, the lay academies in Germany, the Zoe Community in Greece, the Kerk en Wereld Institute in Holland, and the Ecumenical Institute in Bossey, Switzerland. He came into contact with prominent clergy and lay people active in an emerging ecumenical lay movement in Europe. In an article describing what he learned from these centers, Lewis wrote, "in addition to Sunday punch delivered by the clergy, the church must train her laymen as 'in-fighters' in office, factory, shop, and neighborhood" (Lewis 1952, 5). Lewis returned to Texas in 1951 with new models of organizational forms that might make religion more relevant to university students and train them to be these infighters. He returned to Austin intending to establish "alongside the University of Texas . . . a residential center for the education of lay leaders" (*Letter to Laymen* 1957, vol. 3, no. 8).

In the early to mid-1950s, there was nothing else quite like the Community in the United States: an intentional religious community to train lay student leaders, an ecumenical student monastery for the laity built to engage the university and the world. Resources for the founding of the CFLC came from the rapidly expanding churches in Texas. As the CFLC grew and received national attention, Lewis took his fundraising on the road, traveling from state to state and internationally to support his emerging lay educational center. Lewis described the Community as an "experiment" that aimed to push to students to "to enter into all human relationships as men of faith responding to the gracious activity of God who meets them in the concrete situations of every moment"

(*Letter to Laymen* 1959, vol. 6, no. 2). For Lewis this meant encouraging students to make "venturesome" religious incursions into secular life. The experiment encouraged students "to come to a realistic Christian self-understanding so that they [could] bring their critical intelligence to bear upon the pressing social, economic, political and educational problems of our time" (*Letter to Laymen* 1959, vol. 6, no. 1). The experiment aimed to alter not just the world but also the Church in the world, to revive faith as much as to breath religion into the secular.

In the mid-1950s, the Community was a leading edge of a broader special-purpose initiative by Protestants to influence the realm of the research university and the national drive for mass, popular college education. By the 1960s, imitations of the CFLC appeared in universities across America, but in the 1950s the Community was a unique expression of the emerging ecumenical lay movement in America (Sloan 1994; *Letter to Laymen* 1959, vol. 5, no. 7).

The leaders of this lay movement in America took their theology very seriously. The theological renaissance of neo-orthodoxy shaped their thoughts about religious engagement with the world. They believed Christian engagement with the broader culture promised to have a recursive effect on the Church and the world. Many, like Lewis, viewed the university as the nerve center of the technological and administrative advances of the modern world and the strategic point to simultaneously exercise religious influence on the secular and revive the Church through a renewed mission in the world (Sloan 1994, 76). Yet higher education appeared to them to be religiously challenged, tone-deaf to the spiritual call for deeper meaning. They hoped that through new religious organizations they could help the university answer this higher calling and infuse the emerging information age with a moral sensibility.

As envisioned by Lewis, the CFLC was a lay center built alongside the university to lead Christian students to answer this calling. An appealing figure with clear but offbeat charisma, Lewis personally recruited many of the thirty charter members of the Community. In 1955 the CFLC added a women's dormitory. In 1956 he expanded the staff with the help of a $41,250 grant from the Danforth Foundation (*Letter to Laymen* 1956, vol. 3, no.1). At the start of the 1957–58 school year, the Community had expanded to include eighty students: forty-eight men, thirty-two women; thirty-three Presbyterians, twenty-five Methodists, ten Baptists, and a score from a range of smaller denominations. Lewis capitalized on his connections within church and educational institutions in Texas to attract respected names to the board of trustees including leading figures from the UT administration and Texas churches and businesses. Although the trustees were, as a whole, considerably more conservative than Lewis, through the 1950s they remained vocal, public supporters of the Community and its program.

In fact, the Community became a place off campus where the UT administration encouraged experiments it was worried about rushing into as an institution. In the wake of *Brown v. Board of Education*, as the university dragged its feet on racial integration on campus—particularly in the realm of sociability like dorms, sports, and the arts—some of its leaders backed Lewis's vision of a racially integrated CFLC. In 1956, the CFLC admitted Albertine Bowie, the first African American woman to live in a UT dormitory, school-owned or private, with white students (Goldstone 2006).

Joseph Mathews and CFLC

In 1956, Lewis appointed Joseph Mathews to lead the religious education at the Community. Mathews, a theologian from Southern Methodist University in Dallas, was known for his electrifying pedagogy. CFLC students wildly admired lectures Mathews gave during a visit to campus the year before and pressed Lewis to invite him to design and implement a curriculum at the Community. Lewis gave Mathews total control of the educational program and turned his energies to securing funds for the Community and "interpreting" its experiment for a wider audience across the United States, Europe, and Australia.

Mathews grew up in Appalachia, in the small town of Ada, Ohio. He was the son of a Methodist minister who was forced to quit his pulpit because he suffered from manic depression. During the Great Depression, Mathews hitchhiked to Los Angeles in the hopes of becoming an actor. As a vagabond in a boxcar headed to the West Coast, his conversion to Christ began. In Los Angeles it was completed under the Holiness tradition. After a short but transformative stay, he returned east for college, earning a bachelor's degree in 1936 from Asbury College in

Wilmore, Kentucky—an Evangelical college with Wesleyan connections and in the Holiness tradition.

In a paper written years later at Yale Divinity School, he reflected on the Holiness roots of his religious awakening as a young man. He criticized his religious roots as narrowly fundamentalist, but "I absorbed from them a certain temper for which I am grateful" (Mathews 2006, 109). His brother James described that temperament in an account of their early work together as rural revival preachers. They worked hard to save souls in Lee County, Virginia, the most western part of the state, squeezed by the Cumberland Gap.

> Joe was made of sterner stuff than I, and his manner tended to emphasize the wrath and judgment of God. My inclination was to stress the love of God. Between these two poles a fruitful ministry seemed to develop. It was a kind of "divine pincer movement," which had the effect of embracing everyone. (Mathews 2006, 109)

In 1938, after graduating from Asbury and working the backwoods of the Bible Belt, the brothers enrolled in Biblical Seminary in New York.

In New York, Joe turned theologically away from his fundamentalist roots and the emphasis of God's wrath and embraced the left hand of God. After graduating with a bachelor's in divinity, Mathews earned a pastoral position in Sharon, Connecticut, and enrolled in Union Theological Seminary. At Union he studied with Reinhold Niebuhr and Paul Tillich. In the years just before the war, he was ordained as deacon and elder and became a member of the New York Conference of the Methodist Church. When the United States entered World War II, Mathews became a chaplain in the Army.

He served in the Pacific theater and witnessed the bloody battles of Eniwetok, Saipan, and Okinawa. He buried hundreds and hundreds of young men. When the war ended, he was shattered, and worried about his training as a minister. His experience of ministering to scared young men facing death on the battlefield convinced him that most Christians knew very little about their faith. From his perspective as an Army chaplain, religious leaders had failed to interpret Christianity for their age. He also grew insecure about his own abilities as a minister.

After the war, he went back to school seeking deeper knowledge of Christian theology. He enrolled at Yale Divinity School and H. Richard Niebuhr became his advisor. At Yale, he committed to the following goals and principles: "clarification of the Christianity experience," "a reconstruction of our religious education programs," "an ecumenical Church," "a united Christian voice on glaring social problems," and a "rethinking of missions—more action (Christian) than talking" (Mathews 2006, 106).

After three years of study, with his dissertation unfinished, he took a teaching appointment at Colgate as an instructor of philosophy and religion. He taught there for three years and then took an appointment in the Perkins School of Theology at Southern Methodist University. After four years at SMU, he felt restless. His career trajectory as an academic looked impressive, but Mathews remained unsatisfied. He was a rising theologian and professor at a rapidly expanding Texas seminary, but Mathews sought a more engaged and wider orbit of social influence. He hoped to find this influence at the CFLC.

His move in 1956 from SMU to Austin to direct the curriculum of the CFLC was daring, even downwardly mobile, but the Community was emerging as a key institution in a lay movement that was attracting the attention of a wide range of dissenting Christians. CFLC presented a model others were beginning to follow on campuses across America. It was also a place unlike a liberal arts college or a seminary where Mathews could revolutionize the Church's mission in the world. Mathews was also beginning to seize on the particular issue of race as an Archimedean point for what he would term "intensive and extensive renewal." Directing the curriculum of an integrated lay community offered an opportunity that the Perkins School of Theology could not.

With the aid of the Danforth grant money, Mathews tripled the size of the faculty. He recruited a devoted and ecumenical group that included clergy and laymen representing Methodist, Baptist, and Presbyterian traditions. Mathews unveiled a new curriculum for the fall which, in the words of Lewis, "knive[d] through extraneous material and [got] to the heart of the matter" (*Letter to Laymen* 1956, vol. 3, no. 1). With the new curriculum, Mathews planned an overarching form to the academic cycles of the Community. The first academic year of 1956–57 was dedicated first to "corporate study," second to "corporate worship," and the third to "corporate living." The arc of the curriculum then finished in the fourth year, 1959–60, with the study of "corporate mission" (*Letter to Laymen* 1959, vol. 6, no. 1).

As the Community began to take shape under Mathews, he guided students through a curriculum designed to shake their worldviews and stir a critical approach to society, church, and the individual. In the pages of the official newsletter, the *Letter to Laymen*, Community members criticized American Protestants for losing their sense of mission in the world. They attacked the religious establishment for its shallow transactional ethos that offered Americans "pie in the sky" in exchange for being Christians on Sunday (*Letter to Laymen* 1959, vol. 6, no. 4). They warned that the Church was suffering from a malaise. Mathew's curriculum sought to extend religion into the everyday lives of its students—or perhaps more accurately, to extend the urgent matters of everyday life into their religion. He was training Lewis's "infighters."

Bringing spiritual meaning to the research university was at the center of the Community's experiment in renewing the Church's mission in the world. The university was at the heart of a new age and the Community wanted to teach university students "the way to a new Christian style of life" (*Letter to Laymen* 1958, vol. 5, no. 1). The *Letter to Laymen* referred to this new age as one of anxiety in which people lived in the shadow of the atom bomb and under the restless temptation of meaningless materialism. This Christian style of life required new symbols and new meanings that would resonate within a new world. Mathew's curriculum was a search for these symbols and meanings.

Students at the Community covenanted to attend morning worship and short services before dinner each day. They also committed to attend a seminar at the Community that amounted to a time commitment comparable to one university course. Connected to this seminar were Friday lectures by distinguished academics from UT and elsewhere. Mathews's curriculum was designed to guide student discussions during these seminars. It was steeped in Christian existentialism. The students were reading Dietrich Bonhoeffer, Rudolph Bultmann, Paul Tillich, and Rollo May. Following Tillich, Mathews understood sin to be alienation: self-alienation, alienation from others, alienation from the "ground of being." He taught students to understand the meaninglessness of their university education, the malaise in their church, and the collective mood of anxiety that haunted them and their generation in terms of this understanding of sin. Introspection alone trapped the self in anxiety and alienation. That said, Mathews and his faculty did much to heighten student anxiety and existential introspection with seminar topics like "Who am I?" They clearly sought to agitate their students with difficult, soul-searching questions, but they had an action plan to push the students through the anxiety and out the other end. Following Rollo May, they believed that anxiety could inspire exalted states of being; anxiety could push us to do our best if we acted on it.

The effect of this psychologically experimental curriculum on students is registered in their accounts of their experiences at the Community. If Mathews aimed to unsettle his wards, he succeeded. In 1964, Millard Research Associates, Ltd, surveyed 286 former residents of the Community. The research was funded by a grant from the Hogg Foundation of Mental Health at the University of Texas. The survey asked respondents to "describe their experience there in terms of the meaning it has had for their lives" (Millard Research Associates 1964). The opening pages of the report written from this survey analysis included excerpts from ten such descriptions that the researchers said "were not uncommon." Here are two examples:

> I will say that the Community was one of the most important times of my life, but in the most unpleasant way possible . . . the Community completely upended me by forcing a re-examination of everything that had meaning to me. Paradoxically, however, the Community was one of the best things in which I ever had part . . . the Community produced the doubt that skylights faith into supreme relevance for life. For that favor in disguise, I shall ever be thankful. (Millard Research Associates 1964, 2066)

> My experience at XKO was personally traumatic in several respects: I came there questioning my vocational decision to enter the ministry. Out of a conservative background theologically, I entered a highly-pitched existential program geared to tear down nominal and irrelevant belief and rebuild it again, this time shorn up with pillars of Tillichian theology and Freudian psychology. That experience is traumatic for anyone. My theological criticism of the XKO both then and now is that existentialism

is a thorough enough instrument of questioning, and, indeed, of destruction; however, it does not serve to rebuild a constructive faith which will prepare laymen to revitalize the Church. (Millard Research Associates 1964, 531)

The faculty at the Community aimed to dismantle the religious beliefs students arrived with in order to prepare them for a revitalized faith.

In the 1959–60 academic year, Mathews and his faculty pointed the way out of the agitated condition he and his faculty had fueled and interpreted for the students. They designed what they termed a "breakthrough." The approach was certainly unorthodox but not out of step with Jack Lewis's vision of the Community as he described it in 1958:

Each year is different in the Community. Each year our sinfulness is revealed to us anew. . . . When we meet the living God in flesh-and-blood events, that is when we hide. And that is when we reject God because we know that in His claims there is a cross. . . . As the Church we are not called to be either world-denying or world-affirming. We are called to be . . . world-transforming. . . . To be the people of God knowing we are weak sinners. (*Letter to Laymen* 1958, vol. 5, no. 1)

Mathews taught students that the pressing social problems of the day, in Lewis's terms the "flesh-and-blood events" that make us want to hide, were "Christ-events." He prepared his students not to shrink from them, but to embrace their cross, to find freedom in the Christ-event.

Lois Boyd traveled from Norman, Oklahoma, to a "spiritual retreat" at the CFLC in the winter of 1960–61. Even though she had "heard that what they had down there was pretty 'way-out' for most folk," she was not prepared for what turned out to be a "kookie" but transformative forty-four hours in Austin. As she and her friends left the Community to return to Norman, they clearly felt revitalized.

I remember how good the afternoon sunlight and soft Texas air felt on my face. I took a deep breath and realized that we hadn't been out of that house for a whole week-end. The air was sweet—Life was good—and—I KNEW IT WAS SO! Every cotton pickin' thing They had told us was SO. LIFE . . . THE CHRIST-EVENT . . . FREEDOM . . . COSMIC

PERMISSION TO LIVE . . . EVERYTHING . . . IT WAS ALL THERE . . .
IT WAS THE WORD!

What word? Oh, that Word. Well, why didn't you say so? What is so
wonderful about that little, old word. Haven't I heard it all my life?

We got in the car, the wheels started to roll—and the dialogue began,
all of us trying to talk at once—and it was in the midst of Us—LIFE—

Such conversation—all about "what I saw" . . . and "what I know" . . .
and "what do you think They . . . ? (the Living Ones we now thought of
as Our Fathers in the Faith) meant by . . .". Everything we said was so full
of meaning because, you see, We had known each other ever since our
Lives began . . . Only our Lives were so very new . . . and birth is such a
delicate, fragile thing—and violent—and personal. But good! Only the
newly Alive can know how good! (*Letter to Laymen* 1961, vol. 8, no. 5)

Race and the CFLC

The CFLC position on race and integration first emerged from the
experiences and observations of Lewis during his European travels
and surfaced in his writings as early as 1951. Lewis, the visionary and
organizing force behind the CFLC, wrote regular articles for his denominational periodical, the *Presbyterian Outlook*, in which he attempted
to both report on the emerging forms of church engagement by laity
in postwar Europe and to pose possible applications of these forms to
the American context. Over the course of his tour abroad, he became
convinced that "one key toward discovering the Christian answers to
problems of the modern world is in the confrontation and conversation
of informed, articulate Christians from different segments of society—
races, classes, cultures, denominations—all in the search for the truth,
fall where it may" (Lewis 1952, 6).

If for Lewis racial equality was a means to an end, Mathews turned
racial equality into an end in itself. From notes to a 1958 lecture and
a published lecture given in the early 1960s, it is clear that Mathews
saw racial integration as *the* Christ event of the time (Mathews 1958,
Mathews n.d.). From the notes to the earlier lecture he gave on the
"Negro in America," he framed "living integration" at the Community
as "a sign for the South." By living integration alongside UT, the CFLC
could provide "a new image as mission" and "a new demand on the

Church" that could spread out across Texas and the world. He concluded the Church "must stop sentimentality and press for Justice" in "this new age" through "new institutions" like the integrated Community (Mathews 1958).

Although the pages of the *Letter to Laymen* dedicated less space to the problems of race as compared to nuclear war, shallow materialism, and the meaninglessness of traditional religious and secular education, a deep concern with the sin of racial bigotry and hope for integration nonetheless breaks through. Gretta Rutherford, a student at the Community who traveled to Germany in the summer of 1957, described her feelings in the *Letter to Laymen* about the exclusion of Barbara Smith, a black student, from a UT opera production that same year:

> [W]hen the University of Texas' action in removing a Negro student from her part in an opera hit the front pages of the German papers, someone laid one down in front of me and said, "This is your state, isn't it?"
>
> At that moment I felt as though I were all American ideals and all American failures rolled up together. This was when a feeling of responsibility for more than my own individual actions first came to me.
>
> And many German students have this for their country, too, even though their parents were far more directly involved in the war. They understand that we are responsible for the situation which we are in, not because we caused it, particularly, but simply because we're in it. They are often more realistic than the older Germans about facing up to the moral choices they made during the Nazi regime. Among the latter there is a tendency to evade responsibility by claiming ignorance.
>
> I feel that this utter responsibility cannot be faced, cannot be endured except in faith. But, then, only in the context of faith are we aware of this responsibility as a personal one. (*Letter to Laymen* 1957, vol. 4, no. 2)

"Living integration" was part of this new Christian style of life and its sense of "utter responsibility." Even if the *Letters* handled the problem of race delicately, the responsibility of facing racial prejudice stirred the students at the Community. Dorothy Dawson Burlage in her memoir described how it disturbed her right from the start of her experiences at the CFLC:

> On the day I moved in [to the Community], my life took a dramatic and an irreversible turn, when all the contradictions of my southern upbringing and my emerging social consciousness came together during a ten-minute car ride. I got in my pink and gray Chevrolet Belaire to drive from the Community's women's dorm to the men's dorm, where the lectures were held. I offered a ride to a white student who then saw two black students coming out of the building, so he offered them a ride as well. One of the black men got in the front seat of the car. In a split second, I felt my world turn upside down. For the first time in my life, I experienced being in a situation of apparent social intimacy with a black man—not just in a meeting or a class, but in my mother's car, breaking my mother's rules and violating nineteen years of her training. Although I felt physically sick with fear that I had crossed the color line and worried about possible retribution for breaking this southern tradition, the very intensity of my reaction taught me how deep had been my socialization into the racist system and how irrational it was to have such a reaction. I did not want white children to be raised the way I had been. (Burlage 2000, 96)

Dorothy's reflection retains the mark of Mathews's curriculum and what it taught students about how to interpret deeply unsettling experiences. The fear of having crossed the color line, the physically sick feeling of transgression, was actually the appearance of a moral opportunity for personal and social renewal.

Starting in 1959, members of the CFLC started to push through their personal feelings and responsibility for what Dorothy called a racist system toward the collective action their faith demanded. In a spring article in *Letter to Laymen*, John Lee Smith, a Baptist faculty member at the CFLC, invited the UT community to join the mission to be "world-transforming." In his piece, he foreshadowed not only the themes of the upcoming year's curriculum but also events that would break out on the streets of Austin in 1960:

> There are people who in faith have recognized the power of the Gospel of Jesus Christ, who no longer have to defend the Lord with theological arguments or ecclesiastic programs, but in radical freedom and faith can

become transparent to His power working through us in our decision to be responsible in our witness and mission. Some of us poor derelicts have sobered up enough to realize the desperate need of raising the question "what must I do" and being done with our obsession with "who am I." Something is being born into existence—a call to witness, to action, and to mission. It is my hope that there are people associated with the University of Texas who are demanding an occasion and opportunity for expressing their existence in the world in terms of creativity, productivity, witness, mission, and purpose in action. (*Letter to Laymen* 1959, vol. 5, no. 7)

That same spring, George Todd from the East Harlem Protestant Parish addressed the CFLC from Matthew's Gospel (10:39): "He who finds his life will lose it, and he who loses his life for my sake will find it." Todd cautioned the Community that it is a "temptation for the church to think of itself as exempt from this call to give her life away"; after all, "we strive to build up the church." But this was to shrink from the mission and Todd told students and faculty that the church must "risk" taking upon "itself the suffering of the world" even if it threatens its material well-being.

From time to time there becomes apparent human need that calls for action on the part of the church. This may be the action of making public the existence of injustice and of proclaiming God's opposition to the suffering of men at the hands of men. . . . Such action may not have clear rewards for building up the life of the church. No members may be won. Some may be alienated. It may cost the church in money, time, and property that could be used for the well-being of the Christian congregation. Yet we must not count the cost any more than did Christ when the sins of men led him to death on a cross. We are called to faithful action. (*Letter to Laymen* 1959, vol. 5, no. 9)

That summer, Sandra Cason, now better known as Casey Hayden, a student member of the Community, joined the East Harlem Protestant Parish to work in its group ministry for the summer. She was finding her Christ-event.

The CFLC Breakthrough

In the fall of 1959, around fifty men and thirty women enrolled in the Community's College House. In September, the first of two CFLC publications entitled "Breakthrough" announced the arrival of "THE NEW MAN":

> With the new world has come a breakthrough in the human spirit. Howsoever rare, the post-modern man is emerging. The tomorrows are in his hands. His essential characteristic is intensive and extensive consciousness of his situation in an utterly new world.

A special calling confronted this new person with her intensive and extensive consciousness:

> To [r]ecover that kind of genuine dialogue among contemporary men which will issue in creative social structures capable of mediating authentic personal existence and new possibilities for justice for all.

In November, the second "Breakthrough" publication appeared.

> The Community looks upon its own life as an Experiment on behalf of the Church . . . an attempt to articulate a style of life; and endeavor to recover secondary symbols which can freight meaning in the various communities of family, labor, and politics.

Within months, social protest became part and parcel of the search for authentic life and the overcoming of alienation at the CFLC.

Casey Hayden recalled her personal experience the following spring:

> When the sit-ins broke out across the South in the spring of 1960, I was back in Austin in graduate school. . . . I went to the meetings of the Austin Movement with black women who lived across the hall from me in the only integrated housing on campus, the Christian Faith and Life Community (CF&LC), known by us simply as "the Community"—the third of the life-changing religious organizations of my college years. Here I roomed with Dorothy Dawson, my oldest friend.

Calling itself a lay training center, the Community was established and staffed by ministers who had been through World War II, an event that, speaking conservatively, had challenged their beliefs. I learned at the Community to reject absolute constructs and abstractions of civilization, following the lead of existentialists. I learned to believe my own experience and join others to create meaning through intentional living. Intentional living was supported by honesty and, through covenant, a promise to be present and accountable to each other. At the CF&LC I experienced the creation of empowering community; and within it an image of myself, in terms of which I then lived. Later, I understood the movement on this model. Our image of ourselves in the Southern Freedom Movement was that of the Beloved Community, created by activity, the experience, of nonviolent direct action against injustice. (Hayden 2000, 339)

Intentional living at the Community became a model for Casey Hayden of the "Beloved Community" she craved in the Southern Freedom Movement.

When the pickets started on a Friday in early March, Ronnie Dugger, a liberal reporter from the *Observer* who had fallen under Casey's spell, took in their significance (Dugger 1974):

Now, suddenly, the hesitant liberals are irrelevant. They do not matter. The students are saying, "This is wrong. We do not care what anybody says. We know this is wrong." "I know this is wrong. I am going to protest. This is wrong." And so the plain, confronting force of a moral idea: the dignity of a person sweeps all else before it. The nation is called by the single conscience; and they become many; they speak from many places; they become a brotherhood of protest. (Dugger 1960)

That summer, Casey Hayden, a representative of a UT contingent, spoke to a national audience at the convention of the National Student Association (NSA). As a Southern white woman on a panel of white students tasked to address the challenge made by African American students that the NSA should support the spreading sit-ins, it may have been expected by organizers that Casey would speak against backing the protests (Rossinow 1998). If so, they had failed to do their homework. Here is part of what she said in that speech:

I am thankful for the sit-ins if for no other reason than that they provide me with an opportunity for making a slogan into a reality by making a decision into an action. It seems to me that this is what life is all about. While I hope that the NSA Congress will pass a strong sit-in resolution, I am more concerned that all of us, Negro and white, realize the possibility of becoming less inhuman through commitment and action. (Rossinow 1998, 104)

The sit-ins provided a critical moment for students to be more fully human, to counter alienation by turning slogans into decisive action, to attack meaninglessness with a sense of authenticity grounded in action that reveals "what life is all about." Quoting Thoreau, Casey ended the speech with a taunt: "What are you doing out there?"

In the audience was Tom Hayden, the emerging voice of the nascent Students for a Democratic Society, who recalled the speech as "putting into words the transformation I was undergoing" (Hayden 1988, 42). The following year, Mathews presided over the marriage of Casey and Tom in a ceremony held at the Community in Austin.

In the fall of 1960, UT students launched the "stand-ins" at the segregated movie theaters on "the Drag"—Guadalupe Street, which forms the western boundary of the campus. Activists at the campus Y and the CFLC organized the stand-ins, and according to historian Doug Rossinow, the largest share of participants from any particular organization on or off campus came from the Community (Rossinow 1998). Impatience with segregation had been brewing for a while in the integrated CFLC. Living integration at the Community clashed with racist routines that governed interaction elsewhere in Austin. As Dorothy Dawson Burlage remembers, "if you wanted to go to the movies or go out it was pretty insulting to go where other students that we lived with couldn't go" (Evans 1980, 35). One evening in the fall of 1960, Dick Simpson recalls that the Community "en masse" spontaneously walked to the Drag to join the protest (Rossinow 1998, 127). The stand-ins on the Drag were the first sustained protests to roil the campus but not the last.

Casey Hayden, a crucial leader in this first phase of new Left protests, moved away from Austin in 1961 to go work with SDS and SNCC. When she left, other CFLC members during the breakthrough year took the lead of an expanding wave of protest. Jim Neyland, a student of Mathews's 1959–60 breakthrough curriculum, became the president of the campus Y. Neyland and other student activists at the Y started articulating arguments that would soon be associated with the attack on the "multiversity" and its complicity in a culture of war and materialism. Neyland's early attacks on materialism show the clear influence of the CFLC breakthrough:

> The materialistic values, the values of security have been followed with such intensity and zeal that the values of freedom have been overshadowed. It is the omission of the "spiritual," the philosophical, the aesthetic that has made the dehumanization and perhaps more important, the depersonalization of our society. (Rossinow 1998, 99)

The student activism of members and former members of the CFLC created a serious controversy among the trustees at the Community and administrators at UT. In the spring of 1962, Mathews was asked to resign. He left with his entire faculty. They followed what they taught, and sacrificed the material existence of the Community for the spiritual mission of renewal. The experiment at the CFLC ended shortly thereafter, but some of it leading residents like Casey Hayden, Dorothy (Dawson) Burlage, Jim Neyland, Dick Simpson, and Vivien Franklin had already moved on to lead the developing protests of the new Left in Austin and across the country.

REFERENCES

Berger, Peter L. 1961. *The Noise of Solemn Assemblies: Christian Commitment and the Religious Establishment in America.* Garden City, NY: Doubleday.

Blumer, Herbert. 1939. "Collective Behavior." In *An Outline of the Principles of Sociology*, edited by Robert E. Park, 221–280. New York: Barnes and Noble.

Burlage, Dorothy. 2000. "Truths of the Heart." In *Deep in Our Hearts: Nine White Women in the Freedom Movement*, edited by Constance Curry et al., 85–130. Athens: University of Georgia Press.

Christian Faith-and-Life Community. N.d.(a). Promotional booklet. CFLC file. Austin History Center, Austin, Texas.

Christian Faith-and-Life Community. N.d.(b). "One Positive Answer." Promotional pamphlet. CFLC file. Austin History Center, Austin, Texas.

Christian Faith-and-Life Community. 1959. "Breakthrough." Pamphlet. Two issues. CFLC file. Austin History Center, Austin, Texas.

Dugger, Ronnie. 1960. "Chilled Sunlight." *Observer*, March 11.

Dugger, Ronnie. 1974. *Our Invaded Universities: Form, Reform, and New Starts*. New York: W. W. Norton.

Evans, Sara. 1980. *Personal Politics: The Roots of Women's Liberation in the Civil Rights Movement and New Left*. New York: Vintage.

Goldstone, Dwonna. 2006. *Integrating the 40 Acres: The Fifty-Year Struggle for Racial Equality at the University of Texas*. Athens: University of Georgia Press.

Hayden, Casey. 2000. "Fields of Blue." In *Deep in Our Hearts: Nine White Women in the Freedom Movement*, edited by Constance Curry et al., 333–376. Athens: University of Georgia Press.

Hayden, Tom. 1988. *Reunion: A Memoir*. New York: Collier Books.

Lewis, Jack. 1952. "America: Lessons from Abroad Applied at Home." *Presbyterian Outlook*, January 7, 1952, pp. 5–7.

Mathews, James K. 2006. *Brother Joe: A 20th-Century Apostle*. Lutz, FL: Resurgence Publishing.

Mathews, Joseph W. N.d. "The Christ of History" for the Corporate Ministry of the Christian Faith-and-Life Communty. CFLC file. Austin History Center, Austin, Texas.

Mathews, Joseph W. 1958. Notes to Lecture on Negro in America. Wesley Theological Seminary Library, Washington, D.C.

McAdam, Doug, John D. McCarthy, and Mayer N. Zald (eds.). 1996. *Comparative Perspectives on Social Movements*. Cambridge, UK: Cambridge University Press.

McCarthy, John D., and Mayer N. Zald. 1977. "Resource Mobilization and Social Movements: A Partial Theory." *American Journal of Sociology* 82(6): 1212–1214.

Melucci, Alberto. 1989. *Nomads of the Present: Social Movements and Individual Needs in Contemporary Society*. London: Hutchinson Radius.

Melucci, Alberto. 1996. *Challenging Codes: Collective Action in the Information Age*. New York: Cambridge University Press.

Millard Research Associates. 1964. "The College House of the Christian Faith and Life Community at Austin, Texas." Pelham, New York.

Morris, Aldon D. 1984. *The Origins of the Civil Rights Movement: Black Communities Organizing for Change*. New York: Free Press.

Niebuhr, H. Richard. 1951. *Christ and Culture*. San Francisco: Harper and Row.

Riesman, David, with Nathan Glazer and Reuel Dennney. 1961. *The Lonely Crowd*. New Haven, CT: Yale University Press.

Rossinow, Doug. 1998. *The Politics of Authenticity: Liberalism, Christianity, and the New Left in America*. New York: Columbia University Press.

Sloan, Douglas. 1994. *Faith and Knowledge: Mainline Protestantism and American Higher Education*. Louisville, KY: Westminster John Knox Press.

Tilly, Charles. 2004. *Social Movements, 1776–2004*. Boulder, CO: Paradigm Publishers.

Whyte, William H. 1956. *The Organization Man*. New York: Simon & Schuster.

Wuthnow, Robert. 1988. *The Restructuring of American Religion: Society and Faith since World War II*. Princeton, NJ: Princeton University Press.

9

Religious Culture and Immigrant Civic Participation

JUAN R. MARTINEZ

In 2005, the United States House of Representatives introduced and passed the Border Protection, Anti-Terrorism, and Illegal Immigration Control Act (H.R. 4437). This legislation proposed additional measures to deter undocumented migration and settlement in the country, including increased security along U.S. borders and harsher penalties for anyone who knowingly provided aid to undocumented immigrants. The passage of H.R. 4437 was met with much public resistance by allies of undocumented immigrants. In early 2006, an estimated 3.5 to 5 million people participated in pro-immigrant public demonstrations in the form of parades and rallies across the United States (Fox, Selee, and Bada 2006). These public demonstrations reflected a diverse constituency of individuals and organizations in support of undocumented immigrants' presence in the country. Among the demonstrators were members and representatives of Christian faith-based organizations. Crowds of demonstrators marched behind church banners carrying rosaries, crosses, and portraits of Our Lady of Guadalupe, a Mexican Catholic ethno-religious portrayal of Jesus Christ's mother, Mary. Christian leaders, including Catholic priests and Protestant ministers, gave speeches calling for U.S. politicians to "welcome the stranger," halt the deportation of undocumented families, and enact fair and humane immigration legislation. The prevalence of Christian imagery, coupled with religiously imbued claims during the pro–immigrant rights public demonstrations in 2006, suggested that the matter of undocumented immigration is not only a political issue, but a deeply religious one as well.

This chapter examines how pro-immigrant advocates used religious culture to justify undocumented immigrants' inclusion and encourage civic activism of a politically marginalized group in the United States.

Drawing on public documents and participant observations of pro-immigrant public demonstrations in a major metropolitan area[1] that I will call "Midwest City" between 2006 and 2011, I explore how undocumented immigrant advocates—individuals as well as secular and faith-based organizations—deployed religious culture to construct narratives that framed undocumented immigrants as deserving citizens and, at the same time, encouraged their civic participation in the United States. I found that pro-immigrant advocates drew upon religious culture to rearticulate the meaning of socio-political belonging and advance a progressive form of citizenship, and specifically, a model of substantive citizenship. Substantive citizenship refers to a form of belonging where societal membership is predicated on civic inclusion and activism, rather than a formal citizenship status recognized by the state. It entails acting as a citizen, being seen as one, and ultimately, investing in the host society (Staeheli 1999). In constructing and projecting a narrative of substantive citizenship, advocates used religious culture to justify undocumented immigrants' presence in the United States. Thus, religion provided a cultural toolkit (Swidler 1986), which pro-immigrant advocates drew upon to construct claims justifying undocumented immigrants' presence in the country and, at the same time, to cultivate civic activism. Religious culture—in the form of religious beliefs, biblical stories, and narratives—provided the resources for pro-immigrant advocates to construct moralistic arguments to legitimize claims supporting undocumented immigrants' societal membership and encourage their civic engagement, despite their occupying a politically marginalized status.

Substantive Citizenship and Religious Culture

Substantive citizenship refers to a type of socio-political belonging indicative of civic engagement and activism that promotes and reflects a claim or stake within a broader social system (Staeheli 1999; McEwan 2001; Davis, Martinez, and Warner 2010; Nakano Glenn 2011). According to Staeheli, substantive citizenship differs from formal citizenship whereby citizens are "entitled to certain rights and . . . expected to fulfill certain responsibilities" (63). For instance, democratic nation-states grant (in theory) formal citizens the right to vote and entitlement to government benefits. Formal citizens are also expected to participate in the nation-state through actions such as military service or paying taxes. Substantive citizenship, on the other hand, refers "to the ability to act as a citizen and to be respected as one" and it "is affected by much more than a set of legal conditions or characteristics" (64). Thus, formal citizenship is an *ascribed* status, assigned by the nation-state. Substantive citizenship is an *achieved* status, enacted by the individual. However, they are not mutually exclusive. Certainly, a formal citizen can "act" as a citizen by voting, paying taxes, and enrolling in the military. Alternatively, non-citizens can be civically engaged and politically active despite lacking full formal citizen rights. Still, the main distinction remains: nation-states do not extend to non-citizens the same legal rights, nor have the same expectations of them, as they do of citizens.

The concept of substantive citizenship is useful for reconsidering traditional ideas of belonging, whereby membership is fixed and static. Nakano Glenn (2011) posits that the concept of substantive citizenship provides a holistic understanding of societal membership. For instance, despite formal and informal barriers to fair and equal political participation, women and racial minorities in the United States contested social and institutionalized discrimination through collectively mobilizing, participating in public demonstrations, and petitioning the government to obtain the rights entitled to all formal citizens. Thus, despite occupying a politically marginalized status, these groups laid claims to the rights of formal citizens by embodying the characteristics of democratic citizenry.

However, claims to fair and equal participation in the United States do not solely emanate from political beliefs, but religious ones as well. Beliefs in the U.S. about the rights of the individual have their roots in Protestant Christianity, giving rise to ideas about religious liberty and political autonomy that have shaped the country's domestic and foreign policy. Influential Protestant Christians (both clergy leaders and politicians) have often conveyed these beliefs to U.S. leaders and the general public, reminding the nation it will be held accountable for transgressions against God's laws and followers. For example, as Gutterman (2006) shows, civil rights leaders, such as Martin Luther King Jr., drew on the Exodus story to link Jews' struggles for freedom to African-Americans' fight against racial oppression during the U.S. civil rights movement of the 1950s and 1960s. In this way, the Black Church and black religious leaders spent their moral authority to combat institution- alized racism, acknowledge the plight of African Americans, and legiti- mize progressive social change. Hence, the Black Church, as one of the central institutions in African American life and a key mobilizing agent in the U.S. civil rights movement, provided the religio-cultural resources for activists to draw upon and legitimate claims of socio-political inclu- sion and facilitate collective mobilization (Morris 1986).

Policy makers, although not deaf to influential religious leaders' mes- sages or immune to an influential Christian electorate, must often contend with translating religiously inspired initiatives into government policies palpable to a secular democratic society. As Braunstein (2012) found, this matter was not lost on liberal religious advocates in supporting pro- gressive types of policies. She finds that these advocates often engaged in religious storytelling, drawing on a repertoire of religious narratives and linking them to general issues of morality. In doing so, they used religious storytelling to appeal and reframe faith-based social movement claims in a way that was more palpable to policy makers and a broader U.S. secular public.

Similarly, Wood (1999) has argued that religious institutions are "generators of religious culture" (307) and can offer cultural resources that give rise to social action. Yet there has been relatively little analy- sis of how social movement actors strategically employ religious culture to promote social and political action among *non-citizens*. Part of this omission is due in large part to a focus on how those minorities (women and people of color) who *already hold* U.S. citizenship collectively or- ganize to secure the social and political rights that the U.S. Constitu- tion grants to formal citizens. Essentially, individuals of marginalized groups who hold formal citizenship in a democratic nation-state may, in theory, legally justify why they should have full political rights while non-citizens cannot. This poses a unique problem for understand- ing how liberal religious advocates encourage politically marginalized groups such as undocumented immigrants to engage in their own ad- vocacy. Undocumented immigrants may be resistant to participate in social movement actions in public (demonstrations) and private (let- ter writing campaigns) arenas because doing so may have significant consequences as it may increase the risk of detection by political authorities and chances of detention and deportation. Following this, we may ask how pro-immigrant social movement groups draw on religious culture to motivate individuals to align with the broader aims of the pro-immigration movement.

In the remainder of this chapter, I examine how faith-based advocates of undocumented immigrants draw on religion to facilitate social-political belonging of non-citizens, and advance a model of substantive citizenship. In the first section, I describe how advocates integrate religious culture into public demonstrations to lay claims of undocumented immigrant worthiness of belonging. These public demonstrations occurred at weekly vigils at an immigrant detention center and at an annual religious street procession. In the second section, I explore how advocates employ religious culture to encourage undocumented immigrant civic participation. Specifically, I detail how pro-immigrant organizations employed religious elements to encourage undocumented immigrants to complete the 2010 U.S. Census enumeration. I argue that religious culture provided the resources to pro-immigrant advocates to construct a progressive conceptualization of belonging that legitimizes social inclusion and encourages civic activism for a politically marginalized group.

"All Are Welcome in This Place": Public Demonstrations and Religious Culture in Creating the Legitimate Citizen

On a cold December day at 6:30 in the morning, I jumped into a white cargo van at the entrance of Our Lady of Pompeii Catholic Church in Midwest City. The van and the other passengers—one male Italian immigrant, two priests (one Italian and one Latino), and six teen-aged Latinas—were headed to the Metropolitan Detention Center (MDC), an undocumented immigrant holding and processing center located two miles away. We arrived at the MDC within ten minutes to a crowd of nearly 100 people. Most of those in attendance were Latinos. Non-Latinos in the crowd included white clergy leaders, nuns, and pro-immigrant activists as well as an African Catholic priest and an Indian woman.[2] Over the next half hour, the number of attendees grew as vans from Catholic and Protestant religious congregations dropped off passengers, adding to the number of bystanders holding candles, rosaries, and yellow pamphlets with the words to songs. Two Latino men, one holding a nearly three-foot-high wooden cross flanked with rosaries and the other carrying an equally sized portrait Our Lady of Guadalupe, stood at the front of the MDC entrance.

On this Friday, as they have done every Friday morning at 7:15 a.m. since 2007, pro-immigrant activists gathered in front of the MDC to hold prayer vigils, sing songs, and give speeches protesting the arrest, detainment, and deportation of undocumented immigrants held inside the building. The gathering is a public demonstration against what advocates see as cruel and unjust treatment of undocumented immigrants who sit in the MDC's jail cells. The MDC, operated by the U.S. Immigration and Customs Enforcement (ICE), serves as a temporary detention and processing center for undocumented immigrants arrested by law officials. Here detainees are held, with little or no interaction with family or friends on the outside, until they are processed and transported to an airplane bound for their country of origin.

The weekly demonstrations at the MDC are both a political and spiritual act. The most visible and consistent attendees were members of religious organizations, in particular, a group of Catholic nuns. Sister Patricia McNally and Mary Perry spearheaded the weekly demonstration two years prior. They come every Friday morning—the day that detainees are transported out of the center—to denounce what they see as inhumane policies and practices. Though demonstrators are of different backgrounds, the weekly event operates as a religious, and distinctively Catholic, vigil. Traditional Catholic prayers and recitations are said in unison: the Rosary, the Our Father, the Apostles' Creed, and *Gloria Patri*. The next hour consists of speeches and prayers. Father Lorenzo, head pastor and priest at Our Lady of Pompeii, works as the master of ceremonies this day, passing the microphone to participants and (mostly) religious leaders who also denounce the detention and deportation of those inside. In between speeches, clergy and non-clergy lead the crowds in prayers. Between prayers they sing songs from pieces of paper, distributed by religious organizers. Lyrics for each song are printed in English and Spanish to accommodate the majority of participants. The only exception is one song entitled "All Are Welcome," written in English.

Let us build a house where hands will reach
Beyond the wood and stone
To heal and strengthen, serve and teach
And live the Word they've known.
Here the outcast and the stranger bear the image of God's face;
Let us bring an end to fear and danger:
All are welcome,
All are welcome,
All are welcome in this place.

The weekly MDC pro-immigrant vigils reveal how social movement actors use religious culture to contest what they see as harsh and unjust actions committed against undocumented immigrants. They do so by strategically adapting and integrating religious culture in the form of imagery, prayers, religious narratives, and songs to project a political claim that undocumented immigrants in the U.S. are worthy of full membership in the nation-state. In doing so, pro–immigrant rights demonstrators at the MDC constructed a counter-narrative that repositioned undocumented immigrants as welcomed and worthy of the rights afforded to formal citizens. Along with song, the MDC demonstration was filled with religiously infused speeches. Whereas the dominant anti-immigrant narratives frame MDC detainees as "criminals" or "illegal aliens," speeches at the demonstration discussed the severance of families, and specifically, those of the detainees and their U.S.-born children who are often left in the U.S. without a parent. Likewise, religiously infused performances were aimed at constructing an image of detainees (as well as undocumented immigrants as whole) as worthy members of society who embody the characteristics of model citizens.

In this way, religious culture and organizations provide the sources through which socially and politically marginalized groups (citizens and non-citizens) substantiate their struggles. In essence, religion provides the cultural schemas to justify, legitimize, and substantiate claims of citizenship (Wood 1999). Aldon Morris's (1986) examination of African American mobilization during the U.S. civil rights movement identifies how the Black Church connected the plight of black Americans with religious meaning. Morris writes:

The black church supplied the civil rights movement with a collective enthusiasm generated through a rich culture consisting of songs, testimonies, oratory, and prayers that spoke directly to the needs of an oppressed group. Many black churches preached that oppression is sinful and that God sanctions protest aimed at eradicating social evils. (4)

Though the Black Church and civil rights activists did not need to contend with issues of formal citizenship as the majority of its constituents were already citizens, black religious leaders and lay members drew on religious themes to contest African Americans' second-class citizenship status. Similarly, demonstrators at the MDC drew on religious songs to convey the claim that undocumented immigrants awaiting deportation inside the building were unjustly detained and that the "outcast" and the "stranger" were "welcome." As Powell (2011) writes, "Once members of a group adopt a frame, their narratives become shaped by the frame in such a way that propels and legitimates the movement" (456). However, demonstrators were singing not just to comfort those detained on the inside (the song was sung in English, which not all detainees may speak) but to also counteract anti-immigrant sentiment and discourse in the United States. Hence, the MDC organizers drew on a performance piece imbued with Christian imagery, which sought to legitimize the undocumented immigrants' presence and the broader aims of the movement.

Public demonstrations, like the weekly vigil at the MDC, are both religious and political acts. Pro-immigrant activists contest what they see as morally wrong and call for political action to remedy what they see as harsh anti-immigrant measures. For this reason it is imperative that social movement actors get their message out to the broader U.S. public. One way that pro-immigrant activists raise awareness is through public demonstrations across spaces. In the spring of 2006, undocumented immigrant activists and organizations participated in mass-scale demonstrations throughout U.S. cities. In the form of rallies and parades, activists and organizations voiced their dissent over anti-immigration laws. The largest of them occurred in metropolitan areas, including Los Angeles, Chicago, and Dallas (Fox, Selee, and Bada 2006). National media took notice of the hundreds of thousands of pro-immigrant activists who marched down city streets calling for fair, humane, and comprehensive immigration reform. These public demonstrations showed the power that undocumented immigrants yielded and, perhaps more pragmatically, the power of supporters who held formal citizenship.

A great number of the participants in these demonstrations were members of religious organizations. Reflected in the mass coordination of faith-based organizations and numerous depictions of religious symbols, pro-immigrant activists and organizations repeatedly drew upon and deployed religious culture to legitimize undocumented immigrants' journey to the United States in search of a better life for themselves and their families. Though public mass demonstrations have dwindled, faith-based organizations continue to mobilize for pro-immigrant legislation. One way that these organizations do so is by linking religious cultural traditions to social movement aims. Many Catholic churches in the United States and beyond coordinate annual religious processions to celebrate the lives of saints, religious stories, and church anniversaries. Though religious processions occur in many different types of localities, they are often associated with areas that have a distinctive and sizeable ethnic community. For instance, Italians in New York City's East Harlem coordinate a yearly procession that marks the religious celebration of Our Lady of Mount Carmel Catholic Church. The annual festival and procession serves as a symbol of Italian Catholics' deep spiritual devotion to the patroness and their connection to the neighborhood, particularly in light of non-white racial succession. In this sense, religious processions are about not only religious identity but reaffirming social identities as well (Orsi 1985; Sciorra 1999).

However, while Italian Harlem's procession serves as a link between ethno-religious identity and place, many Catholic churches include performances that dramatize the social plight of the disadvantaged in their religious processions. For those with a large Mexican immigrant population, procession organizers (both clergy and laity) actively connect religious themes with the political struggles of undocumented immigrants. For instance, Chicago's Via Crucis, or Good Friday, procession, a public reenactment of the events leading up to Jesus Christ's crucifixion, is organized and jointly coordinated by Mexican parishes and often incorporates contemporary themes regarding the plight of undocumented immigrants. In Midwest City, pro-immigrant activists, many of whom are members of faith-based organizations, help coordinate the Posada, a Mexican Catholic religious tradition that reenacts the journey of Jesus

Christ's parents, Joseph and Mary, from Nazareth to Bethlehem. The re-enactment is a nine-day event that begins on December 16 and ends on Christmas Eve. The centerpiece of the event is a procession that reenacts the biblical story of Joseph and Mary's migration, with the roles often played by children and young adults. Along the way, Christ's parents-to-be, who are followed by a contingent of marchers, stop and seek shelter at designated spots (symbolic of the inns and barns in the biblical story) but are turned away. Finally, on December 24, both migrants are granted shelter in a "barn" where Christ is born.

Both secular and faith-based pro-immigrant organizations in my observations saw the Posadas as a way to create awareness of the undocumented immigrant struggle. Though Posadas reenactments generally occur within the surrounding vicinity of the churches organizing them, this year Our Lady of Pompeii's Posadas was strategically coordinated to begin at the MDC and end at the church two miles away. This year's actors consisted of ten Latino youth, between the ages of 15 and 24, who wore traditional biblical-era costumes and led the crowd of the Posadas observers from the MDC back to Our Lady of Pompeii Church. An orange mesh fence surrounded them, differentiating actors from observers. This procession, though a reenactment of a biblical story, is fraught with real dangers. Our journey back to the church was during morning rush hour and on busy major streets. However, local police departments stationed squad cars in front of and behind the marchers to alert passing motorists and guide procession participants. Additionally, some (including myself) wore neon green jackets and monitored the procession to ensure that participants did not wander beyond the right-hand lane into adjacent traffic.

The focal pieces of the Posadas that day were three stops that symbolized the migration of Christ's parents from Nazareth to Bethlehem. At each stop, Mary and Joseph pled with innkeepers to give them shelter. They were turned away at the first two, but given room and board at the third. Though traditionally a religious event and a marker leading up to Christmas, the Posadas integrated contemporary and relevant themes directly related to the challenges that undocumented Mexican immigrants encounter. The procession was coordinated to symbolize the undocumented immigrant experience and the hostile receptions they often receive in the United States. The procession stopped at three pre-planned areas: (1) outside a factory; (2) along a set of train tracks; and (3) in front of the church. At each stop, the orange fence was un-furled around Mary and Joseph and their robed followers, followed by readings and prayers (in English and Spanish) by three people. The first reader began with "*Mi alma os doy con ellos mi corazón también*" ("My soul I give them my heart also") and identified the significance of each stop as it relates to the undocumented experience. The factory signified undocumented immigrant labor, work ethic, and investment in a new land; the train tracks were symbolic of the dangerous journey across the U.S.-Mexico border; and the church represented the aspirations un-documented immigrants have for their families in the United States. The second and third readers followed, describing the political and social challenges that undocumented immigrants encounter.

Through their melding of religious and political languages and sym-bols, the Posadas procession functioned as a public demonstration that intertwined a religious narrative with progressive political activism. As Ashley (1999), drawing on Davis (1986), writes: "dramatic represen-tations, parades, and public ceremonies are political acts. People use these public displays as tools for building, maintaining, and confronting power relations" (342). Though the Posadas was initially a traditional Mexican Catholic religious event, those who organized the procession from the MDC to the church incorporated explicitly political overtones. The narrative neatly overlapped with the challenges that undocumented Mexican immigrants encountered in light of the absence of progres-sive immigration policy. Both the readers and the pre-staged responses from marchers acknowledged and conveyed the hardships that undocu-mented immigrants face. In doing so, they worked to legitimize the rea-sons for undocumented immigrants' decision to migrate while making claims to justify their presence.

Moreover, the presence of pro-immigrant social movement orga-nizations and respected religious leaders who coordinated with local law officials to stage the public demonstration sanctioned the event as a safe one for undocumented immigrants to participate in. The crowd included both documented and undocumented immigrants as well their U.S. citizen allies. Among those who were undocumented was Jaime, who played the role of Joseph. Born in Mexico, Jaime came to the United States with his parents as a young child, and recently became active in pro-immigrant issues though a community organization based at Our Lady of Pompeii in Midwest City. He was joined by a contingent of other marchers—citizens and immigrants, both undocumented and documented—and a group of white marchers from a local religious congregation. Through the representation of the holy family as undocumented immigrants, the Posada was reconfigured in a way to legitimize undocumented immigrant struggles and social actions. According to Nagel (1994), "Cultural claims, icons, and imagery are used by activists in the mobilization process; cultural symbols and meanings are also produced and transformed as ethnic movements emerge and grow" (165). In this way, religious processions such as the Posadas provided a unique opportunity for social movement actors (documented and undocumented) to integrate religious culture to combat anti-immigrant measures and rhetoric while encouraging public civic activism.

By linking Joseph and Mary's migration to undocumented Mexican immigrants' journey and settlement in the United States, activists (citizens, documented immigrants, and undocumented immigrants) sought to legitimize their struggles. "Belonging" involves much more than a drive to leave one's birth country—it also means a willingness to contribute and invest in a new one. Writing about civic integration, Peter Skerry (2004) notes that faith-based organizations aim to address the immediate material needs of undocumented immigrants while facilitating their long-term investment in the communities in which they live. For these organizations, civic integration, he writes, "holds the promise of addressing immigrants' material needs and self-interest, while also taking into account their broader responsibilities to the political community, even if they are not citizens" (29).

As I have shown in this section, pro-immigrant activists strategically integrated religious culture into public demonstrations at the MDC vigils and the Posada procession. Their aim was to construct a narrative to legitimize undocumented immigrants' journey to the U.S. as well as to highlight their social and material investments in and social contributions to the country. To achieve this end, they linked shared moral interpretations of religious stories to secular ideas of citizenship. In doing so, they advanced a model of substantive citizenship that suggested it is a moral imperative that undocumented immigrants be seen as model members of society and worthy of belonging. Still, situating undocumented immigrants as ideal citizens worthy of belonging does little to support these claims if they do not act as substantive citizens. In the following section I describe how advocates drew on religious culture to encourage undocumented immigrants' participation in the U.S. Census.

"Make Yourself Count": Religious Culture and Undocumented Immigrant Civic Participation in the U.S. Census

Substantive citizenship requires more than rearticulating ideals of belonging in order to counter anti-immigrant policies, narratives, and notions of formal political rights. It also entails *acting* as a citizen through civic engagement. Yet barriers to immigrant civic participation remain a concern for pro-immigrant activists. One concern revolves around the lack of Latino immigrant participation in the U.S. Census, which results in undercounting the population. Government officials and analysts use census data to make policy decisions regarding the distribution of resources and the drawing of political district boundaries. Those who do not participate in the U.S. Census run the risk of losing community resources and political representation. This is particularly a concern for social service organizations and representatives of Latino immigrant communities who fear their constituents will not participate in the census. Due to either a lack of knowledge or fear, many undocumented immigrants may be reluctant to provide personal household and financial information. Still, pro–immigrant rights activists implored all Latinos to participate in the census. As one Latino pro-immigrant advocate relayed, "We have to go back to everybody and say, 'Just as you marched, just as you naturalized, just as you voted, now you have to be counted'" (Preston 2009).

The U.S. Census has, additionally, adopted social and technological advances to enhance its ability to reach out and accurately count various populations in a diversifying society. In 2000, the U.S. Census distributed census forms in 17 different languages (Elliot 2010). In 2010, the number increased to 28. Along with these changes, there has been a shift in strategy to target particular racial and ethnic minority groups, especially Latino immigrants. As the second largest ethno-racial group, there is much at stake for Latino immigrant communities. Hence, the U.S. Census has focused on ways to encourage immigrants—documented and undocumented—to fill out the census. One way has been to high-light the importance of completing it. As one Latina marketing executive who consulted with the U.S. Census to increase Latinos' participation said, "it's critical people [Latinos] participate because this will bring our children a better future" (Elliott 2010). Rather than conveying participation in the U.S. Census as a *civic* duty, Latino immigrant advocates often sought alternative ways to frame why it was important to be counted, particularly by linking participation to family well-being.

Still, these appeals may hold relatively little sway over many immigrants, both documented and undocumented, who are reluctant to provide any personal information to government organizations. The message to participate must be legitimized through a credible source to reassure that it is safe to do so. For many immigrants, religion and religious organizations are that source. One example is the initiatives of Latino political organizations who frame civic participation in religious terms, such as the National Association of Latino Elected Officials (NALEO), who, in 2009, constructed and distributed a Christian religious–themed poster encouraging people to participate in the census. The blue-and-white poster depicted the journey of Joseph and Mary from Nazareth to Bethlehem. The top of the poster read, "THIS IS HOW JESUS WAS BORN" and "JOSEPH AND MARY PARTICIPATED IN THE CENSUS." Toward the bottom, it implored readers to "Participate in the Census in March 2010" and "Make yourself count," along with the words the angel Gabriel spoke to Mary, "DON'T BE AFRAID."

Distributed widely across both secular and faith-based organizations, the NALEO poster intentionally used a Christian biblical story to encourage and legitimize participation in the census. Though aimed at encouraging the participation of Christians of different ethnic backgrounds (the poster was distributed in English, Spanish, and Polish), it was specifically directed toward undocumented immigrants. Despite some Latino religious leaders being openly critical of the conflation of religion and secular politics, many congregations were supportive of the initiative.[3] The poster was reportedly going to be displayed in over 7,000 Evangelical churches. Reverend Samuel Rodriguez Jr., an Evangelical pastor and president of the National Hispanic Christian Leadership Conference, commented on the importance of Latino immigrant civic participation, saying, "I believe we pastors have a moral responsibility to educate our flock in an action that will help our communities move forward on the path of political empowerment" (Preston 2009).

Christian biblical narratives have long been used to justify the collective mobilization of groups (Morris 1986; Gutterman 2006). During the U.S. civil rights movement, Black Church leaders drew upon numerous biblical stories to encourage their congregation toward civic participation and activism. Perhaps the most cited example is the story of the Jews' migration from Egypt to Israel, found in the biblical books of Exodus and Deuteronomy. In the story, the Israelites, who were enslaved by Egypt's pharaohs, were led by Moses to Israel, or the "Promised Land." The most noted incorporation of the story was in Martin Luther King's speech "I've Been to the Mountaintop," delivered at a religious gathering in Memphis, Tennessee, on April 3, 1968, one day before his assassination:

> We've got some difficult days ahead. But it doesn't really matter with me now. Because I've been to the mountaintop. I don't mind. Like anybody, I would like to live—a long life; longevity has its place. But I'm not concerned about that now. I just want to do God's will. And He's allowed me to go up to the mountain. And I've looked over. And I've seen the Promised Land. I may not get there with you. But I want you to know tonight, that we, as a people, will get to the Promised Land. So I'm happy, tonight. I'm not worried about anything. I'm not fearing any man. Mine eyes have seen the glory of the coming of the Lord![4]

In acknowledging the "difficult days ahead" and the possibility that he "may not get there," King called upon pro–civil rights activists to march ahead. Similar messages to combat black racial oppression were echoed in many southern black churches during the civil rights movement. As Aldon Morris (1986) writes:

> For the first half of the twentieth century most black churches taught that the meek would inherit the earth; that God would judge the oppressor according to his wicked deeds; that God loved the dispossessed and would provide them with just rewards after they long Christian fight; and that a good Christian was more concerned with perfecting his or her spiritual life rather than material wellbeing. These messages were

expressed through elaborate and eloquent rituals, songs, prayers, and sermons. It was a religion of containment, the opiate of the masses, a religion that soothed the pains and of economic, political and social exploitation. (97)

Hence, biblical narratives—and in many cases migratory stories—were strategically used and aimed to inspire and promote political activism despite the consequences. Like African Americans were and continue to be, undocumented immigrants are marginalized within U.S. society. As non-citizens, they are ineligible to vote in U.S. elections and are further constrained from publically voicing their concerns due to fears of deportation. Yet, participating in the 2010 U.S. Census did not require participants to hold formal citizenship.

Still, despite calls for undocumented immigrants to participate in the census, many may be reluctant to do so. Undocumented immigrants may be wary of answering the doors to census takers because they may be seen as immigration officials. Thus, posters telling undocumented immigrants "DON'T BE AFRAID" may offer little assurance against real dangers of deportation. This was illuminated during the monthly Neighborhood United (NU) meetings held at Our Lady of Pompeii. Formed in 2005, NU was a coalition of volunteers from over 40 community-based organizations. It consisted of community members and representatives from area schools, churches, and local governments. The mission of NU was to streamline services and resources in the areas of social services, education, youth outreach, parental participation, and immigration. The organization was co-chaired by Father Lorenzo and Victoria Salas, a second-generation Mexican American woman who was employed by a state social service agency.

The church served as a broker between NU members, agencies, organizations, and undocumented Mexican immigrants in the area. Beyond providing a meeting space and connecting religious and secular organizations, it became a hub for social service organizations and pro-immigrant groups to exchange information and create joint initiatives. This became clear during one NU meeting in early 2010 where various members discussed the logistics of counting undocumented immigrants in the census. Questions revolved around issues of numerical accuracy ("Do babies count?"), census workers' backgrounds ("What are the racial backgrounds of the census door knockers?"), and confidentiality ("Does the Patriot Act change confidentiality?"). The exchange of information, including many questions that members were asked by their undocumented clients, was important to clarify and confirm matters of the enumeration in order to maximize responses. However, to do so meant getting the word out. On this matter, Our Lady of Pompeii served a central purpose in two ways. First, the church provided a space for community organizations to operate and access a large population of undocumented immigrants. One such group was the Metropolitan Action Project (MAP), whose aim was to improve the quality of life of the predominantly Latino families in the surrounding area. Members consisted of mostly Latino youth and young adults, some of whom who were undocumented. Along with working to improve the quality of life of Latino residents, MAP collaborated with other pro–immigrant rights organizations on initiatives, demonstrations, and political lobbying. For instance, members often coordinated pro-immigrant events and initiatives at meetings at Our Lady of Pompeii. The group also coordinated trips to Washington, D.C., to lobby elected officials for progressive immigration reform. Second, the church provided an opportunity for pro–immigrant rights organizations to access a large contingent of undocumented immigrants. In late 2009, in anticipation of the upcoming U.S. Census, MAP members disseminated information in the form of announcements and materials regarding the logistics of enumeration. In addition, members also conducted door-knocking campaigns to inform residents about the importance of participating in the census. This was done in the hopes of improving participation, but also to quell residents' fears about providing personal household information and the threat of detainment and deportation. Hence, Our Lady of Pompeii served as a hub from which pro-immigrant right SMOs could organize, collaborate, and disseminate information to undocumented immigrants.

Conclusion

The ratification of H.R. 4437 by the House of Representatives in December 2005 unleashed a mass-scale response by undocumented immigrant advocates. Central to the mass mobilization and public demonstrations were the joint coordination efforts of activists who contested the criminalization of immigrants and those who knowingly aided them. The response led to the death of H.R. 4437 in the Senate and prompted elected leaders to reconsider their positions on immigration and seek out alternative policies aimed at including undocumented immigrants in the fabric of U.S. social life, rather than excluding them from it. Though mass demonstrations have dwindled, pro-immigrant advocates and organizations remain persistent in contesting anti-immigrant policy while continually working to integrate undocumented immigrants by reframing them as model and worthy members of U.S. society and encouraging civic participation. As this chapter has shown, pro-immigrant activists strategically drew on religious culture to rearticulate the meaning of belonging to the public as well as to encourage undocumented immigrants' civic participation and activism. Religious culture, in the form of music, ethno-religious traditions, and biblical narratives provided the resources for advocates to advance a progressive conceptualization of socio-political belonging aligned with the idea of substantive citizenship. Doing so, they advance a progressive model of citizenship that challenges dominant conceptualizations of societal membership, rearticulate meanings of belonging, and work toward a larger goal of undocumented immigrant inclusion in the United States.

ACKNOWLEDGMENTS

The author would like to thank Todd N. Fuist, Stephen P. Davis, R. Stephen Warner, and Rhys H. Williams for their comments on previous versions of this paper.

NOTES

1 With the exception of publicly available information from documents (newspapers, national organizations, and fliers), all information about people, places, and local organizations has been changed.

2 I did not know her religious affiliation or whether she was a religious leader.

3 Not all Latino Christian religious organizations supported the NALEO poster. The National Coalition of Latino Clergy and Christian Leaders saw it as blasphemous (Elliot 2010).

4 Martin Luther King Jr., "I've Been to the Mountaintop," April 3, 1968, *American Rhetoric*, www.americanrhetoric.com.

REFERENCES

Ashley, Wayne. 1999. "The Stations of the Cross: Christ, Politics, and Processions on New York City's Lower East Side." In *Gods of the City: Religion and the American Urban Landscape*, edited by Robert A. Orsi, 34–66. Bloomington: Indiana University Press.

Braunstein, Ruth. 2012. "Storytelling in Liberal Religious Advocacy." *Journal for the Scientific Study of Religion* 51(1): 110–127.

Davis, Stephen P., Juan R. Martinez, and R. Stephen Warner. 2010. "The Role of the Catholic Church in the Chicago Immigrant Mobilization." In *¡Marcha!: Latino Chicago and the Immigrant Rights Movement*, edited by Amalia Pallares and Nilda Flores-Gonzalez, 79–96. Urbana: University of Illinois Press.

Davis, Susan G. 1986. *Parades and Power: Street Theatre in Nineteenth-Century Philadelphia*. Philadelphia: Temple University Press.

Elliott, Stuart. 2010. "A Census Campaign That Speaks in Many Tongues." *New York Times*, January 14.

Fox, Jonathan, Andrew Selee, and Xóchitl Bada. 2006. "Conclusions." In *Invisible No More: Mexican Migrant Civic Participation in the United States*, edited by Xóchitl Bada, Jonathan Fox, and Andrew D. Sellee, 35–40. Washington, DC: Woodrow Wilson International Center for Scholars.

Gutterman, David S. 2006. *Prophetic Politics: Christian Social Movements and American Democracy*. Ithaca, NY: Cornell University Press.

McEwan, Cheryl. 2001. "Gender and Citizenship: Learning from South Africa?" *Agenda* 16(47): 47–59.

Morris, Aldon D. 1986. *The Origins of the Civil Rights Movement*. New York: Free Press.

Nagel, Joane. 1994. "Constructing Ethnicity: Creating and Recreating Ethnic Identity and Culture." *Social Problems* 41(1): 152–176.

Nakano Glenn, Evelyn. 2011. "Constructing Citizenship: Exclusion, Subordination, and Resistance." *American Sociological Review* 76(1): 1–24.

Orsi, Robert A. 1985. *The Madonna of 115th Street: Faith and Community in Italian Harlem, 1880–1950*. New Haven, CT: Yale University Press.

Powell, Rachel. 2011. "Frames and Narratives as Tools for Recruiting and Sustaining Group Members: The Soulforce Equality Ride as a Social Movement Organization." *Sociological Inquiry* 81(4): 454–476.

Preston, Julia. 2009. "Latino Leaders Use Churches in Census Bid." *New York Times*, December 23.

Sciorra, Joseph. 1999. "'We Go Where the Italians Live': Religious Processions as Ethnic and Territorial Markers in a Multi-Ethnic Brooklyn Neighborhood." In *Gods of the City: Religion and the American Urban Landscape,* edited by Robert A. Orsi, 310–340. Bloomington: Indiana University Press.

Skerry, Peter. 2004. "Citizenship Begins at Home: A New Approach to the Civic Integration of Immigrants." *Responsive Community* 14(1): 26–37.

Staeheli, Lynn A. 1999. "Globalization and the Scales of Citizenship." *Geography Research Forum* 19: 60–77.

Swidler, Ann. 1986. "Culture in Action: Symbols and Strategies." *American Sociological Review* 51(2): 273–286.

Wood, Richard L. 1999. "Religious Culture and Political Action." *Sociological Theory* 17(3): 307–332.

10

Progressive Activism among Buddhists, Hindus, and Muslims in the U.S.

GRACE YUKICH

On January 13, 2013, over 200 people gathered in a small city in the Northeast to celebrate the life and legacy of Dr. Martin Luther King, Jr. While people around the U.S. frequently commemorate Dr. King at this time of year, this particular celebration stood out for the diversity of those present: not just their racial diversity but their religious diversity as well. Protestants, Catholics, and Jews joined with Hindus, Buddhists, Muslims, Sikhs, Jains, and Baha'is to affirm their hard-won civil rights, to call for continued activism, and to share their religious traditions with one another. After singing "We Shall Overcome" and listening to excerpts of Jesus's Sermon on the Mount, a Hindu American woman performed Bharatanatyam, a classical Indian dance, and a Buddhist woman guided the crowd in contemplative meditation. While interfaith gatherings like this one have become more common in the U.S., many groups—especially ones focusing on community engagement and activism—lack the diversity represented in this gathering. Most primarily include Christian and Jewish activists and perhaps an occasional Muslim, while members of other religious traditions are rare in such coalitions (Wood, Fulton, and Partridge 2012).

Does this mean that members of these religious traditions are less likely to be involved in working for social change, or that they are just less likely to be involved in this specific type of activism, the kind that has typically been recognized by scholars? Partly because of its focus on congregation-based organizing, both in "interfaith" community organizations and larger-scale social movements, sociological research on religious activism has significant blind spots that make it difficult to answer these questions. Namely, virtually all of the sociological research on religion's role in activism in the U.S., including research on "progressive religion," has been based on activism in Christian and Jewish communities. As Bender et al. write in their recent critique of the state of the sociology of religion, "broadly shared conception[s] of American religion [are] directly linked to Protestant American theological conceptions" (2012, 5). The maxim that religious institutions remain some of the most important civic institutions for democratic life by developing congregation members' social and political capital has been based largely on national surveys that include few non-Judeo-Christian voices (Djupe and Gilbert 2006; Putnam and Campbell 2010). Likewise, research on faith-based community organizing has revealed the important roles religious organizations often play in creating social change in their communities, but the vast majority of the religious communities involved in these organizations are Christian or Jewish (Wood 2002; Lichterman 2005; Swarts 2008; Wood, Fulton, and Partridge 2012). Lastly, studies of larger-scale social movement activism have documented the role that religious groups and individuals often play in providing resources that help movements mobilize, but with few exceptions, these movements have been made up of Christians and Jews (see Morris 1984; Smith 1996; Harris 1999; Nepstad 2008; Yukich 2013). As a result, we still know very little about activism in Buddhist, Hindu, and—to a somewhat lesser extent—Muslim communities in the U.S., particularly outside of the context of interreligious events like the one depicted above.

This hole in existing knowledge is a gaping one in many respects. While the Judeo-Christian roots of the U.S. are often discussed and debated, over the past several decades, the number of Buddhists, Hindus, and Muslims in the U.S. has grown exponentially. Estimates of the number of Buddhists, Hindus, and Muslims in the U.S. range from 1.7 percent of the total population—about the same size as the Jewish population (Pew Research Center 2008)—to closer to 4 percent of the population (Pluralism Project 2013), and immigration projections indicate that their numbers will only continue to grow in coming years (Passel and Cohn 2008; Pew Research Center 2012). The increasing size of other religious groups not only challenges the idea held in some communities that the U.S. remains (or should remain) a Christian nation, it also creates a demand for a place in public life for religious traditions that some Americans see as foreign to or incongruent with American culture (Wuthnow 2005; Kurien 2007). This demand is slowly resulting in greater religious diversity among the nation's leaders: in the 2012 congressional elections, Americans elected the first Buddhist to the Senate and the first Hindu to Congress, building on the elections of two other Buddhists and of two Muslims to congressional positions during the previous five years.

Thus, current accounts of progressive religious activism run into two problems. First, existing definitions of progressive religion often ignore non-Judeo-Christian traditions and are therefore too restrictive. Second, partly as a result of this, existing definitions of what counts as religious activism are too restrictive as well. By neglecting these religious communities in sociological research on activism, we are missing an increasingly important piece of the American religious-political landscape and potentially misunderstanding what "progressive religion" actually looks like in the U.S. today.

Instead, in order to understand how religion shapes activism in today's world, including progressive religious activism more specifically, it is essential that scholars do at least four things, which I will discuss in more detail below. First, we must pay more attention to religious traditions other than Christianity and Judaism, especially since differences in religious traditions' beliefs, practices, organizational forms, and relationship to U.S. society suggest that they might have very different kinds of relationships to activism. In particular, sociology's growing emphasis on congregation-based community organizing, while interesting, is limiting due to the dearth of Buddhists, Hindus, and Muslims in these organizations.

Second, since congregations play a less central role in these religious traditions than in Christianity and Judaism—especially Protestantism—we must look beyond congregations and congregation-based organizing to observe and explain Buddhist, Hindu, and Muslim activism in the United States. Third, we must look for "religious activism" in places that may be less public or less collective than in the past, since Buddhist, Hindu, and Muslim activism may take less public and collective forms for a variety of theological and organizational reasons. Finally, we should look for activism with targets that are not necessarily political, since new religious groups may be especially concerned about the structure and legitimacy of their own religious institutions.

In sum, in articulating an agenda for research on progressive religious activism in the U.S., we need to pay special attention to groups on the margins, perhaps especially because progressive groups themselves are more likely to hold values and goals related to pluralism and ecumenical cooperation (Safi 2003).

What Do We Mean by Progressive Religion?

This volume is focused on a category of religiosity we are calling "progressive religion," a characterization that supposedly reaches across the boundaries of specific religious traditions. But does it, in fact, do this in practice? Does the label "progressive religion" apply to followers of non-Judeo-Christian traditions like Buddhism, Hinduism, and Islam? To begin interrogating this question, we must first explore what we mean by progressive religion. Among other things, progressive religion could refer to how individuals self-identify (i.e., as a "religious progressive"); to affiliation with particular denominations, traditions, or political groups typically identified with progressivism; to a particular set of theological and/or political beliefs and attitudes deemed to be progressive; to individual or group engagement in a particular set of religious and/or political practices defined as progressive; or to a group or movement primarily defined by what it is *not* (e.g., NOT the religious Right). To incorporate these various forms of measurement, the introduction to this volume puts forward the notion of a "progressive religious field of action"—a field of intersecting individuals and organizations that is defined partly through one's self-understanding as someone with progressive values, progressive theology, a progressive identity, or who engages in progressive action, as well as in relation to other fields, such as the religious Right or secular progressivism.

According to this definition, Buddhist, Hindu, and Muslim activism could fall under the umbrella of progressive religion at least some of the time. But several important questions remain: does this actually happen in practice? How do current and historic uses of the term "progressive religion" constrain the ways in which we most often define and look for progressive religion? How might emerging forms of Buddhism, Hinduism, and Islam in the United States both fit into a progressive religious field of action and simultaneously challenge how we define and where we look for progressive religion?

Religious Diversity, the New Immigration, and Progressive Religion

In recent decades, religious diversity in the United States has increased in significant ways. While the numbers of religious minorities remain relatively small, they have grown exponentially recently. The newness of many Buddhists, Hindus, and Muslims in the U.S. has at least two important implications for their inclusion in the progressive religion umbrella. First, recent immigrants (especially first-generation immigrants) tend to have fewer connections to civic organizations in their new country, due in part to language and other cultural barriers to incorporation and assimilation (Cadge and Ecklund 2007). They are also more connected to their countries of origin than are second generation immigrants, meaning that they are more concerned about and influenced by the religious and political debates and categories in other countries than those in the U.S., at least compared with the second generation (Kurien 2013).

Second, the newness of their presence in the United States means that Christian and Jewish individuals and organizations that might see Buddhists, Hindus, and Muslims as potential partners in a progressive religious field of action often do not have the cultural and social capital they need to form genuine partnerships with followers of these traditions (Yukich 2013). For instance, a lack of knowledge about Buddhist holidays might lead faith-based organizing groups to hold meetings during times that are impossible for Buddhists to attend or a lack of familiarity with Muslim scriptural references may make it difficult for groups to frame their work in ways that will resonate with non-Judeo-Christian groups.

Further, the very category of progressive religion has Judeo-Christian and American roots, making it a foreign and unfamiliar category for many first-generation Buddhists, Hindus, and Muslims. As John Cobb, Jr. (2008), founder of the group Progressive Christians Uniting, has written, widespread use of the term "progressive religion" is relatively recent. While it was occasionally adopted to mean a variety of things in the past, its recent, more prevalent use emerged due to the need for an alternative to the growth and predominance of the religious Right in the United States. Those who did not identify with the religious Right sought a different term to describe themselves, though they had problems with the term "liberal religion" because of its association with liberal Protestantism as well as stereotypes that liberal religion simply meant watered-down religion (Cobb 2008). Instead, "progressive religion," as the term is most frequently used today by those identifying with it, has roots in the legacies of American Reform Judaism, liberal Protestantism, and liberation traditions in Catholicism, a combination that is peculiarly American, though some individual aspects of it have roots outside of the U.S.

As such, the degree to which "progressive religion" as a category or identity resonates with recent immigrants, particularly immigrants from non-Judeo-Christian traditions, is unclear (Yukich 2013). The religious players and battles are different in other nations and in other religious traditions: does "progressive religion" apply to them in the same ways that we are applying it to American, Judeo-Christian forms of activism, or must we define progressive religion differently if we want to include Buddhists, Hindus, Muslims, and other religious minorities in the progressive religious umbrella?

Moving beyond Christocentrism in Studies of Religious Activism

As discussed, despite the growth in religious diversity, accepted knowledge about how religion shapes activism in the U.S. is almost entirely based on research on Christianity and, to a much lesser degree, Judaism. But there are exceptions to this general rule that provide a foundation on which we can build. A few studies examine Hindu activism in the U.S. (Lal 1999; Rajagopal 2000; Kurien 2007). Similarly, several scholars have explored themes of "socially engaged Buddhism," though many of these have focused both on U.S. and non-U.S. contexts (Queen and King 1996; Queen 2000; Keown, Prebish, and Queen 2003; King 2009). And while most research on Muslim political engagement focuses on civic activity (e.g., Jamal 2005; Dana, Barreto, and Oskooii 2011; Pew Research Center 2011) or politics and activism in non-U.S. contexts (e.g., Meyer,

Tope, and Price 2008; Davis and Robinson 2012), a small number of studies have examined Muslim activism in the U.S. (see Leonard 2007; Hondagneu-Sotelo 2008; Ahmed 2011; Hammer 2012). However, of all of these studies, only a few connect Buddhist, Hindu, or Muslim activism in the U.S. to theories concerning the relationship between religion and activism (e.g., Stanczak 2006; Hondagneu-Sotelo 2008), and none has addressed how greater attention to these traditions might help illuminate the phenomenon of progressive religion more specifically.

This gap will not be addressed by simply conducting more research on these religious communities; indeed, there is reason to believe that many of our underlying assumptions about the relationship between religion and activism are Christocentric and require significant revision in order to adequately make sense of a wider range of cases (Kurien 2007; Levitt 2007; Bender et al. 2012). First, theory suggests that religion can be an asset in efforts to mobilize activists because of its emphasis on transcendence, divine guidance, and absolute moral codes (see Smith 1996; Harris 1999; Nepstad 2008). But these characteristics of religious belief are not common to all religious traditions, nor is the primacy of religious belief in general. As Lichterman (2012) argues, "It is easy to take for granted partly because of a Protestant-derived, American cultural tendency to understand religion as identity-pervading belief . . . [which] may capture very clumsily the religious understandings of non-Christians" (117). For instance, Buddhism has a different understanding of transcendence and divine guidance compared to Christianity and even Judaism, particularly since the notion of a personal god is not part of most Buddhist traditions (Cadge 2005; Seager 2012). This suggests that the role of religious beliefs in motivating activism—and the times and places in which people actually express these sentiments (Lichterman 2012)—may be different for followers of different religious traditions, and that current theories do not reflect that diversity.

Second, theorists have highlighted the ways in which Christianity—and to a lesser degree, Judaism—holds a special place in American history and public life, giving its leaders moral authority that legitimates their public claims. As a result, it has been argued that religion can act as a resource for activists by lending authority and legitimacy to their cause (Smith 1996; Williams 1996; Lichterman 2005; Hondagneu-Sotelo 2008; Nepstad 2008). However, this history of public moral authority is not shared by religious newcomers like Buddhists and Hindus, and prejudice against Muslims might actually make their support of a cause seem less, rather than more, legitimate in the public eye (Leonard 2007; Hondagneu-Sotelo 2008; Ahmed 2011; Haddad 2011).

Finally, the most accepted idea regarding the role of religion in activism is its propensity to provide financial and organizational resources that movements need for mobilization, such as members, social networks, funding, meeting space, and material and technological supplies (Morris 1984; Smith 1996; Harris 1999; Wood 2002; Lichterman 2005; Nepstad 2008; Swarts 2008; Yukich 2013). As preexisting organizations with regular meetings and, frequently, a formal structure, *congregations* can fill many of the most pressing needs of a growing movement (McAdam 1982; McAdam, Tarrow, and Tilly 2001).

In the U.S., Christian and Jewish communities—but especially Protestant groups—have usually taken a congregational form, encouraged by laws that provide tax breaks to religious organizations that possess these qualities (see Kurien 2007). Some research suggests that immigrant Buddhist, Hindu, and Muslim groups become more "congregational" in the U.S. context, partly in order to meet these legal regulations (Warner and Wittner 1998; Ebaugh and Chafetz 2000; Williams and Massad 2006; Kurien 2007). Even so, these traditions are not rooted in congregationalism to the same extent that Christianity and Judaism are, leading other scholars to posit that Buddhist, Hindu, and Muslim activism may be less likely to follow the congregation-based models that have become the dominant form of religious activism in Christian and Jewish communities (Joshi 2007; Kurien 2007; Levitt 2007; Hondagneu-Sotelo 2008; Min 2010; Bender et al. 2012). Even mosques, which are probably more "congregational" than Buddhist and Hindu temples, often serve primarily as sites for prayer rather than as meeting or gathering spaces (Hondagneu-Sotelo 2008).

Thus, the question emerges: how does the relationship between religion and activism differ in Buddhist, Hindu, and Muslim communities compared to Christian and Jewish communities, and how might this challenge existing understandings of how religion shapes activism in the U.S.? While a growing body of research on Buddhist, Hindu, and Muslim activism in the U.S. and its relation to progressive religion guides our inquiries, there is still much we do *not* know. We are unsure as to whether progressive religion is a meaningful category for organizing Buddhists, Hindus, and/or Muslims, or whether the category is not resonant or applicable to the forms of social engagement in which members of these traditions are involved. We also do not know whether congregations play an important role in organizing members of these traditions (as they do for Christians and Jews), since they tend not to be involved in congregation-based community organizing. If congregations are not important in organizing religious activism, by which mechanisms do religious activism occur among Buddhists, Hindus, and Muslims? In order to obtain a fuller picture of progressive religion in the United States, we need a research agenda that better enables us to interrogate the degree to which current conceptions of progressive religion include or exclude growing religious minorities in the U.S.

Initial Explorations

My current research has used in-depth interviews to describe and explain religious activism among Buddhists, Hindus, and Muslims in the United States. Preliminary findings suggest their activism does not fit easily into the categories of progressive or conservative. To include forms of social engagement that may lie outside of typical definitions of "religious activism," I am conceptualizing activism broadly as intentional work to challenge or defend existing institutional or cultural authority, whether through organized groups or via other means, and calling it "social engagement" to make sure my respondent pool includes people who may not identify with the somewhat stigmatized label of "activist." While this research is in process and its findings are therefore highly preliminary, it serves alongside existing knowledge about these religious traditions to stimulate a conversation about how conceptualizations and operationalizations of "progressive religion" should expand if they are to include non-Judeo-Christian forms of activism in the U.S.

Progressive Buddhism

While it is not clear that progressive and conservative are meaningful identities for Buddhists internationally or even in the U.S., there is a tradition of "engaged Buddhism" that resembles Fuist et al.'s (this volume) definition of progressive religion in several ways. Donald Rothberg, a key participant in both the U.S.-based Buddhist Peace Fellowship and the International Network of Engaged Buddhists, describes engaged Buddhism as a focus on linking the inner spiritual transformation most commonly associated with Buddhism to the need for social transformation. He writes, "There is the irony of attempting to overcome self-centeredness through spiritual practice while ignoring the cries of the world. . . . And there is the danger of not seeing how the world is not just 'out there' but also 'in us,' internalized through our self-images" (2006, 5). For Rothberg and other proponents of engaged Buddhism, inner transformation is impossible without attention to social transformation. While there is some overlap in the areas of focus common among those involved in "engaged Buddhism" with the concerns of progressive religious activists (e.g., peace and environmentalism), engaged Buddhism is not necessarily collective or organized in the way scholars typically conceive of activism. Instead, the emphasis is often on living daily life in both personally and socially responsible ways (e.g., "right livelihood"), whether that includes organized, collective forms of contentious politics or not.

A second important example of something that might resemble progressive religious activism in the American Buddhist realm is the Buddhist Peace Fellowship. Started and largely sustained by white, native-born American converts to Buddhism and modeled in part on the religious peace fellowships founded by American Christians and Jews during the mid-20th century, the Buddhist Peace Fellowship includes a more explicitly activist orientation (Seager 2012). Still, its membership is individual rather than institutional (Buddhist congregations do not typically join), indicating that the largest form of "progressive Buddhist activism" in the U.S. is a non-congregational form of activism. Other forms of "progressive Buddhism" may be even less collective and organized, more localized, and relatively unidentified with either progressive traditions or with other, non-Buddhist religious groups.

An interview I conducted with a highly educated, white, native-born American Buddhist convert in her 40s is suggestive of these trends. While she volunteers for environmental organizations and has traveled to Asia several times to distribute health care in poor communities, she is not an activist in the traditional sense. Instead, she sees Buddhism as primarily focused on inner transformation to mindful living: it is a route to social change insofar as this inner transformation guides Buddhists to make more socially responsible decisions in their lives rather than through inspiring collective action. For instance, she told me:

> I see my professional work as a contribution in the spirit of "right liveli-hood." I am a [health] researcher, and my work is a small attempt at pre-venting [disease] and helping people live with [disease]—especially the underserved who are at greater risk but do not have good access to health care. I don't think my own work makes a big contribution in that regard, but I feel like I am a small part of the solution, rather than doing nothing.

While she is not organizing contentious actions to address social inequities, she sees her own daily work in the health care field as an attempt to create social change, a goal and a method influenced in part by her Buddhist practice. Thus, existing knowledge about Buddhism in the U.S. and my preliminary research suggest that looking for "progressive Buddhism" might necessitate focusing attention on different forms of practice compared with progressive Christianity, for instance. Progressive Buddhism may resemble the types of phenomena being studied by scholars of "lived religion," which requires not only observation of everyday practices but an exploration—often through interviews—of the meanings (including religious ones) people attach to those practices (e.g., Ammerman 2006). Moreover, it requires researchers to look in different places for progressive Buddhism—not in faith-based community organizations or national or regional Buddhist activist organizations, but in the daily lives and practices of Buddhists (whether individuals or groups) that desire to create social change. In other words, perhaps progressive religion need not always be collectively organized and enacted.

Progressive Hinduism

Most research on American Hindu activism has focused on Hindu nationalists, who are better characterized as fundamentalist or right-wing than as progressive (see Kurien 2007, 2013; Falcone 2012). Still, there are two ways in which something we might categorize as progressive Hindu-ism exists in the U.S. today. First, some Hindu Americans have engaged in activism challenging popular stereotypes of Hindus and seeking to create more legal space for Hindus in the American public sphere (Kurien 2007, 2013). In fighting for the expansion of rights and representations for a marginalized minority group, this type of activism might be characterized as progressive, even though it is not associated with popular progressive causes like poverty, the environment, or peace. Second, like Buddhists who engage in social change efforts primarily through mindful living and decision-making in their everyday interactions with individuals, groups, and institutions, many Hindus may be guided by religiously progressive values in their decisions about their work, their families, or other types of social engagements in a way that might be characterized as progressive.

Both of these were the case for one of my interview respondents, a highly educated first-generation Indian immigrant in her 60s. She does not consider herself an activist but thought of herself as engaged in her local community in multiple ways. She does not regularly attend or "belong" to a Hindu temple, but she identifies as Hindu and wears a sari and a bindi, suggesting that her religious practice is more individual than collective, though not necessarily "private." In this way, she resembles most American Hindus, who despite evidence that American Hinduism is more congregational than its Indian counterpart (Kurien 2007) still practice their religion outside of organized communities that we might call congregations (Pew Research Center 2012). Still, she is regularly involved in several interreligious groups, where she sees her goal as educating others about Hinduism. Finally, she volunteers for several local charitable organizations seeking to aid impoverished populations, including serving on the board of a local food pantry. In explaining why she does these things, she mentions several Hindu poets and her parents as inspirations, but she never mentions involvement in any Hindu activist groups.

Together, existing knowledge about Hinduism in the U.S. and my preliminary research suggests that finding progressive Hinduism in the U.S. may require researchers to look outside of faith-based community organizations and national or regional Hindu activist organizations, instead focusing on the daily lives and practices of Hindus and the meanings (religious or otherwise) they attach to those practices. It may also require researchers to examine Hindutva (right-wing) activists to see who they feel their opponents are, since that may provide clues to who the comparatively progressive Hindus in the U.S. are.

We can also take away a second important lesson from what we already know about Hindu activism in the United States: that "progressive religion" may be focused not only on changing political policy but also on changing religious groups themselves and the ways in which they are perceived and treated by other groups. Rather than emphasizing participation in coalitions working on progressive causes like environmental care, this may take the form of participation in interreligious dialogue groups that allow religious minorities to educate others about their traditions, or forms of activism designed to challenge laws regulating religious freedom, expanding them to better include non-Christian traditions. While fighting for religious freedom is often considered a conservative cause, when its purpose is to create more room for religious pluralism and, in particular, to expand the rights of religious minorities, we might instead characterize it as progressive. Looking for progressive Hinduism thus requires not only different methodologies and settings for locating religious progressivism but also a more contextualized approach to determining which "causes" are deemed progressive versus conservative.

Progressive Islam

While the terms "progressive" and "conservative" are not particularly common as descriptors for different forms of Islam in Muslim-majority countries, some American Muslim scholars have argued that there is "a nascent community of Muslim activists and intellectuals" who identify as "progressive Muslims" (Safi 2003, 3), with the label "progressive Islam" signifying a focus on issues of social justice, gender justice, and pluralism. However, this identity may not easily align with the left-right political continuum currently popular in the U.S., with 70 percent of American Muslims saying they lean Democrat and prefer bigger government with more services, but 45 percent saying homosexuality should be discouraged (Pew Research Center 2011).

In terms of progressive religious activism, the landscape is even more complicated. Because American Islam is very diverse, made up of both African American Muslims and immigrant Muslims from many countries around the world, many local mosques include attendees with vastly different political, cultural, and religious backgrounds, making it difficult to find enough consensus to act collectively to create social change. One of my interview respondents, a highly educated, native-born American Muslim in his 30s with a mixed ethnic background (including Arab ancestry), is an imam at a large, immigrant mosque with a great deal of diversity in individuals' national origins. In addition to providing a place for prayer, the mosque works with youth, helps families with the assimilation process, participates in interreligious groups, and raises money for charities. However, it is not involved in any more organized efforts to create social change, such as congregation-based organizing. This stands in contrast to African American mosques, which are more likely to participate in political organizing (Bagby 2004). My respondent offers insight into why more diverse, immigrant-majority mosques may refrain from participation in this kind of work:

> We participate in charitable programs and we participate in interfaith programs. But beyond that it's difficult, because we [leaders] in a way represent the entire community, which is a thousand people. So it's hard to speak with one voice. Though we have taken a very strong position about moderation within the religion.

Though it is difficult to achieve enough consensus for the mosque to engage in something we might recognize as progressive religious activism around social issues like inequality or the environment, one thing the community members as a whole shared was a commitment to encouraging religious change within Muslim communities, supporting moderation as opposed to more fundamentalist directions within their religious institutions.

In thinking about progressive Islam, we find both similarities to and differences from Buddhism and Hinduism. Because of their faith's greater degree of congregationalism (Hondagneu-Sotelo 2008), we might be more likely to find Muslims involved in efforts like congregation-based organizing: and indeed, while their involvement in such organizations is relatively rare, it is still more common than involvement from Buddhists and Hindus (Wood, Fulton, and Partridge 2012). Still, certain elements of American Islam make it more likely that we might locate progressive social engagement in places and forms other than faith-based community organizations.

As with Hindus, progressive social engagement may take the form of participation in interreligious dialogue groups that allow religious minorities to educate others about their traditions; this may be especially important for American Muslims, who must counter the negative stereotypes many Americans have of Islam (Pew Research Center 2011). Further, Muslims and other small but growing religious minorities may be especially concerned about the shape that their religious institutions take in the U.S. context, both because of a concern about religion itself but also because of a recognition that the shape of the religion might influence the degree to which it is accepted in American society. For this reason, focusing not only on political targets but also on other targets, such as religious institutions themselves, may be especially important for locating forms of non-Judeo-Christian progressive religion such as progressive Islam.

Conclusion: Toward an Inclusive Research Agenda

What does examining the cases of religious minorities, who have often been left out of research on religious activism in general and progressive religion more particularly, tell us about progressive religion, how to study it, and where to find it? As a reminder, the shared definition we are using in this volume asks us to look for progressive religion in progressive action, progressive values, progressive identities, and/or progressive theology. Also, in trying to sketch out a "progressive religious field of action," it suggests that we define the field in part by its relation to other fields such as the religious Right and secular progressivism or liberalism.

While this definition is a fine place to begin, this chapter suggests that preliminary evidence on religious groups commonly ignored in studies of religious activism—Buddhists, Hindus, and Muslims—demand that we proceed carefully. Indeed, a research agenda on progressive religion that includes the diversity of American religious traditions requires that our shared definition be expanded, or at least further emphasized, in four key ways.

First, common categories and labels in the U.S.—"religious Right" and "religious Left," "conservative religion" and "progressive religion"—may not have the same resonance for religious minorities, particularly for new immigrants. Instead, they may more readily identify with categories associated with their religious traditions in their countries of origin, which may draw boundaries among their followers in very different kinds of ways. If this is the case, it may be harder for them to identify with activist groups in the U.S. organizing under a progressive religious umbrella, as some interfaith activist coalitions do.

Second, for some religious minorities, advocating for a place in the public religious landscape is a motivating factor for their engagement in social change efforts. While they may also care about causes typically associated with progressivism in the U.S., these causes may take a backseat to the need to create more acceptance of and legitimacy for their own religious traditions in a sometimes hostile environment. Because the dominant shape and content of a religious tradition may affect the degree to which followers are accepted in the U.S., religious activism with religious targets may be especially likely among religious minorities. Still, their current marginal status can sometimes act as a constraint to public contentious action (Yukich 2013), a calculation Hindus and Muslims especially must consider even more carefully than Christians and Jews before they engage in progressive religious activist coalitions. These additional costs may make it more likely for religious minorities to engage in contentious action when those actions have clear benefits for them (e.g., by creating greater freedom of religious practice) rather than in actions that have similarly high costs but few direct benefits.

Third, while existing knowledge about variation in organizational forms between different religious traditions (i.e., whether they are more or less congregational) suggests that Buddhists, Hindus, and Muslims may be less inclined toward congregation-based organizing than more congregational traditions like Christianity and Judaism, organizational form may not be the only variation between traditions that shapes involvement in progressive religious activism. Patterns of practice—whether practice tends to be more collective or individual, enacted in particular times and places or "lived" in the everyday—may also shape the possibilities for engaging in what we typically identify as religious activism.

Finally, the multiple social change efforts emerging from these preliminary data that do not fit contentious politics definitions of activism suggest that common definitions of activism may be too restrictive. While social movement scholars have traditionally conceptualized activism as disruptive, public struggle over political issues (see McAdam et al. 2005 for a summary of this), in more recent research this traditional definition is being deconstructed in several ways. Using a multi-institutional politics approach, some scholars are recognizing that activism can target many arenas for change, not just political ones, including religious institutions (e.g., Armstrong and Bernstein 2008; Yukich 2013). Yet these approaches often leave the definitions of activism (as disruptive and public) relatively intact. Instead, we should consider expanding our definitions of activism to include less disruptive, more private, less organized efforts to create social change. Expanding our definitions will better recognize the multitude of tactics involved in intentional social change and will allow us to build new theories regarding how these different tactics produce change.

We must increase the amount of overall attention paid to religious minorities if our theories of progressive religion are to hold water. Not only are these traditions growing in number and importance, they are central to what many define as the progressive religious vision, which holds ecumenism as a key value and goal. Broadening our empirical scope will help produce more accurate, more generalizable theories of progressive religion.

More broadly, examining how American Buddhists, Hindus, and Muslims engage in efforts to create progressive social change in their communities has the potential to complicate widespread assumptions about religious minorities, which often depict these groups as quiescent or—particularly Muslims—as fundamentalist or even terrorist. Challenging public misconceptions is an urgent task in a national context in which much of the public remains ignorant about members of these traditions, ignorance that at its worst results in hate crimes against members of these communities. Highlighting how Buddhists, Hindus, and Muslims are both similar to and different from Christians and Jews (and each other), while also demonstrating how followers of these traditions engage in practices of justice and care for those around them, can transform popular images of religious minorities: from outsiders who threaten America to fellow Americans who are integral parts of their communities.

REFERENCES

Ahmed, Leila. 2011. *A Quiet Revolution: The Veil's Resurgence, from the Middle East to America*. New Haven, CT: Yale University Press.

Ammerman, Nancy T., ed. 2006. *Everyday Religion: Observing Modern Religious Lives*. New York: Oxford University Press.

Armstrong, Elizabeth A., and Mary Bernstein. 2008. "Culture, Power, and Institutions: A Multi-Institutional Politics Approach to Social Movements." *Sociological Theory* 26: 74.

Bagby, Ibsan. 2004. "The Mosque and the American Public Square." In *Muslims' Place in the American Public Square: Hope, Fears, and Aspirations*, edited by Zahid H. Bukhari, Sulayman S. Nyang, Mumtaz Ahmad, and John L. Esposito, 323–46. Walnut Creek, CA: Altamira Press.

Bender, Courtney, Wendy Cadge, Peggy Levitt, and David Smilde, eds. 2012. *Religion on the Edge: De-centering and Re-centering the Sociology of Religion*. New York: Oxford University Press.

Cadge, Wendy. 2005. *Heartwood: The First Generation of Theravada Buddhism in America*. Chicago: University of Chicago Press.

Cadge, Wendy, and Elaine Howard Ecklund. 2007. "Immigration and Religion." *Annual Review of Sociology* 33: 359–79.

Cobb, John B., Jr., ed. 2008. *Resistance: The New Role of Progressive Christians*. Louisville, KY: Westminster John Knox Press.

Dana, Karam, Matt A. Barreto, and Kassra A. R. Oskooii. 2011. "Mosques as American Institutions: Mosque Attendance, Religiosity and Integration into the Political System among American Muslims." *Religions* 2(4): 504–24.

Davis, Nancy J., and Robert V. Robinson. 2012. *Claiming Society for God: Religious Movements & Social Welfare*. Bloomington: Indiana University Press.

Djupe, Paul A., and Christopher P. Gilbert. 2006. "The Resourceful Believer: Generating Civic Skills in Church." *Journal of Politics* 68(1): 116–27.

Ebaugh, Helen Rose, and Janet Saltzman Chafetz, eds. 2000. *Religion and the New Immigrants: Continuities and Adaptations in Immigrant Congregations*. Walnut Creek, CA: Altamira Press.

Falcone, Jessica Marie. 2012. "Putting the 'Fun' in Fundamentalism: Religious Nationalism and the Split Self at Hindutva Summer Camps in the United States." *Ethos* 40(2): 164–95.

Haddad, Yvonne Yazbeck. 2011. *Becoming American?: The Forging of Arab and Muslim Identity in Pluralist America*. Waco, TX: Baylor University Press.

Hammer, Juliane. 2012. *American Muslim Women, Religious Authority, and Activism: More than a Prayer*. Austin: University of Texas Press.

Harris, Fredrick C. 1999. *Something Within: Religion in African-American Political Activism*. New York: Oxford University Press.

Hondagneu-Sotelo, Pierrette. 2008. *God's Heart Has No Borders: How Religious Activists Are Working for Immigrant Rights*. Berkeley: University of California Press.

Jamal, Amaney. 2005. "The Political Participation and Engagement of Muslim Americans: Mosque Involvement and Group Consciousness." *American Politics Research* 33(4): 521–44.

Joshi, Khyati Y. 2007. *New Roots in American Sacred Ground: Religion, Race, and Ethnicity in Indian America*. New Brunswick, NJ: Rutgers University Press.

Keown, Damien, Charles S. Prebish, and Christopher Queen, eds. 2003. *Action Dharma: New Studies in Engaged Buddhism*. New York: Routledge.

King, Sally B. 2009. *Socially Engaged Buddhism*. Honolulu: University of Hawaii Press.

Kurien, Prema. 2007. *A Place at the Multicultural Table: The Development of an American Hinduism*. New Brunswick, NJ: Rutgers University Press.

Kurien, Prema. 2013. "Majority and Minority Religious Status in India: Homeland-Oriented Activism in the US." Presentation at the Annual Meeting of the Society for the Scientific Study of Religion, Boston.

Lal, Vinay. 1999. "The Politics of History on the Internet: Cyber-Diasporic Hinduism and the North American Hindu Diaspora." *Diaspora* 8(2): 137–72.

Leonard, Karen. 2007. "Finding Places in the Nation: Immigrant and Indigenous Muslims in America." In *Religion and Social Justice for Immigrants*, edited by Pierrette Hondagneu-Sotelo, 50–58. New Brunswick, NJ: Rutgers University Press.

Levitt, Peggy. 2007. *God Needs No Passport: Immigrants and the Changing American Religious Landscape*. New York: New Press.

Lichterman, Paul. 2005. *Elusive Togetherness: Church Groups Trying to Bridge America's Divisions*. Princeton, NJ: Princeton University Press.

Lichterman, Paul. 2012. "Studying Public Religion: Beyond the Beliefs-Driven Actor." In *Religion on the Edge: De-Centering and Re-Centering the Sociology of Religion*, edited by Courtney Bender, Wendy Cadge, Peggy Levitt, and David Smilde, 115–36. New York: Oxford University Press.

McAdam, Doug. 1982. *Political Process and the Development of Black Insurgency, 1930–1970*. Chicago: University of Chicago Press.

McAdam, Doug, Robert J. Sampson, Simon Weffer, and Heather MacIndoe. 2005. "'There Will Be Fighting in the Streets': The Distorting Lens of Social Movement Theory." *Mobilization* 10(1): 1–18.

McAdam, Doug, Sidney G. Tarrow, and Charles Tilly. 2001. *Dynamics of Contention*. New York: Cambridge University Press.

Meyer, Katherine, Daniel Tope, and Anne M. Price. 2008. "Religion and Support for Democracy: A Crossnational Examination." *Sociological Spectrum* 28(5): 625–53.

Min, Pyong Gap. 2010. *Preserving Ethnicity through Religion in America: Korean Protestants and Indian Hindus across Generations*. New York: NYU Press.

Morris, Aldon D. 1984. *The Origins of the Civil Rights Movement: Black Communities Organizing for Change*. New York: Free Press.

Nepstad, Sharon Erickson. 2008. *Religion and War Resistance in the Plowshares Movement*. New York: Cambridge University Press.

Passel, Jeffrey, and D'Vera Cohn. 2008. *U.S. Population Projections: 2005–2050*. Washington, DC: Pew Hispanic Center.

Pew Research Center. 2008. *U.S. Religious Landscape Survey*. Washington, DC: Pew Forum on Religion and Public Life.

Pew Research Center. 2011. *Muslim Americans: No Signs of Growth in Alienation or Support for Extremism*. Washington, DC: Pew Research Center.

Pew Research Center. 2012. *Asian Americans: A Mosaic of Faiths*. Washington, DC: Pew Research Center.

Pluralism Project. 2013. *Harvard University—The Pluralism Project*. www.pluralism.org.

Putnam, Robert D., and David E. Campbell. 2010. *American Grace: How Religion Divides and Unites Us*. New York: Simon & Schuster.

Queen, Christopher S., ed. 2000. *Engaged Buddhism in the West*. Somerville, MA: Wisdom Publications.

Queen, Christopher S., and Sallie B. King, eds. 1996. *Engaged Buddhism: Buddhist Liberation Movements in Asia*. Albany: State University of New York Press.

Rajagopal, Arvind. 2000. "Hindu Nationalism in the United States: Changing Configurations of Political Practice." *Ethnic and Racial Studies* 23(3): 467–96.

Rothberg, Donald. 1998. "Responding to the Cries of the World: Socially Engaged Buddhism in North America." In *The Faces of Buddhism in America*, edited by Charles S. Prebish and Kenneth T. Tanaka, 266–86. Berkeley: University of California Press.

Safi, Omid, ed. 2003. *Progressive Muslims: On Justice, Gender, and Pluralism*. Oxford: Oneworld.

Seager, Richard Hughes. 2012. *Buddhism in America*. Revised and expanded edition. New York: Columbia University Press.

Smith, Christian, ed. 1996. *Disruptive Religion: The Force of Faith in Social-Movement Activism*. New York: Routledge.

Stanczak, Gregory C. 2006. *Engaged Spirituality: Social Change and American Religion*. New Brunswick, NJ: Rutgers University Press.

Swarts, Heidi J. 2008. *Organizing Urban America: Secular and Faith-Based Progressive Movements*. Minneapolis: University of Minnesota Press.

Warner, R. Stephen, and Judith G. Wittner, eds. 1998. *Gatherings in Diaspora: Religious Communities and the New Immigration*. Philadelphia: Temple University Press.

Williams, Rhys H. 1996. "Religion as Political Resource: Culture or Ideology?" *Journal for the Scientific Study of Religion* 35(4): 368–78.

Williams, Rhys H., and John P. N. Massad. 2006. "Religious Diversity, Civil Law, Institutional Isomorphism." In *Religious Organizations in the United States: A Study of Identity, Liberty, and the Law*, edited by James A. Serritella, Thomas C. Berg, W. Cole Durham, Jr., Edward McGlynn Gaffney, Jr., Craig B. Mousin, 111–28. Durham, NC: Carolina Academic Press.

Wood, Richard L. 2002. *Faith in Action: Religion, Race, and Democratic Organizing in America*. Chicago: University of Chicago Press.

Wood, Richard L., Brad Fulton, and Kathryn Partridge. 2012. *Building Bridges, Building Power: Developments in Institution-Based Community Organizing*. Interfaith Funders. www.interfaithfunders.org.

Wuthnow, Robert. 2005. *America and the Challenges of Religious Diversity*. Princeton, NJ: Princeton University Press.

Yukich, Grace. 2013. *One Family Under God: Immigration Politics and Progressive Religion in America*. New York: Oxford University Press.

11

Religious Beliefs and Perceptions of Repression in the U.S. and Swedish Plowshares Movements

SHARON ERICKSON NEPSTAD

As social movements gain momentum, their opponents may respond with intimidation and sanctions. Authorities often resort to repression in hopes that it will deter further protest, thereby causing movement decline. Although this may happen, repression can also have the opposite effect of strengthening a movement. While numerous scholars have analyzed the differing effects of repression, the literature has a couple of notable gaps. First, many researchers give limited attention to activist agency, assuming that those who face repression have only two choices: persist or desist. In reality, protesters can respond in numerous ways and more scholarly attention ought to be given to activists' diverse reactions. A second limitation is that studies of movement repression have largely been immune to the cultural turn within the field of collective action. In other words, there is an assumption that all protesters are rational actors who calculate the costs and benefits of mobilizing in risky conditions; there has been virtually no attention given to the role that collective identity, values, group style, or ideology may play in activists' deliberations.

This chapter examines movement responses to repression through a cultural lens. I argue that activists' beliefs, worldviews, and group culture shape how they interpret and respond to repression, which in turn influences the impact that sanctions have. To support this claim, I compare the U.S. and Swedish Plowshares movements. The Plowshares movement began in the United States in 1980, when radical Catholic activists broke into a General Electric (GE) plant outside of Philadelphia that was producing first-strike nuclear weapons. The activists were armed with household hammers and bottles filled with their blood. When they located components of GE's nuclear missiles, they enacted the prophet Isaiah's vision of a day when "nations shall beat their swords into plowshares and their spears into pruning hooks" (Isaiah 4:2). They hammered upon the missiles, poured blood, and then prayed until they were arrested. The eight were convicted of burglary, conspiracy, and criminal mischief, receiving sentences ranging from five to ten years (Polner and O'Grady 1997). Within a few months, other Plowshares actions took place and a movement was underway. The U.S. judicial system attempted to stop the movement by imposing severe prison sentences. While the courts obliged, the repression did not work. The U.S. Plowshares movement continued, generating dozens more actions and persisting well into the 21st century.

By the late 1980s, the Plowshares movement had spread to Australia and Europe (Nepstad 2008). One of the most active "branch" movements was in Sweden, where participants employed the same tactics of property destruction to challenge the Swedish weapons trade. While Swedish activists were sent to prison for this provocative form of activism, they were incarcerated for much shorter periods. Despite the more moderate sanctions imposed, the Swedish movement began to founder. After ten years, it collapsed.

While several factors influenced each movement's trajectory, I posit that one factor that contributed to the U.S. Plowshares movement's longevity was its religious interpretation of repression, which had positive consequences for the movement. In contrast, the Swedish movement viewed arrests and imprisonment as a strategic opportunity to stimulate national dialogue and recruit new members. While the Swedish movement did manage to stir widespread debate about the arms trade, this strategic view of movement repression had negative consequences for the movement, contributing to its demise.

Movement Repression

Why did state repression strengthen the U.S. Plowshares movement but weaken the Swedish movement? This finding—that repression can have differential effects on social movements—is not new (Lichbach 1987; Davenport, Johnston, and Mueller 2005; Earl 2006). Numerous studies have found that as repression increases, protest rates decline since people become unwilling to take on the higher risks and costs of activism (Tilly 1978; DeNardo 1985; Carley 1997; Olzak, Beasley, and Oliver 2003; Saxton 2004). Yet other researchers have found that repression can increase protest rates as people become so outraged at government crackdowns that they believe change is imperative (Barkan 1984; White 1989; Opp and Roehl 1990; Khawaja 1993, 1994; Meyer and Staggenborg 1996; Smithey and Kurtz 1999; Goldstone and Tilly 2001; Almeida 2003; Einwohner 2003; Francisco 2005; Schock 2005; Hess and Martin 2006; Martin 2007; Stephan and Chenoweth 2008). Still others argue that the relationship between repression and mobilization is not unidirectional but curvilinear: low levels of repression may initially allow protesters the freedom to express their dissent. However, if repression becomes extreme and highly dangerous, then protest levels drop off (Muller 1985; Weede 1987; Muller and Weede 1990; Brockett 2005; Davenport 2005).

One explanation for these conflicting findings is that many studies assess whether a movement is expanding or declining during repressive periods by measuring changes in the quantity of protest events. But, as several scholars note, a decrease in public activities does not necessarily indicate movement demise. Movements may actually gain participants but be less visible due to a decision to switch to covert tactics or to engage in alternative organizing activities. Thus, another way to gain insight into the effects of repression is to examine the qualitative changes that occur when a movement faces sanctions (Chang 2008, 652).

Several scholars have taken this approach, documenting the changes that movements may make during repressive episodes. For example, state-sponsored repression may compel protesters to adopt new tactics—either to avoid further repression or to throw the opponent off balance by taking an unanticipated course of action (McAdam 1983; Lichbach 1987; Moore 1998). Repression may additionally lead organizers to forge new alliances to expand their base of resistance and to increase the chance of survival if one movement segment or organization is decimated (Boudreau 1996, 2004; Loveman 1998; McCammon and Campbell 2002; Van Dyke 2003; Almeida 2005; Chang 2008). Finally, repression may foster militancy, as activists may conclude that peaceful change is not possible and thus shift toward armed struggle (Koopmans 1997; Zwerman and Steinhoff 2005).

These studies are significant because they restore agency to challengers and reveal various responses to repression. Yet none of these studies consider how a movement's collective identity or cultural beliefs may shape their responses. There is still an assumption that such changes in tactics, frames, and movement activities are driven by an instrumentalist mindset of achieving goals while avoiding or minimizing sanctions.

What we need is a close examination of how activists talk about and interpret the meaning of repressive experiences. In other words, we need to analyze movement repression through a "culture in interaction" approach that examines "group style" (Eliasoph and Lichterman 2003). As Epstein (1991) reveals in her account of jail experiences with the Livermore Action Group in the 1980s, a movement's cultural norms, beliefs, and practices can determine whether activists view repression as a punishment to avoid or an empowering event. Similarly, in the worldwide Plowshares movement, I argue that each movement branch had a distinctive group style that influenced how activists responded to repression and whether sanctions had destructive or constructive consequences. To demonstrate this, I compare the way that the U.S. and Swedish Plowshares movements viewed repression and evaluate the effects it had on each group.

Methodology

To explore perceptions of repression in the international Plowshares movement, I draw on data that I gathered using a multi-method approach. I began by conducting participant observation at Jonah House—a faith-based resistance community where numerous Plowshares leaders and activists live. I also participated in an Atlantic Life Community retreat, attended by many Plowshares participants. During this time, I took extensive field notes and conducted exploratory interviews. Drawing upon this qualitative data, I designed a survey that addressed demographic information, religious beliefs, political practices, and so forth. Using movement documents to compile a list of participants, I was able to locate 112 people out of 161 living Plowshares activists; 54 of them completed the surveys, generating a 48 percent response rate.

Since the survey results were drawn from only one-third of the movement, I collected additional data. At the end of the questionnaire, I asked if the respondent would be open to participating in an in-depth interview. Almost everyone agreed. From those who indicated that they were willing, I selected a sample based on legal status (i.e., I did not interview those who were incarcerated at the time). In all, I conducted 35 semi-structured interviews in the U.S. and Europe. All interviews were tape-recorded and transcribed. Finally, I also drew from the DePaul University Plowshares movement archives. This triangulated approach enabled me to verify the accuracy of participants' oral accounts.

Background on the Plowshares Movement

United States

The Plowshares style of activism was influenced by radical Catholic responses to the Vietnam War. Despite escalating protests, the White House did not change its foreign policy, and thus some Catholic activists argued that protest was not enough; they called for war obstruction. This shift from protest to resistance occurred when Father Philip Berrigan and several others raided a Selective Service office in Baltimore and poured blood over draft files. Several months later, Philip Berrigan organized a second action and his brother, Jesuit Daniel Berrigan, joined him. They broke into another Maryland draft board office and burned hundreds of conscription files with homemade napalm (Klejment and Roberts 1996).

The brother priests spent several years in prison for the draft board raids. When they were released in the mid-1970s, they and their supporters wanted to use similar tactics to challenge the escalating nuclear arms race. The activists' vision of using dramatic tactics to obstruct the arms race culminated in 1980, when eight people entered a General Electric plant that was producing first-strike nuclear warheads. After destroying components of these warheads, the activists were sentenced to five to ten years in prison (Polner and O'Grady 1997). Although these long sentences were designed to deter others, the General Electric action actually inspired new campaigns. Consequently, judges imposed even harsher prison sentences, ranging up to 18 years. Nonetheless, Plowshares actions continued, culminating in over 50 campaigns throughout the United States (Laffin 2003).

Sweden

The roots of the Swedish Plowshares movement can be traced to Syracuse, New York. This is where Swedish activist Per Herngren was sent in 1983 when he participated in an international peace organization exchange program. During his time in New York, a Plowshares action took place at Griffiss Air Force Base, a short distance from Syracuse. Several individuals had entered the base and hammered upon B-52 bombers. Herngren was inspired—several months later, he and seven others destroyed components of a Patriot missile launcher at a Martin Marietta plant in Orlando, Florida. They left an indictment that charged Martin Marietta with violating international law (Laffin 2003).

The Swedish news agencies covered Herngren's trial extensively. When he was deported back to Sweden, he received considerable support from the peace movement. Several activists saw the effect that Herngren's incarceration had in raising awareness about nuclear weapons and thus they began working with him to establish a Swedish Plowshares movement. From the beginning, Swedish organizers realized that they would need to reduce the U.S. movement's religious references. In their secular nation, where roughly 4 percent of the population attends church, the religious symbolism would not resonate. Thus they eliminated the use of blood—which is used in the U.S. movement to signify sacrifice and redemption—and reduced the biblical justifications for radical peacemaking, focusing instead on the ideas of Gandhi and Thoreau.

While they rejected such religious elements, Swedish activists did adopt the infrastructure of the U.S. Plowshares movement by forming an intentional community called Omega that paralleled Jonah House. After a few years, however, Omega collapsed due to internal conflicts. The group also decided that communes were not well suited to the Swedish context and thus established a formal movement membership organization called Svärd till Plogbillar (Swords into Plowshares).

Swedish Plowshares activists made other changes as well. Rather than engaging in symbolic acts of moral witness, as the U.S. movement does, they wanted to build a mass movement that could genuinely influence Swedish policies. They recruited widely, drawing in atheists, Pagans, secular anarchists, and so forth. But given the heterogeneous nature of the movement's membership and their commitment to consensus decision-making, the group's internal dynamics quickly became contentious since participants held highly divergent views.

Despite these tensions, Swedish activists successfully carried out 11 Plowshares actions from 1988 to 1998. Since Sweden has no nuclear weapons, the activists focused on Swedish weapons companies. They hammered upon Swedish-made anti-aircraft missile launchers and bazookas. They also targeted the Saab Corporation, which was producing attack reconnaissance planes (Laffin 2003).

To deter others from joining the movement, the Swedish judicial system prosecuted and sentenced the Plowshares activists, albeit to shorter prison terms than their U.S. counterparts faced (see Table 11.1). But these sanctions did not hurt the Swedish movement nearly as much as their internal conflicts did. By the mid-1990s, disagreements among activists escalated. Some felt that male leaders dominated the movement despite an explicit commitment to egalitarianism. Others felt that those who went to prison were excessively glorified while those who did critical behind-the-scenes tasks were not valued. Due to the internal fighting, no Plowshares actions occurred during a two-year period. Eventually, the roughly 200 members of the Plowshares organization decided that they could take no more; they disbanded the organization in 2000.[1]

TABLE 11.1. Comparison of Plowshares Activists' Prison Sentences by Region (percentages)

Sentence	United States	Sweden
5 months or less	11.5	60.9
6–11 months	3.8	17.4
12–23 months	42.4	21.7
2–3 years	11.5	0
3–4 years	3.8	0
4–8 years	19.3	0
8+ years	7.7	0
Total	100.00	100.00
Mean	52.2 months	4.6 months
Median	18.0 months	1.0 months

The U.S. Plowshares Movement's View of Repression

Why did the U.S. Plowshares movement persist, despite heavy sanctions, while the Swedish Plowshares movement collapsed under the weight of its internal problems? As I explain in my earlier work, numerous factors contributed to these divergent outcomes—including the decision-making systems, organizational forms, and recruitment and retention practices that each movement adopted. While it is not possible to determine the relative weight of each factor in these movements' divergent outcomes, I propose that one plausible explanation is that U.S. activists interpreted their repression in religious terms that reinforced their collective identity as radical Catholics. This not only blunted the negative effects of state-sponsored sanctions, it also generated positive effects that strengthened the movement. To illustrate this, I elaborate on the U.S. Plowshares movement's religious view of repression below.

Repression as a Sign of Christian Fidelity

Repression sometimes inspires activists to greater resistance since it may indicate that the movement is genuinely posing a threat to the powers that be, thereby increasing actors' sense of efficacy. However, in the U.S. Plowshares movement, repression was not interpreted as a sign of political success but Christian fidelity. U.S. Plowshares activists view their stigmatization and incarceration as an indication that they are faithfully following in Christ's steps. Specifically, they note that Christ was imprisoned by Roman rulers and executed on charges of political sedition—i.e., "stirring up the people for revolt, forbidding payment of tribute [taxes] to Caesar, and calling himself a king" (Luke 23:2). Anyone seeking to follow him, they argue, should also challenge unjust governments. When they do, they should expect to suffer, just as Christ did. One U.S. Plowshares participant stated:

> Jesus said, "Take up your cross, deny yourself, and follow me." We interpret taking up the cross to mean risking punishment by the state because, at that time, the cross was the Roman means of execution. So following Jesus means risking our lives and being punished by the state, the

empire—the Roman empire at that time and the U.S. empire today. (interview with author, 2000)

U.S. Plowshares activists emphasize that members of the early church were also repressed. To support this claim, they point to a story in the scriptural book of Acts where Peter and other apostles are thrown into a Jerusalem jail. During the night, an angel sets them free. When the authorities discover that they have escaped, they send out guards to search for them. When they are found, the authorities have the apostles whipped and then order them to stop preaching the gospel. How do the apostles respond? They continue their "crime" of preaching and "they went out rejoicing that they were considered worthy of suffering disgrace for the sake of the Name" (Acts 5:41). For Plowshares activists who see themselves as part of the apostles' tradition, experiences of state repression are not something to be ashamed of but rather an honor. Moreover, this biblical story underscores the importance of not retreating, but faithfully following one's religious convictions despite the threat of imprisonment (McKenna 1996). In short, part of the U.S. movement's group style is the expectation that participants will be imprisoned for acting on their faith.

But government authorities are not the only ones who repress activists. Counter-movements and those in the broader public may also try to discredit or undermine a movement by stigmatizing, ridiculing, or threatening activists (Lo 1982; Meyer and Staggenborg 1996; Earl 2003; Ferree 2004; Fetner 2008). U.S. Plowshares activists have been exposed to this type of repression as well, as the following letter reveals. This letter, written by an angry citizen, was sent after several Plowshares activists damaged a nuclear-equipped ship called *The Sullivans* at Bath Iron Works (BIW) in Maine:

> I am incensed at . . . [those] who desecrated *The Sullivans*. . . . The Berrigan mob might just as well go and urinate on the Viet Nam wall memorial or overturn gravestones at Arlington. In saner times, the Navy guard at BIW would have been armed and the vandals would have been shot on the spot. Having shot a lot of enemy soldiers whom I respected more, I would gladly volunteer right now to blow these ungrateful bastards

away. . . . Hopefully, there are some people behind bars who are at least patriotic enough to beat these traitors into plowshares themselves so we won't have to feed and house a bunch of sick vandals for decades to come. (Berrigan-McAlister Collection, DePaul University archives, Box 36A)

While U.S. Plowshares activists are frequently subjected to such scathing condemnations, most consider this an indication that they—like Christ and the early apostles—are speaking a truth that others will despise. As one activist priest reflected:

I get tons of hate mail, even death threats. But the thing is, I'm a Christian and I read in the gospel that Jesus was harassed and persecuted every day he opened his mouth . . . and he's the guy I claim to follow. . . . Dorothy Day said that if you're not in trouble, then you need to reflect on your life. *It's a measure of your discipleship.* (interview with author, 2003, italics mine)

Prison as a Redemptive Experience

U.S. Plowshares activists experience more than public ridicule and threats. Nearly all of them spend time in prison. But by and large, the prison experience is perceived as a religiously redemptive experience, not punishment. Prison provides an opportunity to deepen one's spirituality. One Catholic activist stated, "Jail serves the same purpose today for peacemakers as the desert did for early Christian contemplatives" (Douglass quoted in Dear 1994, 241). This attitude is very prevalent in the movement as activists commonly state that "prison is more monastic than punitive" (author's field notes, 2001).

Prison also offers an opportunity to engage in "works of mercy," helping inmates who are often from underprivileged or oppressed backgrounds. One activist explained:

I always used the time to write letters for people and be an amateur counselor to others . . . [and] teach GED classes. So [it's about] Matthew 25: "Feed the hungry, visit the sick and imprisoned." It seems to me that aside from the action, going to jail is a good thing for Christians to do. . . . [B]eing in prison voluntarily—since very few people are there voluntarily—gives you an opportunity to be a willing ear to people who rarely have anyone who is a willing ear. Illiteracy is rampant, and very few people are willing to write letters and make themselves available to help out in a multitude of ways. People in jail could really use the assistance. So I always felt that my time in jail was well spent, helping people who wouldn't have gotten help from anyone else. (interview with author, 2003)

Going to prison, therefore, puts one in the tradition of Christ and the apostles while giving activists yet another context to act on their faith convictions.

Repression as Evidence of the State's Evil Nature and the Need for Ongoing Resistance

U.S. Plowshares organizers also use the prison experience to reinforce activists' beliefs that the U.S. government is oppressive, ruthless, and evil. The U.S. uses military violence and threats of mass destruction to maintain its power and economic privilege in the world, and it uses incarceration to maintain its power at home by removing, demoralizing, and silencing its domestic critics. One activist described the violent nature of U.S. prisons:

I thought I had seen it all but what I saw this last time in a Texas prison was something so diabolical. . . . This was a prison for women with health issues but what I saw was deliberate, calculated indifference. . . . Sometimes I saw tumors growing out of people; when they got there they went untreated, undiagnosed to the very end. . . . I consider these prisons and jails as weapons of mass destruction now because of the impact on . . . the lives inside. It's the biggest civil rights abuse of this decade. (interview with author, 2003)

These direct experiences with government cruelty reinforce group boundaries, deepening activist beliefs that the U.S. government is an intrinsically oppressive, evil system.

Consequences

These religious views of movement repression have had three constructive consequences for the U.S. Plowshares movement. First, it has given activists motivation and a rationale for continued resistance regardless of the costs and risks involved. In fact, U.S. movement participants refuse to calculate the costs associated with disarmament actions; they persistently engage in resistance because, according to their faith tradition, it is the right thing to do and the ensuing repression is evidence that they are following in Christ's footsteps. Second, these views minimize the likelihood that Plowshares activists will be co-opted by the government since such devoutly religious individuals are unlikely to compromise with an avowedly evil state. Third, these beliefs generate internal movement unity. While Plowshares activists do have differences of opinion on certain issues, such as abortion, those internal differences are seen as relatively unimportant in light of the urgent need to stop the government from committing military atrocities (Nepstad 2008). In short, this movement's religious beliefs and group style mean that repression is unlikely to deter activists; on the contrary, repression deepens their commitment and strengthens the movement's internal unity.

Swedish Plowshares Movement's Views of Repression

Since Swedish organizers rejected many of the religious elements of the U.S. movement, and since they recruited a heterogeneous group of activists, the Swedish Plowshares movement's group style is notably different from that of its U.S. counterpart. One Plowshares activist described these differences:

> [U.S. Plowshares activists] exercise a radical Christian faith based on Bible study, political reflection, community living and worship, often hospitality work and regular acts of nonviolent resistance. . . . Practically all the actions have leaned towards symbolic levels of military property damage, the symbolic communicating that three or four people cannot achieve disarmament—the hands of God and others are needed. Largely ignored by the media, the [U.S.] activists talk about the essential value to the actions that does not depend on results. . . . The [Swedish] Plowshares

movement describes and views itself in very strategic terms, almost devoid of the religious language and images prevalent in the U.S. movement. The movement is a fusion of radical liberalism and nonviolent anarchism and understands the dynamic of Plowshares actions as acts of civil disobedience attempting to create dialogue and to reach a consensus of both morality and action, especially around the issue of Swedish weapons exports. . . . In the wake of their 1993 . . . action, the movement was extensively covered by the media, such that it is now a household name. (Hancock 1996, 6)

With a distinctively secular orientation, Swedish activists interpreted movement repression in more strategic ways, which I explain below.

Repression as an Opportunity to Stimulate Debate about the Swedish Weapons Trade

As in many social movements, Swedish Plowshares activists intentionally engage in civil disobedience because they know that the trials that follow provide a chance to raise public awareness of militarism. By dramatically hammering upon Swedish weaponry, the activists hoped that the population would question why they would undertake such drastic action, thereby stirring debate about the morality of the global arms trade. The amount of coverage that the Swedish media devoted to activists' trials helped the activists achieve this goal. In fact, after an action in 1993, several Swedish Plowshares activists participated in a nationally televised debate with military personnel (Nepstad 2008). Thus state-sponsored sanctions have been perceived as a strategic opportunity.

Sanctions as a Way to Challenge the Mentality of Obedience

Swedish activists use their imprisonment in another strategic way: to challenge the nation's culture of obedience. Specifically, movement participants believe that many of their fellow citizens share their conviction that it is immoral to profit from killing. If this is true, why aren't more people challenging weapons manufacturers? The answer, according to the Swedish activists, is that people fear the punitive consequences of protest. Thus Plowshares activists intentionally embrace these sanctions to inspire others to overcome their fear so that they can act on their convictions. One activist explains:

> The arms race could not continue without the obedience of citizens, which is caused mainly by people's fear of the consequences of disobedience. But there are no methods of control today that could be used against an entire population that is prepared to take the consequences of their disobedience. Therefore, vulnerability to the consequences becomes the prerequisite of breaking obedience's hold on us. (Herngren 1993, 96–97)

Consequences

The Swedish Plowshares movement's strategic view of state-sponsored sanctions did not generate the same benefits that the U.S. Plowshares religious interpretations yielded. Specifically, because they did not view stigmatization or repression as a sign of Christian fidelity, going to prison did not strengthen Swedish activists' commitment to the movement. In fact, many participants dropped out after one action because they felt they had made their contribution to disarmament; it was time for others to do their part in achieving this goal. And, according to one of the movement founders, some participants merely wanted to experience radical political action. For them, it was something interesting to do, like going on an African safari. But once you've done it, you don't need to do it again (author's field notes, 2003).

Moreover, the view that sanctions were merely a way to instigate debate made activists more susceptible to government co-optation. As activists gain a greater voice, influence, and a national profile, they may stop using disruptive tactics and begin engaging in institutional politics (Meyer 1993). This occurred to some degree in the Swedish Plowshares movement, as one activist noted:

> Today you will find people that have been part of our movement are now in parliament. . . . We end up on TV shows. We end up on lists of the most powerful people in Sweden. . . . If you are in opposition to the government here, you become an advisor to the government. You are co-opted. They give money even to the most angry anarchist groups, if they will

accept it. . . . It's clever in terms of a power play because you have a stronger hold on the opposition when you say, "We'll give you money in order to sustain your opposition but we won't accept this or that." . . . That creates a totally different environment to do radical politics. (interview with author, 2003)

Finally, because Swedish activists did not vilify their government and Swedish weapons manufacturers—that is, they did not depict their struggle as one against evil—they did not prioritize the need to fight militarism as more urgent than their internal fights. In other words, they did not experience the internal cohesion that is generated from an imminent external threat. As a result, they continued to focus on their internal disputes—over leadership issues, gender dynamics, and movement policies—so that they eventually spent more time arguing than organizing. According to Swedish Plowshares activists, this is ultimately what destroyed the movement.

Discussion

What theoretical insights can be derived from this comparative analysis of repression in the U.S. and Swedish Plowshares movements? First, those movements (like the Swedish movement) that view repression as a strategic opportunity to mobilize are likely to be more reliant on visible gains—such as rising public support or growing numbers of participants—to keep such actions going. If activists do not see these gains, they are likely to determine that such high-risk tactics are not effective and shift to alternative tactics that have less punitive consequences. In contrast, those with religious worldviews that interpret repression as a sign of spiritual fidelity will be better at sustaining high-risk actions precisely because the experience of repression is intrinsically valuable and personally gratifying.

A second insight is that movements that view repression as a strategic opportunity will be more prone to co-optation than those that view it in terms of a religious struggle against an evil system. The Swedish Plowshares movement used controversial tactics of property destruction to stimulate dialogue about the morality of Swedish military policies and its weapons trade—not to prophetically denounce an evil system. As these became issues of national debate and Plowshares leaders gained greater visibility, they were invited to participate in government task forces and policy discussions. This opened the door to involvement in institutionalized politics, which some pursued since it provided activists with another venue for achieving their goals. In contrast, U.S. Plowshares activists, who see their struggle against U.S. militarism in terms of a religious battle against evil, are far less susceptible to co-optation since it would mean compromising their faith. Moreover, since they perceive U.S. political leaders as modern-day Herods, they are less willing to work with governmental leaders. From their view, people of faith should repudiate evil systems, not collaborate with them.

These religious interpretations of movement repression created another valuable consequence: the generation of internal movement unity. The good versus evil view generated internal movement solidarity, enabling U.S. Plowshares activists to avoid the damaging personal disputes that plagued and undermined the Swedish Plowshares movement. As Lewis Coser (1954) noted long ago, an external threat generates internal cohesion.

While I argue that activists' beliefs and perceptions of repression can profoundly shape the impact of sanctions, I also recognize that perceptions are not the only thing that matters. In the cases examined here, it was much easier for the U.S. Plowshares movement to persuade others that the U.S. government and its military policies are evil because the U.S. possesses (and has actually used) weapons of mass destruction. In contrast, Sweden has a policy against nuclear weapons. Additionally, the social problems and inequalities in the U.S. are far greater than those in Sweden, which has one of the strongest social welfare systems in the world. Swedish Plowshares activists acknowledged this. One man stated, "In the U.S., you live in this world empire where you have huge military spendings, nuclear weapons, and huge social problems, so it's really easy to see the state as more or less evil. In Sweden, that state is not that way . . . [and] most activists don't see the Swedish state as Babylon" (interview with author, 2003).

These different views of the government are most evident in Plowshares activists' experiences in state correctional facilities. While U.S.

Plowshares activists recount abuse by guards and brutality among prisoners, Swedish Plowshares activists describe the pleasant character of their prison system. One Swedish activist wrote:

> Never having served time in prison I was naturally anxious about what I was going to face. I was surprised by the friendliness I met, both from guards and fellow inmates. During the time I have been in prison so far . . . I have not been met by even a harsh word, threat, or any physical abuse whatsoever. Neither have I seen any violence, physical or psychological, between any one in prison. The heaviest weapon the guards carry is a pepper spray. . . .
>
> [In this prison] everyone has their own private cell equipped with a bed, desk, chair, bookshelf, wardrobe and TV. . . . They only lock the door to the floor at nine in the evening and unlock it at eight in the morning. During all the other hours you are free to walk outside, go to the gym, etc. . . . At my prison you are required to either work or study. . . . My newfound passion is happiness research within the field of psychology. For some time now I have had the idea to write a book in Swedish about happiness. . . . So that is what I do during the weekdays—writing about the science of happiness. Prison is a perfect place for writing a book—very few distractions and plenty of time. . . .
>
> The guards invite us many times a week to jogging, indoor hockey, beach volleyball, and soccer. We also play badminton, table tennis, and tennis. There has never been a time in my life when I have been more physically fit than now! The food here is also good. I am the only vegan at this prison but . . . they have provided me with delicious and well-balanced vegan meals for which I am very thankful. . . .
>
> I will face trial again on an appeal for the disarmament action I was a part of . . . last year. . . . [Whatever the outcome], I will accept it with peace, since now I know that I feel pretty good about serving time in a Swedish prison. A chance to finish my book and to stay in shape![2]

In short, while both the U.S. and Swedish government used imprisonment as a means of stopping these movements, it was far easier to vilify the U.S. government—thereby minimizing U.S. activists' chances of co-optation and increasing their internal unity.

Conclusion

U.S. Plowshares activists have experienced more severe repression than their Swedish counterparts, but they have also been more successful at persisting through this repression. I have argued that this is partly due to their group style, which is rooted in a radical Catholic worldview that interprets repression as a sign of genuine discipleship. By viewing repression in these positive terms, U.S. Plowshares activists have muted the power of state-sponsored sanctions. In contrast, Swedish activists also put forth alternative interpretations of repression, hoping to strategically use their arrests, trials, and prison sentences as a way to encourage greater public dialogue on the Swedish weapons trade and to encourage others to break free from a mentality of disobedience. While having time to exercise and write a book might sound appealing to some, the Swedish view of repression did not help sustain the movement. In fact, since the Swedish state was not perceived as evil, Swedish activists were not unified by having a dreadfully dangerous opponent, as the U.S. activists did. Moreover, since the Swedish state was to some degree willing to listen to the movement's criticism, the danger of co-optation increased and tensions within the movement grew over whether to dialogue with policy makers. Without the "benefits" of harsh sanctions or a deeper religious significance associated with their tactics, the movement succumbed to its internal tensions.

Yet this comparison of the U.S. and Swedish Plowshares movements reveals that activists cannot just adopt any group style or interpretation of repression. Such interpretations are constrained to some degree by the structural conditions and institutions that we confront. Hence Swedish activists would have found it difficult to promote a Manichean view of their state since the Swedish government is significantly less bellicose than the United States government. Similarly, if Swedish Plowshares leaders promoted a strong Christian interpretation of movement repression as a sign of discipleship, it might not have resonated with Swedish activists, who live in one of the most secular nations in the world. In short, while activists' beliefs and interpretations do shape the consequences of repression, those interpretations are also structurally and culturally circumscribed.

In sum, this chapter argues that activists' views of repression can influence whether a movement persists or falters. The radical religious beliefs of the U.S. Plowshares movement were particularly effective in sustaining resistance to nuclear weapons, even when the costs were severe. In fact, the Catholic culture of this group reveals that religious activists may not fit neatly into traditional social movement theories that view repression in strategic and utilitarian terms. Religious values can lead some activists to reinterpret costs as honors or indications of a vital, engaged faith. This underscores the importance of investigating religion within progressive movements, with an emphasis on how faith can shape the way that people do politics.

ACKNOWLEDGMENTS

I would like to thank Rhys Williams, Ruth Braunstein, and Todd Fuist for comments on earlier drafts of this chapter. Segments of this chapter were previously published in Nepstad, Sharon Erickson. 2008. *Religion and War Resistance in the Plowshares Movement* (New York: Cambridge University Press). Reprinted with permission.

NOTES

1 The Swedish movement's formal organization, Swords into Plowshares, was never revived. Independent Plowshares activists conducted the Swedish actions of 2008 and 2009, not former members of this still defunct organization.
2 Letter written by Swedish Plowshares activist Martin Smedjeback, 2009, *Jonah House*, www.jonahhouse.org.

REFERENCES

Almeida, Paul D. 2003. "Opportunity Organizations and Threat-Induced Contention: Protest Waves in Authoritarian Settings." *American Journal of Sociology* 109(2): 345–400.
Almeida, Paul D. 2005. "Multi-Sectoral Coalitions and Popular Movement Participation." *Research in Social Movements, Conflicts and Change* 26: 65–99.
Barkan, Steven. 1984. "Legal Control of the Southern Civil Rights Movement." *American Sociological Review* 49(4): 552–656.
Boudreau, Vincent. 1996. "Northern Theory, Southern Protest: Opportunity Structure Analysis in Cross-National Perspective." *Mobilization* 1(2): 175–89.
Boudreau, Vincent. 2004. *Resisting Dictatorship: Repression and Protest in Southeast Asia*. New York: Cambridge University Press.

Brockett, Charles. 2005. *Political Movements and Violence in Central America.* Cambridge, UK: Cambridge University Press.

Carley, Michael. 1997. "Defining Forms of Successful State Repression of Social Movement Organizations: A Case Study of the FBI's COINTELPRO and the American Indian Movement." *Research in Social Movements, Conflicts and Change* 20: 141–76.

Chang, Paul Y. 2008. "Unintended Consequences of Repression: Alliance Formation in South Korea's Democracy Movement." *Social Forces* 87(2): 651–77.

Coser, Lewis. 1954. *The Functions of Social Conflict.* New York: Free Press.

Davenport, Christian. 2005. "Repression and Mobilization: Insights from Political Science and Sociology." In *Repression and Mobilization*, edited by Christian Davenport, Hank Johnston, and Carol Mueller, vii–xli. Minneapolis: University of Minnesota Press.

Davenport, Christian, Hank Johnston, and Carol Mueller, eds. 2005. *Repression and Mobilization.* Minneapolis: University of Minnesota Press.

Dear, John. 1994. *The Sacrament of Civil Disobedience.* Baltimore: Fortkamp Publishing.

DeNardo, James. 1985. *Power in Numbers: The Political Strategy of Protest and Rebellion.* Princeton, NJ: Princeton University Press.

Earl, Jennifer. 2003. "Tanks, Tear Gas, and Taxes: Toward a Theory of Movement Repression." *Sociological Theory* 21(1): 44–68.

Earl, Jennifer. 2006. "Introduction: Repression and the Social Control of Protest." *Mobilization* 11(2): 129–43.

Einwohner, Rachel. 2003. "Opportunity, Honor, and Action in the Warsaw Ghetto Uprising of 1943." *American Journal of Sociology* 109: 650–75.

Eliasoph, Nina, and Paul Lichterman. 2003. "Culture in Interaction." *American Journal of Sociology* 108(4): 735–94.

Epstein, Barbara. 1991. *Political Protest and Cultural Revolution: Nonviolent Direct Action in the 1970s and 1980s.* Berkeley: University of California Press.

Ferree, Myra Marx. 2004. "Soft Repression: Ridicule, Stigma, and Silencing in Gender-Based Movements." *Research in Social Movements, Conflicts and Change* 25: 85–101.

Fetner, Tina. 2008. *How the Religious Right Shaped Lesbian and Gay Activism.* Minneapolis: University of Minnesota Press.

Francisco, Ronald A. 2005. "The Dictator's Dilemma." In *Repression and Mobilization*, edited by Christian Davenport, Hank Johnston, and Carol Mueller, 58–84. Minneapolis: University of Minnesota Press.

Goldstone, Jack, and Charles Tilly. 2001. "Threat (and Opportunity): Popular Action and State Response in the Dynamic of Contentious Action." In *Silence and Voice in the Study of Contentions Politics*, edited by Ronald R. Aminzade, Doug McAdam, Elizabeth J. Perry, William H. Sewell, Jr., Sidney Tarrow, and Charles Tilly, 179–94. Cambridge: University of Cambridge Press.

Hancock, Stephen. 1996. "Ploughshares Activists Find Unity in the Vulnerability, Despite Trans-Atlantic Tension." *Peace News*, August/September: 6.

Herngren, Per. 1993. *Path of Resistance: The Practice of Civil Disobedience*. Philadelphia: New Society Publishers.

Hess, David, and Brian Martin. 2006. "Repression, Backfire, and the Theory of Transformative Events." *Mobilization* 11(2): 249–67.

Khawaja, Marwan. 1993. "Repression and Collective Action: Evidence from the West Bank." *Sociological Forum* 8(1): 47–71.

Khawaja, Marwan. 1994. "Resource Mobilization, Hardship, and Popular Collective Action in the West Bank." *Social Forces* 73(1): 191–220.

Klejment, Anne, and Nancy Roberts. 1996. "The Catholic Worker and the Vietnam War." In *American Catholic Pacifism: The Influence of Dorothy Day and the Catholic Worker Movement*, edited by Anne Klejment and Nancy Roberts, 153–69. Westport, CT: Praeger.

Koopmans, Ruud. 1997. "Dynamics of Repression and Mobilization: The German Extreme Right in the 1990s." *Mobilization* 2(2): 149–64.

Laffin, Arthur. 2003. *Swords into Plowshares: A Chronology of Plowshares Disarmament Actions, 1980–2003*. Marion, SD: Rose Hill Books.

Lichbach, Mark. 1987. "Deterrence or Escalation?: The Puzzle of Aggregate Studies of Repression and Dissent." *Journal of Conflict Resolution* 31: 266–97.

Lo, Clarence. 1982. "Countermovements and Conservative Movements in the Contemporary U.S." *American Review of Sociology* 8: 107–34.

Loveman, Mara. 1998. "High-Risk Collective Action: Defending Human Rights in Chile, Uruguay, and Argentina." *American Journal of Sociology* 104: 477–525.

Martin, Brian. 2007. *Justice Ignited: The Dynamics of Backfire*. Lanham, MD: Rowman & Littlefield.

McAdam, Doug. 1983. "Tactical Innovation and the Pace of Insurgency." *American Sociological Review* 48(6): 735–54.

McCammon, Holly J., and Karen E. Campbell. 2002. "Allies on the Road to Victory: Coalition Formation between Suffragists and the Women's Christian Temperance Union." *Mobilization* 7(3): 231–51.

McKenna, Margaret. 1996. "The Angel of Recidivism." In *Apostle of Peace: Essays in Honor of Daniel Berrigan*, edited by John Dear, 92–96. Maryknoll, NY: Orbis Books.

Meyer, David. 1993. "Institutionalizing Dissent: The United States Structure of Political Opportunity and the End of the Nuclear Freeze Movement." *Sociological Forum* 8(2): 157–79.

Meyer, David, and Suzanne Staggenborg. 1996. "Movements, Countermovements, and the Structure of Political Opportunity." *American Journal of Sociology* 101(6): 1628–60.

Moore, Will H. 1998. "Repression and Dissent: A Substitution Model of Government Coercion." *Journal of Conflict Resolution* 44(1): 107–27.

Muller, Edward N. 1985. "Income Inequality, Regime Repressiveness, and Political Violence." *American Sociological Review* 50(1): 47–61.

Muller, Edward N., and Erich Weede. 1990. "Cross-National Variation in Political Violence: A Rational Action Approach." *Journal of Conflict Resolution* 34(4): 624–51.

Nepstad, Sharon Erickson. 2008. *Religion and War Resistance in the Plowshares Movement*. New York: Cambridge University Press.

Olzak, Susan, Maya Beasley, and Johan Oliver. 2003. "The Impact of State Reforms on Protest against Apartheid in South Africa." *Mobilization* 8(1): 27–50.

Opp, Karl Dieter, and Wolfgang Roehl. 1990. "Repression, Micromobilization, and Political Protest." *Social Forces* 69(2): 521–27.

Polner, Murray, and Jim O'Grady. 1997. *Disarmed and Dangerous: The Radical Lives and Times of Daniel and Philip Berrigan*. New York: Basic Books.

Saxton, Gregory D. 2004. "Structure, Politics, and Ethnonationalist Contention in Post-Franco Spain: An Integrated Model." *Journal of Peace Research* 41: 25–46.

Schock, Kurt. 2005. *Unarmed Insurrections: People Power Movements in Nondemocracies*. Minneapolis: University of Minnesota Press.

Smithey, Lee, and Lester Kurtz. 1999. "We Have Bare Hands: Nonviolent Social Movements in the Soviet Bloc." In *Nonviolent Social Movements: A Geographical Perspective*, edited by Stephen Zunes, Lester Kurtz, and Sarah Beth Asher, 96–124. Malden, MA: Blackwell.

Stephan, Maria, and Erica Chenoweth. 2008. "Why Civil Resistance Works: The Strategic Logic of Nonviolent Conflict." *International Security* 33(1): 7–44.

Tilly, Charles. 1978. *From Mobilization to Revolution*. Reading, MA: Addison-Wesley.

Van Dyke, Nella. 2003. "Crossing Movement Boundaries: Factors That Facilitate Coalition Protest by American College Students, 1930–1990." *Social Problems* 50(2): 226–50.

Weede, Erich. 1987. "Some New Evidence on Correlates of Political Violence: Income Inequality, Regime Repressiveness, and Economic Development." *European Sociological Review* 3(2): 97–108.

White, Robert W. 1989. "From Peaceful Protest to Guerrilla War: Micromobilization of the Provisional Irish Republican Army." *American Journal of Sociology* 94(6): 1277–302.

Zwerman, Gilda, and Patricia Steinhoff. 2005. "When Activists Ask for Trouble: State-Dissident Interactions and the New Left Cycle of Resistance in the United States and Japan." In *Repression and Mobilization*, edited by Christian Davenport, Hank Johnston and Carol Mueller, 85–107. Minneapolis: University of Minnesota Press.

PART IV

Distinctive Styles of Progressive Religious Talk in the Public Sphere

Finally, this section focuses on a dilemma related to the role of religion in political life—most of the progressive religious actors profiled in this book respect the liberal democratic premise that all citizens should be able to participate in public debates, yet the use of religious language in these debates is often perceived as exclusionary, and thus counterproductive to this goal. While the reasons for this perception are complex, it is at least partly rooted in anxieties about conservative and fundamentalist religious voices, which are viewed as unwilling to engage in the open-minded and reasoned style of debate and compromise about the public good that is expected of citizens in a democratic public sphere.

In addition to anxieties about *how* religious conservatives engage in public debate, there are also concerns about the *content* of their messaging. Namely, they have relied heavily on Christian nationalist rhetoric, pairing an understanding of the U.S. as a "Christian nation" with a celebration of rural, small-town communities, or what conservative Christian figures such as Sarah Palin refer to as "real America." While the religious Right is not monolithic, and while some conservative Christian figures and groups have championed racial diversity, this vision of small-town America as the backbone of a Christian nation has typically meant that those citizens viewed as most capable of speaking on behalf of "real Americans" are white and Christian. In contrast, as we have seen, contemporary progressive religious groups highlight the religious and racial diversity of the nation, and work to lift up voices that are often marginalized from public debates.

Yet when these progressive religious groups participate in public debates, they must reckon with the fact that many Americans associate *all* religious activists with their stereotypes about *conservative* religious groups. As such, religious progressives are conscious of the possibility that they will be met with distrust about their motives and interests, or with an unwillingness to take religious arguments seriously. As this section demonstrates, they navigate this dilemma in a variety of ways. Some progressive religious groups have developed careful and creative ways of expressing the connection between faith and politics. Meanwhile, others *avoid* making these connections, preferring to present themselves as nonpolitical or neutral actors intervening in issues of *moral* concern. Still others have developed multivalent styles of expression—like storytelling—that carry religious and secular meaning, depending on the identities of the speakers and the audiences.

These groups are also careful to highlight the religious, racial, and socioeconomic diversity of their communities, partners, and allies. Whether they are lifting up stories from the U.S.-Mexico border or from soup kitchens across the Midwest, the progressive religious activists highlighted in this section work to bring a diverse range of voices into public debates. Many also draw on civil religious language, symbols, and narratives as an alternative to Christian nationalist rhetoric. Although civil religious discourse has always competed with more particular and exclusive religious (and secular) languages for dominance in American public life, proponents of American civil religion contend that, because it is widely accessible and meaningful, it has the unique capacity to bind together a diverse people.

Together, these cases demonstrate that progressive religious actors draw on various forms of religious and religio-political talk when they participate in public life. In so doing, their efforts trouble theoretical assumptions that religiously inspired actors cannot productively engage with religious and secular "others" in the public sphere, and offer new ways of understanding *how* religious actors engage in public debates within diverse democratic societies.

12

Reviving the Civil Religious Tradition

PHILIP S. GORSKI

"We the people, in order to form a more perfect union." Two
hundred and twenty one years ago . . . a group of men gathered and . . . launched America's improbable experiment in
democracy. . . . The document they produced was . . . stained
by this nation's original sin of slavery. . . . Of course, the answer to the slavery question was already embedded within
our Constitution. . . . And yet words on a parchment would
not be enough. . . . What would be needed were Americans
in successive generations who were willing to . . . narrow
that gap between the promise of our ideals and the reality of
their time.
—Barack Obama, "Speech on Race," March 2008

It was mid-February, 2008, and Barack Obama appeared well on his way
to securing the Democratic presidential nomination. After holding his
own in the "Super Tuesday" primaries on February 5, the young senator
from Illinois racked up an impressive series of victories against his only
remaining opponent, Hillary Clinton. Then, on March 18, ABC News
broadcast incendiary excerpts from sermons preached by the Obamas'
then pastor, Jeremiah Wright. "God bless America?" Wright asked in
one. "No, God *damn* America, for taking innocent lives!" he thundered.
In truth, there was nothing all that unusual about this rhetoric. Wright
was just being true to his name and preaching a jeremiad, a staple of
Protestant homiletics since Puritan times.[1] But this bitter salt fell on the
still-open wounds left by the 9/11 attacks. Howls of outrage ensued.

Suddenly, Obama was in trouble. His polling numbers plummeted.
His campaign seemed in peril. At first, he waited for the news cycle to
wash away the controversy. Next came efforts to situate Wright's words

within the "black church tradition." All to no effect: media commentators began drafting Obama's political obituary. Then, on March 25, Obama delivered his famous "speech on race." Few politicians had dared speak so forthrightly on this subject before a national audience. Within days, millions had watched the speech. Suddenly, miraculously, Obama was back on a glide path to the nomination.

The race speech was widely praised and rightly so. But it was unusual in certain ways not often remarked. Take the setting: instead of an iconic site from the Civil Rights Movement, Obama chose the National Constitution Center in Philadelphia. The rhetoric was also unusual, at least for a Democratic presidential candidate. The opening lines were taken from the Preamble to the Constitution: "We, the People . . ." And the initial framing was lifted from the Hebrew Bible. There was talk of founding covenants (the Declaration and the Constitution), original sins (slavery), of a people backsliding and wandering (Jim Crow and civil rights) and a Promised Land just over the horizon (racial harmony).

To some, this rhetoric may have seemed new, even unprecedented. In truth, it was old, older than the republic itself. In a famous essay written in 1967, at another moment of national optimism, Robert Bellah described this characteristically American mixture of sacred and secular themes as the "American civil religion" (ACR) (Bellah 1967). In a book-length follow-up, published almost a decade later, at a moment of widespread cultural malaise, he pronounced it a "broken and empty shell" (Bellah 1975).

Was he right? The Obama campaign certainly suggested otherwise. Anyone who attended an Obama rally could see—could feel—that the ACR still awoke deep feelings of collective purpose in many Americans. But the birth of the Tea Party a few months later painted a gloomier picture. Evidently, the culture wars were still not over.

The goals of this chapter are twofold. The first is to describe the internal anatomy of the ACR and of its two main rivals: religious nationalism and radical secularism. The ACR is a synthesis of two distinct traditions: the prophetic religion of the Hebrew Bible and an Anglo-American version of civic republicanism. Religious nationalism is comprised of two different discourses: Biblical narratives of conquest and apocalypse. Radical secularism weaves together the rhetorics of "total separationism" and militant scientism. Or so I argue.

The second goal is to assess the promise and perils of a revived ACR. The promise is an end to the culture war between religious nationalists and radical secularists and the renewal of America's "vital center." Because it combines secular and sacred elements in an overarching narrative of national purpose, the ACR can potentially speak to people of faith and of no faith and provide a shared language that bridges long-standing divides. A revived ACR would not end debate. Rather, it would enable *meaningful* debate. Or so I believe.

The perils that confront a renewed ACR are multiple. One is internal imbalance. Prophetic religion is alive and well, but civic republicanism is weak and ailing. Another peril comes from without. The ACR's two powerful rivals—religious nationalism and radical secularism—have both grown stronger in recent decades, and both now feed off of one another. The third peril comes from below, from the gradual hollowing out of the ACR's social basis: liberal Protestantism.

What Is American Civil Religion?

Following Bellah, I understand the ACR as a dynamic synthesis of "prophetic religion" and "civic republicanism." By "prophetic religion," I mean a certain understanding of the Hebrew Bible centered on the idea of a "national covenant" that God has concluded with his peoples. By "civic republicanism," I mean a certain understanding of political community that derives from Ancient Rome and Greece.

In the prophetic tradition, as I interpret it, the covenant is dynamic rather than static. In the Hebrew Bible, recall, the covenant is originally established with Abraham, but then repeatedly renegotiated with both Noah and Moses. In the process, it becomes less sacramental and ritualistic and more legalistic and ethical. America's covenant has also evolved over time. For instance, it has become steadily more egalitarian and inclusive. It now encompasses many previously excluded groups: non-whites, non-Anglos, non-Protestants, and women.

Covenants can grow, but they can also decay. Most often, the covenant is undermined by the powerful and the prideful, who are perennially tempted to exploit the poor and trample on the weak. The role of the prophet is to speak truth to power and call the people back to the covenant. There has been no shortage of backsliding on America's covenant, particularly as regards race. But there has also been a steady stream of civic prophets as well, who have repeatedly invoked the Declaration's promise that all are created equal.

Prophetic religion entered into American political culture via Puritan New England. Like the Israelites, the Puritans were a covenanting people. Their churches were established by the swearing of covenants; so, too, were their cities and towns. Over time, the scope of the covenant was expanded to include the nation as a whole. In this vision, the American project was the creation of a "New Israel." This vision echoes on in contemporary movements—religious and secular—that seek to build national community and achieve social justice.

The second strand of the ACR is civic republicanism. It is rooted in the twin ideals of the polis and the *res publica*. The polis ideal stems from the Ancient Greeks. It refers to a free people that governs itself by means of general laws. The notion of the *res publica* is inherited from Ancient Rome. It is variously translated as "the public thing" and, less literally, as "the public good" or "the common wealth." Republicanism strives for positive freedom as well as negative rights, and it links individual well-being to the common good. In both of these regards, it is more demanding than its liberal cousin.

Like covenants, republics are subject to corruption and decay. Corruption occurs when a particular social group or political faction is able to dominate others and pursues its private interests at the expense of the common good. Decay occurs when civic virtue erodes and citizens become unwilling to abridge their private welfare for the sake of the commonwealth. From the republican perspective, corruption and decay are two sides of the same coin. One side is structural, the other cultural. To a civic republican, the liberal understanding of corruption as a "few bad apples" engaging in "quid pro quos" appears laughably naïve. Corruption doesn't stop at the fruits; it goes to the roots.

The republican tradition influenced Continental thinkers such as Machiavelli and Rousseau. But it reached American shores via "Whig" and "Commonwealth" thinkers such as John Harrington and Thomas Gordon. The roots of American republicanism are more British than European. And this was important because British republicanism was religion friendly in ways that Continental republicanism was not, allowing for a uniquely American melding of republicanism and prophetic religion—prophetic republicanism for short.

Historical Origins and Inner Logic of the ACR

What do prophetic religion and civic republicanism have to do with one another? In the traditional historiography: very little. The centrality of covenant for Puritan political theology has been well known since the 1930s, that of republicanism for the American Revolution since the late 1960s. Taken together, this work implies a deep caesura between the Puritans and the Founders. It makes Reformation and Enlightenment into two chapters in a secularization narrative. But this is far too simple.

Recent research has uncovered some deep continuities and connections between Puritanism and republicanism. On the one hand, Puritan thought and institutions contained many republican and proto-republican elements. Colonial historian Michael Winship has recently shown that the Puritan polity aspired to an ideal of "godly republicanism" (Winship 2006). Meanwhile, Eric Nelson and other intellectual historians have demonstrated that the republican ideology of the American Revolution had Biblical as well as classical roots (Nelson 2010). Many Americans believed that the Ancient Israelites—rather than the Greeks or Romans—had created the first and best republic. The dominant vision of civic republicanism in the Revolutionary era—and long after—can be fairly described as "Hebraic republicanism."

This uniquely American synthesis of civic republicanism and prophetic religion may have been historically contingent, but it was not internally incoherent. On the contrary, there are deep affinities between the two traditions. For example, civic republicanism and prophetic religion both presume that the health of the polity depends on the morality of the citizenry—"civic virtue" in the republican idiom, "righteousness" in the prophetic one. Both also insist that individual morality involves social obligations: "self-sacrifice" in the republican lexicon, "charity" in the Biblical one. Both further conceive of historical time in circular rather than linear terms. Following Plato and Polybius, classical republicans believed that political regimes went through periodic cycles of corruption and renewal. Similarly, the prophetic tradition narrates a cycle of covenants made, broken, and remade. Finally, both presume that a political community must periodically revisit its founding values, not simply to reinstate its original form, but to rearticulate them in light of present circumstances.

If there are affinities between the two traditions, there are also tensions. Generally speaking, civic republicanism is more optimistic about human nature than prophetic religion is. For republicans, moral virtue is easily achieved through proper education. In the Biblical tradition, the crooked timber of humanity is not so easily straightened. On the other hand, prophetic religion is more hopeful about social progress than civic republicanism is. The prophetic tradition contains a providential component. The republican tradition knows of golden ages but not promised lands. A final contrast concerns the relationship between political freedom and social equality. Classical republicans believed that inequality was the price of freedom; the labor of women and slaves underwrote the freedom of the citizen. The Biblical prophets were often more concerned with social equality than political freedom. Historically, these tensions have often been productive ones, with one tradition checking the enthusiasms of the other.

What Is a Tradition?

I have repeatedly referred to prophetic religion and civic republicanism as "traditions." By "tradition," I mean a culture that is conscious of itself. To be part of a tradition is to know certain stories, read certain texts, and admire certain people. So, the first three elements of a tradition, as I define it, are narrative, canon, and pantheon. The fourth is archive, a set of lesser-known stories, texts, and exemplars that can be retrieved in times of crisis or uncertainty.

This theory of tradition draws primarily on the work of Alasdair MacIntyre and Paul Ricoeur (Ricoeur 1990; MacIntyre 1994). Tradition is often set in opposition to rationality. With MacIntyre, I believe that rationality is possible only from within a tradition, and only to the degree that one has achieved some mastery of that tradition, whether that tradition be "sociological theory" or "abstract expressionism." Traditions are often conceived as static. Following Ricoeur, I believe that the truth of a tradition is disclosed only through time, as the meaning of its values is probed in various contexts. A tradition does need foundations. But it is built up over time. Properly understood, traditions are dynamic rather than static.

Elsewhere, I have shown at greater length that prophetic religion and civic republicanism do constitute dynamic traditions in this sense. In this context, I will give one example of how the ACR has changed and grown over time. The Preamble to the Declaration of Independence asserted that "all men are created equal." However, Article 1, Section 2 of the U.S. Constitution tacitly defined an African slave as "three-fifths" of a person. Antebellum thinkers attempted to resolve this contradiction in various ways. Some claimed that Africans had no souls. Others argued that slaves were just "animated tools." Still others insisted that republicanism required slavery, invoking Athens and Rome—and ignoring Florence and Holland. In the end, these arguments failed, not just by force of arms, but also by force of logic. They failed because they were falsified by black preachers, black writers, and black orators who demonstrated that African Americans had souls and minds and civic spirit. And they failed, too, because free men and free soil went together in the Northern states, just as they had in Renaissance Europe. They failed, finally, because the letter of the Constitution was shown to violate the spirit of the Declaration. Of course, even the Civil War did not definitively settle the argument. Jim Crow and civil rights are proof enough of that. Nor is that argument over, even today. The riots in Baltimore are just the most recent reminder.

But why should a progressive care about tradition? After all, isn't progress at odds with tradition? Not necessarily. Tradition can actually be quite radical. The American Revolution drew heavily on the republican tradition. The Civil Rights Movement was largely inspired by prophetic religion. Tradition should not be confused with traditionalism. Traditionalism is static and inherently conservative; tradition is dynamic and potentially progressive.

Perhaps, the critical reader may respond, but why should a secular progressive care about the prophetic religious tradition? For at least two reasons: first, because it is the main historical source of many of her most cherished political values, including social equality and social justice; and second because it is the main source for much of our civic poetry. "Let justice roll down like waters, and righteousness like an ever-flowing stream." Martin Luther King? No, King citing the Hebrew prophet Amos. Progressives who choose a technocratic idiom over a prophetic one should not be surprised if their rhetoric falls flat. It will not evoke America's "mystic chords of memory."

Prophetic republicanism is not the only political tradition in the United States though. There are at least two others: religious nationalism and radical secularism. They are the principal protagonists in the Culture Wars.

Religious Nationalism

Just when did the Culture Wars begin? With the counter-culture's credo of "sex, drugs and rock and roll"? With Nixon's attack on "acid, amnesty and abortion"? With the foundation of Jerry Falwell's Moral Majority? However one dates them, the Culture Wars have helped set the terms of our civic conversation for at least three decades now. In the process, they have turned it into an unproductive shouting match.

By "American religious nationalism," I mean the toxic blend of WASP nativism and chauvinistic hyper-patriotism that has fueled so many of America's witch hunts and imperial misadventures over the centuries. By "radical secularism," I mean the equally noxious blend of militant atheism and overreaching scientism that has been steadily gaining ground on the American left.

The roots of American religious nationalism (ARN) are very deep. They go back to the Puritans' clashes with the Native Americans during the late 17th century. Like the ACR, the ARN is a synthesis of two discourses, in this case, the Conquest Narrative and premillennial apocalypticism. Like prophetic religion, the Conquest Narrative draws on the Hebrew Bible. Specifically, it draws on the stories of violent conquest contained in the books of Judges, Samuel, and Kings. Where prophetic religion defines political community in terms of covenant, the Conquest Narrative defines it in terms of blood: blood conquest, blood sacrifice, and blood belonging.

Unlike the ACR, ARN also draws heavily on the eschatological texts of the Christian Bible, especially those contained in the Book of Daniel and the Revelation of John. Historically, the Christian churches have interpreted these texts in analogical terms, that is, as symbolic representations of the inner struggles of the Christian life. Since the early 20th century, however, American Protestants have increasingly read these texts in literal terms as coded predictions of a cosmic war between good and evil, which will culminate in the "rapture" of all believers, the Second Coming of Christ, and his 1,000-year reign on earth. They embrace a narrative of premillennial apocalypticism.

The influence of ARN has grown significantly since World War II. There are several reasons for this. The first is the steady growth of American militarism and imperialism. Historically, these tendencies were checked by a long tradition of geopolitical isolationism, deep currents of Christian pacifism, and, not least, the age-old republican suspicion of standing armies. During the Cold War, however, these checks were systematically dismantled, and the War on Terror has eroded them further still.

The second reason for the expanding footprint of ARN is the growing influence of premillennial apocalypticism within American Protestantism, especially since World War II. This is due both to the decline of liberal Protestantism and the spread of "prophecy belief" within Evangelical circles. In recent years, apocalypticism has seeped into secular culture via popular media such as the "Left Behind" novels and films.

Why should a religious believer reject religious nationalism? Because it is an irreligious creed. It is national self-worship disguised as American patriotism. Being a Christian and a patriot does not make one a religious nationalist. Confusing the two does.

American Radical Secularism

There is also another reason for the continuing appeal of ARN: it draws energy from its Culture War against radical secularism. American radical secularism (ARS) is a synthesis of two distinct discourses: aggressive secularism and militant scientism. Aggressive secularism may be distinguished from passive secularism (Kuru 2009). Passive secularists are primarily concerned with the preservation of religious freedom and civic equality under conditions of religious pluralism. In America, for example, passive secularists would oppose the creation of religious establishments and the imposition of religious tests for public office. Passive secularism has deep roots in American history. They extend back to Puritan dissenters such as Roger Williams and Anne Hutchinson. Its legal foundations were set down in the U.S. Constitution, specifically in the First Amendment's "no establishment" and "free exercise" clauses and in Article VI's prohibition of "religious tests."

Aggressive secularism is a much newer tradition in the United States. Aggressive secularists wish to eliminate religion from public life. Accordingly, they advocate a "total separation" not only of church and state but, more expansively, of religion and politics. They seek to erect a "wall of separation" that is so thick and so high that nothing can pass through it—no money, no symbols, no arguments—even if this restricts the freedoms and ties the tongues of their religious co-citizens.

If total separationism is the first article of the secularist creed, then militant scientism is the second. By "militant scientism," I mean the view that science and religion are fundamentally incompatible and, more broadly, that natural science and human knowledge are fully coterminous. In other words, if you accept science, you must reject religion; more, you must base all of your beliefs on science. Militant scientism invokes the authority of science to contest the legitimacy of religion.

How deep does this tradition go? Radical secularists often claim a Revolutionary pedigree, and on two grounds. First, they argue that the American Revolution was an Enlightenment project and thus a secular project. But this argument is doubly false: the Enlightenment was not the sole source of Revolutionary ideology; indeed, it was arguably not even the dominant one; nor was the American Enlightenment a purely secular Enlightenment; on the contrary, it was at least as much a religious Enlightenment. To be sure, there were a few champions of "radical Enlightenment" amongst the Revolutionary generation. One thinks especially of Ethan Allen and Thomas Paine. But the "Founding Fathers" were arguably more influenced by the moderate and religious versions of Enlightenment.

Radical secularists also like to argue that the American Constitution mandates total separation. More specifically, they claim that Jefferson and Madison authored the First Amendment, and that they were total separationists. This argument is mostly wrong as well. The First Amendment was collectively authored; Jefferson and Madison did not get the last word. Nor did they establish a "wall of separation" between religion and politics. That phrase is not even in the Constitution; rather, it is taken from a letter that Jefferson penned years later. Nor is it clear that Jefferson and Madison were "total separationists" in the contemporary sense. They certainly advocated "disestablishment." But they recognized that religious belief could be an important source of civic virtue.

One reason that radical secularists lay claim to a Revolutionary pedigree is that the actual pedigree of radical secularism is not so distinguished. Radical secularism first crystallized during the 19th century. It was catalyzed by two developments: mass immigration and Darwinian theory. The doctrine of total separation was first embraced by Protestant nativists such as Paul Blanshard, who used it to parry Catholic demands for educational reform. Militant scientism often went together with Social Darwinism and cultural elitism. What do social classes owe one another? asked Yale sociologist William Graham Sumner. Absolutely nothing. Sink or swim (Sumner 1883). And failing that? Why eugenics, of course, answered H. L. Mencken (Mencken 1914). Radical secularism is no longer linked to Social Darwinism. But it sill emits a strong odor of cultural elitism.

So why should a radical progressive reject radical secularism? Because it is an illiberal creed dressed up in liberal garb. Because it is cultural condescension disguised as radical egalitarianism.

Civil Religion as Vital Center

Writing shortly after World War II, in the wake of Europe's tragic self-immolation, the Harvard historian Arthur Schlesinger spoke of the urgent need to fortify America's vital center against the centrifugal forces that threatened to pull it apart (Schlesinger 1949). By "vital center" he meant an alliance between the non-Communist left and the non-Fascist right. By "centrifugal forces" he meant social changes and radical ideologies that were tearing at America's social fabric.

Today, America's vital center is threatened by a new set of centrifugal forces: by a growing divide between the have-nots and the have-mores; by the partisan polarization between red states and blue states; and by the geographical sorting of the population into residential enclaves defined by class and culture. These social forces are pulling Americans apart.

The vital center is also threatened by radical ideologies. Some have old roots, such as the neo-nativism inspired by the latest wave of mass immigration. Others have roots that are older still, such as the "states' rights" backlash of recent years. But others are newer, such as the Randian libertarianism that is steadily gaining ground among the younger generation. The polarization has proceeded so far that respectable commentators now call for violent revolution—Chris Hedges from the left and Charles Murray from the right, for instance (Hedges 2015; Murray 2015). The American mosaic cannot survive these pulls much longer.

What is needed today is a new vital center, an alliance between the non-libertarian left and the non-chauvinist right. It cannot be constructed around religious or ethnic identity; Americans are too diverse a people for that. Nor can it be built around secular humanism or "public reason"; Americans are too metaphysical a people for that.

The civil religious tradition provides a more promising starting point. It contains both religious and secular elements and can be construed in both religious and secular terms. It defines the national community in terms of choice and ideals rather than blood and conquest and in terms of political values rather than ethnic culture. Unlike religious nationalism and radical secularism, it can encompass a diverse and metaphysical people.

Obama's 2008 presidential campaign can be seen as a first effort at reconstructing the vital center.

Barack Obama and Civil Religion

In his first campaign for the presidency, George W. Bush famously promised to be "a uniter, not a divider." And in the early months of his first term, he seemed sincere about keeping that promise. His ideology of "compassionate conservatism" and his support for "faith-based" social programs steered a middle course between the "tough love" of the market fundamentalists and the welfare statism of the social-democratic left. On foreign policy, he tried to "speak softly" and tend alliances.

Then came September 11, 2001, and the Second Iraq War. A brief efflorescence of national unity slowly gave way to a deepening of partisan divides. In truth, Bush's rhetoric was more cautious than many of his followers'. But it was not cautious enough. Bush eschewed talk of a war between Christianity and Islam, but not talk of a war between good and evil. He avoided the apocalyptic rhetoric of Gog and Magog, but embraced millennial rhetoric about an end to all evil. Bush's version of religious nationalism was more muted than some, but still easily recognizable to the trained ear.

In his first campaign for the presidency, Barack Obama also promised to be a uniter rather than a divider. He famously rejected the slicing and dicing of the American people into red states and blue states, insisting that all were members of the same United States. And he openly embraced the prophetic vision of the American project, skillfully weaving Scripture into many of his speeches.

Then came the Great Recession and the Second Health Care War. Once again, a brief moment of national unity gave way to a deepening of partisan divides. Obama's rhetoric was also more cautious than many of his supporters', partly because of his temperament but also because of his race: the first black president could not allow himself to be cast as an "angry black man."

But the real problem was not caution so much as inarticulacy. Obama could still be quite articulate about certain issues. He could summon the prophetic voice of the Civil Rights Movement to speak about racial inequality. And he could pull on the Christian Realism of Reinhold Niebuhr to address foreign policy. But other topics tied his tongue. When he tried to explain the bank bailouts, he quickly slipped into the technocratic idiom of macroeconomics. And when he tried to explain his health care law, he spoke the hoary language of the New Deal.

The reason for this curious mixture of inspiring rhetoric and *langue de bois* is the gross imbalance between the prophetic and republican dimensions in Obama's version of the civil religious tradition. To be sure, one sometimes hears distant echoes of civic republicanism as in his occasional calls for civic activism. But they are faint indeed when compared to the explicit and forthright invocations of King and Niebuhr that are threaded through so many of his pronouncements. If prophetic religion is Obama's first language, then the various dialects of modern liberalism are his second, with the ancient language of civic republicanism a halting third.

To fully revive the civil religion, we need to more fully recuperate the republican tradition—and distance ourselves from modern liberalism. Doubling down on liberalism will only deepen our problems.

Religious Progressivism and Civic Republicanism

Religious and secular progressives speak the same two languages but with differing levels of fluency. For religious progressives, prophetic religion is their mother tongue and modern liberalism a second language; for secular progressives, it is the reverse. But both tend to speak the language of liberalism when engaged in public debate.

Why does this matter? Because liberal arguments for progressive causes tend to be weak arguments—so weak, in fact, that they easily collapse under the weight of their inner contradictions. Consider a few examples.

The first concerns the relationship between personal freedom and government intervention. Modern liberalism tends to conceive of this relationship in zero-sum terms: more intervention equals less freedom. This is because liberals define freedom as "non-interference" and intervention is a kind of interference. This makes it very difficult for American liberals to make a coherent argument in favor of government action.

The second concerns the relationship between free markets and human well-being. Modern liberalism tends to conceive of human well-being in utilitarian terms and of free markets as the best means of maximizing utility. This makes it very difficult for American liberals to make a coherent argument against a market society.

The third concerns "constitutional balance." Modern liberalism envisions constitutional balance in terms of negative rights and the separation of powers. But this makes it very difficult to combat political corruption. Don't the Koch brothers have a right to their opinions, too?

In many cases, arguing for progressive causes in liberal terms is like coming to a fistfight with one hand tied behind your back. I believe that republicanism provides a more powerful vocabulary for the progressive.

How so?

First, because the republican understanding makes it easier to argue for certain forms of government intervention. Republicans understand freedom as "non-domination," which is to say, immunity from the arbitrary will of other persons (Pettit 1997). Republicans also view the rule of law as the most effective means of checking the exercise of arbitrary power. Hence, they do not see individual freedom and government intervention in zero sum terms. On the contrary, they can easily imagine situations where regulation will actually enhance freedom: for example, labor laws that require employers to provide "cause" when terminating a worker. Removing the threat of arbitrary termination checks the domination of employers.

Second, because the republican vision makes it easy to argue against market fundamentalism. Republicans understand human flourishing as the purposeful exercise of human capacities—for speech and reason, in the classical account, but also for art, play, and nurturance in modern ones. Of course, some measure of material affluence is a precondition of the human good in this sense and a market economy may be a useful instrument for achieving it. However, from a republican perspective, overwork and overconsumption are actually inimical to human well-being and to the degree that markets encourage this, they must be contained—by limiting work hours and expanding vacation and leave time, for example, and also more generally by preventing the instrumental and utilitarian logic of the market from colonizing non-economic areas of human activity.

Third, because the republican vision makes it easier to argue for greater social equality. For liberals, there is no contradiction between social inequality and political freedom. Vast differences in wealth can go hand in hand with equal rights and equal protections. For republicans, the liberal view is hopelessly naïve. Great concentrations of wealth lead to great inequalities in power—in a word: oligarchy. From the republican perspective, the problem with inequality is not simply that it is unjust, though it is surely that, too; it is that it is inimical to popular government, because the few use their wealth to nullify the power of the many. From a republican perspective, then, there are compelling *political* reasons for limiting economic inequality.

Fourth and finally, because the republican vision makes it easier to argue against the influence of big money in American politics. On the liberal definition, corruption is defined narrowly in terms of quid pro quos between bad actors. The obvious remedy is therefore criminal prosecution—*if* intent can be proven. On the republican definition,

corruption is understood expansively in terms of dependency and ser-
vility. If candidates for president have to "audition" for billionaires, that
is a problem in and of itself, even if there are no explicit quid pro quos.

Conclusion: Religious Progressives and the Vital Center

On June 17, 2015, the Rev. Clementa Pinckney and eight of his parishioners were shot down in cold blood by Dylann Storm Roof, a young
white supremacist. The murders took place during an evening Bible
study group at an African Methodist Episcopal Church in Charleston,
South Carolina. The group had invited Roof in when he appeared at the
church door. Founded during the early republic, Emanuel AME was an
epicenter of abolitionism and, later, of the struggle for civil rights.

Nine days later, on June 26, 2015, President Barack Obama strode to
the pulpit at Emanuel and delivered a eulogy for Pinckney. There were
echoes of the famous speech on race that he had delivered in Philadelphia seven years before. Once again, Obama decried chattel slavery as
the nation's original sin and called its citizens to a more perfect union.

Still, the tone of the speech was different: less academic and more
homiletic. The race speech had been filled with invisible footnotes to
scholarly studies. The grace speech was filled with unmarked citations
from Christian scripture.

For that was the governing theme of the speech—grace. "According
to the Christian tradition," Obama reminded his listeners, "grace is not
earned. Grace is not merited." It is not merited, he added, because "we
are all sinners." Sinners! Not since Jimmy Carter had an American president dared suggest that the American people were anything but inherently good, not since Ronald Reagan had publicly absolved them of all
their sins some three decades earlier.

Nor was Obama speaking solely of individual sins; he urged his
listeners to reflect on the "collective sins" of the American people, on
their support for slavery, and Jim Crow and "massive resistance" to civil
rights. Nor would acts of "individual charity" be enough to atone for
these sins, he added; that would require the pursuit of "social justice."

Obama had opened his eulogy with a verse from Paul's letter to the
Hebrews. But his main focus was the last line of the first verse of "Amazing Grace": "I once was blind, but now I see." By God's grace, Obama

said, we—not an accusatory "you," but a generous "we"—are now able to see the wrongness of our ways—the wrongness of flying the Confederate flag over the state capitol of South Carolina, for example, and of our callous indifference to hungry children languishing in dilapidated schools without any prospects for the future.

Midway through the speech, Obama declaimed the first verse of "Amazing Grace." Then, at its close, by way of peroration, he began to sing, slowly, haltingly, a little off-key, more parishioner than soloist, as other members of the congregation joined in one by one, sotto voce. The most powerful man on earth was, for a brief second, just another man in the pews.

No one who saw that speech, who felt that speech, who sang along with that speech, could possibly conclude that the American civil religion is just an empty and broken shell. No, there is still life in that tradition. The main source of that life is the prophetic religion that lives on in the Black Church, and in other churches and synagogues, too.

Still, anyone who knows the full history of that tradition, who knows the language of civic republicanism, who can still speak that language today, will also worry that the ACR is only fighting at half strength, with one hand tied behind its back or, better, dangling at its side. Speaking truth to power is important; the prophetic tradition addresses that need. But so, too, is a robust vision of political community. There, the republican tradition is crucial.

Nor is this the only peril. The Black Church is a sturdy reed, but it is too thin to carry the weight of the civil religious tradition all by itself. Historically, liberal Protestants and Jews have helped to shoulder the burden as well. But both have been afflicted by a steady loss of members over the last half century and, perhaps, too, by a crisis of confidence.

So, rebuilding the vital center will involve more than a recuperation of the republican tradition. It will also require the creation of a new alliance. Where might the new "social carriers" of the civil religious tradition come from? Perhaps from young Evangelicals who care as much about social justice as about sexual morality. Perhaps from cradle Catholics inspired by the new pope or Latino Catholics who remember a liberationist faith. Hopefully also from the ranks of the "poster children," the young "post-Protestants" who are still devoted to the core values of their ancestral religion, if no longer to its liturgy or rites.

288 PHILIP S. GORSKI

NOTE

1 Meanwhile, President Obama had more difficulty connecting with the American people than candidate Obama had. He could articulate a national vision, but he had trouble translating it into a political agenda. Anger on the Right was accompanied by disappointment on the Left.

Bellah, Robert. 1967. "Civil Religion in America." *Daedalus* 96: 1–21.

Bellah, Robert Neelly. 1975. *The Broken Covenant: American Civil Religion in Time of Trial.* New York: Seabury Press.

Hedges, Chris. 2015. *Wages of Rebellion: The Moral Imperative of Revolt.* New York: Nation Books.

Kuru, Ahmet T. 2009. *Secularism and State Policies toward Religion: The United States, France, and Turkey.* Cambridge, UK: Cambridge University Press.

MacIntyre, Alasdair. 1994. "The Concept of a Tradition." In *Communitarianism: A New Public Ethics,* ed. Markate Dale, 123–126. Belmont, CA: Wadsworth.

Mencken, Henry L. 1914. "The Mailed Fist and Its Prophet." *Atlantic Monthly* 114: 598–607.

Murray, Charles. 2015. *By the People: Rebuilding Liberty without Permission.* New York: Crown Forum.

Nelson, Eric. 2010. *The Hebrew Republic: Jewish Sources and the Transformation of European Political Thought.* Cambridge, MA: Harvard University Press.

Pettit, Philip. 1997. *Republicanism: A Theory of Freedom and Government.* Oxford: Clarendon Press.

Ricoeur, Paul. 1990. *Time and Narrative.* Pbk. ed. 3 vols. Chicago: University of Chicago Press.

Schlesinger, Arthur Meier. 1949. *The Vital Center: The Politics of Freedom.* Boston: Houghton Mifflin.

Sumner, William Graham. 1883. *What Social Classes Owe to Each Other.* New York: Harper & Brothers.

Winship, Michael P. 2006. "Godly Republicanism and the Origins of the Massachusetts Polity." *William and Mary Quarterly* 63(2): 427–462.

13

Strategic Storytelling by Nuns on the Bus

RUTH BRAUNSTEIN

The stories are endless. . . . It touches the heart. We spend a
lot of time shedding a tear or two.
—Sister Simone Campbell to *Pittsburgh Press*
(June 28, 2012) (Riely 2012)

When a group of Catholic Sisters set off on a national bus tour to critique Republican congressman Paul Ryan's proposed cuts to the federal
budget (Ryan 2012), this unlikely vision captured the media's attention.
The "Nuns on the Bus," as they called themselves, bore little resemblance
to the ruler-wielding disciplinarians of the American cultural imaginary,
who care more about sexual depravity than economic deprivation. As
they logged miles driving through America's heartland, these Sisters
showed Americans a different picture of their community: they were pragmatic stalwarts who had long since traded their habits for simple street
clothes, and who ran underfunded soup kitchens and service organizations
in America's poorest communities. Most of these women had toiled in relative obscurity for decades, until an unlikely series of events thrust them
into the spotlight.

Although one could choose to begin this story much earlier, for our
purposes it suffices to begin in April 2012.[1] It was then that the Vatican
Congregation for the Doctrine of the Faith called for a major reform—or
"renewal"—of the Leadership Conference of Women Religious, an umbrella organization that speaks for the majority of Catholic Sisters in
the United States. Among the concerns outlined in the Vatican's doc-
trinal assessment was that Catholic Sisters were focusing too much on
"promoting issues of social justice," while they were relatively "silent"
on issues like abortion and same-sex marriage. Perhaps more problem-
atically, the Sisters' efforts to promote social and economic justice had

occasionally placed them at odds with the (male) bishops, who were, according to the assessment, "the Church's authentic teachers of faith and morals." Against the backdrop of a growing political divide between "social justice Catholics" and "right to life Catholics," this censure had the unintended effect of transforming the Sisters (at least for a time) into the public face of social justice Catholicism.[2]

In June 2012, NETWORK—a Catholic Sisters–led social justice advocacy organization that had been explicitly criticized in the Vatican assessment—capitalized on this newfound attention and launched a bus tour intended to raise national awareness of the harm that proposed federal budget cuts would cause struggling families around the country.[3] This small band of lobbyists became the Nuns on the Bus, known by swelling crowds as the "Soul Sisters," and received everywhere they went, at least for a time, as unlikely "rock stars" (Boorstein 2012).

After three months on the road, Sister Simone Campbell, the leader of the campaign, spoke at the Democratic National Convention, making visible to millions of Americans the work that progressive religious activists were doing to shape the moral contours of the policy debate. During this televised appearance, she shared the stories of four people she had met during the campaign, highlighting the ways in which they relied on programs and services that received funding from the federal government.

By placing ordinary people's stories at the forefront of this appearance—and of the campaign more generally—the Nuns on the Bus engaged in a practice that is common within the progressive religious advocacy field. As this chapter will show, the style of storytelling that was central to this campaign not only helped the Nuns overcome various communications challenges they faced as progressive religious advocates, but also enabled them to recast both individual policy issues and the very nature of policy debates in moral terms.

Progressive Religious Advocacy and Communication Challenges

Organizations like NETWORK participate in the competitive field of interest group politics in Washington, DC, where they work alongside a range of other lobbyists and interest groups—religious and secular, progressive and conservative—that seek to influence the policymaking process. What unites the diverse array of *religious* advocacy organizations is that they bring their varied faith perspectives to bear on policy debates. They do so by lobbying for public policies that are consistent with their communities' religious values or with values that are broadly shared across multiple faith communities, like peace, social justice, or the common good. Many also seek to mobilize grassroots support for their efforts, by engaging in public campaigns that highlight the moral valence of issues and calling upon people of faith to pressure their representatives (Hertzke 1988; Wuthnow 1988; Hofrenning 1995; Yamane 2005; Fowler et al. 2010).[4]

Whether they are progressive or conservative, religious advocates face a number of communications challenges. The first of these is due to the fact that the policymaking process is increasingly dominated by moneyed interests—armed with large checkbooks—and professional policy experts—armed with surveys, statistics, and advanced degrees in economics (Schlozman, Verba, and Brady 2012). Religious advocates do not typically have sufficient material resources or expert knowledge to compete with these actors on their own terms. Instead, they derive their authority to intervene in debates from their status as representatives of large moral communities, which are either impacted directly by policies or work closely with impacted populations through direct service organizations. In this way, they argue they add local knowledge and "prophetic vision" to the policymaking process (Hertzke 1988; Hofrenning 1995; Moody 2002; Olson 2002; Steensland 2002).

But the fact that this authority is rooted in their religious identities is complicated when we consider the second challenge they face: the fact that policymaking is widely viewed as a secular endeavor, at least in the context of a value-diverse democracy. Policymaking here must be distinguished from politics, in which religious expression is encouraged and commonplace. But a line is typically drawn between the two—in theory, if not in practice, policies applying to all citizens should be justified using arguments that are persuasive and accessible to all, irrespective of their religious views (Habermas 1989, 2006; Rawls 1993; Audi 1997).

This has been interpreted—particularly among political liberals anxious about the antidemocratic potential of public religion—to mean that there is no place for religious discourse in policy debates. While many conservative religious groups reject this concern, arguing that policies can legitimately be justified in terms of Christian (or Judeo-Christian) values, liberal religious groups have responded by building broad-based interfaith support for their positions, and attempting to speak in terms that resonate across religiously diverse and non-religious publics (Wood 2002; Lichterman 2005).

Liberal groups have struggled, however, to cultivate a broad-based moral voice that allows them to speak to and for a broad set of religious communities, as well as their secular liberal partners. Some speak in technical, moral, or ethical terms that should, at least hypothetically, broaden the appeal of their message while also enhancing their credibility as policy professionals (Hertzke 1988; Dillon 1996; Yamane 2000; Jelen 2005). But because these advocates justify their existence by reference to the authenticity and distinctiveness of their *religious* voices (Moody 2002; Olson 2002), these communications strategies can appear shallow, and can ultimately undermine their authority (Steensland 2002; Wood 2002).

A Dilemma and a Solution

Simply put, these actors face a dilemma. The context in which they operate requires they simultaneously speak to multiple audiences—the policymakers they seek to persuade, the media they need to carry their message to the general public, and the members of their own religious communities that they seek to mobilize around issues. Across all of these audiences, they must demonstrate their authority to intervene in policy debates—which is rooted in the knowledge they carry as representatives of faith communities—while also speaking in terms that are broadly accessible to their various audiences, regardless of their religious commitments.

One solution that many of these groups have developed involves storytelling (Braunstein 2012). Stories, prepackaged in a format that appeals to journalists, allow activists to make complex problems tangible to the broader public (Ryan 1991). For this reason, a wide range of political actors engages in storytelling (Davis 2002; Polletta et al. 2011). But because storytelling also fulfills the various requirements outlined above, it can be a *particularly* useful communications strategy for progressive religious groups.

One reason for this is that stories supply a clear interpretive frame—the *moral* of the story—yet do not *moralize* in terms specific to any religious tradition (Stone 2001; Polletta 2006). Put differently, storytelling allows progressive religious advocates to (re)frame policy debates in broad-based moral terms, creating a context in which their particular brand of authority becomes most relevant. Moreover, as I will show, the specific storytelling style that these groups have developed allows them to highlight: (1) *their own moral status as storytellers*, (2) *the moral status of the characters in their stories*, and (3) *the moral status of storytelling itself.*

First, advocates highlight their status as representatives of their faith communities as the basis of their credibility as storytellers. As Rhys Williams and Jay Demerath (1991) have argued, despite secular anxieties about the role religion can play in policy debates, religious communities are still considered the "carriers of the moral" in American society, and religious leaders are widely recognized as moral authorities on issues of public concern. Through their relationships to their religious communities (and to networks of faith-based care providers), they have direct access not only to the hearts, minds, and concerns of large swaths of the American public, but also to vast wells of stories of suffering, which they can tap into as evidence of proposed policies' negative impacts. Their status as moral authorities rests upon demonstrating the strength of these relationships, and moreover, in Jeffrey Stout's (2010) terms, that they have "earned" the authority to speak on behalf of their communities.

Second, advocates tell stories about the suffering that people in their faith communities have experienced firsthand or confronted through their direct service work. Although the way in which this is done varies widely, one common strategy is to highlight the ways in which (current or potential) beneficiaries of government spending conform to widely shared conceptions of deservedness, or what Brian Steensland (2006) calls "cultural categories of worth." This may involve reframing "undeserving" groups as worthy of government assistance, or selectively highlighting stories of individuals that are already most likely to be viewed as worthy.

Finally, advocates assert the *moral necessity* of taking stories seriously, by arguing that policymakers have a moral obligation to face the human realities of an issue before making decisions that will impact people's lives.[5] More specifically, they argue that the *form* in which this information is delivered to policymakers has moral implications. The intimacy of stories is contrasted to the relative coldness of statistics, which obscure individuals behind trends. If, as the historian Theodore Porter (1995, ix) has argued, "quantification is a technology of distance," then storytelling is a technology of closeness. While the former enables indifference, the latter encourages empathy. As such, stories not only provide policymakers with more grounded information about how impacted populations experience hardships and interact with the system in question; they also force an emotional connection with these populations.

That said, the data delivered via stories is anecdotal, and may be viewed as inferior to more representative forms like survey data. Yet stories are actually quite difficult to refute, as Andrew J. Perrin (2009, 72) found, based on an analysis of political conversations. He observed that people would readily refute others' arguments, but their stories took "the form of an objective fact. . . . A challenger can raise objections to the anecdote's *relevance*, or offer alternative anecdotes or alternative interpretations of the same anecdote. She cannot, however, easily challenge the logic underlying the anecdote's recital." By asserting the authority status of ordinary people's experiences—delivered via stories—as a complement to other forms of data in policy debates, religious advocates challenge not only the content of policy debates, but also their structure. Put differently, stories not only expand *what is known* about the impacts of policy, but also *how we can know*.

The sections that follow present an in-depth analysis of storytelling by Nuns on the Bus in order to demonstrate how this works in practice.

Nuns on the Bus

On June 6, 2012, NETWORK (2012) announced that a group of Catholic Sisters, many of whom were also registered lobbyists, would embark on a "multi-state bus trip . . . highlighting the work Sisters do to meet the needs of people at the economic margins and revealing how federal budget cuts proposed by Rep. Paul Ryan (R-WI) and passed by the House of Representatives will hurt struggling families in these states." Coming on the heels of the Vatican's rebuke, this campaign—called "Nuns on the Bus: Nuns Drive for Faith, Family and Fairness"—harnessed the unprecedented flood of media attention the Sisters were receiving by shining a spotlight on the hardships that Catholic Sisters encountered every day. While NETWORK is part of this broader network of Catholic Sisters, it is also a lobbying organization, so the participating Sisters also intended to meet with members of Congress in each of the states they visited. They announced they would use these lobby visits as occasions to "lift up" the stories they encountered on the road.

On June 17, they kicked off their tour in Des Moines, Iowa, with a celebration and prayer service for a crowd of approximately three hundred people (Johnson 2012). Over the next fifteen days, they traveled twenty-seven hundred miles through nine states. They made a high-profile stop in Ryan's hometown of Janesville, Wisconsin, and at Speaker John Boehner's district office in West Chester, Ohio. But most days involved visits to the people who would be most affected by cuts: a food pantry in Dubuque, a dental clinic in Milwaukee, a "children's day camp and hunger center" in Cleveland, the Dorothy Day House in Youngstown. On several evenings, the nuns were occupied with "Friend Raisers."

Everywhere they went, large and enthusiastic crowds greeted the bus. When they arrived in South Bend, Indiana, on the fifth day of their trip, they were met by "the same sort of enthusiastic crowds that often greet Notre Dame teams coming home after big wins on the road," according to the *National Catholic Reporter*. On June 27, the *Washington Post's* Michelle Boorstein (2012) summed up the Nuns' newfound fame:

> The bus Sister Simone Campbell is using for her cross-country publicity tour is the type typically used by rock bands. To some, this seems appropriate. The D.C. nun was greeted in Jackson, Mich., with "Saint Simone" signs, and in Janesville, Wis., people inside a downtown office-building atrium lined the balconies chanting and snapping photos.
>
> In the past couple of weeks, the dry-humored lobbyist has been on the "The Colbert Report." "The Daily Show," which will feature Campbell in July, made her a satiny, "Grease"-like jacket emblazoned with "Bad Habitz" on the back.

On July 2, they concluded the tour in Washington, DC, with a rally where they announced they would "Bring Stories of Hardship to Capitol Hill," and introduce their vision for a "faithful budget." Campbell, as mentioned, later spoke at the Democratic National Convention, where she shared the stories of individual Americans she had encountered during the bus tour. And on July 31, 2013—having just returned from a second Nuns on the Bus campaign promoting comprehensive immigration reform—Campbell testified before Ryan's own House Budget Committee, at a hearing dubbed "The War on Poverty: A Progress Report" (NETWORK 2013). According to NETWORK's (2013) press release describing her testimony, Campbell "not[ed] that she had met with many people whose lives are directly impacted by programs such as these, [and] told some of their stories."

By placing stories at the forefront of this campaign, the Nuns on the Bus leveraged their moral authority as social justice–minded people of faith in order to convey broadly accessible information about the ways in which struggling Americans relied on programs and services that received funding from the federal government.

Moral Framing through Storytelling

As I have argued, this communications strategy provided the Nuns with one way to overcome the dilemmas they face as progressive religious actors seeking to influence public policy debates. It did so by providing them with opportunities to highlight their own moral status as storytellers, the moral status of the characters in their stories, and the moral status of storytelling itself. More specifically, through their storytelling performances, they framed religious communities, and in this case Catholic Sisters, as morally superior to political elites like Paul Ryan as carriers of knowledge about the effects of cuts in government spending; they framed vulnerable people and the programs that serve them as morally worthy beneficiaries of government spending; and finally, they asserted the moral necessity of taking stories seriously alongside other forms of more abstract and impersonal data that inform the policymaking process.

The Storytellers

When NETWORK first announced the campaign, the press release noted, "Because of their work, Sisters see the suffering of people in poverty on a daily basis. As a result, they recognize the harm that the Ryan budget will cause" (NETWORK 2012). By noting that many Catholic Sisters work directly with individuals and organizations that require government spending to survive, they grounded their authority to intervene in this debate in their community's unique capacity to understand the impact of proposed budget cuts.

When the Nuns mobilized their network of Catholic Sisters to stand alongside them at each stop on their bus tour, they sought to demonstrate the depth of their relationships with this community and the people it serves, and by extension their credibility to tell their stories. They underscored this point on nearly every stop on their tour and during countless media appearances. For example, in an interview with National Public Radio (2012), Campbell was asked, "Why did you choose this method to address the federal budget cuts?" Her response was:

> All over our nation, Catholic Sisters are working at the margins of our society to serve people who are struggling in this economy, people who are hungry, people who are left out of the economy, people who have lost their jobs or people working at low wage jobs. We thought the best way to bring an education to our nation about what's happening here in Washington is if we went on the road and lifted up their work and the consequences they would face if this Republican House budget goes through. . . . We thought, we need to illustrate the problem because people outside the Beltway don't know.

This comment not only underscores the Sisters' credibility as carriers of the stories of "people who are struggling in this economy"; it also suggests that *without* their voices, "people outside the Beltway" would not fully understand the consequences of "what's happening here in Washington." This, they suggested, was because the voices that Americans *were* hearing (including those of political elites like Paul Ryan and Governor Mitt Romney, the Republican nominee for president who had recently selected Ryan as his running mate) were not providing

Americans with an accurate picture of how the budget would impact people's lives.

In other appearances, Campbell made this comparison more explicitly. For example, after the Nuns invited Romney to join their campaign for a day, Campbell offered the following reason during a visit to *The Ed Show* (2012):

> I think he doesn't know how those at the lowest 20 percent of income in our society live. He doesn't know how hard they work, how they struggle every day, and he's making some gross generalizations about them being lazy or not working. *And that's just plain wrong.* We found on our bus trip over and over that people who are the working poor, working at low-wage jobs, are using our social safety net to keep their families alive, to keep a roof over their head or food on the table. *And Governor Romney doesn't appear to know this at all.* We would like to introduce him to the reality of our nation. (emphasis added)

Here, Campbell went subtly beyond highlighting the credibility and knowledge of her network of Catholic Sisters; she also aligned herself (and the other Nuns on the Bus) with them by referencing what "*we* found on our bus trip." Although Campbell and her colleagues are lobbyists whose home base is Washington, DC, the bus trip was an opportunity to distance themselves—literally and figuratively—from the elitist DC bubble in which they portrayed Ryan and Romney living.

Together, comments like these frame those individuals working with vulnerable populations as more credible carriers of information about the potential impacts of policies than elite and out-of-touch Washington insiders.

The Characters

The bus tour provided the Nuns with a supply of stories that they could "lift up" when they were advocating for their version of a "faithful budget." As far as these stories themselves were concerned, the Nuns told stories about individuals that they encountered during their travels or provided platforms for individuals to tell their own stories firsthand.[6] In each case, the stories illustrated how virtuous and hard-working yet struggling Americans relied on programs and services that were supported by government funding.

For example, at the Democratic National Convention, Campbell used well over half of her speaking time to recount the stories of four people she had met during the campaign, including Billy:

> In Milwaukee, I met Billy and his wife and two boys at St. Benedict's dining room. Billy's *work hours were cut back* in the recession and Billy is *taking responsibility* for himself and his family. But right now, without food stamps, he and his wife could not put food on their family table. We share responsibility for creating an economy where *parents with jobs* earn enough to care for their families. In order to cut taxes for the wealthy, the Romney/Ryan budget would make it even tougher on *hard-working Americans* like Billy to feed their families. Paul Ryan says this budget is in keeping with the moral values of our shared faith. I disagree. (emphasis added)

In this same speech, she also spoke of two ten-year-old boys in Toledo, Ohio, who were having trouble at school because they were the sole caregivers of their bed-ridden mother, and of a Cincinnati woman who lost her job, lost her health insurance, and soon after developed cancer and died.

The stories that the Nuns shared during the campaign were not likely selected at random; indeed, they served as direct rebuttals to the claims made by Republican proponents of the budget cuts. Consider Campbell's comment above about Romney. She explicitly noted that his "gross generalizations" about beneficiaries—as "being lazy or not working"—were "just plain wrong." Rather, she explained that they regularly encountered "people who are the working poor, working at low-wage jobs, are using our social safety net to keep their families alive, to keep a roof over their head or food on the table"—people like Billy.

Although some progressive groups make a case for the provision of social rights to all members of society, regardless of their participation in the labor market, many of the stories that the Nuns told featured individuals who were working, attempting to find work, or had recently lost jobs. Other stories featured innocent children and families. And nearly all of the stories featured "average Americans" from heartland cities like

Milwaukee, Toledo, and Cincinnati.[7] Taken together, we can see that the individuals they "lifted up" tended to be members of groups that are widely viewed by the American public as morally worthy and deserving of government assistance. Thus, even though Campbell was careful to note later in her convention speech that the Nuns "care for the 100 percent," by highlighting this subset of all possible stories, they reinforced the elevated moral status of these categories of citizens over others.

Groups wishing to challenge this moral hierarchy might criticize this strategy. But with the possibility looming of major rollbacks to social spending, one could also make the case that the more urgent need was to defend *existing* spending patterns, rather than attempt to *broaden* the public's conceptions of deservedness. In the short term, stories that resonated with preexisting understandings of deservedness would be mostly likely to achieve this goal: they were more likely to feel familiar to average Americans, pull at the heartstrings of conservative and liberal politicians alike, and trigger feelings of moral obligation among the general public.

The Stories

Finally, in addition to highlighting the Nuns' moral authority as storytellers and the moral worth of current beneficiaries, Campbell also repeatedly asserted the moral status of the stories themselves and why they should play a role in this debate. Specifically, she argued that policymakers have a moral obligation to consider the real people that will be directly impacted by their decisions. Where statistics afford a cold detachment from the human implications of public policies, stories of actual people have an emotional impact on policymakers that cannot be easily dismissed. As Campbell told Greg Kaufman (2012) of *The Nation*:

> KAUFMAN: You said that the Nuns went on the road to explain to people about the Ryan budget, but instead the people explained to you. You've worked your whole life on poverty-related issues. What is it that you learned on this trip?
> CAMPBELL: The stories of people who broke our hearts over and over and over again. To meet people like Margaret's family who came

directly from her memorial service to our "friendraiser" because they wanted to raise up Margaret so that no more people would die without health insurance because they lost their job. Or Shiesha in Chicago, who is pulling her life together in this little oasis of hope on the South Side—to see her determination and work in getting her college diploma. Or Billy trying to feed his family when he can only afford to either put a roof over their heads or food on the table, so he uses the food program at St. Benedict's dining room. Or the man who just got out of jail in Youngstown who now has this place to stay that's like a bed and breakfast, who never felt his dignity until he had that experience. And it's all because of the programs of Sisters in these public-private partnerships.

When the Nuns returned to Washington, DC, after the first stage of the campaign, Campbell reiterated this message. When she was asked what their next steps were, she responded:

Probably in September we'll do a briefing on Capitol Hill that's not just about data. They've got enough data! But I want to break their hearts with the people we saw and met. Because it's so easy to arrogantly just dismiss programs because you can argue about numbers and effectiveness. But tell me that Margaret should die again, and I'll fight you tooth and nail. It's just wrong. (Kaufman 2012)

Nearly a year later, she followed through on this promise to do a briefing that was not "just about data." NETWORK's (2013) press release describing her testimony before the House Budget Committee placed stories front and center:

Noting that she had met with many people whose lives are directly impacted by programs such as these, she told some of their stories. She spoke of a Milwaukee couple, both with jobs but whose work hours had been cut back, who needed food stamps and church-provided food so their children could be fed. Another story was of a young homeless Iowa mother who was moving to self-sufficiency because of "federal programs that helped fund the shelter, transition housing, SNAP, Medicaid and a Pell grant."

She also spoke of an Ohio woman who died of cancer after she lost her job and health insurance, which meant she could not afford the health screenings and early treatment that would have saved her life. The Affordable Care Act and Medicaid expansion will make tragic stories like hers less prevalent.

The press release concluded by highlighting Campbell's call for the committee to "avoid the easy sound bites that cast poor families as 'other.'" In so doing, it subtly reinforced the importance of considering the complexities and humanity of real people's stories when making policy choices.

Conclusion

By using this style of storytelling, the Nuns highlighted: (1) the moral authority of their faith communities as knowledgeable witnesses to poverty and credible carriers of stories; (2) the moral status of beneficiaries as hard-working Americans and families who deserve help when they are in need; and (3) the moral necessity of taking stories seriously in policy debates.

The problem, they argued, was not that politicians like Ryan or Romney did not have access to enough data. Rather, the Nuns argued that certain kinds of data are insufficient—the statistics and expert opinions that politicians rely on can be distorting, depersonalizing, and distancing. Instead, the Nuns argued that stories—which convey the experiences and humanity of beneficiaries—are necessary complements to these other sources of data.

Of course, storytelling is not without its critics. When activists rely too heavily on stories of individual suffering, they may neglect more complex impersonal and/or structural accounts of the root causes of this suffering (Iyengar 1991; Tilly 2002). Yet there are ways to mitigate this concern. "Subversive" stories, for example, portray individual experiences as embedded in larger power structures (Ewick and Silbey 1995). That most of the stories this campaign lifted up embedded individuals' suffering in broader social and economic patterns suggests an effort to address this shortcoming.

Another critique comes from those concerned about inequalities in the "distribution of storytelling authority" (Polletta 2006, 168; see also Blommaert 2001). Public debates are structured by inequalities that shape who speaks, whose voices are viewed as credible, and whose voices ultimately shape the direction of conversation. Although creating space for storytelling might help to level the playing field, it does not guarantee parity: all storytellers are not treated as equally credible (Gamson 1992; Fung 2003; Polletta and Lee 2006; Perrin 2009).

In this case, the Nuns benefitted from high levels of storytelling authority, rooted in cultural reverence and moral credibility that extended well beyond the Catholic community. That they found it necessary to highlight their religious identities only underscores their recognition of this inequality. But they also used their unequal supply of moral authority in order to create platforms for other storytellers—many of whom would not have been treated with the same reverence had they not been anointed by the Nuns as credible storytellers.

Overall, storytelling may be most useful for progressive religious groups like the Nuns because stories show, rather than tell. The Nuns did not simply *tell* people that Ryan's budget was *wrong* (based on their specific version of moral wrongness); they *showed* people how *bad* it would be (in tangible ways, for real people). In general, stories offer a way to provoke emotional reactions before intellectual rebuttals. And stories can hypothetically reach everyone at this more basic level, regardless of the theological or philosophical frameworks through which they might ultimately interpret the information communicated through the story.

In this way, storytelling also provides a solution to secularist concerns about the inaccessibility of public religious speech in religiously diverse societies. Although there are a number of ways in which religious groups can and do communicate across religious differences, storytelling appears to serve as one useful method of doing so, particularly for groups that desire to speak to multiple audiences simultaneously. As such, storytelling potentially serves as a multivocal form of moral communication that *transcends* specific religious divisions.

NOTES

1 Over the past several decades, Catholic Sisters and lay Catholics have increasingly challenged the male leadership of the US Catholic Church on questions about women's authority and role within the church and in public life. See Katzenstein (1998) for a discussion of these activities. This longer history provides context for the Vatican's 2012 calls for reform.

2 The 2012 American Values Survey found significant political divides between those who identified primarily as "social justice Catholics" (60 percent) and those who saw themselves as "right to life Catholics" (31 percent). In the 2012 presidential election, for example, "social justice Catholics" strongly favored Obama (Democrat), while "right to life Catholics" strongly favored Governor Mitt Romney (Republican). Moreover, "social justice Catholics" believed that "the Catholic Church should focus more on social justice and the obligation to help the poor, even if it means focusing less on issues like abortion and the right to life" (Jones, Cox, and Navarro-Rivera 2012:3).

3 Despite the tensions caused by the Vatican assessment, the Nuns repeatedly noted that they "stood with the bishops" on this issue. Indeed, the US Conference of Catholic Bishops *also* spoke out against Ryan's budget, calling the proposed cuts "unjustified and wrong," and urging Congress "to resist for moral and human reasons unacceptable cuts to hunger and nutrition programs [that would] hurt hungry children, poor families, vulnerable seniors and workers who cannot find employment" (Blaire and Pate 2012). But in relative terms, the Nuns' campaign received far more attention than the bishops' did.

4 Although most studies of religious advocacy have focused exclusively on lobbying organizations, advocacy today is undertaken by a broader range of actors representing people of faith. Participants in these efforts include faith leaders; membership-based advocacy organizations affiliated with religious communities; the Washington offices of certain religious denominations; faith-based peace, social justice, and service organizations; national networks of congregation-based community organizations and other grassroots groups; and media and consulting groups (Dionne 2008; Jones 2008; Sullivan 2008).

5 Representative democracy rests on the premise that political elites and specialized experts are best qualified to make public policies because they have the knowledge and wisdom to "refine and enlarge" (in the words of James Madison) citizens' myriad preferences and needs (Schlozman, Verba, and Brady 2012, 104–5). Yet this requires they seek out and listen to a wide range of citizens—a difficult task in light of rising inequalities in whose voices are heard in these debates. Advocates offer stories as one means of lifting up underrepresented voices.

6 In addition, many of the stories they "lifted up" were not about individuals but about *organizations* that served people in need. In light of the campaign's call for a moral budget that provides "Reasonable Revenue for Responsible Programs," these stories were intended to highlight the work being done by some of these "responsible programs." But these stories ultimately communicated a similar "moral" as those

that portrayed individuals: they showed that these programs helped disadvantaged yet hard-working individuals become productive members of their communities; that despite resource constraints, they have been effective; and that they required continued funding or these individuals and their communities would suffer.

7 As Rhys Williams (2004) has argued, the Midwest—or "the heartland"—is often evoked within politics and popular culture as a symbol of a "true" or "average" America. Of course, politicians need not reference this vision with nostalgia or longing in order to acknowledge the strategic reality that "'Will it play in Peoria?' is an all-purpose way to think of a large, loosely defined, white, more or less middle-class, cultural sensibility" (204).

REFERENCES

Audi, Robert. 1997. "Liberal Democracy and the Place of Religion in Politics." In *Religion in the Public Square*, edited by Robert Audi and Nicholas Wolterstorff, 1–66. Lanham, MD: Rowman & Littlefield.

Blaire, Bishop Stephen E., and Bishop Richard E. Pate. 2012. Joint Letter to Senate Appropriations Subcommittee on Agriculture, FY 2013. *United States Conference of Catholic Bishops*, April 16. http://origin.usccb.org.

Blommaert, Jan. 2001. "Investigating Narrative Inequality: African Asylum Seekers' Stories in Belgium." *Discourse and Society* 12(4): 413–49.

Boorstein, Michelle. 2012. "The Nuns on the Bus Tour Promotes Social Justice—and Turns a Deaf Ear to the Vatican." *Washington Post*, June 27.

Braunstein, Ruth. 2012. "Storytelling in Liberal Religious Advocacy." *Journal for the Scientific Study of Religion* 51(1): 110–27.

Davis, Joseph E., ed. 2002. *Stories of Change: Narrative and Social Movements*. Albany: State University of New York Press.

Dillon, Michele. 1996. "Cultural Differences in the Abortion Discourse of the Catholic Church: Evidence from Four Countries." *Sociology of Religion* 57(1): 25–36.

Dionne, E. J., Jr. 2008. *Souled Out: Reclaiming Faith and Politics after the Religious Right*. Princeton, NJ: Princeton University Press.

The Ed Show with Ed Schultz. 2012. August 9. MSNBC.

Ewick, Patricia, and Susan S. Silbey. 1995. "Subversive Stories and Hegemonic Tales: Toward a Sociology of Narrative." *Law and Society Review* 29(2): 197–226.

Fowler, Robert Booth, Allen D. Hertzke, Laura R. Olson, and Kevin R. den Dulk. 2010. *Religion and Politics in America: Faith, Culture, and Strategic Choices*. Boulder, CO: Westview Press.

Fung, Archon. 2003. "Survey Article: Recipes for Public Spheres: Eight Institutional Design Choices and Their Consequences." *Journal of Political Philosophy* 11(3): 338–67.

Gamson, William A. 1992. *Talking Politics*. Cambridge, UK, and New York: Cambridge University Press.

Habermas, Jürgen. 1989. *The Structural Transformation of the Public Sphere: An Inquiry into a Category of Bourgeois Society*, trans. Thomas Burger. Cambridge, MA: MIT Press.

Habermas, Jürgen. 2006. "Religion in the Public Sphere." *European Journal of Philosophy* 14(1): 1–25.

Hertzke, Allen D. 1988. *Representing God in Washington: The Role of Religious Lobbies in the American Polity*. Knoxville: University of Tennessee Press.

Hofrenning, Daniel J. B. 1995. *In Washington but Not of It: The Prophetic Politics of Religious Lobbyists*. Philadelphia: Temple University Press.

Iyengar, Shanto. 1991. *Is Anyone Responsible?* Chicago: University of Chicago Press.

Jelen, Ted G. 2005. "Political Esperanto: Rhetorical Resources and Limitations of the Christian Right in the United States." *Sociology of Religion* 66(3): 303–21.

Johnson, Annysa. 2012. "Nuns on the Bus En Route to Wisconsin." *Milwaukee Journal Sentinel*, June 18.

Jones, Robert P. 2008. *Progressive and Religious: How Christian, Jewish, Muslim, and Buddhist Leaders Are Moving beyond the Culture Wars and Transforming American Life*. Lanham, MD: Rowman & Littlefield.

Jones, Robert P., Daniel Cox, and Juhem Navarro-Rivera. 2012. "The 2012 American Values Survey: How Catholics and the Religiously Unaffiliated Will Shape the 2012 Election and Beyond." *Public Religion Research Institute*. http://publicreligion.org.

Katzenstein, Mary Fainsod. 1998. *Faithful and Fearless: Moving Feminist Protest inside the Church and Military*. Princeton, NJ: Princeton University Press.

Kaufman, Greg. 2012. "This Week in Poverty: The Soul Sisters." *Nation*, July 6.

Lichterman, Paul. 2005. *Elusive Togetherness: Church Groups Trying to Bridge America's Divisions*. Princeton, NJ: Princeton University Press.

Moody, Michael. 2002. "Caring for Creation: Environmental Advocacy by Mainline Protestant Organizations." In *The Quiet Hand of God*, edited by Robert Wuthnow and John H. Evans, 237–64. Berkeley: University of California Press.

National Public Radio. 2012. "Born to Be Wild: Catholic Nuns Hit the Road." *NPR News*, June 8.

NETWORK 2012. "NETWORK Nuns Launch Nine-State Bus Tour Highlighting How Federal Budget Cuts Harm Struggling Families" (press release). http://www.networklobby.org.

NETWORK. 2013. "Sister Simone Campbell Testifies on Poverty before Rep. Paul Ryan's Committee" (press release). http://www.networklobby.org.

Olson, Laura R. 2002. "Mainline Protestant Washington Offices and the Political Lives of Clergy." In *The Quiet Hand of God*, edited by Robert Wuthnow and John H. Evans, 54–79. Berkeley: University of California Press.

Perrin, Andrew J. 2009. *Citizen Speak: The Democratic Imagination in American Life*. Chicago: University of Chicago Press.

Polletta, Francesca. 2006. *It Was Like a Fever: Storytelling in Protest and Politics*. Chicago: University of Chicago Press.

Polletta, Francesca, and John Lee. 2006. "Is Telling Stories Good for Democracy? Rhetoric in Public Deliberation after 9/11." *American Sociological Review* 71(5): 699–721.

Polletta, Francesca, Pang Ching Bobby Chen, Beth Gharrity Gardner, and Alice Motes. 2011. "Sociology of Storytelling." *Annual Review of Sociology* 37: 109–30.

Porter, Theodore M. 1995. *Trust in Numbers: The Pursuit of Objectivity in Science and Public Life.* Princeton, NJ: Princeton University Press.

Rawls, John. 1993. *Political Liberalism.* New York: Columbia University Press.

Riely, Kaitlynn. 2012. "Nuns on the Bus Hear Stories of Formerly Homeless in Clairton." *Pittsburgh Press,* June 28.

Ryan, Charlotte. 1991. *Prime Time Activism: Media Strategies for Grassroots Organizing.* Boston: South End Press.

Ryan, Paul. 2012. "A Budget That Trusts the American People." Speeches and Statements. *Committee on the Budget: U.S. House of Representatives.* http://budget.house.gov.

Schlozman, Kay Lehman, Sidney Verba, and Henry E Brady. 2012. *The Unheavenly Chorus: Unequal Political Voice and the Broken Promise of American Democracy.* Princeton, NJ: Princeton University Press.

Steensland, Brian. 2002. "The Hydra and the Swords: Social Welfare and Mainline Advocacy, 1964–2000." In *The Quiet Hand of God,* edited by Robert Wuthnow and John H. Evans, 213–37. Berkeley: University of California Press.

Steensland, Brian. 2006. "Cultural Categories and the American Welfare State: The Case of Guaranteed Income Policy." *American Journal of Sociology* 111(5): 1273–1326.

Stone, Deborah A. 2001. *Policy Paradox: The Art of Political Decision-Making.* Revised edition. New York: W.W. Norton.

Stout, Jeffrey. 2010. *Blessed Are the Organized: Grassroots Democracy in America.* Princeton, NJ: Princeton University Press.

Sullivan, Amy. 2008. *The Party Faithful: How and Why Democrats Are Closing the God Gap.* New York: Scribner.

Tilly, Charles. 2002. *Stories, Identities, and Political Change.* Lanham, MD: Rowman & Littlefield.

Williams, Rhys H. 2004. "Religion and Place in the Midwest: Urban, Rural, and Suburban Forms of Religious Expression." In *Religion and Public Life in the Midwest: America's Common Denominator?,* edited by Philip Barlow and Mark Silk, 187–208. Walnut Creek, CA: AltaMira Press.

Williams, Rhys H., and N. J. Demerath III. 1991. "Religion and Political Process in an American City." *American Sociological Review* 56(4): 417–31.

Wood, Richard L. 2002. *Faith in Action: Religion, Race, and Democratic Organizing in America.* Chicago: University of Chicago Press.

Wuthnow, Robert. 1988. *The Restructuring of American Religion: Society and Faith since World War II.* Princeton, NJ: Princeton University Press.

Yamane, David. 2000. "Naked Public Square or Crumbling Wall of Separation? Evidence from Legislative Hearings in Wisconsin." *Review of Religious Research* 42(2): 175–92.

Yamane, David. 2005. *The Catholic Church in State Politics: Negotiating Prophetic Demands and Political Realities.* Lanham, MD: Rowman & Littlefield.

14

"Neutral" Talk in Educating for Activism

GARY J. ADLER, JR.

Begun as the "educational arm" of the 1980s Sanctuary Movement, for a quarter century BorderLinks has hosted thousands of travelers from seminaries, congregations, and colleges across the United States. A transnational brokering organization, BorderLinks arranges weeklong immersion trips across the U.S.-Mexico border as part of its strategy of "raising awareness, inspiring action" against the numerous injustices done to undocumented migrants, immigrant communities, and border cities.

Outside the door at BorderLinks is a bright-blue barrel retired from serving desert duty as a water station for undocumented migrants crossing near Tucson, Arizona. The main meeting area at BorderLinks has a U.S. immigration history timeline that recounts dark moments of immigrant exclusion. Elements of a synthetic, immigrant-connected religion abound: a folk-art cross from Central America, *ropa típica* from Chiapas, a *papier-mâché* Virgin of Guadalupe statute, and liberation theology books (Menjívar 2007). The organization's founders were Sanctuary Movement luminaries; its first two directors were nationally known social justice ministers from Mainline Protestant denominations. The majority of the staff consider themselves religious and maintain close linkages to progressive religious groups involved in activism.

And yet, despite these elements characteristic of religiously connected progressive advocacy and activism, BorderLinks constructs an organizational culture of *formal neutrality*: a set of practices and meanings that demarcates a space for personal transformation toward progressive goals but avoids both coercion and issue politicization. To wit, the organization includes voices from "all sides" of the immigration debate—including the Border Patrol and the anti-immigrant Minutemen—instead of presenting one viewpoint as just. As a staff member explained to trip participants: "We don't tell you what to do. It's about falling in love. Go back and get connected and do *something.*"

This orientation to formal neutrality is surprising when compared to the contentious discursive styles characteristic of other progressive collective action forms such as community organizing, or classic social movement organizations, or even new social movements (Wood 2002; Tarrow 2006). It is also surprising because previous research on immersion travel in progressive, religious activism has shown that trips motivate awareness and action by producing moralized issue frames and encouraging specific actions, in contrast to BorderLinks' approach (Smith 1996; Nepstad and Smith 2001; Nepstad 2008).

As this chapter will show, BorderLinks *does* attempt to motivate awareness and activism, but it does so in a way that is less familiar to scholars of progressive religious activism, but possibly more familiar to the many people that inhabit a range of progressive religious organizations and settings whose organizational work is not primarily activist (Beyerlein and Chaves 2003; Ammerman 2009). BorderLinks inhabits a middle ground between education and activism, between the prophetic and quiet styles of action that comprise the repertoire of action among Mainline Protestant religious organizations (Wuthnow 2002). Its niche in the organizational field of progressive religious action resides between, on the one hand, feeder organizations—congregations, seminaries, and colleges—that supply adherents oriented to progressive ideas about immigration reform and, on the other, activist organizations hoping to mobilize constituents who will support humanitarian aid and immigration reform activism (Fligstein and McAdam 2011).

BorderLinks provides fertile theoretical ground for observing variation in organizational forms of progressive religious action and tracing the social forces that shape a commitment to a non-contentious, socially aware, personalistic style of motivating action (Mische 2007). The concept of formal neutrality may help to illuminate how the link between education and activism, between feeder organizations and activist organizations, is made among religious groups by the use of midwife or brokering organizations, and how that might compare to other historical examples of that link, whether Mainline or Evangelical (Morris 1986; Polletta 2002; Gahr and Young 2014). The details of the case also help explain why the immensely popular tool of immersion travel produces activist outcomes less regularly than might be predicted. Earlier research on immersion travel as a mobilization strategy tended to work backward—beginning with the end product of travelers who became activists, then crafting an explanation for how travel was a necessary part of the process. The "view from the beginning" of the mobilization sequence that I present here has the benefit of clarifying how an organizational commitment to formal neutrality may channel the outcomes of immersion travel.

The Case

This chapter draws on research conducted between 2008 and 2010, especially on participant observation done with six groups from different feeder organizations traveling through BorderLinks on weeklong immersion trips. Up to six months after trip completion, 36 of the 44 travelers I observed completed in-depth interviews. These are supplemented with interviews from nine BorderLinks staff members from both sides of the border, two federal government agents that talk to groups, four leaders of local non-profits that speak with groups, and three leaders of groups that canceled their BorderLinks trip. This ethnographic and interview data is contextualized by a survey given to travelers immediately after travel.[1] All names of persons and organizations, except BorderLinks, have been changed.

According to an activist involved with its founding, BorderLinks was designed to be become the "educational arm" of the local Sanctuary Movement. BorderLinks would help to motivate individuals involved in feeder organizations that would, in turn, support the work of providing sanctuary to undocumented migrants. Headquartered in Tucson, the organization could easily connect travelers from across the United States with evidence of immigrant suffering.

The organization's approach was conceived within the context of liberal Christian theology in the 1980s. BorderLinks' founding director, Rick Ufford-Chase, was the son of a Presbyterian Church USA (PCUSA) minister with wide experience in connecting social analysis, theology, and activism. During its first decade, a number of liberal theologians and religious activists helped to construct BorderLinks' mission and identity, including Robert McAfee Brown, John Fife, and Ched Myers

(Gill 1999). An anthropologist studying the Sanctuary Movement in the early 1990s wrote that BorderLinks "didn't provide just any kind of immersion but one that resonated with Sanctuary's political critique of the US state" (Cunningham 2001, 373).

As the Central American Peace Movement and Sanctuary Movement declined in the early 1990s, BorderLinks continued on as a place to cultivate progressive identities in a religious organization. In the early 2000s, as undocumented immigration swelled again, BorderLinks increasingly focused its work on undocumented immigration and the economic conditions behind this rise. In 2008, the organizational mission was to be "an international leader in experiential education that raises awareness and inspires actions around global political economics."

Each of the weeklong trips I observed was led by two BorderLinks staff members: one a monolingual Mexican national and the other a bilingual U.S. national who provided simultaneous translation. Trips included a range of activities to provide information, make relationships, and reflect on the experiences of the week. Nearly all groups (91 percent) visited at least one shelter, aid agency, or soup kitchen where they interacted with migrants. Over 95 percent of groups visited with an activist organization or their members, such as No More Deaths activists. About one-third of all groups met with a U.S. border control agent. Most groups (82 percent) observed a federal mass deportation hearing in Tucson. Over half (68 percent) of groups did a homestay in Mexico. Each evening, BorderLinks staff led a reflection of the day's experiences, with ample informal time in the van for discussion.

Formal Neutrality

What is formal neutrality? Formal neutrality is a component of "internal organizational culture" (Williams 2004) that shapes how opinions are formed, information is moralized. and future action is imagined. The key aspect of formal neutrality is a discursive space that signals neutrality by downplaying organizational expertise, deliberately including conflicting information, and being purposefully non-directive about action possibilities. Other non-discursive elements of the organization—staff identities, organizational partners, and symbolic material—may be non-neutral. BorderLinks thus straddles the constrained-expansive dichotomy that Stephen Hart (2001) has argued structures the styles of progressive groups. BorderLinks constrains its own discursive presence so that groups from feeder organizations can engage in their own styles of talk during travel (though not all do). Intriguingly, this *discursive* constraint exists alongside the organization's expansive *symbolic* life. Its internal art, posters, dress, food consumption, and staff biographies tilt toward a progressive interpretation of undocumented immigration.

With both constrained and expansive cultural elements, the organization orients travelers to a goal of inspired awareness, without coercing or directing them in a way that would run afoul of the individual-conscience-respecting logics of their feeder organizations. Similar to what Nina Eliasoph (1998) has shown about Americans' avoidance of talking politics, BorderLinks provides experiential material for producing religious, progressive identities while simultaneously limiting certain modes of conflictual, focused speech that more pointedly promote collective action. The organization creates a space of exploratory conversation, emotional talk, and spiritual reflection devoid of politicized pressure. The result is an environment that provides elements that *could* motivate action, but not in a directive, coercive way that formulates clear conclusions or encourages specific actions. Instead, the organization relies on the epistemic power of experientially encountering suffering and injustice, as well as the already constituted visions and networks of feeder organizations, to orient travelers' new opinions and actions.

Endogenous Practices of Formal Neutrality

Three practices constituted formal neutrality at BorderLinks. First, the organization's staff avoided asserting expertise in the diagnosis of immigration injustice and the prognosis of ameliorative action. As staff members accompanied travelers during the week, they served as *guides*, not experts. For example, the staff leader George resisted the requests of travelers from Central College throughout their trip to give *his* opinion about solving immigration injustice. As the group prepared to cross into Mexico, a Central College student excitedly asked George about one of the trip activities: "How much of the industrial park [of maquilas] will we get to see? Can we explore the buildings?" George replied rather curtly: "We'll drive through and get out [of the vans] to look at one point. Ophelia [the Mexican BorderLinks staff member] can talk about changes in Nogales over time." Susan, another Central College student, was listening but had not caught onto George's attempt to avoid preempting the ensuing experience. She asked George, "With all the news about drug cartels that we've been hearing about, how does it affect immigrants?" George looked uncomfortable, blew the air out of his mouth with a sense of deflation, ran his hand through his hair, and squirmed in his chair. His answer to Susan was vague and short: "The war on drugs and the war on immigrants have parallels. In my mind, they are the same dynamic." Sensing that George might actually be opening up, the group's leader, Mike, asked a question that would continue to be asked of George throughout the trip: "Will we get *your* ideas on the solution?" George squirmed in his chair some more and looked frustrated, but refused to give his opinion.

This avoidance of expertise, by locally embedded people who *are* experts, made BorderLinks' discursive character surprisingly open-ended and unfocused. BorderLinks staff members avoided overinterpreting what travelers saw, generally refusing to provide synthetic summaries. The staff tried to guide participants through the course of a week, allowing travelers' own intuitions to come to the fore through discussions with various actors at the border. The organization went so far in this *laissez-faire* direction that it did not offer a coherent frame of analysis, critique, or suggestion, a finding about BorderLinks confirmed by others (Piekielek 2003).

A second practice that created formal neutrality at BorderLinks is evident in the organization's efforts to provide a supply of "expert" voices so that groups would hear "balance" between all possible viewpoints. According to the official history of BorderLinks, this means:

> A concerted effort [is] made to provide opportunity for participants to hear and respect a wide spectrum of voices and points of view. Indeed, a positive balance is sought between the perspective of a manager of a maquiladora and that of its workers, as well as between that of a Border Patrol agent and a migrant person. (Gill 2004, 21)

BorderLinks tried to have "both sides" of immigrant issues represented, usually meaning immigrants themselves or immigrant activists on one side and members of anti-immigrant social movements or state border enforcement authorities on the other. BorderLinks attempted to create an inclusive field of voices that participants could query through deliberation (Schneiderhan and Khan 2008). At the end of a week, participants would, hopefully, have a complete set of ideas and opinions to navigate and choose from. The specific speakers BorderLinks recruited included migrants, activists, attorneys, ranchers, ministers, and federal border agents. Their grouping of different positions as "sides" informally signaled an antagonistic field of immigration-related positions that BorderLinks perceived as already existing.

In reality, BorderLinks struggled to recruit enough "opposing voices" to fill the itineraries of the dozens of groups it hosted each year. For example, the availability of border enforcement authorities fluctuated greatly. In the first half of the 2000s, a generally amenable local Border Patrol official made agents regularly available to talk at BorderLinks. In 2008, with a change in Border Patrol leadership, BorderLinks was told it could have only one visit with Border Patrol officials each month. This meant that only about one-quarter of trips would have a meeting with an official. The organization had similar trouble scheduling speakers from other governmental organizations, such as Customs and Border Protection and Immigration and Customs Enforcement (ICE). In the six trips that I participated in, I heard two presentations by Customs agents and one presentation from an ICE official. Despite BorderLinks' and participants' commitment to "hearing all sides," not all sides appeared interested in representing themselves.

In attempting to construct an identifiable field of positions that need to be heard, BorderLinks encouraged distinct listening practices that enlisted participants in producing formal neutrality. Just inside the door to BorderLinks' dorm area, all participants were shown a list of values, one of which was "open communication." During one orientation, the staff member Janice explained to us the need to use a "listening posture" with interlocutors, which she said would be modeled by her. This posture meant looking directly at the speaker and showing interest in the conversation. BorderLinks' goal of "respecting" speakers led to the suppression of participants' dissent in favor of respectful listening. Participants *rarely* challenged what speakers said even if they made empirically dubious statements, such as Customs agents that presented their work as "fighting terrorism" creeping across the U.S.-Mexico border. After a 30–60-minute presentation, travelers would engage in a short question-and-answer period with a speaker. A line of respect was marked by BorderLinks staff as they never challenged what these speakers said to groups.

The importance of reining in challenges, and protecting formal neutrality, was evident to me one day with my own reaction to something Pam, a staff member, said. It was the end of a long day and Pam said that the next day we would have a visit from "ice, ice baby," using a cadence referencing the 1990s hit song by Vanilla Ice. She was mocking the visit we would have the following day from ICE. As our group chuckled at the cheesy tune, Pam seemed to notice she was overstepping a line of respect. She sarcastically commented: "We should sing this tomorrow, it'd be very disrespectful." The group chuckled again. The next day, though, the group did no such thing. By respecting all speakers through the silencing of public disagreement, BorderLinks civilized the field of conflicting positions that it helped create in the first place.

One outcome of equitably including so many voices was the possibility that participants would have trouble distinguishing a just position and/or be swayed by the rhetorical strategies of a well-trained speaker. After all, many speakers had a vested interest in drawing participants toward their interpretation of immigration. This became clear when I interviewed an ICE agent about his willingness to make agents available to BorderLinks. He saw BorderLinks as an important part of the agency's mission to communicate its work to the public. As he recounted, it was an opportunity for the agency to point out the *real* danger of terrorists and drug dealers that ICE was protecting against, while also letting them know that the media images of agents raiding migrant residences was inaccurate. For him, BorderLinks was actually doing his agency a service by constituting small publics that his efforts could influence.

BorderLinks' respectful inclusion of many different positions left open the possibility that conclusions taken away from a BorderLinks trip were at odds with BorderLinks' generally pro-immigrant orientation. At the very least, the discursive experience of BorderLinks could create a troubling sense of complexity: that the causes of immigration were complex, that the amelioration of immigration injustice was complex, and that a traveler's response should be complex. At the end of a week, participants were left with the difficulty of sorting through new knowledge without an organizationally articulated principle as to what was right and what was just. The creation of complexity worked against a unified consolidation of message, something usually understood by scholars as crucial to motivating action (Snow et al. 1986; DiMaggio 1997; Jasper 1997).

The third practice of formal neutrality was the organization's restraint from suggesting pathways of action to individuals. BorderLinks' delegation leaders went to great lengths to avoid suggesting what participants could do in response to what they had seen and heard. On the trip with Central College, the students and professors repeatedly pinned George into conversation to ask what he thought they should do. George's reply to the group on the last day, given with a look of exasperation, was, "I have no idea, but I hope you do something." When the BorderLinks staff member Nancy spoke with groups, she often gave a similar message: "We don't tell you what to do. It's about falling in love. Go back and get connected and do something. And, hopefully, something with the poorest and the marginalized. We didn't bring you here to be worker bees in immigration reform. We want that [immigration reform], and people do need it, but just become involved!"

A parting message like this would seem to go *against* the organization's formal neutrality by mentioning immigration reform. Instead, it worked to publicly note the organization's progressive orientation, but reinforce its non-didactic, non-coercive approach. Travelers themselves were attuned to whether the deck was stacked during a BorderLinks trip. In follow-up interviews I asked travelers whether they thought BorderLinks had an agenda. A number replied, "Yes," that BorderLinks' message was that the immigration situation was bad and more humane policies were needed. So participants were aware of entering a space with a progressive, moral orientation. Yet a majority of travelers also reported feeling non-coerced. *No* participant mentioned feeling pressured to accept a certain party line or being ostracized for differences of opinion. Most participants replied that they had "no idea" what Border-Links hoped they might actually do after the trip. Participants stated that BorderLinks' agenda was for them "to be aware" of what was happening at the border. One traveler termed the group's message "incredibly complicated," saying that it "open[ed] more questions than it close[d]."

Through these three practices, avoiding asserting expertise, balancing different voices, and avoiding suggesting pathways to action, Border-Links constructed and sustained a discursive space of formal neutrality. In the next section I discuss forces that constructed and gave meaning to this local organizational orientation.

Influence One: Cultural Predilections

Formal neutrality developed at BorderLinks not because of a single conscious choice by founders but, rather, through a range of shaping forces linked to the identity of the people and organizations involved at its founding. From its genesis, BorderLinks balanced a mix of underlying values, sustaining an identity of being both religious and progressive without being overtly political.

One organizational value construed social action as an outgrowth of spirituality. In the organization's view, spiritual growth was the first step toward activism. In his organizational history, Gill (1999; 2004) noted ideological tensions at the founding of BorderLinks between organizations in the Sanctuary Movement. As he described it:

> The Chicago style [of Sanctuary] was one of political action, seeking to change national policy, while the Tucson style was more in line with Quaker values of providing assistance in a peaceful manner. . . . Those in Tucson . . . felt that the spiritual aspect of their work had been the primary focus at the outset and should continue to be so. (Gill 1999, 15)

This focus on a spiritual first step disentangled personal growth in the present from specific future action. As Gill noted about BorderLinks' work, "the encounter [with the range of voices] must be structured with a minimum of direct teaching or of pressure to come to any specific conclusions" (1999, 37). The protection of individuals' social conscience was a result, preparing the conditions for transformation without demanding any particular transformation.

A second value orientation viewed education through experience as the appropriate means of transformation toward awareness and action. BorderLinks' trips to locations of suffering were a way to get people "seeing with their own eyes." BorderLinks assumed that the embodied experience of visiting and viewing the border would produce moralized judgments that participants could channel into social, civic, or activist work. The language that BorderLinks used to describe its approach valorized the ability of travelers to come to know reality through direct experience.

This organizational vision hinged on the belief that, given the right experiential conditions, the true causes of suffering would reveal themselves to individuals open to understanding them. The belief in this happening was so strong that at BorderLinks, "[t]here is no attempt to stack the deck in favor of the Mexican experience, since the realities of the border will always manage to reveal themselves" (Gill 2004, 21). The theory of suffering's moral power was based in the past experience of staff members and previous travelers for whom this transformation did occur. Sharon Erikson Nepstad (2007, 665) captured the essence of this possibility, noting that in Central American immersion trips "direct encounters with oppression evoke[d] a visceral rejection of such inequitable treatment."

What these organizational orientations produced was a trust in the liberatory potential of experiential education to simultaneously be a tool of personal and social transformation. By focusing its work on experiential education—helping individuals transform—the organization mapped out its terrain as something different than, but related to, direct action or political critique. The organization made overt and frequent allusions to the work of Paulo Freire, the founder of what has come to be known as popular education. A central concern in Paulo Freire's work was the ideological role of expertise in most systems of education. According to his popular education model, the traditional teacher-student education relationship actively recreated a subordination that served the ideological interests of power in society. Quoting directly from Freire's *Pedagogy of the Oppressed* (1970) in one of its 2009 fundraising mailers, BorderLinks wrote:

> "Education either functions as an instrument which is used to facilitate integration of the younger generation into the logic of the present system and bring about conformity or it becomes the practice of freedom, the means by which men and women deal critically and creatively with reality and discover how to participate in the transformation of their world."

This assumption of popular education resulting in liberatory outcomes and social action was deep in the organizational history. Gill (1999, 37) writes that "while BorderLinks is not essentially an activist organization, it is committed to the belief that all real learning leads naturally and *inevitably* to action." The pillars of spiritually based growth and experiential growth within the organization elevated a respect for conscience and resulted in disfavoring conflictual, didactic, or even strongly framed modes of motivating participants.

Influence Two: Historical Context

Alongside the shaping power of cultural predilections was a changing historical context that made critical social analysis more difficult for BorderLinks. Between 1990 and 2002, the U.S.-Mexico border context shifted from relatively low flows of refugees fleeing Central American war zones to massive flows of migrants driven north by free-trade policies and Mexican economic reform beginning in the mid-1990s. BorderLinks' official history noted a parallel shift in focus: as the Central American refugee plight ended in the mid-1990s, the focus moved from political themes to the economic forces structuring the border (Gill 1999). An anthropologist who had studied the Sanctuary Movement participated in a BorderLinks delegation in 1990 and then again in 1999, using that gap in time to determine changes in the organization's focus (Cunningham 2001, 2002). During that time, BorderLinks transitioned from a focus on Central American politics, with a clear marking of the U.S. government as the controller of the border, to a broader focus on various aspects of free trade and neoliberal economics. These economic forces—often portrayed to travelers through individual migrant testimonials of depressed hometowns and lost jobs—were difficult to explain as a clear cause of injustice compared to the state-based repression of the 1980s. This change in causal forces demanded a different diagnosis, one that dealt with multiple forces of repression and with diverse migrant trajectories.

The social analysis provided during a BorderLinks trip became less incisive over time. BorderLinks staff admitted to struggling with the purpose of immersion trips in a radically changed political and economic environment. As an example, by 1999 BorderLinks travelers gave sympathetic reactions to a Border Patrol officer, something that seemed impossible on a trip a decade earlier (Cunningham 2002). Historical complexity had overtaken BorderLinks' original ability to provide clear social analysis. It was not impossible for the organization to do so, but neoliberalism was daunting in its ideological power.

Influence Three: Environmental Pressures and Feeder Organizations

Just as important as cultural roots and historical context, BorderLinks was shaped by forces in its own organizational field (DiMaggio and Powell 1983). BorderLinks conducted a fair amount of boundary maintenance work, which demarcated its neutral stance compared to other groups, deepening its commitment to this positioning. BorderLinks' boundary maintenance work occurred in two directions: distinguishing itself from "short term mission trips" and distinguishing itself from border activists.

In one direction, the organization distinguished from the charitable actions characteristic of the burgeoning "short-term mission trip movement," which sends U.S. citizens abroad to paint houses, construct buildings, and donate goods (Beyerlein, Adler, and Trinitapoli 2011). BorderLinks advertised education, not (charitable) action, during immersion travel. This contrasting approach was articulated right at the point of first contact between the organization and potential travelers. The staff person in charge of scheduling trips reported frequent conversations with youth groups, high school teachers, and college student groups interested in "serving" Mexican communities or migrants. This staff person would try to bend these inquiries towards BorderLinks' educational work of awareness-raising, away from what it saw as the creation of dependency through charity. The emphasis at BorderLinks was on open exploration and learning, not service work.

In another direction, the organization distinguished itself from the activist organizations and actions that made up the social movement sector in Southern Arizona. So, while BorderLinks introduced participants to organizations doing the work of placing water in the desert, organizing day laborers, and lobbying politicians, the organization did not do that work itself. George explained this distinctive vision to a new group of trip participants on the first day of their trip, asserting, "We are not activists here, so we're not doing lobbying or things like that. We do education."

BorderLinks' success at embodying this complex mission can be seen in survey answers given by participants immediately after their trip ended. Asked if the trip was oriented more towards education or activism, 30 percent said mostly educational, 7 percent said mostly activist, and 60 percent said it was a mix of both. The work of distinction places the organization between other ways of being progressive and religious, while reaffirming the possibility of education to produce change. Furthermore, the groups that actually came to BorderLinks from feeder organizations had a constant shaping effect on its internal culture (Morris 1986). BorderLinks recruited groups from feeder organizations that shared a similar orientation toward education and personal growth. This bloc recruitment (Oberschall 1973) made generating travelers easier, but it had implications for the way that feeder organizations influenced BorderLinks.

There were two types of organizations that sent participants to Border-Links: educational, encompassing secular colleges and universities, and religious, encompassing churches, seminaries, religious colleges, and high schools. Both of these types of organizations shared three broad characteristics. First, the engagement of politics was a sensitive boundary that was patrolled, such that political speech in the name of the organization was generally considered an illegitimate activity. Second, both types of organizations understood individual discernment and transformation to be important. Third, these organizations existed for purposes *other* than social movement involvement.

Feeder organization leaders planning to participate in a BorderLinks delegation had to articulate to their internal audiences how such participation aligned with the feeder organization's goals and values. If BorderLinks was seen as an activist outfit, the feeder organization courted contamination. To accomplish this balancing, group leaders made the case to their feeder organization that BorderLinks investigated political issues without being political, encouraged social activism without advocating one strategy, and inspired individuals without heavily determining the content or direction of that inspiration. BorderLinks was legitimate to groups from these organizational types precisely *because* it was non-partisan and lacked action scripts. With no strong frame and no sure prescriptions for change, BorderLinks was essentially a shell: it created a context for feeder organizations to bring their members into. BorderLinks hollowed its own viewpoint out so that the particular interests, ideas, and values of feeder organizations could fill it. This was an attractive identity since it allowed feeder organizations—where travelers really have a membership commitment—to interpret the experience and imagine future action through their own organizational lens. This was deeply meaningful for leaders from feeder organizations, who reported that BorderLinks trips were more authentic, meaningful, and transformative than their traditional environments. Dana, a professor on one trip, remarked that this was exactly the sort of "transformative education" she wanted to be doing. She noted that her institution was "behind the curve" in supporting this, even though she made the case to the university that "this isn't service-learning [which her university supported] . . . but it's that idea of going beyond the books."

Conclusion

It is easy to think of BorderLinks as "not quite." Not quite educational, not quite activist, not quite effective enough. This middling position can be frustrating for scholars who study successful mobilization strategies. It is also frustrating for progressive religious activists who seek something more. A nationally known social science colleague who is a Mainline Protestant, and who had personally been on a BorderLinks delegation, exemplified this consternation. He confided his perplexity to me by simply saying: "they don't *do* anything."

In being "not quite," though, BorderLinks is actually formulating a distinct moralization strategy that represents a portion of the field of progressive religion which lies at the intersection of education and activism. At that intersection are religiously connected, non-activist organizations full of adherents—those who *might* become part of a widespread movement for immigration reform (McCarthy and Zald 1977). Feeder organizations that send groups view BorderLinks as an ideal venue to connect the dots for these people, using experiential education as a moralization and mobilization tactic. This is a stretched vision of education, one that includes experience and orients toward spiritual, moral implications. The belief in experiential education to lead to social change, and for social reality to be grasped through "real" education, is a hallmark of progressive action (Hart 2001). Such an educational approach is a central way for progressives to be religious in the United States (Edles 2013).

But BorderLinks' stretch toward activism is neither politicization, nor cognitive liberation, nor direct mobilization (Nepstad 1997). Formal neutrality characterizes the approach that an organization may take as part of its role in the organizational division of labor that defines the field of progressive religion. BorderLinks is attempting to form a felt awareness through encounter with the U.S.-Mexico border while respecting the boundaries of individual conscience and diverse feeder organization logics. It is creating a politics that avoids the most controversial aspects of partisanship and activism. It is characterized by what Edles (2013) has recently termed a "living the question" mode of being progressive and religious. That mode involves openness and an ongoing search for truth, precisely the sorts of values that BorderLinks' practices of formal neutrality support. BorderLinks' travelers are learning to be religious and political in ways that equip them for specific religious and political journeys, journeys that are likely to be navigated individually in a multitude of contexts with varying religious and political identities (Lichterman 1996; Wuthnow 1998). The organizational culture of formal neutrality may be a distinctive characteristic of religious advocacy organizations that, while liberal, resists overt partisanship.

What are the hurdles to social action that this orientation produces, what Hart (2001) calls the cultural dilemmas of progressive politics? One hurdle is that travelers may miss a critical engagement with immigration injustice. This is the potential outcome that critics of "poverty tourism" have in mind (Meschkank 2011). This outcome would be at odds with the orientation of those pedagogues that inspired BorderLinks' work to begin with. As Paulo Freire said in a recorded dialogue with Myles Horton of the Highlander Folk School: "While having on the one hand to respect the expectations and choices of the students, the educator also has the duty of not being neutral. . . . The educator as an intellectual has to intervene. He [sic] cannot be a mere facilitator" (Bell, Gaventa, and Peters 1990, 180). Inserting "BorderLinks" as the educator in this quotation and "travelers" as the students, the duty to "intervene," to push beyond a formal neutrality, is something that the organization does not accept. An overly moral reading of experience would be seen as coercive by the organization and as a didactic response to a complex social reality.

A second hurdle is that travelers usually leave without a concrete sense of what action they could actually take to respond to immigration injustice. The most frequent suggestion from BorderLinks was to simply "become more aware," despite the organizational hope that awareness would spur action. Post-travel action can and did happen among travelers, but it was usually clearly connected to another critical mobilizing element like an activist background, a biographical turning point, travel with an ideologically critical group, or a preexisting connection to immigration rights organizations. BorderLinks had no control over these factors, which helps to explain the difference in the causal importance of travel between this "view from the beginning" study and other cases (Nepstad 1997, 2007). And yet, one wonders whether BorderLinks could, and should, do more in guiding the imaginations of its freely "captive" audience.

To conclude, what does BorderLinks tell us about progressive religion? Mainliners, as Wuthnow (2002) once noted, tended to work "quietly" at the intersection of religion and politics. The phenomenon of *formal neutrality* suggests that, in addition, their parachurch organizations like BorderLinks may tend to work "carefully" so as to build religion and awareness for individuals who may connect to a variety of different organizations and actions (Lichterman 1996). Particularly in a moment of national political life when religious people have felt the reverberations of publicly divisive religious argument, formal neutrality is a boundary marker. It marks the line on a map made by religious progressives between a moralistic, preached mode of religion in the world and one that appears more educational and less coercive (Lichterman 2008). It has deep roots in the progressive version of American voluntarism, in which religious and political identity relate with great "complexity" to collective behavior. At BorderLinks, complexity is, indeed, the result.

NOTE

1 Of 217 eligible participants drawn from 22 traveling groups, 201 (93 percent) responded to the immediate post-trip survey.

REFERENCES

Ammerman, Nancy. 2009. "Building Religious Communities, Building the Common Good: A Skeptical Appreciation." In *The Civil Life of American Religion*, edited by Paul Lichterman and C. Brady Potts, 48–68. Palo Alto, CA: Stanford University Press.

Bell, Brenda, John Gaventa, and John Peters. 1990. *Myles Horton and Paulo Freire: We Make the Road by Walking: Conversations on Education and Social Change*. Philadelphia: Temple University Press.

Beyerlein, Kraig, Gary Adler, and Jennifer Trinitapoli. 2011. "The Effect of Religious Mission Trips on Youth Civic Participation." *Journal for the Scientific Study of Religion* 50(4): 780–95.

Beyerlein, Kraig, and Mark Chaves. 2003. "The Political Activities of Religious Congregations in the United States." *Journal for the Scientific Study of Religion* 42(2): 229–46.

Cunningham, Hilary. 2001. "Transnational Politics at the Edges of Sovereignty: Social Movements, Crossings and the State at the U.S.-Mexico Border." *Global Networks* 1(4): 369–87.

Cunningham, Hilary. 2002. "Transnational Social Movements and Sovereignities in Transition: Charting New Interfaces of Power at the U.S.-Mexico Border." *Anthropologica* 44(2): 185–96.

DiMaggio, Paul. 1997. "Culture and Cognition." *Annual Review of Sociology* 23(1): 263–87.

DiMaggio, Paul, and Walter W. Powell. 1983. "The Iron Cage Revisited: Institutional Isomorphism and Collective Rationality in Organizational Fields." *American Sociological Review* 48(2): 147–60.

Edles, Laura Desfor. 2013. "Contemporary Progressive Christianity and its Symbolic Ramifications." *Cultural Sociology* 7(1): 3–22.

Eliasoph, Nina. 1998. *Avoiding Politics: How Americans Produce Apathy in Everyday Life*. Cambridge, UK: Cambridge University Press.

Fligstein, Neil, and Doug McAdam. 2011. "Toward a General Theory of Strategic Action Fields." *Sociological Theory* 29(1): 1–25.

Freire, Paulo. 1970. *Pedagogy of the Oppressed*. New York: Sebury Press.

Gahr, Joshua, and Michael Young. 2014. "Evangelicals and Emergent Moral Protest." *Mobilization* 19(2): 185–208.

Gill, Jerry H. 1999. *BorderLinks: The Road Is Made by Walking*. Tucson, AZ: BorderLinks.

Gill, Jerry H. 2004. *Borderlinks II: Still on the Road*. Tucson, AZ: BorderLinks.

Hart, Stephen. 2001. *Cultural Dilemmas of Progressive Politics: Styles of Engagement among Grassroots Activists*. Chicago: University of Chicago Press.

Jasper, James M. 1997. *The Art of Moral Protest: Culture, Biography, and Creativity in Social Movements*. Chicago: University of Chicago Press.

Lichterman, Paul. 1996. *The Search for Political Community: American Activists Reinventing Community*. Cambridge, UK: Cambridge University Press.

Lichterman, Paul. 2008. "Religion and the Construction of Civic Identity." *American Sociological Review* 73(1): 83–104.

McCarthy, John D., and Mayer N. Zald. 1977. "Resource Mobilization and Social Movements: A Partial Theory." *American Journal of Sociology* 82(6): 1212–41.

Menjivar, Cecilia. 2007. "Serving Christ in the Borderlands: Faith Workers Respond to Border Violence." In *Religion and Social Justice for Immigrants*, edited by Pierrette Hondagneu-Sotelo, 104–22. New Brunswick, NJ: Rutgers University Press.

Meschkank, Julia. 2011. "Investigations into Slum Tourism in Mumbai: Poverty Tourism and the Tensions between Different Constructions of Reality." *GeoJournal* 76(1): 47–62.

Mische, Ann. 2007. *Partisan Publics: Communication and Contention across Brazilian Youth Activist Networks.* Princeton, NJ: Princeton University Press.

Morris, Aldon. 1986. *Origins of the Civil Rights Movement: Black Communities Organizing for Change.* New York: Free Press.

Nepstad, Sharon Erickson. 1997. "The Process of Cognitive Liberation: Cultural Synapses, Links, and Frame Contradictions in the U.S.-Central America Peace Movement." *Sociological Inquiry* 67(4): 470–87.

Nepstad, Sharon Erickson. 2007. "Oppositional Consciousness among the Privileged: Remaking Religion in the Central America Solidarity Movement." *Critical Sociology* 33: 661–88.

Nepstad, Sharon Erickson. 2008. *Religion and War Resistance in the Plowshares Movement.* Cambridge, UK: Cambridge University Press.

Nepstad, Sharon Erickson, and Christian Smith. 2001. "The Social Structure of Moral Outrage in Recruitment to the U.S. Central America Peace Movement." In *Passionate Politics: Emotions and Social Movements*, edited by J. Goodwin, J. M. Jasper, and F. Polletta, 158–74. Chicago: University of Chicago Press.

Oberschall, Anthony. 1973. *Social Conflict and Social Movements.* Englewood Cliffs, NJ: Prentice Hall.

Piekielek, Jessica. 2003. "Visiting Views of the U.S.-Mexico Border: Reflections of Participants in Experiential Travel Seminars." M.A. thesis, Anthropology, University of Arizona, Tucson.

Polletta, Francesca. 2002. *Freedom in an Endless Meeting: Democracy in American Social Movements.* Chicago: University of Chicago Press.

Schneiderhan, Erik, and Shamus Khan. 2008. "Reasons and Inclusion: The Foundation of Deliberation." *Sociological Theory* 26(1): 1–24.

Smith, Christian. 1996. *Resisting Reagan: The U.S. Central America Peace Movement.* Chicago: University of Chicago Press.

Snow, David A., E. Burke Rochford, Jr., Steven K. Worden, and Robert D Benford. 1986. "Frame Alignment Processes, Micromobilization, and Movement Participation." *American Sociological Review* 51(4): 464–81.

Tarrow, Sidney. 2006. *Power in Movement: Social Movements and Contentious Politics.* Cambridge, UK: Cambridge University Press.

Williams, Rhys H. 2004. "The Cultural Contexts of Collective Action: Constraints, Opportunities, and the Symbolic Life of Social Movements." In *The Blackwell Companion to Social Movements*, edited by David A. Snow, Sarah A. Soule, and Hanspeter Kriesi, 91–115. Malden, MA: Blackwell.

Wood, Richard. 2002. *Faith in Action: Religion, Race, and Democratic Organizing in America*. Chicago: University of Chicago Press.

Wuthnow, Robert. 1998. *Loose Connections: Joining Together in America's Fragmented Communities*. Cambridge, MA: Harvard University Press.

Wuthnow, Robert. 2002. "Beyond Quiet Influence?: Possibilities for the Protestant Mainline." In *The Quiet Hand of God: Faith-Based Activism and the Public Role of Mainline Protestantism*, edited by Robert Wuthnow and John H. Evans, 381–404. Berkeley: University of California Press.

15

How Moral Talk Connects Faith and Social Justice

TODD NICHOLAS FUIST

In 2010, Stephen Colbert, then the host of the satirical news show *The Colbert Report*, testified before Congress about migrant workers' rights. As many expected, Colbert used the opportunity to speak in character, cracking jokes as the parody right-wing pundit he played on his show. Perhaps the most revealing moment, however, was when Representative Judy Chu asked Colbert why he was interested in speaking on migrants' rights. Becoming visibly emotional as he broke character, Colbert, a devoutly Catholic Sunday school teacher, explained:

> I like talking about people who don't have any power, and [it] seems like [some] of the least powerful people in the United States are migrant workers who come and do our work, but don't have any rights as a result . . . and that's, that's, uh, an interesting contradiction to me. And, you know, "whatsoever you do for the least of my brothers," and these seem like the least of our brothers right now.

With this statement, Colbert uses a saying of Jesus, "whatsoever you do for the least of my brothers," to sacralize a contemporary political issue, the rights of migrant workers, integrating theology and progressive politics in his analysis of power and inequality.

The way we talk about politics has the power to shape our understandings of the world by drawing boundaries, creating categories, and deeming certain topics or communication styles off limits in discussion (Eliasoph 1998; Perrin 2006). This can be especially pronounced in faith communities, where shared understandings of the world carry a great deal of cultural and spiritual weight. For example, Dawne Moon (2004) found that churches that understand politics as divisive and dirty have trouble discussing lesbian and gay rights, while Korie Edwards (2008) demonstrated that even a well-meaning interracial church can reproduce white dominance when its members lack languages to talk about racial inequality in structural terms (see also Emerson and Smith 2001). Inaction and quiescence, though, are not the only possible outcomes. In fact, researchers have shown that religion can provide narratives, identities, and ideas that can be useful in making sense of the political world (Morris 1984; Wood 2002; Gutterman 2005; Lichterman 2005; Nepstad 2008; Braunstein 2012). Understood in this way, religion represents a powerful cultural resource (Williams 1995; Kniss 1997) for groups and individuals seeking languages to speak about politics. We may ask, then, how do faith communities integrate religion and politics in their conversation, and what moves these conversations in a direction that encourages progressive engagement, rather than either conservatism or disengagement?

This chapter explores three models of how religious progressives integrate faith and social justice in their talk that emerged through observing a diverse panel of religious groups. These models are:

1. The Teacher Model: Religious figures are presented as teachers or exemplars of justice. They were discussed as role models for how to live a just and moral life.
2. The Community Model: Local spaces and networks are imbued with sacred significance as groups focus on how to properly live in their social milieus.
3. The Theological Model: Existing religious beliefs and practices are creatively applied to contemporary social situations, bringing them into the sacred cosmos of the observed groups.

Through these three overlapping models, religious groups create the necessary categories of thought for faith-based, progressive social engagement. By examining the content of these three models in a variety of progressive religious groups, we can better understand how social justice and faith are integrated.

Studying Progressive Religion

This chapter emerges out of a larger study examining progressive religious groups in Chicago, Illinois, and Seattle, Washington. I selected groups for the study based on a number of criteria. First, they must meet at least one of our agreed-upon "progressive" markers (delineated in this volume's introduction), including espousing progressive theologies or ideologies, participating in progressive activism, or holding progressive identities. Second, I selected groups with an eye toward diversity of faith tradition, demographics, and polity structure, in an effort to capture a wide range of beliefs, practices, and experiences. The groups include two communes, two non-profit organizations, and six congregations. The data for this chapter come from 86 interviews with participants in the observed groups, along with ethnographic observations that range from approximately 40 hours to several hundred hours per group depending on how often and consistently the group meets. My goal with each group was to get a sense, through talking to members and participating in their social lives, of how they understood the connections between their faith and their politics and how they actualized those understandings in the world. Below, I explore the main patterns that emerged through my analysis.

Three Models of Integrating Faith and Politics

To review, I observed three key models of integrating faith and justice in these communities. These were: (1) the Teacher Model, (2) the Community Model, and (3) the Theological Model. I will explore each model in turn before considering them together at the end of the chapter.

The Teacher Model

Each community I observed routinely held up religious figures as *teachers and exemplars of just and moral behavior*. In doing so, they provided role models of what constitutes right socio-political practice. These exemplars were mentioned both in formal settings, such as in sermons during services, as well as in more casual conversations and one-on-one interviews with me. Additionally, these exemplars included both foundational figures of faith traditions, such as Jesus Christ and Mary, as well as more contemporary figures, such as Rabbi Heschel, Jean Vanier, or Martin Luther King, Jr. Further, the sharing of both certain figures and interpretations of their lives and teachings among the communities

I studied demonstrates the degree to which progressive religious groups share reference points that organize them into a field of action. I will first discuss some of the foundational and contemporary figures the groups referenced, then turn to how these figures drew connections between them.

As I sat drinking coffee with Maria, a young Latina employee of Cornerstone Community Outreach, a Christian homeless shelter in Chicago's Uptown neighborhood, she explained to me what it meant to be a "Christian homeless shelter" in her understanding. Primarily, she said, it meant doing what Jesus would do, explaining,

> Jesus, when he realized that things were messed up, when somebody had this bad lifestyle, or whatever, that's when he was, like . . . hanging out with them all the time. Teaching them stuff and lovin' on them, you know? So the people who are the *most* destitute and looked upon as nothing, *that* is who really needs to be ministered to, and that's the reason that Cornerstone is different from the other shelters, because we are Christian. . . . Even if someone is totally difficult and ridiculous and it seems hopeless we are *still* gonna try and get you somewhere that can help you and listen to you.

Maria presents a fairly typical understanding for members of Cornerstone, reiterated by the staff, volunteers, and clients, of how to follow the example of Christ in the context of a homeless shelter. In fact, while having lunch with Cornerstone's staff one day, some members of the security team amicably joked with the caseworkers that they are too forgiving of the residents of the shelter because they're always trying to emulate the example of Jesus. Confirming this, as I walked around the Uptown neighborhood with Cliff, another employee of Cornerstone, he suggested to me that if Jesus were alive today he'd be helping out at a shelter like Cornerstone. Cliff said this is because Christ's ministry directly points to a concern with issues of inequality, racism, and prison reform, an interpretation of Jesus's life that I will refer to in the next section.

The Teacher Model was particularly prominent at Dignity/Chicago, a small lesbian, gay, bisexual, and transgender (LGBT) identified Catholic congregation in Chicago's Boystown neighborhood. Members of

Dignity/Chicago routinely held up specific religious figures, both historical and contemporary, as models of proper Christian behavior. For example, Elaine, one of Dignity/Chicago's woman priests, used Mary as a religious exemplar in a sermon on her experiences as a woman priest.

> When I was young, I was wounded by not seeing my body represented on the altar, by not hearing my voice emanating from the pulpit. As a woman and a Roman Catholic priest, I've encountered my share of disappointments, and sometimes it is easy to give in to fear. But then I think of Mary. Mary was just an ordinary woman who said "yes" when called by God to serve. And as a Roman Catholic woman priest, Mary's "yes" fills me with hope.

The implication was obvious: if God can call on an ordinary woman such as Mary to take on such an important role in the history of Christianity, what earthly institution can deny that other women may hear God's call in their life? The political repercussions of Elaine's sermon were not lost on members of Dignity/Chicago, who understood their use of women priests to say mass in explicitly feminist terms. One member, Doug, commented that the decision to bring in women priests came about because "the rules [in the Catholic Church] around sexuality and who gets to preside are based in deep social misogyny" and Dignity/Chicago was seeking ways to actively counter that. As such, at Dignity/Chicago, feminism is embodied by Mary, who is held up as an exemplar of a woman who listened to God's call for her life. Through this, Dignity/Chicago circumvents the Catholic Church's rejection of women priests by identifying the issue with one of the great exemplars of faithfulness in the Catholic tradition.

Similarly, members of Dignity/Chicago often mentioned particular contemporary clergy or theologians as models for right behavior. Several interviewees for example, brought up Sister Jeannine Gramick, a nun who has been an outspoken advocate for LGBT rights. One member named Mark enthusiastically recounted all the ways he could think of that the Church has tried to censure Sister Gramick and marveled at how they haven't been able to silence her. Another member of Dignity/Chicago, Carl, spoke at length about growing up idolizing nuns and priests who participated in the civil rights and anti-war movements of the 1950s and 1960s, For members of Dignity/Chicago, Catholic exemplars who stand up for issues the community is concerned about, such as peace, feminism, and LGBT rights, serve as religious role models of how a Catholic can integrate faith and social justice in their life and work.

Members of other communities, as well, brought up notable religious exemplars from their particular faith tradition to promote proper socio-moral behavior. For example, members of Mind, Body, and Soul Church, an African Methodist Episcopal congregation in the Black Church tradition, regularly referenced their denomination's founder, Richard Allen. Members often related the story that he was literally pulled off of his knees as he was praying because he was in the white section of a church, a racist indignity that lead him to found the historically Black denomination. Likewise, members of LGBT-identified Jewish group Welcome and Shalom Synagogue often discussed well-known Jewish theologian and activist Rabbi Abraham Joshua Heschel as a religious exemplar because of his work with Martin Luther King, Jr., in the civil rights movement. Heschel was often discussed by members of Welcome and Shalom as evidence that a concern for civil rights has long been a central tenet of what it means to be Jewish.

The connection between Rabbi Heschel and Martin Luther King, Jr. highlighted by members of Welcome and Shalom is particularly notable. King was, not surprisingly, a common reference point for almost all of the observed groups. Reba Place Fellowship, for example, a Mennonite commune in and around Chicago of about 80 members, had a picture of King hanging in their meetinghouse's main room, and often favorably cited him during meetings. One meeting of the Fellowship began with a prayer that quoted King's "Letter From a Birmingham Jail," saying "if we are extremists, let us be extremists for love." King, though, was not the only shared reference point among the groups. In fact, the commonality of teachers and exemplars represents a key way that the groups exist in a shared progressive religious field, even when they don't directly communicate with each other. For example, the prayer that Reba Place said that quoted King was taken from a prayer book called *Ordinary Radicals*. One of the authors of this book, Shane Claiborne (whom I will discuss further below), is a well-known Christian activist in the New Monastic movement and was regularly referenced by several of the groups I observed. For example, Dignity/Chicago had an event where members gathered to share dinner while watching a video recording of a speech given by Claiborne. Additionally, the members of Neighborhood Church, a multi-racial congregation in Chicago, regularly mentioned Claiborne as an author they read in conversations with me. Another author members of Neighborhood Church frequently mentioned was Jean Vanier, the Catholic theologian who founded the L'Arche communal living federation. Along with Neighborhood Church, members of both Reba Place Fellowship and another communal group, Jesus People USA (JPUSA), cited to me Jean Vanier's understanding of community as influential on their development as communes. In fact, one member of Reba Place I interviewed lived in a L'Arche community for several years before moving to Reba Place, saying that L'Arche was the group that first piqued his interest in the possibilities of communal living and Christian activism. A number of other figures, including René Girard, James Cone, Tim Otto, and Dorothy Day, were mentioned to me as exemplars by members of multiple observed groups.

As is evident by this (partial) list of role models and exemplars, the communities I observed shared a constellation of religious figures, both historical and contemporary, that served as models of moral behavior. In fact, despite many of the groups having no *explicit* social connections to each other, they often referenced the same exemplars, as indicated above. King, Claiborne, Vanier, and others serve as teachers for members of communities with very different focuses and from different faith traditions. Following from this, there are several implications of the Teacher Model of integrating religion and politics. First, religious figures are used as exemplars of right behavior in an effort to sacralize specific political practices. Feminism, communal living, LGBT advocacy, or civil rights activism are given a *sacred* significance as communities tell stories about religious figures who embody these practices and values and were motivated to act because of their spiritual convictions. Second, these figures create a history of progressive religion that connects contemporary issues to past religious figures such as Christ and Mary. By discussing Christ as a champion of the downtrodden or Mary as a proto-feminist, the communities create sacred historical narratives that contextualize contemporary practices. Finally, the shared panel of exemplars serves to map the field of action the groups are situated in. Even groups that have no direct connections to each other share role models, meaning that they often read the same books, reference the same history, and draw on similar languages, theologies, and narratives to understand their behavior. Through these shared references, the groups are able to identify with a wider field of progressive religious activism.

The Community Model

Several of the groups I observed sacralized the local by discussing the importance of the community around them or the social networks they were embedded in. To be a person of faith for many of the observed communities was to be in right relationships with your neighbors. How these right relationships were conceptualized reflected the particular political theologies of the communities (which I will discuss in greater detail below when I explore the third model).

For the communes and non-profit organizations I observed, community was especially important because both kinds of groups are (1) inherently connected to the politics of a particular place, and (2) forced to think about their relationships with other people in highly intentional ways. The Mennonite commune Reba Place Fellowship, for example, was intentionally founded in a diverse neighborhood in the 1950s with the intention of, as one of Reba's founders put it, fostering "brotherhood between races," as well as sharing "financial resources as a way to combat . . . materialism" (quoted in Jackson and Jackson 1987). The commune's efforts to combat materialism and foster community are reflected in their official policy. In 1964, the community decided to limit their spending to whatever the current income for families on welfare is. This reflects the community's desire to, in one member's words, live "in solidarity with the poor." This policy, though, continues to be debated from the perspective of how to best sacralize the local. While I was observing Reba Place, two members made a proposal to shift from living on the welfare standard to spending more money to consume locally grown, organic food. They argued that Reba's low-income neighbors lack healthy, non-processed food to eat and, as such, living in poverty and having to buy cheap food actually *contributes* to the food scarcity problems faced by many poor neighborhoods. Rather, they said, buying healthier food and then sharing it with their neighbors represented a better way to truly "live in solidarity" with the poor. To make this argument, the two members presented an impassioned speech before the community in which one of them said that Christians were called to disinvest in "Pharaoh's economy," by which they meant corporate capitalism. To *truly* be in solidarity with the poor, they said, was to reinvigorate the local food culture by eschewing "Pharaoh's economy" and follow the example of Jesus and the apostles, who lived relationally with their neighbors.

Similarly, members of Cornerstone Community Outreach use Biblical paradigms to talk about the politics of their local community. For example, Cliff, the employee of the shelter mentioned in the previous section, walked me around the neighborhood one day pointing out landmarks including where one gang's territory ended and another's began, or where recent shootings were. Cliff regularly goes on walks like this to maintain a presence in the neighborhood and, on every block, people walking by struck up conversations with Cliff, asking how his family was, checking in on someone who lived or worked at the shelter, or just greeting him. When I asked Cliff about the dense array of connections he has in the neighborhood, he said,

> I think it is important because, you know . . . this is what the incarnation is all about. It's like, Jesus came to earth to live with people, you know? And we, being in the neighborhood . . . they know where we live and they see what we do . . . I think it helps the relationship to be able to help one another and see each other.

In this understanding, Cliff connects the importance Christians place on Jesus's ministry on earth to the work of living in the neighborhood you serve when you work for a shelter. I asked Cliff to elaborate on how his work at Cornerstone connects to Christ's ministry and, becoming animated, Cliff said that Jesus would be against the contemporary prison system, which he sees as destroying neighborhoods.

> If you walk down Wilson Avenue [a major thoroughfare by Cornerstone], [you see the police] lock up young Black men, not lock up young white men, you know? For marijuana, or even crack, or whatever, because the [laws] have been made *just* like the laws in the New Testament. They suit some people and they don't suit others. . . . When [Jesus] would be, like,

healing people on the Sabbath, they'd say you can't heal people on the Sabbath, you know? It's, like, here are these laws, which *they* can make to bring about *their* form of justice or law or finance or whatever they want to do.

Cliff understands the inequality in his neighborhood through a lens that combines a focus on structural racism in the criminal justice system with a Biblical paradigm, sacralizing the fight for civil rights within his neighborhood by seeing it as similar to how Christ had to deal with local authorities when challenging unjust laws. Workers at Cornerstone reiterated this understanding of a ministry of presence time and time again. For example, Lizzie, another employee of Cornerstone, drawing on the same Bible verse that Stephen Colbert quoted at the beginning of the chapter, said, "Jesus says . . . 'whatever you do to the least of these you do to me,' you know? So there is a tremendous amount of scriptural backing to taking care of impoverished people." She went on to add, though, that it is difficult to do that when you lack a "vested interest" in the community you're serving and, as such, she posits a need for Christians to live where they serve if they wish to follow the example of Jesus's ministry of presence.

The two congregations that practiced the community model of integrating faith and justice were the aforementioned African Methodist Episcopal congregation Mind, Body, and Soul Church and multi-racial congregation Neighborhood Church. Race and ethnicity are often tied to space in complicated ways (McRoberts 2003). As such, because faith groups are often connected to various racial and ethnic histories, the sacralization of the local can create a powerful mixture of history, space, and identity, for members of certain communities.

Pastor Diana of Mind, Body, and Soul Church explicitly discussed this when she talked about the history of the Black Church. Pastor Diana was raised without religion but became attracted to the Black Church tradition as an adult for reasons that mixed the spiritual and the political.

As the Black Church began to grow, it became the hub. It was the place, the *only* place our children could learn to read . . . . That idea, of the Black Church being the heart of the community is what attracted me, and it's what holds me. . . . So I think the church has the power to be that voice to the community, that voice that helps to realize and reclaim and continue to fight for the freedoms that the community deserves.

I asked Diana how she actualizes her understanding of the Black Church as the heart of the community in her ministry and she told me two stories. The first was about going to local PTA meetings to use her moral authority as a pastor to speak out about the racism in the school system. The second was about cooking dinner for a family from the church whose mother was in the hospital. What united these seemingly different instances, in Diana's understanding, is the commitment to a sacred understanding of the local community. When members face problems, whether they are structural problems or personal troubles, it is the job of the church to see those problems as opportunities for ministry.

Congregants at Neighborhood Church, a multi-racial church with a large immigrant population in a diverse neighborhood, understood the connection between neighborhood, politics, and religion similarly to people at Mind, Body, and Soul Church. For example, in an interview with a couple named Will and Miranda from Neighborhood Church, they mentioned that the neighborhood was so important for their understanding of how to do church with their congregation that they "moved five blocks closer to be across the street from the meetinghouse." In Miranda's words, "to say that this physical location affects how we love one another is really important." Knowing this about the congregation, I asked Neighborhood Church's pastor, Wendy, about the connection between the congregation and the community. She answered that the church was intentionally planted in a diverse, urban area for reasons that reflected the political theology of the community:

> I think Acts is a strikingly multi-cultural and multi-ethnic book. . . . There are passages in Luke . . . where between three sentences they're switching back and forth between . . . speaking in Aramaic, in Greek, in Hebrew, all in like the space of three or four verses. . . . The reality is that this was a multi-ethnic congregation. And the great commission! It's going and making disciples of all nations. I feel like we, here, in our neighborhood, have this amazing opportunity to do that because all the nations are here.

Wendy connected this understanding of a diverse ministry to progressive racial politics, saying, "My vision for Neighborhood Church is that we would have a multi-racial, multi-ethnic leadership . . . . If the people that are making the decisions are all white . . . that doesn't shift the power dynamics." For Wendy, and other members of Neighborhood Church, the call for the Church to represent "all nations" does not simply mean having a diverse-looking congregation but, rather, represents a statement about the distribution of power. For example, here's Wendy talking at length about the difference between how Neighborhood Church responded to a shooting near the meetinghouse and how a local politician did:

> We held, immediately after that . . . a prayer vigil on the corner. . . . We partnered with several other churches and . . . community groups to make a statement about how we, as a community, want to have this be a safe community for everyone. . . . I would contrast that with our alderman. The next week, he held what he referred to as a "positive loitering" event. . . . [My husband] and I showed up for the positive loitering thing. The difference was, it was really important for the events that *we* organized as a church congregation [to] be well represented in terms of Black leaders and white leaders, that the crowd include the youth that were friends of one of the victims, the mother of the boy who was shot was present, because it was really important to us to say that we want a neighborhood that is safe for these kids, as well as for me and you, whatever your skin color. We stand against violence *and* we stand against the systems that lead to the violence. . . . The positive loitering event was very white, it was very much about getting rid of the people that we're afraid of, getting them to move away, and that feels wrong to me.

We see in Wendy's comments how the political theology of Neighborhood Church draws on the great commission not merely to suggest evangelism but, rather, to sacralize the diversity of its community. She specifically discusses "power dynamics" and "the systems that lead to violence," suggesting that structural understanding of inequality is at the heart of her political theology. These statements, illustrative of everyone I spoke with from Neighborhood Church, indicate that making believers of all nations is not a call for *conversion*, but rather a statement about how equality and social justice must be enacted at the local level in the congregation and community.

In each of these examples, we see how members of the various communities sacralize the local. On the one hand, they sacralize the relationships they have with each other by understanding themselves as participating in the "beloved community" or behaving in ways that put them in right relationship with their neighbors. Additionally, the groups understand the local community as a sacred space that connects them to particular histories or allows them to embody specific political theologies about how people of faith should live in the world. This leads us to the final way that politics and faith were integrated: through the direct application of theology.

The Theological Model

As indicated in the above examples, the groups I observed drew on and developed political theologies to integrate faith and social justice. Peter Scott and William T. Cavanaugh (2006) define a "political theology" as "the analysis and criticism of political arrangements (including cultural-psychological, social and economic aspects) from the perspective of differing interpretations of God's ways with the world" (2). The groups I observed both used existing theological work and developed their own ideas through interaction to construct theologies they could apply to political arrangements. The groups' political theologies underpin the two previously discussed models. Following an exemplar such as Christ requires a particular interpretation to make sense of his actions. Similarly, to sacralize a particular space or relationship requires a group to draw on and apply faith-based understandings.

For example, Rabbi Elliot of LGBT-identified congregation Welcome and Shalom Synagogue explained that his progressive politics emerge directly from reading the Torah, commenting,

> How can you read these texts and preach these texts and not walk the walk in some way? You can't just talk about it! I mean, at least 36 times the Torah says you must not oppress the stranger! You were strangers in

the land of Egypt. You know what it is to be a stranger. You must love the stranger as yourself. Again, and again, and again, and again. So how can you read that and just say, well, you know, I've got mine, so that's all I care about? That doesn't seem left-wing, that just seems, like, *human* to me.

Rabbi Elliot succinctly summarized a fairly typical sentiment among the groups I observed: their political theologies reflect a *common-sense moral application* of the core beliefs of their faith. Other members of Welcome and Shalom Synagogue, for example, followed Rabbi Elliot in the application of Jewish beliefs to understand the world. Many members of the synagogue brought up the concept of "tikkun olam," a rabbinical law that has been influential on Jewish thought. Here is Welcome and Shalom member Sandra discussing the concept and how she hopes to see it enacted:

> For a Jew, if anything exists in the world that is unjust, you're supposed to do something about it. . . . That concept is called *tikkun olam*, which means "repair of the world." . . . For instance, for a concrete goal, it would be very nice to get to full equal rights for gays and lesbians, because I don't see why that should not be.

Throughout our conversation, Sandra reiterated, over and over again, that she felt that she was just applying the basic moral ideas of Judaism to contemporary politics. LGBT people face discrimination and Jews, following the principle of *tikkun olam*, are expected to stand against injustice. When I asked her how she felt about the mixing of faith and politics, she suggested that there is no neat separation of politics from other areas of your life, particularly for LGBT people, whose very existence is politicized in U.S. society. As such, Sandra said, Judaism is a "great fit" for her because it provides a moral framework for her politics and desire to enact social change.

At every community I observed, sermons represented a key time for members of the groups to actively apply theology to contemporary issues. Pastor Diana of Mind, Body, and Soul Church, for example, used the story of a weary and hungry Christ resisting the temptations of bread, power, and wealth offered to him by Satan in the Gospels to suggest to her congregants that they resist the temptation to be successful if it means being immoral. As she walked up and down the aisle of the church preaching, Diana contrasted the behavior of Christ with the selfish actions she suggested typified most people's behavior. "You and I," she said, "keep eating that tempting bread that the Devil offers us!" She then used the evocative image of people climbing up a mountain, stepping on each other and pushing each other down in their quest for monetary success, adding "all of those people climbing that mountain, they keep eating the bread that the Devil offers them." She concluded by telling the church that wealth is not worth it if it means treating others unjustly and creating greater inequality. Rather, she said, the people who follow Christ *resist* the Devil's offer of bread, knowing that a lust for money and power for themselves creates more inequality in the long run.

Similarly, the first time I attended Neighborhood Church, a member named Gary gave a sermon on Christ's triumphant entrance into Jerusalem. Gary said that Christ entered on a donkey, not a warhorse, because Christ was a different kind of king than the Church expected. Christ came in peace, Gary said, and Christ's peace was extended to everyone. Gary went through a number of instances where Christ stood up for the marginalized before rising to a theatrical climax, shouting, "Christ is the illegal immigrant, Christ is the gender nonconformist. Christ is the feminist. And when the Church wants to kill the illegal immigrant, to kill the gender nonconformist, and to kill the feminist, the Church wants to kill Christ!" In both of these examples, we see preachers take particular stories from the Bible and apply them to social issues. For Pastor Diana, Christ resisting the Devil's temptation is a call for contemporary Christians to combat inequality. Gary, likewise, uses various stories about Jesus, including his entrance into Jerusalem, to suggest that Christ promotes peace and centers those on the margins. As such, Gary says, contemporary Christians must see Christ in the marginalized. Additionally, both Gary and Diana critique certain behaviors as flawed. Diana suggests that people who "eat the bread" by acting selfishly when tempted ultimately create an unjust world. Gary, on the other hand, suggests that when the Church, writ large, fails to love those who are oppressed and marginalized, the Church is failing to love Christ.

It is important to note that, as mentioned above, political theologies are drawn both from existing ways of talking about politics using faith-based paradigms, as well as from personal experience, reflection, and conversation. To illustrate, I will use the case of Jimmy, a young member of Reba Place Fellowship. Jimmy grew up in a conservative family in a rural town. He knew he was gay from a young age, but actively denied this because he (correctly) didn't think his local community would have been supportive of his identity. Reba Place had, traditionally, been exclusive of LGBT persons but, after learning about them, Jimmy became enamored with their peace and justice orientation as well as their communal living situation. Jimmy had been reading books by the aforementioned Shane Claiborne, founder of the Simple Way commune, and was looking for a space to live out some of the Simple Way's ideas. When Jimmy contacted Reba Place, he told them that he was gay, but believed celibacy to be God's call for same-sex attracted individuals. Given this, he was allowed to join.

What Jimmy *didn't* know is that a sizable contingent of Reba Place members, particularly in the younger cohorts, were fully LGBT-affirming and were hoping to move the commune in that direction. Several of his new friends in the Fellowship began loaning him books on Queer Theology and Jimmy read them with interest, learning a whole new view on the world. Additionally, Jimmy began to meet other gay Mennonites who, he felt, seemed to have strong spiritual lives. Through these readings and conversations, Jimmy developed his own theological understandings that have allowed him to make sense of, and even sacralize, his sexual identity. For example, Jimmy told me he has come to realize that

> Christ is God hanging out on the margins, with people who are unacceptable to church. . . . As a gay man in church, it puts me on the margins. As a gay man in a rural area, with my family, it puts me *way* out there. So sometimes it puts me right in with Jesus.

In Jimmy's developing theology, because Christ was a marginal figure on earth, the experience of marginality connects one to the lived experiences of Christ. Jimmy furthered this line of thought, saying,

I've always known and believed that God has no gender. . . . But the reality is that when you use only masculine pronouns for God, you give God these kinds of attributes. And I guess I see God as more "other." . . . Especially in the study of Queer Theology, as well, that's important. Understanding God as, you know . . . not fitting in a box.

These theological understandings have allowed Jimmy to shift his understanding of being gay. He has become active in promoting LGBT rights both in the Mennonite Church and the wider society through a variety of activist outlets.

When I asked Jimmy how the officially LGBT-exclusive community at Reba handled his new understanding, he turned to the application of theology again, saying that "people in the fellowship really do believe that you love your neighbor." The end result of this was that the leadership of Reba Place put together a committee, which included Jimmy, to discuss LGBT issues with the intention of moving toward greater inclusion while recognizing that members of the Fellowship held different beliefs on this particular issue. I attended some of the community meetings that emerged out of the committee's work and much of the conversation revolved around building theological justifications for LGBT inclusion that wove together Biblical exegesis, creative application of beliefs, and discussions about personal experience.

In each of these examples, members of the communities both draw on existing theology as well as creatively apply their beliefs to sacralize particular ideas, practices, and groups. For many members of the communities, this represented a commonsense moral application of existing theology. For example, Jews are expected to "heal the world," so one must stand against the inequality that LGBT persons face. Occasionally, though, theology was used to promote ideas that were more radical or countercultural, such as Jimmy challenging the idea of the gender binary using Queer Theology or Gary suggesting that rejecting feminism, undocumented immigrants, and gender nonconformists is tantamount to killing Christ. In every case, though, the political theologies deployed by the groups sacralized their political beliefs and behaviors by integrating them with faith-based understandings, drawing lines of connection between the ideas of their religion and their practices in the world.

Conclusion: The Language of Progressive Religion

The introduction to this book suggested a typology of ways that a group may be considered a "progressive religious group." If a faith-based group participates in progressive action, embodies progressive identities, holds progressive values, or espouses a progressive theology, we argue that they can reasonably be considered part of the wider field of action that compromises the world of progressive religion. In this chapter, I have provided three models that emerged from data collected on progressive religious groups that represent *how* groups may fall into one or more of these categories. To provide some examples, the groups construct progressive identities through identifying with particular role models. Referencing progressive religious figures, such as Martin Luther King, Jr., Sister Jeannine Gramick, Shane Claiborne, and Rabbi Heschel, shapes how the groups understand and talk about what it means to be a person of faith. These teachers additionally suggest particular progressive actions or values, such as promoting civil rights or combating economic inequality. Similarly, when the groups sacralize community by thinking about diversity, local power dynamics, and the way space represents particular group's histories, they promote specific actions as representing right moral behavior. When one sees Christ's work as a call to challenge racism in the community, or the early Church as a model for communal living, it gives sacred authority to progressive ways of relating to one's local surroundings. Finally, as mentioned, progressive theologies underpin these efforts. A feminist reading of the Bible, for example, gives Dignity/Chicago the theological backing to have women priests say mass, while Queer Theology has helped Jimmy and other members of Reba Place sacralize LGBT experiences.

The three models I presented in this chapter are not *inherently* progressive. In fact, one could imagine *conservatives* using similar models. For example, conservative religious groups would obviously posit a different panel of teachers and different political theologies to underpin their political beliefs and practices. What makes these models progressive is not their *form*, but their specific *content* when used in the context of the particular faith groups I examined. Because the observed communities share references to figures associated with more liberal politics and theologies, because they sacralize the local with understandings that highlight structural inequality, and because their political theologies represent progressive applications of religious material to the world, the communities ultimately situate themselves within the progressive religious field.

More broadly, this analysis suggests two key takeaways about religion and politics. First, it highlights the rhetorical flexibility of both politics and religion. Although religion is often conceptualized as having essential conservative qualities, the ease with which the observed groups integrated faith-based and social justice–oriented talk suggests a degree of elasticity not captured by many discussions about religion and politics. Second, we must pay attention to the context that religious narratives emerge out of. Religious narratives do not exist in a vacuum. Rather, identities, relationships, and the availability of different cultural material shape how they are expressed and applied, as evidenced by the above analysis. Taking Jimmy from Reba Place as an example, the meaning and expression of his gay Mennonite identity, and the resources he has to model or understand it, have changed over time as he moved from a small conservative town to a justice-oriented commune in an urban area. As such, religio-political beliefs, practices, and identifications are not static but, rather, represent an ever-shifting process of becoming as groups and individuals creatively apply the materials of their faith to different situations and spaces.

REFERENCES

Braunstein, Ruth. 2012. "Storytelling in Liberal Religious Advocacy." *Journal for the Scientific Study of Religion* 51(1): 110–127.

Edwards, Korie L. 2008. *The Elusive Dream: The Power of Race in Interracial Churches.* New York: Oxford University Press.

Eliasoph, Nina. 1998. *Avoiding Politics: How Americans Produce Apathy in Everyday Life.* New York: Cambridge University Press.

Emerson, Michael O., and Christian Smith. 2001. *Divided by Faith: Evangelical Religion and the Problem of Race in America.* New York: Oxford University Press.

Gutterman, David S. 2005. *Prophetic Politics: Christian Social Movements and American Democracy.* Ithaca, NY: Cornell University Press.

Jackson, Dave, and Neta Jackson. 1987. *Glimpses of Glory: Thirty Years of Community.* Elgin, IL: Brethren Press.

Kniss, Fred. 1997. *Disquiet in the Land: Cultural Conflict in American Mennonite Communities.* New Brunswick, NJ: Rutgers University Press.

Lichterman, Paul. 2005. *Elusive Togetherness: Church Groups Trying to Bridge America's Divisions.* Princeton, NJ: Princeton University Press.

McRoberts, Omar M. 2003. *Streets of Glory: Church and Community in a Black Urban Neighborhood.* Chicago: University of Chicago Press.

Moon, Dawne. 2004. *God, Sex, and Politics: Homosexuality and Everyday Theologies.* Chicago: University of Chicago Press.

Morris, Aldon D. 1984. *Origins of the Civil Rights Movements.* 1st ed. New York: Free Press.

Nepstad, Sharon Erickson. 2008. *Religion and War Resistance in the Plowshares Movement.* New York: Cambridge University Press.

Perrin, Andrew J. 2006. *Citizen Speak: The Democratic Imagination in American Life.* Chicago: University of Chicago Press.

Scott, Peter, and William T. Cavanaugh, eds. 2006. *The Blackwell Companion to Political Theology.* Hoboken, NJ: Wiley Blackwell.

Williams, Rhys H. 1995. "Constructing the Public Good: Cultural Resources and Social Movements." *Social Problems* 42(1): 124–144.

Wood, Richard L. 2002. *Faith in Action: Religion, Race, and Democratic Organizing in America.* Chicago: University of Chicago Press.

Conclusion

What Progressive Efforts Tell Us about Faith and Politics

RHYS H. WILLIAMS

This book has made a case for increasing scholarly and public attention to the religious actors and organizations engaged in progressive social activism. One might say that a part of our justification is a little prosaic—that is, we have noted that so much attention has been devoted to conservative religion and conservative politics that the "other side" needs to get some airtime. That even in what is thought of as a conservative age, and with a documented move to the right by the Republican Party and the incorporation of many self-consciously Christian groups into the Republican Party base, there still exists a "religious Left."

But digging a little deeper, the claim for increased attention isn't so banal after all. A significant thread that runs through current understandings of religion and politics is that there is a great face-off in this country between the *religious* Right and the *secular* Left. And it is true that many organized Christian activists form a key constituency of the Right, while secular people are disproportionately Democrats and/or liberals. But what about the religious Left? Is it really nonexistent, and if not, which we think ought to be pretty obvious after reading this book, why is it so invisible in most journalistic and many scholarly accounts? This volume has demonstrated that a religious Left, or at least religiously based progressive activism, is very much in existence. If one looks carefully, it is everywhere—from the border to urban and suburban settings in the heartland. One finds it involved in high-profile issues such as immigration, but also in battles against economic inequality, poverty and racial discrimination, or protesting militarism, or trying to deal with hunger and homelessness. One would be hard pressed to live in any good-sized community in the United States and not find some example of the type of activism and engagement documented here.

So, a religious Left exists, in numbers that may surprise many. This is, in itself, a point readers should take from this volume. But beyond just the numbers—so what? What is theoretically and analytically significant about this, beyond just "there's a lot of it"? And if this religio-political field really is so big, why is it so invisible, at least in mainstream media depictions of American public life and public politics, and in the worlds of political punditry and social science scholarship? This concluding chapter first offers five interrelated explanations for this invisibility, and then uses those considerations to examine the significance of progressive religious activism for scholarly approaches to religion, politics, social movements, and public life.

Overlooked in Public Discussions

The first explanation for the relative silence about the religious Left involves how the largest media sources cover politics in the United States. It is a cliché to "blame the media," but there is a well-developed literature on the institutional and political processes that determine what gets considered "news" (for example, Schudson 2002). Political media are dominated by "horserace" journalism. Poll numbers, campaign strategy, and winning and losing elections are the overwhelming subjects of attention. As national politics evolve into a perpetual campaign, the analysis of polling data and prognostications about electoral outcomes using sports-inflected languages of winning and losing is ubiquitous. Even as political pundits and reporters call for candidates to eschew symbolism and imagery and focus on issues, they themselves mostly analyze issue positions for their implicit strategy and how they will affect electoral prospects.

This "horserace" approach has two rationales. One is that it can be presented as "objective" journalism, in that it stays focused on numbers, and allows for a notion of "balance" by always quoting a spokesperson from "both sides." After decades of being accused by the political Right of having a "liberal bias," many news organizations avoid too much substantive reporting in lieu of a more "neutral" winners-and-losers approach (Alterman 2003). Second, journalists who work political beats have their own professional circles with distinct institutional norms and practices. Journalists are cultivated by professional campaign consultants and managers, and in return must cultivate them. Reporters gain status within the profession by having inside contacts, scooping stories, and predicting things correctly. Reporters traveling with candidates on the campaign trail must file repeated daily stories when the actual days are often mind-numbingly repetitive. Under these conditions it is not surprising that journalists get drawn into the insiders' world of political consulting and campaign strategy. These dynamics reinforce the tendency to look for short-term effects, to speculate on "who's up and who's down," and to treat civic and social groups mostly as voting constituencies to be cultivated.

Whether media coverage is liberal or conservative, it is clearly the case that the religious Right—as a set of organizations as well as individual voters—has become an integral part of the Republican Party. With the exception of the Black Church, there is no equivalent group in the Democratic Party, although the party has recently begun such an effort with mixed results, as Sager's chapter in this volume illuminated. Thus, groups and voters of the religious Left figure less significantly in the types of counting that political journalism highlights. Even when prominent Democratic politicians speak in a religious register, it is often viewed less as evidence of a progressive religious vision than as a means of positioning themselves as "centrist" or nodding in some obligatory way to "religion in general." Because the religious Left is less connected to campaigns, political consulting, and elections, it receives far less attention.

Some of these dynamics are also apparent in the social science scholarship on religion and politics, a second reason religious progressives are often overlooked. Political scientists, not surprisingly, are overwhelmingly interested in the polity and its institutionalized governing practices. Elections are key to those practices in the U.S., and thus political scientists' interest in religion is often limited to how it influences voting and elections. This is not a criticism, necessarily; understanding political parties, campaigns, and elections is central to the discipline. However, it is also true that elections offer the benefit of a very clear "dependent" variable—one side wins and one side loses. If we think of "politics" as broader than the polity itself, as in the approach outlined in this volume's introduction, the landscape that includes progressive activism emerges more clearly.

But simply broadening our conception of politics would not necessarily be sufficient. Scholarship's blind spot to the religious Left is also an unintended consequence of a scholarly acceptance of the "culture wars" narrative that emerged in the 1990s. This narrative arose among conservative political candidates such as Pat Buchanan, and among social scientists cued by James Davison Hunter's (1991) influential book. Both posited the culture war as being between religious conservatives and liberal or progressive humanists and secularists. The very construction of the culture wars idea had room for only two "sides" (offering a certain clarity in analysis, if sacrificing accuracy), and as such aligned nicely with the American notion of the "two-party system" and our cultural fondness for military and sports metaphors (Williams 1997; see also Wellman [2008] on the "two-party" conception of American Protestantism). Yet public opinion polls, then and now, continue to show more people who are both liberal and religious than who are secularist. Additionally, many public attitudes do not line up in an easily defined bipolar axis. Some analysts worked to offer a more complex accounting of the religio-political scene (e.g., Wuthnow 1989; Wuthnow and Evans 2002; Baker 2005), but this did not stand in the way of the attraction of the culture wars paradigm.

Beyond the institutional and professional conventions of media, political reporting, and a scholarly focus on elections and a culture wars narrative, many progressive religious activists are not so keen on becoming a wing of the Democratic Party. This is a third factor in the low media profile of the religious Left. Activists in many progressive religious efforts differ with the party on some issues, and many feel uneasy with the whole process of electoral politics. Indeed, as the chapters by Fuist and Geraty have shown, many activist groups do not even think of themselves as "political." They are not eager to be counted as foot soldiers in the party base. To be fair, many conservative religious people are not thrilled about such labels either, and it was a source of controversy in the early years of Christian Right organizing in the late 1970s and early 1980s. "Politics" is often thought to be a polluting danger to religion, whether progressive, conservative, or otherwise, and many Americans express distaste for "politics." Nonetheless, the highly visible organizational leaders of Christian Right groups have worked in concert with Republican Party operatives and strategies for over three decades now (see Liebman and Wuthnow 1983; Moen 1992), a phenomenon not matched by the Democrats except within the Black Church.

A fourth characteristic of progressive religious activism that has led to lower levels of media coverage over the last thirty years is that progressive religious activists are not as often engaged in easily mobilized—and easily counted—organizations as are those on the religious Right. It is thus often harder for media and others to find official organizational spokespersons for progressive groups. But more fundamentally, progressive activist coalitions can be quite different in character from conservative ones, and, just as a matter of character and general orientation, liberals are often harder to organize and get moving in a collective direction than are conservatives, as Olson's chapter has shown. The more traditional Left of European politics, or the mid-century U.S. labor movement, were well-organized and disciplined in organizations that pursued political goals. In current U.S. politics, however, what gets called the "Left" is usually "liberal." Being liberal entails a general appreciation for individual conscience and the determination to preserve individual autonomy, discretion, and choice. Moreover, liberals are often more open to diversities of religious, moral, and political viewpoints within progressive coalitions; this leads many of them away from the kind of organizing on the political Left that one sees on the Right. For example, it is hard to imagine a left-wing version of the "Values Voters Summit"—which is essentially a forum to vet candidates based on their conformity to socially conservative moral values, especially around gender and sexuality—as there is much less agreement among liberals about what these moral values should be.

A final factor in keeping progressive religious activism from getting more attention from both journalists and scholars is that the Left has been less "successful" than the Right. In terms of elections and media attention, this is clearly true. The Left has not engaged electoral politics to the same extent, and it is not unreasonable to see the last three decades of American politics as a generally conservative age. Even when Democrats Bill Clinton and Barack Obama were in the White House, religious conservatives were often winning electoral victories and achieving policy goals at the state and local level, in many judicial decisions, and pushing the Democratic Party to the right.

Theoretical Approaches to Religion and American Politics

These five factors—horserace journalism, academic blind spots, unease with party politics, fewer high-profile national political organizations, and fewer successes—explain why progressive religious activism is less reported on, recognized, and analyzed than the religious Right. But this analysis of practical politics and media attention also points to some theoretical and conceptual understandings that we might gain from more attention to the religious Left.

As a scholarly backdrop, the meta-narrative about religion in the modern world has long accepted a general process of "secularization." Some versions of secularization theory have been committed to the idea that this entails religious decline; while those predictions are now less accepted by scholars, more nuanced accounts of secularization recognize that modernity is largely defined by institutional differentiation, and the attendant fact that religious authority must compete for public legitimacy with other sources of authority (e.g., Casanova 1994).

This is relevant because much of our current sociological understandings of religion and American politics, including the "culture wars" account, grew out of engagement with what was first called the "New Christian Right" (NCR) in the late 1970s and early 1980s and the ways it undermined the secularization narrative. In the 1950s, religion had been understood as an important source of social unity (Herberg 1955), and that idea survived much of the activism of the 1960s. That is, while scholars recognized the importance of religion in the civil rights movement (e.g., Morris 1984) and anti–Vietnam War protest (e.g., Quinley 1974), the contours of American politics were more likely to be understood as shaped by race or gender than religion.

That changed when the NCR exploded on the national political stage with the 1980 election of Ronald Reagan to the presidency and a new Republican majority in the Senate. The NCR rejected many if not most of the dimensions of any liberal consensus: it urged a rollback of domestic social programs (including racial integration), objected to many dimensions of changing gender and family relations, and sought to inject Christian symbols and beliefs into the public sphere. These dynamics prompted a thorough reassessment among scholars of the contemporary role of religion in American politics, and more basically, a reexamination of secularization theory (e.g., Hadden 1987).

The visibility of the NCR also contributed to innovation in the sociology of social movements. The vitality of religious movements reasserted for scholars the importance of values and ideology in activism, particularly in understanding the motivations for mobilizing. Social movement studies emerging from "Resource Mobilization" theory (McCarthy and Zald 1977) emphasized organizational resources and social structural understandings of successful social movements. But powerful ideologies such as religion had clearly not gone away, even in an advanced industrial society. Value-based ideologies are a key aspect of collective action, and research demonstrated that religion and religious culture could be a crucial movement resource (see Martinez and Nepstad in this volume). Refocusing on religion in movement politics emphasized the extent to which movements themselves are moral enterprises. And as Pattillo-McCoy (1998), Smith (1996), and others noted, religious congregations could be organizational homes for social movement efforts. They have meeting spaces, membership networks of people who know and trust each other, established practices of decision-making, and attitudes toward reforming the world.

In sum, the rise of conservative religious politics produced lessons for sociological scholarship even beyond the study of religion. But the lessons scholars drew from their renewed focus on conservative religious movements—as valuable as they have been—only captured part of the picture. Progressive religious efforts are different than conservative ones in ways that require us to adjust what is now the "conventional knowledge" about religion's role in activism.

The lessons available in this volume illuminate a weave of institutional and cultural factors. First, our conceptual centering of "organizations" in the study of politics and religion needs to be rethought. As Yukich observed in her chapter, much of the study of religion in American public life assumes that civic engagement efforts are rooted in congregations. That is not necessarily wrong, as the congregation is in many ways the quintessential American form of organizing (Warner 1994, Williams 2007), especially for the Protestant Christians who have long been the dominant social group in American society. But many non-Christian groups are much less focused on congregations as formal organizations, or as spaces for civic and political action. Temples are less for regular gatherings of the laity and more for individualized and family rites.

Further, changes in American Christianity should also caution against an overly organizational focus. There is a well-documented decline in connection to various types of religious organizations among many Americans. For example, religious denominations have been declining in authority and in holding the loyalty of members for several decades. This is particularly true in Mainline Protestantism, but there have been clear changes in Catholicism as well, as lay American Catholics have become more selective in the Church teachings that motivate them, whether it is opposition to contraception or to capital punishment. Indeed, Chaves (1994) uses this decline of institutionalized religious authority as the very definition of secularization.

As noted, the congregation, rather than the denomination, has always been the most significant American religious organization, partly because it aligns with Americans' general preferences for decentralized local authority (see Shain 1994). But as Beyerlein and West discussed in their chapter, there are challenges to congregational mobilization, even when it occurs. Further, recent research has demonstrated that congregational involvement is connected to political commitments in ways that can lead to religious shifting and disaffiliation (Putnam and Campbell 2012). Concomitantly, there has been a decline in congregational involvement, particularly among younger people, and those whose politics are more likely to be progressive. While weekly religious service attendance is associated with conservative politics, other levels of attendance—and types of involvement beyond "worship service attendance"—are not strongly associated with any particular political outcome.

Highly educated, more politically liberal people commonly self-identify as being "spiritual, but not religious," a repudiation of institutionalized authority. Similarly, Marti and Ganiel (2014) analyze the "deconstructed church"—gatherings of self-identified Christians who are determined not to let the spirit ossify in a traditional congregational form. These gatherings are not well-suited for collective civic action. As Wuthnow (2002) notes more generally, American civil society has become less formally organized, with membership numbers in many voluntary associations declining significantly. Unlike many commentators, however, Wuthnow does not interpret this as American civil society falling apart. Rather, he sees an increase in fluid, "loose" connections: people associate, but the form of the formal voluntary organization is less emplaced than it was. Particularly for people with more liberal religious and political persuasions, the organization as such is declining in importance.

If the "organization" as a source of stable resources and settled hierarchies of authority is becoming less of a standard feature of American religion, particularly among liberals, then some assumptions about political action may need reexamining. "Organizing" rather than the "organization" may be a more fruitful conceptual lens. For example, Moore (2008) demonstrates that repeated cases of anti-military activism among American scientists largely existed in networks that were only occasionally formally organized. Rather than focusing on organizations and their "boundaries," Moore shows the fluidity of networks and relationships; these often coalesce for a period into groups with names and some formal structure, but they just as often dissolve, rearrange, and reform. This is particularly true in progressive groups, where commitments to participatory democracy and inclusion align with a religious populism in which authority is largely vested in the individual and often seen as expressed in everyday actions (see Williams 2006). Rather than tightly enforcing symbolic and membership boundaries, progressive organizations often work to decenter internal hierarchies and lower barriers to participation (e.g., Hart 2001; Polletta 2002).

A second distinctive feature of progressive religious activism is how often it is marked by interfaith and interreligious efforts. The liberal/Left is currently more coalitional than the Right and there is thus an increased need for what Diaz-Edelman in this volume calls an "etiquette"—that is, intra-movement practices and discourses—that can accommodate more voices from more traditions. The chapters by Adler, Fuist, Fulton and Wood, and Geraty also discuss collective action efforts that are deliberately and self-consciously internally diverse, especially along religious lines, but also race and class. This volume has shown clearly that such diversities within collective social action identities— even when connected to something as basic as religion—are not necessarily a threat to collective action. But they still must be accommodated, religiously and politically.

More diverse coalitions, along any social or cultural dimensions, are more likely to have a wider range of political and social outlooks among the participants involved. As Lichterman and Williams showed in their chapter, a wide variety of people can be encompassed by the category Mainline Protestant, and while they may agree on some things, that shared territory may be limited. Participants' political commitments may not align along the current liberal-conservative divide, giving Mainline Protestants a particular challenge in articulating their religious rationales for civic and political engagement. This also pertains to groups that are often thought to be more homogenous. The dissolution of the solid "Catholic vote" has been noted for some time and it has led to some particularly polarized politics, with Catholics deeply involved with anti-abortion and anti–same-sex marriage activism as well as integral to anti-military and pro-immigrant movements (e.g., McGreevy 2007).

Indeed, the chapters in this volume have offered dramatic affirmation of the developing understanding among social movement scholars that a shared ideological coherence is not necessarily a prerequisite to collective action. Shared values, and a shared collective identity, can be central resources in mobilizing people and in keeping them together through successes and failures. But how much is "shared" varies, and should not be assumed to be necessary prior to mobilization. Recent scholarship shows that collective identity and ideological coherence often *develop* through activism. Munson (2008), for example, demonstrated that activists can come to ideological clarity and agreement, and sometimes even religious faith, through activism itself, rather than preceding it. Social action is not a mere deduction from extant values but an evolving process.

Thus, attention to progressive religious activism illuminates more general ways in which internal diversity can pose challenges for social movement groups. They must self-consciously handle various identities both strategically and in terms of internal decision-making. But they do get handled, as the chapters in this volume have shown. Social groups develop a "group style" through interaction (Eliasoph and Lichterman 2003) but that style is not immutable and can self-consciously incorporate ways of negotiating difference so that the group can stay together. The forms of collective action that follow from diverse, interreligious coalitions are quite distinct from the image of tightly knit, preexisting social groups who go into collective actions with bright symbolic and social boundaries drawn around their efforts and their visions of the good society.

It is true that progressive religious groups can also create strong identity boundaries that facilitate internal group unity. Among others, Wellman (2008) showed the extent to which liberals defined themselves in large part as not being conservative or fundamentalist—a point also made in the chapters by Adler, Fuist, and Lichterman and Williams. Yet, all progressive religious actors do not engage in this same kind of boundary-work. The symbolic boundaries and social identities they develop are shaped by a range of factors, including the religious, racial, ethnic, and class identities of the participants and the extent to which groups are committed to diversity as a value and goal.

Which leads to the third point, that we must take into account the *content* of ideologies and value orientations. Scholars are rightly dismissive of popular accounts of social movements that focus exclusively on their articulated causes and goals, but ignore many of the commonalities that movements share across political lines. Sociology as a discipline is dedicated to finding common factors across individual cases and illustrating general principles. But the differences in content are significant. To just say "religion matters in much political activism" is true, and has led to a number of useful insights. However, specifying the religious traditions, practices, values, and discourses involved leads to understanding variation; it may complicate our conclusions, but it hones their accuracy.

Thus, it is important to understand the ways that progressive religious activism in the U.S., like liberal and progressive politics more generally, has a basic suspicion of hierarchy, while nurturing ample room for individual choice and room for dissent. As Gahr and Young noted in their chapter in this volume, personal freedom and rebellion were joined in 1960s New Left groups, which in turn could be accommodated more easily by some religious traditions than others. In groups organized for collective action within such traditions, issues of authority can be more complex than those from more hierarchical traditions. Consensus, or at least informed consent, is often required and involves considerable discussion and argument. But the process of making decisions for coordinated action cannot be short-circuited if groups are to be true to themselves. Deliberation itself may well be seen as just as important as any instrumentally oriented achievement (see Epstein 1991; Polletta 2002). Inclusion can be a self-conscious value, especially when one is involved in efforts that are juxtaposed to a political other seen as intolerant (again, how often progressive activists define themselves as "not conservative"). This can align with many religious impulses, from "welcoming the stranger," to "being the change," to "expressing God's love." Simply engaging in activism, properly done, and developing self-identities as "activists," can be understood as "successes" in their own right.

Which leads to a final conceptual concern—how to think about success, or outcomes more generally, when assessing progressive religious activism? Some scholars have argued that liberalism has already "won" in general American culture—that the valorization of tolerance, individualism, diversity, and formal equality means that the "mainstream" is actually liberal. Demerath (1995) argued that to the extent that general acceptance of these values weakened the boundaries between liberal Protestant organizations and the culture, it made defending those organizations a more difficult cause to mobilize around. While an interesting analysis for liberal Protestantism (and not incompatible with Lichterman and Williams's chapter), this volume has illuminated many forms of progressive religious activism beyond that. And more recent turns in American public life have shown that distinctly un-liberal Christian nationalist politics are alive and well (Williams 2013). Nonetheless, we can clearly think of "success" with more nuance than who wins elections.

For example, if we focus on the discourses about our collective, public life, as Gorski has done in his chapter, there are constructions about who is "deserving" within society and who is not. These often shape perceptions and mobilize people to act in civil society distinct from any particular electoral cycle, but are the ground upon which issues emerge. Consider the current public discussions about inequality in American life. While inequality has been increasing in the United States since the 1980s, a clear discussion about whether this is healthy for society, and even more pointedly, whether such a situation is fair or moral, is recent. The Occupy Wall Street movement brought attention to economic inequality (and is credited with the brilliant slogan "We are the 99%"), but other recent efforts have been explicitly religious. In this volume, Braunstein has examined the "Nuns on the Bus"—Roman Catholic Sisters who engaged in a deliberate campaign both to call attention to inequality and to offer pointed messages that this is religiously unacceptable. Similarly, in 2013 a coalition of church pastors and religiously motivated activists began "Moral Monday" protests at the state capitol in North Carolina—arguing that addressing inequality and poverty (among other issues) are religious duties (Berman 2013). This argument has a pedigree. The Rev. Jim Wallis, founder of the liberal Evangelical Protestant group Sojourners, has for several years argued that "budgets are a moral issue" (2005). While not gaining much national traction during the George W. Bush administration, there is more receptivity to that message, and that phrase, now. Given the popularity of Senator Bernie Sanders's 2016 presidential campaign, there is no question that the discourse around economic inequality, including its framing as a moral issue, has changed in the last few years of American politics. Thinking about activism's success needs to be sensitive to many dimensions of outcomes.

Summary

Progressive religious activism is not brand new, of course. Many historically progressive social movements, such as abolition or nineteenth-century populism, had deep religious connections (Young 2006). And the recent scholarly field is not barren, as Demerath and Williams (1992), Hart (2001), Warren (2001), Wood (2002), Nepstad (2004), and Lichterman (2005), among others, have examined both the weaknesses and the possibilities of progressive religious activism. By calling upon, and reaching beyond, these efforts, this volume has brought needed attention to the ways in which the progressive end of the political spectrum is composed not just of secular groups or those fighting only for a classically liberal understanding of individual rights, but also includes religious actors with moral visions for collective life. Our academic and public understandings of religion and politics, social movements and collective action, as well as what visions constitute a good society, can be the richer for this engagement.

ACKNOWLEDGMENTS
I thank Ruth Braunstein, Todd Fuist, and Kelly Moore for their frequent conversations, feedback, and patience.

REFERENCES
Alterman, Eric. 2003. *What Liberal Media? The Truth about Bias and the Media.* New York: Basic Books.

Baker, Wayne. 2005. *America's Crisis of Values: Reality and Perception.* Princeton, NJ: Princeton University Press.

Berman, Ari. 2013. "North Carolina's Moral Mondays: An Inspiring Grassroots Movement Is Fighting Back against the GOP's Outrageous Budget Cuts and Attacks on Democracy." July 17. *Nation.* www.thenation.com/.

Casanova, Jose. 1994. *Public Religions in the Modern World.* Chicago: University of Chicago Press.

Chaves, Mark. 1994. "Secularization as Declining Religious Authority." *Social Forces* 72(3): 749–775.

Demerath, N. J., III. 1995. "Cultural Victory and Organizational Defeat in the Paradoxical Decline of Liberal Protestantism." *Journal for the Scientific Study of Religion* 34(4): 458–469.

Demerath, N. J., III, and Rhys H. Williams 1992. *A Bridging of Faiths.* Princeton, NJ: Princeton University Press.

Eliasoph, Nina, and Paul Lichterman. 2003. "Culture in Interaction." *American Journal of Sociology* 108(4): 735–794.

Epstein, Barbara. 1991. *Political Protest and Cultural Revolution: Nonviolent Direct Action in the 1970s and 1980s.* Berkeley: University of California Press.

Hadden, Jeffery K. 1987. "Toward Desacralizing Secularization Theory." *Social Forces* 65(3): 587–611.

Hart, Stephen. 2001. *Cultural Dilemmas of Progressive Politics.* Chicago: University of Chicago Press.

Herberg, Will. 1955. *Protestant, Catholic, Jew.* Chicago: University of Chicago Press.

Hunter, James Davison. 1991. *Culture Wars: The Struggle to Define America.* New York: Basic Books.

Lichterman, Paul. 2005. *Elusive Togetherness.* Princeton, NJ: Princeton University Press.

Liebman, Robert C., and Robert Wuthnow, eds. 1983. *The New Christian Right.* New Brunswick, NJ: Aldine Transaction Books.

Marti, Gerardo, and Gladys Ganiel. 2014. *The Deconstructed Church: Understanding Emerging Christianity.* New York: Oxford University Press.

McCarthy, John D., and Mayer N. Zald. 1977. "Resource Mobilization and Social Movements: A Partial Theory." *American Journal of Sociology* 82(6): 1212–1241.

McGreevy, John. 2007. "Catholics, Democrats, and the GOP in Contemporary America." *American Quarterly* 59(3): 669–681.

Moen, Matthew C. 1992. *The Transformation of the Christian Right*. Tuscaloosa: University of Alabama Press.

Moore, Kelly. 2008. *Disrupting Science: Social Movements, American Scientists, and the Politics of the Military, 1945–1975*. Princeton, NJ: Princeton University Press.

Morris, Aldon. 1984. *The Origins of the Civil Rights Movement*. New York: Free Press.

Munson, Ziad W. 2008. *The Making of Pro-Life Activists: How Social Movement Mobilization Works*. Chicago: University of Chicago Press.

Nepstad, Sharon Erickson. 2004. *Convictions of the Soul*. New York: Oxford University Press.

Pattillo-McCoy, Mary. 1998. "Church Culture as a Strategy of Action in the Black Community." *American Sociological Review* 63(6): 767–784.

Polletta, Francesca. 2002. *Freedom Is an Endless Meeting: Democracy in American Social Movements*. Chicago: University of Chicago Press.

Putnam, Robert D., and David E. Campbell. 2012. *American Grace*. New York: Simon & Schuster.

Quinley, Harold E. 1974. *The Prophetic Clergy: Social Activism among Protestant Ministers*. New York: John Wiley & Sons.

Schudson, Michael. 2002. *The Sociology of News*. New York: W.W. Norton.

Shain, Barry Alan. 1994. *The Myth of American Individualism: The Protestant Origins of American Political Thought*. Princeton, NJ: Princeton University Press.

Smith, Christian, ed. 1996. *Disruptive Religion: The Force of Faith in Social-Movement Activism*. New York: Routledge.

Wallis, Jim. 2005. *God's Politics: Why the Right Gets It Wrong and the Left Doesn't Get It*. San Francisco: HarperSanFrancisco.

Warner, R. Stephen. 1994. "The Place of the Congregation in the American Religious Configuration." In *New Perspectives in the Study of Congregations*, edited by James P. Wind and James W. Lewis, 54–99. Chicago: University of Chicago Press.

Warren, Mark R. 2001. *Dry Bones Rattling: Community Building to Revitalize American Democracy*. Princeton, NJ: Princeton University Press.

Wellman, James K., Jr. 2008. *Evangelical vs. Liberal: The Clash of Christian Cultures in the Pacific Northwest*. New York: Oxford University Press.

Williams, Rhys H., ed. 1997. *Cultural Wars in American Politics: Critical Reviews of a Popular Myth*. Hawthorne, NY: Aldine de Gruyter.

Williams, Rhys H. 2006. "Collective Action, Everyday Protest, and Lived Religion." Review Essay. *Social Movement Studies* 5(1): 81–87.

Williams, Rhys H. 2007. "The Languages of the Public Sphere: Religious Pluralism, Institutional Logics, and Civil Society." *Annals of the American Academy of Political and Social Sciences* 612 (July): 42–61.

Williams, Rhys H. 2013. "Civil Religion and the Cultural Politics of National Identity in Obama's America." *Journal for the Scientific Study of Religion* 52(2): 239–257.

Wood, Richard L. 2002. *Faith in Action: Religion, Race, and Democratic Organizing in America*. Chicago: University of Chicago Press.

Wuthnow, Robert. 1989. *The Struggle for America's Soul: Evangelicalism, Liberals, and Secularism*. Grand Rapids, MI: William B. Eerdmans.

Wuthnow, Robert. 2002. *Loose Connections: Joining Together in American's Fragmented Communities*. Cambridge, MA: Harvard University Press.

Wuthnow, Robert, and John H. Evans, eds. 2002. *The Quiet Hand of God: Faith-Based Activism and the Public Role of Mainline Protestantism*. Berkeley: University of California Press.

Young, Michael P. 2006. *Bearing Witness against Sin*. Chicago: University of Chicago Press.

Gary J. Adler, Jr., is Assistant Professor of Sociology at Pennsylvania State University and editor of *Secularism, Catholicism, and the Future of Public Life* (2015). His research on culture, activism, and change in religious organizations has been published in *Social Problems*, *Journal for the Scientific Study of Religion*, *The Sociological Quarterly*, and *Journal of Church and State*. He is co-director of The American Parish Project through the Institute for Advanced Catholic Studies at University of Southern California.

Kraig Beyerlein is Associate Professor of Sociology at the University of Notre Dame. He is also a Faculty Fellow in the Center for the Study of Religion and Society, the Center for the Study of Social Movements, and the Institute for Latino Studies. Kraig's research and teaching focus on civic engagement, social movements, and religion. His recent published articles on these topics appear in the *American Sociological Review*, *Journal for the Scientific Study of Religion*, *Poetics*, *Politics and Religion*, and *Social Forces*. Kraig received his Ph.D. from the University of North Carolina at Chapel Hill.

Ruth Braunstein is Assistant Professor of Sociology at the University of Connecticut. Her research explores the ways in which citizens across the political spectrum participate in public life, and the complex role of religion in this process. She is the author of *Prophets and Patriots: Faith in Democracy across the Political Divide* (forthcoming), based on a comparative ethnographic study of progressive faith-based community organizing and Tea Party activism. Her research has also been published in the *American Sociological Review*, *Contexts*, the *Journal for the Scientific Study of Religion*, and *Qualitative Sociology*, among other outlets.

Mia Diaz-Edelman received her doctorate in sociology at Boston University. Her dissertation focuses on collaboration between multicultural, interfaith activists within the Immigrant Rights Movement in San Diego County. Qualitative data was collected in the form of extensive field notes from over two hundred meetings and events, as well as forty-nine formal interviews and hundreds of informal interviews from diverse activists within sixteen organizations. During her data collection, Ms. Diaz-Edelman was a Guest Scholar at the University of California, San Diego's Center for Comparative Immigration Studies. She is currently part of an initiative at Sacred Heart Schools to help promote an authentically inclusive culture and community. Partnering with students, faculty, staff, and families, her work is rooted in Catholic Social Teaching and focuses on multicultural education, equity, justice, privilege, and the LGBTQ+ community.

Todd Nicholas Fuist is Assistant Professor of Sociology at Illinois Wesleyan University. His research interests include religion, politics, identity, and sexuality, with a focus on how culture serves to motivate socio-moral action. His work has been published in the *Journal for the Scientific Study of Religion*, *Qualitative Sociology*, *Critical Research on Religion*, and *Social Movement Studies*. His current research is an examination of the interactive work religious communities do to construct theologically justified political ideologies.

Brad R. Fulton is Assistant Professor in the School of Public and Environmental Affairs at Indiana University, and he was Lead Researcher for the National Study of Community Organizing Coalitions. His research examines the consequences of social diversity within community-based organizations. Fulton's article in the *American Sociological Review* (co-authored with Ruth Braunstein and Richard L. Wood) explains how racially and socioeconomically diverse organizations draw on cultural practices to bridge social differences. His book, *A Shared Future* (co-authored with Richard L. Wood), shows how faith-based community organizing navigates the competing aspirations of universalist and multiculturalist democratic ideals.

Joshua Z. Gahr is Executive Director of Connexion House, Inc. In his spare time, he is working on an oral history and archive of the Christian Faith-and-Life Community.

Kristin Geraty (Ph.D., Indiana University, Bloomington) is Associate Professor of Sociology at North Central College in Naperville, IL. Her research and teaching interests are at the intersection of religion, organizations, and politics. She has published in the *American Sociological Review*, and her current work examines congregational and individual mobilization processes around broad-based community organizations in affluent suburban communities.

Philip S. Gorski is Professor of Sociology and Religious Studies at Yale University. His new book, *American Covenant: A History of Civil Religion from the Puritans to the Present,* will be published in 2017.

Paul Lichterman currently is Professor of Sociology and Religion at the University of Southern California, and formerly was Associate Professor of Sociology at the University of Wisconsin–Madison. He studies civic associations and social movements, religious and secular, and writes on cultural theory and ethnographic methodology. His writings include *Elusive Togetherness: Church Groups Trying to Bridge America's Divisions* (2005), *The Search for Political Community* (1996), *The Civic Life of American Religion* (2009), and a variety of scholarly articles. Paul is completing a book based on a multi-method team research project on housing advocacy in southern California.

Juan R. Martinez is Sociology Instructor in the Social Science Department at Harold Washington College in Chicago, Illinois. He earned a B.A. in General Sociology from Northern Illinois University and an M.A. and Ph.D. in Sociology from the University of Illinois at Chicago. His research interests are in the areas of urban sociology, immigration, racial and ethnic relations, religion, ethnography, and the sociology of place.

Sharon Erickson Nepstad is Distinguished Professor and Chair of Sociology at the University of New Mexico. She is the author of numerous articles and four books: *Nonviolent Struggle: Theories, Strategies, and Dynamics* (2015), *Nonviolent Revolutions: Civil Resistance in the Late 20th Century* (2011), *Religion and War Resistance in the Plowshares Movement* (2008), and *Convictions of the Soul: Religion, Culture, and Agency in the*

Central America Solidarity Movement (2004). She is currently working on a book about lived religion, Catholic Social Thought, and progressive movements in the United States.

Laura R. Olson is Professor of Political Science at Clemson University. She is also Editor-in-Chief of the *Journal for the Scientific Study of Religion*. Her research focuses on contemporary religion, civic engagement, and American politics. Her work has appeared in leading scholarly journals, including *Political Research Quarterly* and *Social Science Quarterly*. She also is the author, co-author, or co-editor of nine books, most recently *Religion and Politics in America: Faith, Culture, and Strategic Choices* (2013).

Rebecca Sager is Associate Professor of Sociology at Loyola Marymount University. Her book, *Faith, Politics, and Power* (2010), examines state implementation of faith-based initiatives and how they reshaped the relationship between church and state at the state level. Professor Sager's research focuses on the intersection of religion, politics, and social movements and has been published in a number of prominent journals. She is currently conducting an extensive research project examining the role of religion in progressive political activism.

A. Joseph West is a doctoral candidate at the University of Arizona, School of Sociology. His research focuses on religion, social movements, and the formal modeling of cultural analysis. His master's research was on congregation-based political mobilization in support of and opposition to gay marriage. His dissertation is a study of insurgency in Afghanistan during the Soviet occupation of the 1980s. His goal with this research is to better understand the role of culture and religion in the mobilization process.

Rhys H. Williams is Professor of Sociology and Director of the McNamara Center for the Social Study of Religion at Loyola University Chicago. His publications include *Cultural Wars in American Politics* (1997), *A Bridging of Faiths: Religion and Politics in an American City* (with Jay Demerath; 1992), and articles in journals such as the *American Sociological Review, Sociological Theory, Social Problems*, and *Theory &*

Society. His research has focused on religion, American culture, and social movement politics; he is currently studying cultural understandings of American national identity, especially as it is expressed in immigration politics.

Richard L. Wood serves as Professor of Sociology at the University of New Mexico. His research and writing focuses on the cultural and institutional bases of democratic life, especially those linked to religion. Wood teaches undergraduate and graduate courses in the sociology of religion, social theory, community organizing, and ethnographic research methods. His most recent book is *A Shared Future: Faith-Based Organizing for Racial Equity and Ethical Democracy* (2015; co-authored with Brad Fulton), and he is the author of *Faith in Action* (2002), which was recognized as best book of 2002 by the American Sociological Association's religion section.

Michael P. Young is Associate Professor of Sociology at the University of Texas, Austin. He is currently working on a book about the radicalization of the U.S. immigrant rights movement.

Grace Yukich is Associate Professor of Sociology at Quinnipiac University. Her research examines how immigration is changing the relationship between religion and public life in the United States. Her book, *One Family under God: Immigration Politics and Progressive Religion in America* (2013), chronicles how religious activists are working both for immigration reform and for greater cultural acceptance of immigrants in the U.S. Her research has also appeared in various journals, including *Social Problems*, *Mobilization*, and *Journal for the Scientific Study of Religion*. She is Founding Editor-in-Chief of *Mobilizing Ideas*, a blog publishing conversations between social movement scholars and activists. For 2014–2016, she was a Young Scholars in American Religion Fellow of the Center for the Study of Religion and American Culture.

INDEX

abolitionist movement, 5, 57, 286, 360

abortion, 57, 78; Mainliners on, 120; "right to life" advocacy and, 101, *106*, 111n1, 290, 304n2

ACR. *See* American civil religion

action, 9, 14; of congregation-based organizing, 76, 94n1; education leading to, 309, 317–19; inclusivity and exclusivity compared for, 125; strategic compared to field of, 21n5. *See also* field of action; political activism and action

activism: civic engagement compared to, 8; contemporary view of progressive, 59–62, 117–18; defining, 181–82, 241; forms of, 8, 15; identities of, 13–14, 116, 165, 174–75, 241; inclusivity in research of religious, 239–41; Mainliners challenges in, 118, 120, 134–35; moral authority in, 181, 182; prospects for future, 134–35; religions impact on, 181–82; religious identity conflict with, 116, 165, 174–75; rhetoric neutrality in, 19–20, 308–10, 312–17. *See also* political activism and action

Affordable Care Act, 69, 111n6

African Americans, 2; in FBCOs, *38, 39, 40*; in IRM leadership, 143; Muslim, 238; religious authority for, 126–27; second-class citizenship of, 212. *See also* Black Church

African Methodist Episcopal Church, 286–87, 333

Akers-Chacón, Justin, 145

Alinsky, Saul, 31, 164–65, 174

American civil religion (ACR), 355–56; congregational history in, 119; defining, 273–75; on morality, 275; Obama and, 3, 19, 272, 283, 287; origins of, 19, 272, 275–76; promise and perils of, 273, 287; rivals to, 272, 273; vital center revival by, 273, 281–82, 287

American radical secularism (ARS), 19; ACR bridging religious nationalism and, 273; components of, 272, 279–80; FBCOs contrasted with, 46; Founders and, 280–81

American religious nationalism (ARN), 19, 272–73, 278–79, 283

American Revolution, 275, 277, 280–81

arrests. *See* convictions and incarcerations

atheists, 117, 130, 251–52

authority. *See* moral authority; religious authority

Baptists, 18, 119, 163

BBCOs. *See* broad-based community organizations

beliefs: CFLC reworking of, 194–95; in repression impact, 249; spiritual over religious, 131, 355

Bellah, Robert, 19, 272, 273

belonging, 206–7, 209, 216–17, 222

Berger, Peter, 186

Berrigan, Daniel, 250

Berrigan, Philip, 250

biblical literalism, 127, 133

bisexuals. *See* LGBT

Black Church: ACR and, 287; in civil
rights movement, 4, 17, 208, 211–12,
219–20; Community Model in, 337–38;
Democratic Party ties with, 70, 350;
Obama and King influenced by, 3–4
Black Lives Matter, 139
Black Protestants: in Arizona, 94n3; in
FBCO field, 35, 36, 37; in LCU, 162–63,
163, 174
Bonhoeffer, Dietrich, 193
border justice movement, 4–5, 319–20
BorderLinks: border maintenance work
of, 320; criticism of, 322; education
emphasis for, 317–19, 320–21; feeder
organizations of, 321–22; formal neutrality approach of, 19–20, 308–10,
312–17, 322–24; formal neutrality influ-
ences for, 317–22; historical influence
on, 319–20; immersion travel as strategy for, 20, 309–11, 317–24; mission
and identity of, 310–11; mobilization
tactics and hurdles in, 315–16, 322–24
Border Patrol, 308, 313–14, 319–20
Border Protection, Anti-Terrorism, and
Illegal Immigration Control Act
(H.R. 4437), 205, 221–22
Bowie, Albertine, 190
broad-based community organizations
(BBCOs), 161–62, 164–65, 166, 178
Buddhism, 241; electoral wins and, 227;
King celebration and, 225; political activism and, 18, 230–33; populations statistics for, 226; as progressive religion,
228–29, 233–35, 240; in progressive
religious movement, 233–35, 240
budget cuts: healthcare and, 301–2; as
moral issue, 129, 299, 303, 304n3,
304n6, 360; policymaker elitism
and, 297–98; poverty and, 296, 297,
300–301. See also "Nuns on the Bus"
campaign
Bultmann, Rudolph, 193
Burlage, Dorothy Dawson, 197–98

Bush, George W., 29, 58, 59–60, 282–83,
360

Calvinist traditions, 132–33
Campbell, Simone, 301–2; Democratic
National Convention speech by, 290,
296, 299, 300; on policymaker elitism
and ignorance, 298, 299; on storytelling power, 289, 297
Cason, Sandra. See Hayden, Casey
Catholic Church, 304n3; collective identity
without solidarity for, 108; in FBCO
field, 35, 36, 37; gender discrimination
in, 289–90, 304n1; in IRM, 209–10, 213;
LCU membership from, 162–63, 163,
174; in mobilization study, 84; morality
debates and, 21n52, 52n21; on movement influence, 104, 105; in pacifist
movement, 21n4, 246, 250, 253; in Plowshares movement in U.S., 246, 250, 253,
264; political divide in, 290, 304n2, 357;
processions of, 213–16; in progressive
religious movement, 5, 17, 52n21, 78, 98;
religious Left and Right identification
of, 101, 107, 107; repression viewed by,
18–19; on social justice historically, 174;
in 2004 presidential election, 59–60.
See also "Nuns on the Bus" campaign
Catholic Social Teaching, 98, 109
Central America movements, 5, 21n4, 79,
311, 318
charity: BorderLinks on education over,
320; justice approach distinction from,
170–72; Perriello campaign focus on,
66–68
Chicago, 178n1, 213; community organizing history in, 167; IAF affiliates in, 173;
progressive religious group study in,
330–31. See also Dignity/Chicago; Lake
County United
Christian existentialism, 187, 193–95
Christian Faith-and-Life Community
(CFLC), 18; Christian existentialism

of, 193–95; early history of, 187–90; experimental nature of, 188–89, 194–96; Mathews leadership in, 190, 192–97, 198, 202–3; membership demographics of, 189–90; New Left emergence and, 183, 202–3; newsletter of, 193, 197–99; Protestant reform movement and, 187, 193; racial equality and, 185, 190, 196–99; social protest of, 200–203

Christian nationalism, 226, 269–70, 359. *See also* American religious nationalism

Christian realism, 174, 283

Christocentrism, 230–33

citizenship, 18; African Americans second-class, 212; framing undocumented immigrants as worthy of, 211, 212, 216–17, 222; substantive compared to formative, 206–7. *See also* substantive citizenship

civic engagement, 354, 357; activism compared with, 8; framing in religious terms, 218–20; for undocumented immigrants, 18, 217–21

civic life and sphere. *See* public sphere

civic republicanism: as ACR component, 19, 272, 274; defining, 273; as dynamic, 277; on freedom, 284–85; historical view of, 275; on human nature, 276; ideals of, 274; on morality, 275; in Obama rhetoric, 283; on political corruption, 285–86; progressive religion activism and, 284–86; prophetic tradition and, 275–76, 287; on social and economic equality, 285

civil disobedience. *See* protests and demonstrations

civil rights movement, 57; Black Church in, 4, 17, 208, 211–12, 219–20; CFLC and, 200–203; congregation-based organizing in, 76, 98; contemporary influence of, 5, 66; Mainliners participation in, 118, 128, 134; prophetic

religion influence on, 277; religious framing in, 1–2, 184, 207–8, 211–12, 219, 353; Teacher Model use of, 333–34, 345

civil society, 8, 31, 42, 355–56, 359

Cizik, Rick, 58

Claiborne, Shane, 333–34, 343, 345

climate change, 69, 121

Cobb, John, Jr., 229–30

Colbert, Stephen, 295, 328, 337

Cold War, 185, 186, 279

collaboration. *See* partnerships and collaborations

collective identity, 358; defining, 99; movement influence and, 100–101, 103–4, *105*; in Plowshare movement in U.S., 253, 257, 262; for religious Left and Right compared, 99, 100, 102–5, *103*, *105*, 108; social movement success with, 16, 99, 253, 262–63, 357; without solidarity, 108

Common Good Strategies, 60, 61

Common Good Summer Fellows, 63, 64, 65–66, 72

communication. *See* discourse; narratives; rhetoric; storytelling; voice

Community Model: in Black Church, 337–38; defining, 20, 329; for immigrant community, 338–39; sacralizing local causes in, 335–40, 345

community organizing, 33; clarity of purpose in, 165–66; history of, 31, 167; suburban municipality challenges in, 163–64, 166–67. *See also* broad-based community organizations; faith-based community organizing; organizing approach

congregation-based organizing, 51n5, 94n1, 163–64, 355; blind spot in study of, 225–26, 227, 233; for Buddhists, 240; causes found in, 82, *82*, 90; in civil rights movement, 76, 98; factors analysis for, 83–85, *85–86*, *87*, 87–92; factors overview for, 78–81, 90–92;

labor unions, 49, 352

Lake County United (LCU): Alinsky legacy and, 164–65; as BBCO innovation, 161–62; charity and justice approach distinction with, 170–72; congregational membership of, 161, 162–63, *163*, 171–72, 174–77; engagement tactics of, 168–72; founding of, 161; geography and identity issues with, 163–64, 172–78; IAF tactics integration for, 166, 178; leadership at, 168–71; Mainliner and Evangelical navigation for, 174–77; purpose and philosophy clarity for, 165–68; Republican base in, 162; socioeconomic makeup of, 162, 166, 177

language: bridge leaders consideration of, 169; FBCOs and, 51n17; IRM consideration of, 148, 154–55. *See also* discourse; rhetoric; voice

Latinos, 217–18, 220–21, 222n3

leadership: in Catholic Church, 289–90, 304n1; CFLC, 190, 192–97, 198, 202–3; development, 149–50; in IRM, 143, 148, 151; in LCU, 168–71; religious Left, 110

Lewis, W. Jack, 187–89, 195, 196

LGBT: progressive religious movement inclusion of, 9–10, 11, 331–34, 345; Theological Model and, 340–41, 343–44

liberalism, 48, 359; Mainliner distinction and variance on, 119–20; progressive cause arguments and, 284–86; secular, 6, 13, 348

lobbying, 88; from Arizona congregations, 77, 82, 84, 90; of "Nuns on the Bus," 294–95; by progressive religious groups, 290–91, 294–95, 304n4

Lutherans, 51n5, 119, 121

MacIntyre, Alasdair, 276

Madison, James, 280–81, 304n5

Mainline Protestants (Mainliners), 94n4, 95n6, 355, 357; BorderLinks relationship to, 308, 309; in civil rights movement, 118, 128, 134; collective identity without solidarity for, 108; cultural challenges for activist, 118, 120, 134–35; denominational identities of, 119–20, 122, 125, 130; discursive field for, 118, 128, 130, 131–32, 134–35; Evangelicals coalition with, 124–25; at FBCO core, 35, *36*, 37; future prospects for activist, 134–35; historical role in progressive religious movement, 17, 97, 118, 120, 132; identities for Evangelicals compared to, 122–25, 126; interfaith and inclusive approach of, 123–25, 127, 134, 135; laity decline for, 109; in LCU, 162–63, *163*, 174–77, *175*; liberal distinction and variances for, 119–20; message framing of, 121–22; mobilization outside of, *87*, 89; mobilization potential of, 79–80; on moral authority, 123–24, 126–27; on movement influence, 104, *105*; political action of Evangelicals compared with, 125–28; progressive views of, 78, 79–80, *87*, 120–21; on religious authority, 125–27, 133; religious Left identification of, 101, 107, *107*; socioeconomic justice focus for, 79–80, 120–21; storytelling of, 127

marginalized population: Census importance for, 220; Christ as exemplar for, 343–44; FBCO focus on, 32–33; IRM on, 138–39; progressive politics focus on, 31–32

marriage, same-sex, 57, 76–77, 78, 82, *82*, 111n6, 120

Mary of Nazareth (Mother Mary): as exemplar in Teacher Model, 330, 332, 334; migration story symbolism of, 214–16, 218

Mathews, Joseph, 190–97, 198, 202–3

May, Rollo, 193–94

May 1st Coalition, 147–48, 149, 150, 153